Information Systems
for
Management
Planning
and
Control

THE IRWIN SERIES IN MANAGEMENT
AND
THE BEHAVIORAL SCIENCES

L. L. CUMMINGS and E. KIRBY WARREN
CONSULTING EDITORS

JOHN F. MEE   ADVISORY EDITOR

Information Systems
for
Management
Planning
and
Control

THOMAS R. PRINCE, Ph.D.

Professor of Accounting
Graduate School of Management
Northwestern University

Revised Edition

1970

RICHARD D. IRWIN, INC. *Homewood, Illinois   60430*
IRWIN-DORSEY INTERNATIONAL *London, England   WC2H 9NJ*
IRWIN-DORSEY LIMITED *Georgetown, Ontario   L7G 4B3*

REVISED EDITION

First Printing, March, 1970

Second Printing, December, 1970

Third Printing, June, 1971

Fourth Printing, April, 1973

Fifth Printing, May, 1974

Library of Congress Catalog Card No. 77–98248
Printed in the United States of America

To
Eleanor

Preface

SIGNIFICANT CHANGES have occurred in the business environment during the past decade, and with each of these changes, the managerial functions relating to the measurement, interpretation, and use of economic data have assumed new meaning in large business organizations. In the more progressive business firms, new titles have been used to designate the modified aspects of these managerial functions: "Manager of Information Systems," "Director of Administrative Services," "Director of Information Intelligence," and "Vice President in Charge of Information."

It is beyond the confines of this discussion to argue over which title should be used to designate individuals performing these expanded managerial functions. Instead, attention is focused on the characteristics of these functions—characteristics determined through analyses of business situations and through interpretations of the expanded managerial functions in the different situations.

Each analysis and interpretation is from the perspective of the systems analyst. It is assumed that the systems analyst has the attribute of being able to simultaneously view, from an objective position, both the total organization and the various segments or parts within the organization. This "double vision" attribute is frequently associated with the professional accountant; however, the systems analyst is used instead of the professional accountant in order to avoid some of the confusion regarding the extent of "economic activity" included within the professional accountant's vision.

The systems analyst also has the ability to perform special observations of the applications of these expanded managerial functions throughout the business organization. Each application relates to a decision-making process; specifically, it involves the information requirements and the data sources needed by the decision-making activity. Thus, the systems analyst focuses upon the information flows (the matching of information requirements with data sources) associated with decision-making activities throughout the business firm. He is concerned with the identification, evaluation, and modification of information flows and with the integration of information flows into information systems. The specific approach that he follows in performing these activities is called the *information systems approach*.

When the first edition of this book was published in 1966, there were only a few corporations in the United States where large-scale, online, management information systems were being designed and implemented. The Mead Corporation case study, dated June 1, 1966, is representative of those selective corporations planning such systems.

During the past three years, several other corporations have conducted large-scale, advanced information systems studies. Based on these extensive efforts, many of the basic concepts of the information systems approach have been reexamined, modified, and expanded; additional concepts have also been developed. For example, specific organizational arrangements have been established for encouraging participation by user department personnel in planning such advanced information systems. A five-phase framework has been developed for planning and implementing an information system. When an advanced information system is designed, it will usually include the following elements: online computer programs for further coding, processing, and assigning of data; common data bases; and online remote terminals for decision centers.

These overall developments in information systems have necessitated an early revision of *Information Systems for Management Planning and Control*. Much of the material in the former Chapter 12, "Total Information Systems," and the former Chapter 14, "Advanced Information Systems," was superseded by these developments; thus, in the revised edition these two chapters are deleted in their entirety.

Three new chapters are included in the revised edition: Chapter 3, "Using Systems for Planning and Control"; Chapter 13, "Advanced Information Systems"; and Chapter 14, "Elements in Large-Scale Information Systems." Two other chapters are extensively expanded: Chapter 4, "Applications to Business Organizations," and Chapter 11, "Marketing Management Information Systems." In addition, flowcharts are included in the revised edition for purposes of clarifying the specific elements and interrelations in the five generalized models of information systems. These latter flowcharts provide a unifying and integrating function for pulling together the conceptual aspects of the *information systems approach*.

The revised edition presents Third Generation Systems Philosophy as it is currently being applied in the most advanced companies. The Amoco Chemicals Corporation case study, dated May 1, 1969, is representative of this type of setting.

Part I of this book presents the foundation and overview for the information systems approach and serves as the frame of reference for the other five parts. The subsequent parts of the book contain general descriptions of information systems in each of the functional areas, the progress toward total information systems encompassing all functional areas, and the special concerns with information systems. Thus, the book is a broad survey of many diverse areas within the business organization that are viewed from the perspective of the systems analyst, or it can be described as a special examination of the information flows associated with decision-making activities throughout the business organization.

The material in this book was developed for use in both a graduate and an undergraduate course at Northwestern University bearing a similar title, "Information Systems for Management Control." After the third offering of these courses, the author modified the tentative title of this book to include "planning." This change was in recognition that planning and marketing models tend to alter the business environment in which they are located, and in such systems it is necessary to view the term "control" as a monitoring of change rather than as a restricting of activity. The author decided that it was easier to modify the proposed title of the book from "Information Systems for Management Control" to "Information Systems for Management Planning and Control" rather than to periodically have to explain in what sense the term "control" is being used.

The material in this book is also used as the general framework for a three-week management training program in a major corporation. The participants in this program are not directly involved in systems design, but are employed in various marketing management and administrative positions. Why was the material selected as the framework for a training program for these participants? The material was selected because of the general applicability and power of the information systems approach. The systems analyst has a meaningful approach toward studying the business process in diverse business environments. Regardless of whether the business firm has advanced information systems or a series of traditional, clerical types of record-keeping systems, the information systems approach suggests a way of getting a "handle on" the business process within these business firms.

Like most other nonintroductory courses, it is suggested that *Information Systems for Management Planning and Control* be used in a scheduled course near the end of the formal academic program: during the spring session of the senior year for undergraduate students and during the spring session of the second year for M.B.A. graduate students. By scheduling this type of course late in the formal academic program, the material will serve as a consolidating and integrating device. The book intentionally reexamines areas with which the reader may already have some familiarity, such as PERT and inventory-control models. However, these areas are reexamined from a new slant that emphasizes the information dimensions of decision-making activities throughout the business organization. Thus, the contents are similar to the policy type of management course, except that where the policy type of course focuses upon the decision process of executive management, the information systems approach focuses upon the *information used in the decision process and the information flow associated with each decision process throughout the business firm.*

The case studies and technical notes included in this book do not require the reader to have a familiarity with any given computer programming language. However, the author has discovered from experience that it is desirable for the reader to complete instruction in some computer programming language before beginning to study the material in this book. This latter instruction should be in sufficient detail that the reader has actually programmed a rather complicated business problem. In the process of developing and testing this program, the reader will gain an increased awareness of the capabilities and limitations of electronic computers.

As far as other prerequisites, the reader should have the equivalent of an introductory course in cost accounting which includes (*a*) an appreciation of the nature of costs, (*b*) an understanding of what is meant by the statement, "different costs for different purposes," and (*c*) a general orientation toward the operation of integrated standard cost- and budgetary-control systems. The reader should have a general understanding of the administrative process and an appreciation of the application of mathematical methods to business. In this latter area, the minimum exposure would include a familiarization with the linear programming technique. All other prerequisites will typically be achieved by scheduling this instruction during the last session of the formal academic program.

The author is indebted to Arthur Andersen & Co. for financial assistance, technical consultation, and other assistance during the initial phase of developing material for this book. Special appreciation is due to the following individuals for their helpful comments on various issues in information systems: Bill Davison and Jack Potter of Amoco Chemicals Corporation; Gene Delves and Irvin Smith of Arthur Andersen & Co.; Basil Regione of the R & R Company (Chicago); and Jim Woodruff, The Special Assistant to the Secretary of the Navy. The author is also indebted to the Ford Foundation and Northwestern University for research and financial assistance during the intermediate phase of developing material for this book.

The author is grateful to the many business firms that cooperated in making available their experience in the area of information systems. Many companies elected to use disguised names; however, in all other respects, the case description is the actual company. The author acknowledges the permission of the Technical Association of the Pulp and Paper Industry to include material in Chapter 3 from his earlier publication with the association. The encouragement and advice of my colleagues at Northwestern University during the writing of this book are appreciated. The comments, questions, and discussions of the many students who studied earlier drafts of this book have significantly influenced this revised edition. The author appreciates the excellent secretarial and typing assistance of Mrs. Laura Hoffman. A final word of gratitude must be said to my wife for her encouragement and understanding during the lengthy period of time I worked on this book.

Evanston, Illinois   THOMAS R. PRINCE
February, 1970

Contents

PART

II. TRADITIONAL INFORMATION SYSTEMS

5. Responsibility Accounting Systems   111

The General Model. Type 1 Information System. Special Characteristics of the Responsibility Accounting System. Responsibility Accounting Reports. Coding Pattern. Accounting Statistical Data. Reporting Guidelines.

6. Profitability Accounting Systems   139

Basic Concept. General Model. Responsibility versus Profitability Accounting Systems. A Note on the Industrial Chemical Industry.

7. Critical Path Planning and Scheduling Information Systems   157

Benefits from This Approach. History. Comparison. CPM Terminology. Illustrative Examples of CPM Technique. Advantages of the Method. Other Considerations. The Method from the Perspective of the Systems Analyst.

PART

III. PRODUCTION AND OPERATION INFORMATION SYSTEMS

8. Production Information Systems   185

The General Model. Type 2 Information System. The Production Function as Viewed by the Systems Analyst. Relation of Production

Function to Other Operations. Predetermined Decision Rules. Special
Concerns.

Case

REQUIREMENTS: The Cost of Carrying Inventory. The Cost of Not
Carrying Inventory. PROCESSING PROCEDURES: Reorder Quantity. Example. Relevant Data for Formulas. Reorder Point.

Cases

Control Procedures. Selective Analysis and Inventory Control. Dollar
Selectivity. Systems Analyst's Perspective.

Case

PART
IV. MARKETING INFORMATION SYSTEMS

INFORMATION SYSTEMS APPROACH: Information Requirements. Data
Sources. Matching Process. INFORMATION ACCUMULATION AND TRANS-
MISSION: TYPE 2.5 Information System. Extensions and Supporting
Systems. TYPE 3 Information System.

Cases

Environmental Changes. Credit Management and Control. Establishing the Credit Rating System. Product Demand and Advertising Management.

Case

PART
V. MOVEMENT TOWARD A TOTAL
   INFORMATION SYSTEM

PART
VI. SPECIAL CONCERNS

PART **I**

FOUNDATION AND OVERVIEW

CHAPTER 1

The Information Systems Approach

THE DECISION-MAKING role of business management has recently been the focus of numerous professional books, papers, articles, seminars, and conferences. Every student of the business process is aware that decisions must be made and that business management must carefully select among alternatives. Business management has been assisted in this latter task by many new tools and techniques which can be used in the preliminary screening of alternatives. In addition, business management has employed control devices where an electronic computer will monitor the programmed responses to a given set of decisions.

But where does the information come from that business management uses in selecting among alternatives? What additional information would business management like to have regarding these alternatives? Is this information available? If not, is it economically feasible to make it available? What is the time lag between the initial accumulation and the subsequent transmission of information to business management? Is all information transmitted to business management, or is some screening device employed so that only exceptional information (according to the management-by-exception procedures) is transmitted to business management? What additional data should currently be accumulated for possible use by business management in a predictable "new set" of decision-making activities in the future?

The previous questions only relate to some aspects of the information dimensions of the decision-making processes of business management in the current complex business environment. Another series of questions might relate to the manner in which business management has used electronic computers, communication equipment, or

3

mathematical tools and techniques in coping with different information flows associated with the decision-making process.

This book is primarily concerned with the information dimensions of the decision-making processes throughout the business enterprise and presents a special approach for viewing and analyzing these information dimensions. But, before describing this special approach, attention is given to citing the historical and environmental changes that permit and support this new approach.

Information Dimensions of Decision-Making Processes

A business organization can be viewed as a series of large information networks connecting the requirements for information in each decision-making process with the sources of data and extending throughout all of the business process, including the actions by users of information. In large complex business organizations, the different operations of a given business organization can be described as separate information networks, with one giant overall information network superimposed on top of the individual information networks.

This idea of viewing a business organization as a series of information networks has been expounded by teachers of management for many years. Until recently, however, this idea was relegated to the general discussions of the business process, and no attempt was made to systematically examine the different aspects of each information network. Previously, any attempt to pursue this idea was quickly discouraged by the overwhelming requirements for (1) information determination, (2) information collection, (3) information processing, (4) information analysis, (5) information transmission, and (6) information interpretation. Methods, tools, techniques, and processing equipment were only recently applied to this management concept in an effort to achieve in practice what had previously been only a vision.

These latter developments within the business environment have been stimulated by the numerous interdisciplinary approaches taken toward studying the business process which have transcended the traditional, functional lines of business. Concurrently with these studies, other developments have occurred in the business environment regarding techniques, procedures, processing equipment, and communication equipment. It is difficult to classify all of these developments during the past decade because each development tends to overlap another development. For purposes of this discussion, however, these dynamic changes are classified according to four movements.

Four Movements

First, the psychological and sociological inquiries were combined to form the behavioral science approach toward studying the business organization, with the human motivational aspects of each area given the greatest emphasis. The behavioral science approach was merged with the interdisciplinary studies resulting in team studies being made of the business organization and of the various departments and operations within the business organization. The membership of these teams consisted of representatives from different departments and functions with the psychologists and sociologists playing dominant positions, in terms of both the area of analysis and the content of the team's report.

Second, extensive studies were made of data flows within the business organization and of the feasibility of installing data processing and communication equipment for coping with these data flows. This type of study is indicative of a change occurring in the business environment. During this period of time, the electronic computer became a familiar expression throughout the United States, and the capabilities and applications of this equipment were significantly expanded. Simultaneous developments in electronic computers and communication equipment provided the necessary means for rapid accumulation, calculation, processing, summarization, reporting, and transmission of information.

Third, mathematical tools and techniques were applied to the study of business events. Many of these techniques have been in existence for years, but were not employed because we lacked a rapid means by which this information could be processed. For example, the ideas of reorder points and reorder quantities (that provide the critical controls around which the integrated inventory control and production control system operates) are candidates for this third classification. The third approach to studying the business process has produced new management control devices and management tools for coping with the various business functions.

Fourth, the scientific method has been applied to the study of the business processes, and applied models (mathematical, descriptive, analytical, or simulated) are frequently used in studying business situations. This fourth approach is primarily a variation of the third approach coupled with formal pragmatic philosophy. However, there are exceptional studies where extensive use has not been made of mathematical tools and techniques, but, instead, a descriptive analysis has been performed which has drawn heavily upon organization theory and formal pragmatic philosophy.

General Systems Theory

While the above four movements have occurred in business, another movement has occurred in the academic setting. Interdisciplinary studies possessing some of the characteristics of each of the four movements are being conducted under a new banner called the "general systems theory."[1] This latter movement is not restricted to the study of business but encompasses all areas of knowledge.

According to Prof. Kenneth Boulding, the quest of general systems theory is to establish a body of systematic theoretical constructs which will discuss the general relationships of the empirical world.[2] These systematic theoretical constructs might be envisioned as analytical and communication vehicles that connect two or more specific disciplines. Thus, the long-term objective would be to develop a set of these analytical and communication vehicles that would connect and interrelate all disciplines.

Most of the efforts to date in applying this concept of a general systems theory have been restricted to the development of specific analytical and communication vehicles that connect common areas of concern in two or more disciplines. Practically no attention has been given to a cataloging of existing analytical and communication vehicles. The next step, of course, would be to integrate these cataloged vehicles in some systematic body of thought.

Although the goal of general systems theory has not been realized, this movement has had significant impact upon the understanding of the business process. In addition to the numerous interdisciplinary studies that are compatible with this movement, the current under-

---

[1] Ludwig von Bertalanffy, "General Systems Theory: A New Approach to Unity of Science," *Human Biology,* Vol. XXIII (December, 1951) , pp. 303–61.

[2] Kenneth E. Boulding, "General Systems Theory—The Skeleton of Science," *Management Science,* Vol. II (April, 1956) , p. 197.

standing of the business process has benefited from another aspect of this movement. The second approach suggested by Boulding for the formation of a general systems theory has been applied by several writers to the task of developing a conceptual framework for each writer's own special area of study.[3]

Boulding describes the second approach as follows: "The second approach is to arrange the empirical fields in a hierarchy of complexity of organization of their basic 'individual' or unit of behavior, and to try to develop a level of abstraction appropriate to each."[4]

Subsequently, he reintroduces and describes again the second approach: "A second possible approach to general systems theory is through the arrangement of theoretical systems and constructs in a hierarchy of complexity, roughly corresponding to the complexity of the 'individuals' of the various empirical fields. This approach is more systematic than the first, leading towards a 'system of systems.' "[5]

This description is followed by a framework containing nine levels of theoretical analysis where each level would be a different type of system.

The approach that is presented in this book for studying the information dimensions of decision-making processes throughout the business organization draws heavily upon some of the basic ideas associated with general systems theory. But, at the same time, there are significant differences.

Description of Approach

The special approach that is presented in this book for studying the information dimensions of decision-making processes is called the *information systems approach*. This can be described as a systematic method of observing, analyzing, evaluating, and modifying a business organization or any segment or part of a business organization.

The term "systematic method" implies that there is a special point of view or perspective toward observing items, guided by theory. For purposes of this book, the term "systems analyst" is used to identify

---

[3] For example, Professors Johnson, Kast, and Rosenzweig have used the previously cited work as a foundation in applying general systems theory to management. See Richard A. Johnson, Fremont E. Kast, and James E. Rosenzweig, "Systems Theory and Management," *Management Science*, Vol. X (January, 1964), pp. 367–84.

[4] Boulding, *op. cit.*, p. 200.

[5] *Ibid.*, p. 202.

an individual who possesses or, at least, is supposed to adhere to, the point of view characterized by the information systems approach. The latter qualification is necessary because some of the case studies included in this book describe systems analysts who may not always fully comply with the information systems approach.

This type of inquiry—information systems approach—is especially appropriate for coping with the current business environment. Concurrent developments in electronic computers, communication facilities, mathematical tools and techniques, and in business technology have significantly changed the business environment and have changed the manner in which most business organizations conduct their operations. Furthermore, these developments have influenced some business organizations to completely change the nature of their business process. In these latter cases, the business organizations are currently engaged in completely new types of business activities.

The information systems approach is an attempt to get a "handle on" the business processes in diverse environments. The applicability of this approach to diverse environments is illustrated in the case studies included in this book. Intentionally, the case studies and technical notes are arranged so that there is a gradual transition from the simple, familiar business environment to the more complex business environment. In other words, in these case studies, the only constant is the approach—the information systems approach; all other aspects are variables.

As previously indicated, the information systems approach does encompass some of the basic ideas of general systems theory. The information systems approach also encompasses some of the basic ideas associated with information theory. Nevertheless, it would be a misstatement of fact to describe the information systems approach and the contents of this book as a blending of general systems theory with information theory. If the reader is searching for a book that is primarily devoted to a blending of these two theories, then the following is recommended: Ira G. Wilson and Marthann E. Wilson, *Information, Computers, and System Design* (New York: John Wiley & Sons, Inc., 1965) .

Characteristics of Approach

The information systems approach represents a new approach toward studying a business organization or any segment or part of a business organization. Basically, the systems analyst is attempting to group major decisions that business management must make (both formally and informally, explicitly and implicitly—thus, all decisions) into categories that are based on a combination of (1) general area that the decision concerns, (2) the time dimension of the decision process, and (3) similar requirements for information in the decision process.

A group of decisions possessing these three characteristics is the nucleus of an *information system*. The systems analyst is concerned with tracing all information flows associated with this group of decisions and with the decision-making processes involved, regardless of the organizational boundaries that must be penetrated. This network of information flows that has been traced and charted for each group of related decisions constitutes a *system*. Since the focus of each network or *system* is upon "information flows," each network is called an *information system*.

Thus, the information systems approach is a special method for viewing and analyzing a business organization or any segment or part of a business organization so that the systems analyst can perceive each major information system within this business process. If the systems analyst is to perceive each major information system, then the systems analyst must be able to identify each major information flow. The latter item—an information flow—represents the organization results of relating or matching the requirements for information with the sources of data for each major decision. This matching process is accomplished by business management and frequently involves the employment of various management science tools and techniques.

In the above description regarding how an information system is formed, one of the fundamental ideas is the matter of *information requirements*. The information systems approach as presented in this book is different from the approach recommended in other contemporary business systems references in that the emphasis is on *information requirements*, not on *information uses*. Therefore, the systems analyst is not concerned with the current "paper flow" and other aspects of existing information uses. Instead, the systems analyst focuses upon the decision-making activities involved and the requirements for information by the decision maker (which may be a team) in each of these decision-making activities.

From another viewpoint, the practical concept of an information system has assumed a new meaning because of the changes that have occurred in the business environment. These changes are the result of the interaction of the previously cited four movements: advancements in behavioral science, developments in electronic computers and communication equipment, developments in mathematical tools and techniques, and the application of the scientific method to the study of business. As a result, the practical concept of an information system has shifted from a traditional *accounting system* to an *economic activity system* which encompasses all types of economic data.

Recognizing that this degree of change has occurred in the business environment and that a state of continuous change is forecast for the immediate future, the systems analyst needs an approach toward studying the business process which transcends the existing flow of documents and the existing processing and communication equipment. Or, from a related perspective, the systems analyst needs an approach to make a diagnosis of the patient rather than treatment of the symptoms. The information systems approach is a systematic method for accomplishing these objectives.

Systems analysis in a given business organization must include the task of treating the symptoms. This important area of concern, however, is reserved for other business systems references, and no attention is given in this book to the patchwork approach of trying to improve the document flow within a given department or division of the business organization.

In summary, the systems analyst attempts to identify, observe, analyze, and specify the requirements for information in decision-making activities throughout the business organization, to determine the sources of data, and to match the information requirements with the appropriate data sources by employing some of the current management science tools and techniques. The systems analyst follows a systematic method in the performance of each of these steps. In order to understand this systematic method, it is necessary to know (1) the special point of view and (2) the theory that guides the observations by the systems analyst. Chapter 2 presents a general frame of reference in which these two aspects, along with other facets of the information systems approach, are fully examined. However, before considering this general frame of reference, special attention is given to the underlying objective of this book.

Objective

The overall objective of this book is to teach the systems analyst to think scientifically about the information dimensions of decision-making activities throughout a business organization and to acquire an approach toward establishing criteria for information flows. A four-step method is followed in trying to teach the systems analyst to perform scientific thinking about information systems.

The first step is to give the systems analyst a conception of the entire business organization and all of its segments. In other words, the systems analyst must possess the ability to simultaneously view both the overall business organization and the individual parts or segments of this overall business organization. Chapter 2 presents a general frame of reference for assisting the systems analyst in achieving the proper perspective for viewing the business process and for identifying, measuring, and evaluating information flows. Chapter 4 describes the extensions of the information systems approach from studying information flows to studying a total business organization or studying major types of activities within a business organization.

The second step is to instill within the systems analyst an understanding of model construction and the ability to formulate models that represent decision-making activities throughout the business organization. This second step is achieved in several ways. First, various parts and chapters of this book are described as being models. At appropriate points in the book, selected models are compared and contrasted with other models. The case studies and topics for class discussion specifically require the reader to express his interpretation of some relation in model form. After these decision-making activities have been expressed in model form, the reader is required to interpret and to justify his model. Furthermore, he must make certain types of extensions from his model. Thus, the second approach is accomplished and reinforced again and again throughout this book.

The third step is to assist the systems analyst in bridging the gap between the ideal, model information system and the operational, practical information system. The selected case studies are presented in an appropriate order so that the variance between the ideal and the operational system is magnified in each successive case study. As this variance increases, the systems analyst must evaluate the various alternative methods, and he must select those methods which he will use for reducing this variance.

The fourth step in the development of scientific thinking about the information system is to instill within the systems analyst the ability to draw a conclusion and make a decision from his analysis. The systems analyst has to learn to choose among alternatives; the information system that is best for one set of conditions may not provide appropriate information for another set of conditions. In searching for the "right" conclusion, the systems analyst may be forced to return to the first step and begin his analysis again. This latter comment is especially applicable where the systems analyst's interpretation of the business situation—upon further study—is discovered to be erroneous. Or, if the business environment has changed (for example, a new method of processing information at a lower cost is introduced by a machine manufacturer), a new analysis may be required. This reexamination process is part of the dynamic dimension of the information systems approach. This last step, of course, is achieved by the various case studies that require the reader to draw a conclusion and to make a decision from his analysis.

While the systems analyst is achieving this overall objective, the contents of this book are so developed that an important secondary objective is also achieved. Various electronic computer equipment, transmission and communication facilities, operations research techniques, management control systems, and information retrieval systems are presented in the selected case studies. The systems analyst views each of these items not from the standpoint of a tool or technique but as a *user, processor,* or *consumer* of information. Emphasis is placed on information sources, information processing means, scientific tools and techniques for analyzing information, information flows in a control network, and information retrieval. Thus, the systems analyst examines each item from the perspective of the information system, and the concept *information* permeates each analysis.

As the systems analyst performs these analyses, he is also acquiring an orientation to some of the recent developments in management science. These developments are presented as part of the business environment in the different case studies and, as such, represent occurrences with which the systems analyst must at least have some familiarization. In other case studies, the problem situations occurring in the application of these management science tools and techniques are featured in a business environment where the systems analyst is asked to respond to the situation. Thus, as the systems analyst responds to these case studies, he is acquiring an appreciation of the *use* of some of these recent developments in management science rather than acquiring a mere description of what some of these recent developments are. This type of orientation to the recent developments in management science is the secondary objective of this book.

TOPICS FOR CLASS DISCUSSION

1. During the past decade, many colleges and universities have added a business policy course which is offered at the end of the formal educational experience. The business policy course is an interdisciplinary inquiry of the business enterprise which transcends the functional lines of business and emphasizes the impact that a given policy type decision has on the total activities of the business organization. Or, from a different perspective, the business policy approach toward studying a business organization emphasizes the necessity for business management to consider the numerous factors in several functional areas of business before reaching a decision on a given policy type of question. How does the business policy approach toward studying a business organization differ from the information systems approach? Contrast and differentiate between the two approaches.

2. What is the difference between the objective of general systems theory and the objective of the information systems approach?

CHAPTER 2

Establishing a General Frame of Reference

THE INFORMATION SYSTEMS approach has previously been described as a systematic method of observing, analyzing, evaluating, and modifying a business organization or any segment or part of a business organization. From another perspective, the information systems approach can be described as a special method for (1) identifying information flows associated with decision-making activities throughout a business organization, (2) evaluating information flows, and (3) designing new information flows.

Before examining this special method, consideration is first given to describing the general characteristics of those individuals who claim that they adhere to the information systems approach—the systems analysts.

The Systems Analyst as a Trained Observer

There are numerous ways an individual may observe an object, event, activity, or relation. Each observer is perceiving the item through a filter composed of his experience, education, and training. Some observers have been trained and conditioned so that they are capable of "role playing." These observers are capable of assuming a special position for viewing an item for a given purpose and are capable of complying with the particular theory or set of theories which is associated with this special position. The application of this latter procedure results in the performance of designed observations for a given purpose.

A trained observer is capable of role playing and is able to compensate in his designed observations for the unique filter through which he perceives an item for purposes of eliminating much of his personal bias. Therefore, in the case of a trained observer, a three-step sequence is followed in designing observations. These steps are indicated by the following questions: What is it that is being observed? For what purpose is this item being observed? What are the theories that are associated with the design of observations for this purpose? This latter question can be restated: How is the item being observed?

A systems analyst is a trained observer who performs designed observations of the information flows associated with decision-making processes throughout the business organization for purposes of evaluating existing information flows and designing new information flows. A description of the above three steps will permit us to comprehend what is meant by this definition of a systems analyst.

What Is Being Observed?

Although the description of the information systems approach states "a business organization or any segment or part of a business organization" is being observed, this is not correct. A business organization or a business enterprise is an invisible creature and, as such, cannot be directly observed. Instead, different manifestations of this creature can be perceived.

A trained observer may study a given type of manifestation from several positions, depending on the set of theories that govern his planned observations. The business profession contains many different types of trained observers, and each type of trained observer may be guided by a slightly different set of theories regarding the nature of this invisible creature. Therefore, different trained observers respond to varying sets of designed observations.

For example, the financial accountant is a trained observer who has been taught to see in a business organization all of those economic activities and events that relate to the measurement of the business organization's financial condition, reported income, flow of funds, and so forth. After the financial accountant has perceived an economic activity or event, he must pass judgment on whether or not the *identified* economic activity meets the given business organization's rules for inclusion in the regular published financial statements (alternative procedures may be employed at the discretion of the business organization's management). Finally, the financial accountant must determine what measurement rules he will follow in expressing the *identified* economic activity that has been *selected* for inclusion in the published financial reports.

Other traditional types of trained observers include the financial manager, the sales manager, and the production manager. The financial manager's view of the business organization emphasizes the relation of the various activities of the enterprise to the external price of stock, to the credit classification of the business organization's long-term securities, and so forth. The sales manager's view of the business organization emphasizes the markets, the products, and the customers. The production manager's view of the business enterprise emphasizes the physical units of output, raw materials, assembly lines, scheduling operations, and selection of alternative inputs.

The systems analyst, like the financial accountant, the financial manager, the sales manager, and the production manager, is concerned with designing observations of certain manifestations of a business organization. But unlike the other cited trained observers, the systems analyst does not respond to any traditional set of theories associated with a functional area of business. Instead, the systems analyst assumes a new, interdisciplinary perspective for viewing manifestations of a business organization.

What manifestations of a business organization does the analyst perceive? The answer to this question has been impl other discussions. The systems analyst is concerned with the informa tion dimension of decision-making activities throughout the business organization, and he must be conditioned and trained to identify the information flows within the business organization.

Actually, the latter statement is an indication of the completion of the first phase of the systems analyst's work, rather than being the first step of the initial phase. Assuming the term "information" refers to relevant data for a given decision-making process, the systems analyst must first be conditioned and trained to perceive *data* only when he views a business enterprise or any segment or part of a business organization. Next, the systems analyst groups "data" into three categories: (1) data that are currently used in some decision process, (2) data that are not currently used in a decision process, but are accumulated for possible use in some predictable future decision-making processes, and (3) data that are not now used nor scheduled for future use in decision-making processes. Data that are classified by this latter grouping are referred to as "noise."

Data has a special meaning to the systems analyst. Data are the representation or symbolization of the systems analyst's perception of economic activity. This representation or symbolization must be at least at an ordinal scale of measurement, which means that the item is capable of being differentiated with a similar item by the notation of "more than" or "less than." We arbitrarily elected to exclude from the "data label" those items which can only be identified at the nominal scale of measurement.

Now the vagueness associated with the term "data" shifts to the term "economic activity." What is economic activity as viewed by the systems analyst? The systems analyst perceives economic activity from an organization theory perspective. To an organization theorist, a business enterprise is a group of people who are united by some common objective in the general sphere of the production and distribution of goods and services. Beyond this general statement, organization theorists will differ as to the identification of the specific objectives, missions, and goals for the particular business enterprise under scrutiny.

While the teacher of management takes this concept of the business enterprise as a point of departure and expounds the administrative process of working with and through people in the pursuit of the organization's objectives, the systems analyst focuses on the information dimension of this concept. Furthermore, the systems analyst sees economic activity as being observed results of the group of people in the business organization responding and interacting through time to the underlying goals, objectives, and missions of the organization. As previously stated, this concept of observed results has been arbitrarily restricted in this book to being at least at the ordinal scale of measurement.

The previous descriptions of data and economic activity are important for purposes of emphasizing the item or manifestation of the business organization that is perceived by the systems analyst. Specifically, the systems analyst does not see the existing document flow within the organization, but views the organization from a more conceptual perspective—he sees the observed results of the group of people in the business organization responding and interacting through time to the underlying goals, objectives, and missions of the organization.

A subsequent discussion of the steps involved in applying the information systems approach to analyzing a business process will assist in further clarifying what it is that is being observed by the systems analyst when he views "a business organization or any segment or part of a business organization." Attention is now focused on the second question.

For What Purpose Is This Item Being Observed?

The information dimension of the decision-making processes throughout the business organization is the primary focus of the systems analyst because of its relation to the basic objective of the systems analyst. This objective was previously included in the description of the information systems approach, which was described as a special method for (1) identifying information flows associated with decision-making activities throughout a business organization, (2) evaluating information flows, and (3) designing new information flows.

There is an "information flow" associated with each decision-making activity which can be described as the network that connects the requirements for information with the sources of data. As previously stated, the numerous networks are classified on the basis of a combination of (1) the general area that the decision concerns, (2) the time dimension of the decision process, and (3) similar requirements for information in the decision process. Each formal group of related networks is called an "information system."

The systems analyst desires to establish the ideal set of information systems that is compatible with the major decision-making requirements in the existing unique environment of a particular business organization. This ideal set of information systems in one organization may make extensive use of computer equipment, communication facilities, and operations research techniques; however, in another organization, limited use may be made of these latter items. Thus, the systems analyst is not trying to develop any standard set of information systems in every business organization; instead, he tries to develop that unique set of information systems in each organization that is most appropriate for the existing conditions in that organization.

Why does the systems analyst desire to establish the ideal set of information systems for each business organization? The answer to this question is self-evident. The ideal set of information systems for a given business organization will be a balancing of the most timely, the most efficient, and the most economical arrangement of information flows for that organization. As a result of establishing these systems, business management will have better information for particular decision-making activities, will typically establish management control devices for coping with reoccurring types of decisions where management will be notified only on an exception basis and overall will generally increase management's understanding of the operations of its own organization. Thus, this development will give management more time for handling unpredicted activities and for short- and long-term planning activities.

The common situation in a given business organization prior to the establishment of this ideal set of information systems is that business management has too large a quantity of certain types of information and has voids in reference to other required information. The systems analyst, therefore, views the manifestations of the business organization from the perspective of the information dimension of the major decision-making activities for the purpose of evaluating existing information flows and, where appropriate, designing new information flows.

How Is the Item Being Observed?

As previously noted, this question can be restated: What are the theories that are associated with the design of observations for the purpose of evaluating existing information flows and, where appropriate, designing new information flows?

Today, many management scientists have training and experience in the biological and physical sciences, and these management scientists use expressions and concepts from these areas in their discussions regarding the information network of a business organization. For example, analogies are frequently made between physical control systems and business information systems. The nervous system of the human being is compared with the information system of a business organization. Other comparisons are made between the ability of the human body to maintain a balance between the chemical composition of the blood and the regulatory and control functions in the business organization. Others argue that the principles of organization theory can be observed in the behavior of very simple animals.

While these analogies and interdisciplinary comparisons are useful generalizations, the systems analyst is cautioned against overreliance on any tangible explanation of information systems. On the other hand, the systems analyst can use these interdisciplinary analogies for purposes of improving his own understanding of some of the facets of this intangible being—the business organization. But the systems analyst must confront the sobering fact that he must cope with the information dimension of decision-making activities if he—the systems analyst—is to achieve his objective.

As implied in the previous discussion of data, the systems analyst draws heavily from organization theory in guiding his designed observations. At all times, the systems analyst is conscious that the business organization is a group of *people* united by some common objective in the general sphere of the production and distribution of goods and services. Business management's role is to coordinate the men, money, materials, machinery, and technology in such a way that it is possible to realize the business organization's long-term, common objective.

The systems analyst is concerned with each major decision-making activity and with the decision maker (including both individuals and teams). The systems analyst desires to study and analyze each major decision-making activity according to a systematic method. The systematic method employed by the systems analyst will vary based on the educational background and training of the systems analyst.

The systematic method presented in this book is not the *definitive* method for performing such analyses, for the current state of the art does not permit students of the business process to know when the definitive method has been specified. Instead, the systematic method presented is a practical scheme that we have successfully employed in several diverse business environments, and it is presented from this context in this book.

The Systematic Method

This systematic method represents a special point of view, guided by theory, for observing the business process and is equally applicable to an analysis of the business process at any level within the business organization. For example, the business process under study might be at any of five levels: (1) a decision-making activity that directly involves only a given problem area in one department, (2) a decision-making activity that directly involves only a particular functional area within a given department, (3) a decision-making activity that directly involves only a given department, (4) a decision-making activity that directly involves only a given division, and (5) a decision-making activity that directly involves the total business organization (such as a major policy type of question that has company-wide implications).

This systematic method will be examined from an abstract position with the decision-making activity under scrutiny being assumed to represent the single, major decision-making activity in the business organization.

As an overview, the systems analyst attempts to specify the requirements for information in this decision-making activity, to determine the sources of data, and to match the requirements for information with the appropriate sources of data by employing some of the current management science tools and techniques. Each of these phases is examined in the following discussion.

Information Requirements

Specifying the information requirements is the last step in a three-step sequence. The first step is to understand the business process for the business organization under study. This requires a familiarization with the unique industry characteristics and practices as well as an appreciation of the general environment in which the business organization is located. This appreciation will include a general insight into how the business organization reacts to its environment.

Before considering how the first step is accomplished, reexamine the wording of this initial step, specifically, "to understand the business process." In other words, what are the general nature and characteristics of the environment in which this decision-making activity is located?

While there are unusual circumstances in which any scheme must be modified, we do not advocate that the systems analyst should immediately go to the physical place of business and observe the operations. Instead, if the systems analyst does not have this understanding of the business environment, it is recommended that he should first go to a public or private business library and make a preliminary review of some of the professional literature regarding the general nature and characteristics of the environment in which the decision-making activity under scrutiny is located.

After the systems analyst has this limited familiarization with the environment, then he can more intelligently observe the operations at the physical place of business and can ask more enlightened and relevant questions. While a checklist of questions may assist the systems analyst in performing this first step, there is no substitute for experience. The experienced systems analyst frequently possesses the knack of quickly gaining an overall "feel" for the environment. For example, we are amazed at the extraordinary ability that some practitioners have in this area; they seem to have perfected the "art" of how to acquire most efficiently this feel for the environment.

The inexperienced systems analyst should not be discouraged by the previous comments. Instead, he should view them from a positive standpoint. The inexperienced systems analyst should exert the additional effort and use the business library facilities in researching this environment. This comment is also applicable to the case studies in this book; if the reader does not have a "feel" for the environment after reading and studying the descriptive material in the case study, then the reader should use the business library facilities *before* he begins to respond to case situations.

In the second step, the systems analyst expands his understanding of the business process for that particular segment of the overall company's operations that has been selected for study. The system analyst must determine the exact missions, goals, and objectives for this business process. In this step as in the first step, experience is a key factor. There is no cookbook approach that is always applicable. The systems analyst observes, he asks questions, and he evaluates replies and observations with his general "feel" for the environment. Thus, the successful accomplishment of the second step will demand all of the systems analyst's analytical abilities.

For example, in a recent consulting engagement, we eventually realized that the objective of a small manufacturing company was not to produce a small group of products in such a manner that they could be sold at a profit. Instead, this particular manufacturing company was primarily engaged in a financing operation. Almost all of the profit was derived from the interest charges on accounts receivable rather than from the margin between cost and selling price of each product. When this general observation was discussed with the small manufacturing company's president, the president commented that his organization has been primarily a "financial institution" for the past two years. Furthermore, because of the competitive situation, the future of this organization appears to be directly dependent upon the successful continuation of these financing activities.

In the third step, the systems analyst must specify the exact requirements for information that are needed for achieving the previously determined mission. As in the other steps, it is easier to state what the systems analyst should not do rather than what he should do. The systems analyst should not begin by asking the decision maker: What information are you currently using? Likewise, the systems analyst should not begin by asking the decision maker: What information do you need?

The systems analyst approaches this third step from another perspective. He asks the decision maker: Will you please describe what occurs in the decision-making process? The systems analyst is concerned with identifying the various questions that must be resolved in the particular decision-making activity under scrutiny. The systems analyst can expedite this step by asking the decision maker: Please cite the issues or questions that must be resolved in this business process. However, the analyst is cautioned from overreliance on this technique. For example, the decision maker may fail to cite some questions because the decision maker feels that the answers to these questions are taken as "givens," when, in fact, they may be the most significant issues in the total decision process under scrutiny.

There is another aspect of this third step which merits attention. There is a difference between the systems analyst viewing the decision-making process from an abstract perspective versus viewing the same process with a concurrent focus on the unique capabilities and characteristics of the decision maker. Although it is a trite expression, the inexperienced systems analyst should remember: The decision maker must be capable of understanding and using the relevant data that are being transmitted to him before these data can properly be classified as "information." Frequently, the systems analyst spends more time in "educating" the decision maker and in "informing" subordinates than he does in designing a new information system. The educational instruction that is given to business management and to employees is one of the major parts of the implementation phase of a new information system.

A different aspect of this third step relates to the matter of electronic computer equipment, communication facilities, operations research techniques, and technology. Are the business organization's current capabilities in these areas considered as "a given" for purposes of this analysis? Or, should the analysis include what has been planned to be available in the near future? The answers to these questions are dictated by the purpose and scope of the investigation.

In summary, the attention that the systems analyst gives to the act of specifying the information requirements in a given decision-making activity is the primary differentiating characteristic of the systems analyst versus other practitioners who do not follow the information systems approach. As a result of this type of attention, this phase of the systems analyst's work approaches some of the attributes of an organization review.

This discussion of information requirements was presented from the standpoint of the inexperienced systems analyst. In the discussion of the first step, some consideration was given to the advantage that the experienced systems analyst has in the sense of performing the step more quickly. In addition, the experienced systems analyst may already have a general appreciation of the environment in which the business process is located; thus, he will only give brief attention to the first step.

The experienced systems analyst also has a significant advantage in the third step. As soon as the decision maker begins to comment on the nature of the decision-making process, the experienced systems analyst will quickly gain a general appreciation of the nature of this process. For example, if the experienced systems analyst believes that the basic problem is in the area of inventory forecasting, then he already knows the significant variables or the typical questions that must be resolved in a normal inventory forecasting activity. If his diagnosis is correct, then the systems analyst will change the focus of his discussion with the decision maker, and will try to determine what unique variables are present in the current situation that are not in the typical situation. Furthermore, the systems analyst will be equally concerned with why some typical variables associated with this general type of problem are not present in the current situation.

These comments on the advantages that the experienced systems analyst has over the inexperienced systems analyst were included for purposes of comparing the above approach to specifying the information requirements with the approach followed by practitioners. As suggested by the above comments, the experienced systems analyst does not formally apply each of three steps; however, subconsciously he may be following similar steps.

Data Sources

The systems analyst does not complete the process of specifying the information requirements before he begins to consider the data sources. In fact, it would be more appropriate to describe these two actions as overlapping.

The systems analyst prepares a "tentative list of information requirements." Next, he looks (1) at the various books, records, documents, and reports within the business organization and (2) at the external published statistical data (including both industry statistics and general business data) and then indicates by each item on his "tentative list" what data sources are available for coping with that requirement. For many items, there may be a choice of several possible data sources.

The systems analyst may not know of any existing data source for a few of the items on the list. Naturally, he must pursue these "listed requirements" for purposes of determining if there are other data sources for coping with these requirements. This second examination frequently reveals data sources for most of the remaining items on the list.

The items on the "tentative list of information requirements" for which there is no specified data source are now individually examined. The systems analyst indicates by each of these items either (1) a new source that might be established for providing data or (2) that there is no known source for the data.

Next, the systems analyst performs an economic evaluation of each item on the "tentative list of information requirements." He must decide if the estimated benefit from using each "tentative requirement" in a decision-making process exceeds the cost of accumulating, processing, and transmitting the data that will directly satisfy that requirement. Of course, there may be overlapping requirements for the same type of data in different decision-making activities. In any case, the systems analyst must decide which of the items on the "tentative list" are considered as valid requirements for the current time frame.

Matching Process

These "valid" requirements for information are matched with the indicated data sources. This matching frequently takes the physical format of a matrix diagram. How far beyond the matrix diagram the systems analyst will go depends on the nature of the decision-making activity under scrutiny and the purpose of the study.

A significant part of this matching process is determined by the existing capabilities in electronic computer equipment, communication facilities, and management science tools and techniques. Another part of this process is determined by the availability of the data sources; for example, there may be two matchings. During the current time frame this data source will be matched with that requirement, but concurrently, a new data source is being created so that in a future time frame (12 months from now, 18 months, etc.) a new matching will occur.

This matching process will be further examined in the context of each of the case studies in this book. In addition, much of the material subsequently presented in this book might be labeled *descriptions of applied management science tools and techniques in the matching of information requirements with data sources.*

Summary

The information systems approach is a special perspective for viewing the business process for purposes of identifying existing information flows, evaluating these information flows, and designing, where appropriate, new information flows. It does not matter which purpose the systems analyst is coping with—identifying, evaluating, or designing—the general method remains constant. The systems analyst specifies the information requirements in each decision-making activity (or in resolving each problem area), lists the data sources that are available or could be made available in satisfying these requirements, and matches the information requirements with the data sources utilizing selective management science tools and techniques.

TOPICS FOR CLASS DISCUSSION

1. If an individual were to analyze a given decision-making process in a business organization, he would identify many uses of information. Explain the difference from both a practical and a conceptual standpoint between the expressions "uses of information" and "information requirements."

2. The financial accountant, the financial manager, the sales manager, and the production manager represent, respectively, the four traditional trained observers for studying a business organization. Explain how the approach followed by the systems analyst differs from the approach followed by each of these traditional trained observers.

3. Explain the perspective that the systems analyst assumes for viewing the business organization. Be specific.

4. Explain the difference between an "information flow" and an "information system."

5. An individual following the ideas of general systems theory might describe the information flows associated with each major activity of the business organization as a "system." The horizontal information flows between a selected group of major activities would also be a "system." The horizontal information flows between the various selected groups of major activities would be a "system" at a higher level. The adherence to this approach would result in the development of a "system of systems" or a hierarchy of systems for the business organization under scrutiny. Explain the difference in the grouping of "information flows" for a general systems theory type of "system" versus the information systems approach type of "information system."

CASE 2–1. LAKEWOOD SERVICE CORPORATION

Representatives of two financial institutions and three insurance companies have been formally organized into a team for purposes of studying the information storage and retrieval problems in each organization as related to the decision-making processes of investment account managers. At present, each organization has its own business library where an up-to-date card system is maintained of the financial statements, reports, and professional articles for most business organizations in the United States whose capital stock is listed on a major stock exchange or regularly sold over-the-counter.

In addition, three of the organizations have selected financial and statistical data for some of these corporations stored in the computer facilities. In each of these three organizations, special computer programs have been developed for selecting for further study those companies that appear to meet certain criteria as to investment opportunity.

During the past year, the investment account managers in these five participating companies were severely criticized for failing to invest in several corporations that experienced tremendous growth. These investment account managers were also criticized for slowly responding to the published statistical data for several major corporations.

As a result of these developments, several investment account managers in the organizations began to respond to this criticism by seeking employment with other similar organizations. Gradually it became apparent to these investment account managers that the problem they were facing was not an individual problem or even a company problem but was an industry problem. Several investment account managers from different business organizations informally met and pondered their common problem. After much discussion within the various organizations and between these organizations, this team of representatives from five participating companies was formally organized.

A preliminary investigation of the financial costs involved versus the estimated benefits from different types of information storage and retrieval systems indicated that it was economically feasible to establish a utility type of online information system for the five participating organizations. The planned system would be financed by the formation of a new corporation, the Lakewood Service Corporation. The capital stock of this latter firm would be sold exclusively to the five participating corporations.

An electronic computer system would be installed at the Lakewood Service Corporation, and a series of communication lines would connect this electronic computer system with inquiry equipment that would be located on the desk of each investment account manager in the five participating corporations. As statistical and financial data would be stored in the electronic computer system, they would become available for use by the investment account managers. In this proposed system there would be no time delay between the point that the investment account manager commences to use his inquiry equipment and the point that this action is recognized in the electronic computer system (thus, it would be "online").

The preliminary plans call for three different information systems. Information System No. 1 would be an online type of system for the retrieval of financial and statistical data for a selected group of active companies. This system would also contain coded statistical data that are based on significant articles, papers, speeches, and other releases that appear in professional sources (such as *The Wall Street Journal, Business Week, Barron's,* and so forth) which relate to these selected business organizations.

Information System No. 2 would contain financial and statistical data for all other companies. The two systems together would contain data on every business corporation listed on any recognized stock exchange in the United States or commonly traded over-the-counter. In Information System No. 2 there would be a time delay in securing answers to inquiries, and these delays would probably be from 15 to 20 minutes.

In this second system the financial and statistical data would be stored in magnetic tape units that are "offline." Periodically, different magnetic tape units would be connected to the computer system and all inquiries of financial and statistical data stored in this tape unit would be answered.

Information System No. 3 would represent a common business library for the participating companies. An up-to-date index would be maintained of the professional literature and releases relating to each corporation included in System No. 1 or System No. 2. This third system would provide each investment account manager with one-day service on copies of any requested article, paper, speech, or release.

The five participating corporations have agreed to the tentative plans for the Lakewood Service Corporation and have asked the coordinating team to continue to study the project. Furthermore, the coordinating team has been asked to submit, as soon as possible, the formal, complete plans covering the general details of the proposed system.

.   .   .

After further study, the coordinating group for the Lakewood Service Corporation has decided on the following approach for designing the information retrieval systems. A survey will be made of the current uses that investment account managers are making of financial statements and statistical data regarding the listed corporations, and a model will be developed which includes a list of all of these uses.

Next, a list will be prepared representing a sample of those business organizations that will be included in the proposed information systems. For each company in this sample, the published annual reports and appropriate statistical data from the professional literature will be accumulated and used as inputs into a computer program. The computer programmers will prepare the appropriate flow charts and the resulting computer program that will be necessary for matching these uses of information (per the list of uses developed from the survey of investment account managers) with the sources of data stored in the program.

This computer program will be run using various sequencing of uses of information, and a close scrutiny of this simulation model will serve a twofold purpose: (1) the uses and sources of data will be matched to see that all uses of information are satisfied by sources of data and (2) a coding pattern will be developed to facilitate the retrieval of information based upon the traditional methods the investment account managers are accustomed to following. While this latter step is being performed, consideration will also be given to the matter of selecting the exact computer equipment and communication facilities that should be purchased as well as determining the financial rate that should be charged for the information retrieval service.

REQUIRED:

1. From the perspective of the information systems approach, evaluate the approach that the coordinating group has decided to follow.
2. Explain step-by-step how a systems analyst would develop the three information systems.

CASE 2–2. MIDWEST ADHESIVE COMPANY

The Midwest Adhesive Company is a relatively small manufacturer of adhesives for industrial purposes, with annual sales of approximately $3,500,000. Frank Martin, president of the Midwest Adhesive Company, was concerned about recent complaints regarding finished goods inventory and asked his new administrative assistant to determine what was required to improve the control of inventories and the writing of resulting production orders.

Dave Miller, the new administrative assistant, had recently graduated from college and was employed at Midwest Adhesive Company earlier in the week. Therefore, the above project was the first significant task that Dave Miller had been assigned.

Dave interviewed the inventory control manager and his associates. During the next few days, Dave talked with sales personnel, production foremen, and the chief accountant. After these discussions, Dave decided that operations research techniques should be employed in developing a system of sales forecasting and inventory control over adhesive inventories. The basic objectives of this proposed system are to:

1. Maintain customer service.
2. Maintain a minimum, balanced inventory.
3. Provide a means for forecasting future sales and inventories by months.

Later that same week, Dave prepared a one-page report for Frank Martin, which stated the above recommendation.

REQUIRED:

1. Evaluate Dave's recommendation.
2. Explain step-by-step how a systems analyst would cope with the president's request.

CHAPTER 3

Using Systems for Planning and Control

THE PROFESSIONAL LITERATURE contained several case studies and reports of surveys which point out where inappropriate decisions have been made by executive management, in planning and implementing large-scale, computer-based systems, and in selecting computer equipment. These studies tend to suggest that, during recent years, most business organizations have made only limited use of large-scale, computer-based systems. Moreover, in most business organizations, the great potential of these systems is yet to be realized by management.

While we may question the economic justification that was submitted in support of many of these computer systems studies, we should also evaluate the role currently being played by the computer systems in business organizations. Many poorly justified computer systems have been installed during the past decade and, subsequently, these systems have become very valuable assets in their respective business organizations.

These computer-based systems have provided the capability for many companies to successfully handle the tremendous increase in transactions that has occurred during recent years. International operations and new product development in marketing activities coupled with business expansion by mergers and acquisitions of other companies have been the major factors responsible for this enormous growth in business transactions. Without the use of these computer systems, it is questionable as to whether many of these companies would have been able to handle this new work load.

We might generalize and state that the majority of the existing large-scale, computer-based systems are currently being used for housekeeping activities rather than for planning and strategic decision-making purposes. In subsequent chapters we will be especially concerned with the systems approach and computer applications for the latter grouping of activities.

Instead of being overcritical about the shortcomings of existing computer-based systems, we might examine the accomplishments of these management efforts. One major accomplishment from management's experience with computer-based systems over the past decade has been the refinement of the "management by systems" concept.

Second, numerous efficient and effective operating systems have been designed and implemented for handling major business functions in many companies. The experiences gained by systems analysts in construction of these systems have caused a reexamination of some of the existing philosophy on the systems concept and the application of the systems approach to business and government. As one management consultant stated, "We know a lot about how not to design a total information system for a diversified major corporation and we have some experience with the design of smaller scale information systems that work."

Third, new organizational forms and arrangements have been created for performing on a centralized basis the information systems function in large corporations. These new arrangements pertain to: (1) the location of the management information systems department; (2) the administrative participation in the scoping phase of an information systems study; and, (3) the assignment of staff and departmental personnel to the information systems study teams. These organizational developments are examined in detail in a subsequent chapter.

This chapter explores different facets of the first two accomplishments cited above. First, the concept "management by systems" is examined. Second, operating systems and information systems are separately explained and differentiated. Finally, an approach is presented toward the construction of a management information system.

I

Management by Systems

A systems analyst may apply the information systems approach to a study of a business or other organizational unit and still not plan or design an information system. As previously explained, the information systems approach is really a special case of the now common term "systems approach" with a special orientation. In using the term "information systems approach" the emphasis is on the unique perspective that the systems analyst assumes and the term in no way relates to the output from the systems analyst's work.

After a systems analyst has studied a given business or organizational unit, he may conclude that either an operating system or an information system should be planned and implemented. The important factor is not which of these two systems should be installed—the systems analyst is more concerned with the administrative skills and perspectives of executive management. Specifically, can management or the members of the management team effectively employ "systems" in the systems concept so as to relieve themselves of significant portions of routine work.

The concept "management by systems" means that management will attempt to establish, where appropriate, a programmed set of decision rules to handle the large volume of reoccurring types of transactions. After these rules have been specified, then subordinates can administer these rules in coping with the daily activities. Where this is successfully employed, management is able to devote most of its efforts to handling the unusual or the nonprogrammed set of transactions.

The concept of management by systems is extremely important in evaluating the success of an operating system or a management information system. There are many cases where these computer-based systems have been established and are successful in handling all of the previous types of transactions. These integrated computer programs have replaced former clerical employees; however, what is missing is that management has not grasped the idea of how to successfully use these new creations.

Education or the reorientation of members of management is one of the major steps in planning and implementing an operating system or an information system. This educational program or training session must assist in reorienting members of management to apply the systems concept in more successfully carrying out their duties and responsibilities. This desire on the part of management to use systems in handling large volumes of reoccurring transactions is a prerequisite to the effective use of either operating systems or information systems. We will see more application of this philosophy as we examine the characteristic of operating systems and information systems.

II

Operating Systems

An operating system is a computer-based, integrated network of information flows representing a significant grouping of the company's activities. The computer programs encompassed in an operating system must be self-contained; that is, they must be capable of operating on a continuous basis without requiring any human intervention. These computer programs can be described as numerous programmed responses to sets of questions that were previously handled by clerical, foreman, supervisory, and middle management personnel.

An operating system is a self-contained unit that may monitor and control a complex operation. The only requirement is that the complex operation must be able to be represented by an integrated set of programmed rules. An example of such an operation is using an IBM 1800 computer system for operating a paper machine. The system may be designed so that we can have human intervention into the system and manually override the programmed activities. The capability of human intervention into the system is an added feature which is not part of the general model of an operating system. The main feature in the basic operating system is a perpetual capacity for handling a defined set of operations in a given manner.

A generalized model of an operating system is presented in Figure 3.1. The heart of the operating system is the set of computer programs that are online and handle the processing of data transmitted through the system. As far as inputs, the operating system may respond to changes in other operating systems and this information is transmitted by tapes. The more typical method of processing data

FIGURE 3.1
A Generalized Model of an Operating System

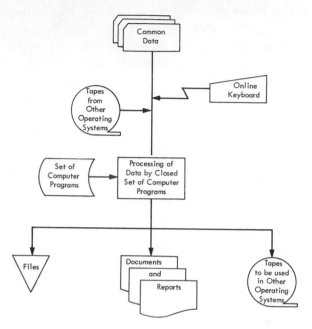

into an operating system is through regular data cards which might be generalized to include punched tape and magnetic-tape types of inputs. The third type of input symbol for the generalized model represents another type of activity. The online keyboard would serve where the operating system is quickly responding to changes in inventory position, changes in production orders, and other status information that is transmitted from an online keyboard located at a remote location.

The outputs from an operating system cover the gamut of communication devices; from documents and reports, to magnetic tape, microfilm, or any other type of filing mode. An important consideration in an analysis of an operating system is what is the major missing dimension. Specifically, there is no return "information flow" from the documents, reports, and other outputs that intersects or connects the input locations. Overall, the operating system, as indicated above, serves to process a volume of transactions. The set of computer programs stored within the computer can be described as programmed-decision rules. However, the overall operating system does not contain any human decision makers as an integral part of the system. An information system will always have human decision makers, and this point will be further developed in the subsequent section.

Evolution. Operating systems have evolved out of the integration of related computer programs. For example, an operating system in personnel might consist of the integration of the following three computer programs related to personnel and manpower planning: (1) a payroll-computer program, (2) a personnel-record computer program, and (3) an employee performance computer program. These three computer programs require the same common data for inputs.

The daily time and attendance report for each employee is the common input for these three programs. When these three computer programs are integrated into an operating system, the newly created operating system should be designed so that it performs the following activities: (1) reads the common input—the daily time and attendance report for each employee, (2) processes these data, (3) stores selected data for payroll purposes, (4) stores selected data for subsequent use in the cost and performance reports, and (5) stores selected data for use in preparing special reports for governmental agencies. It is suggested that the reader should mentally re-label the symbols in the generalized model of an operating system (Figure 3.1) so as to indicate where these five activities are accomplished.

Characteristics. The operating system is a closed network of computer programs for processing a large volume of transactions or inputs. These programs are both closed and self-contained, which means that parameters and variables within this network of computer programs have been specified and continue to operate until management elects to change these values. If no change is initiated, then theoretically this network of computer programs can be employed continuously to process this same set or type of transactions on a perpetual basis.

It is important to grasp the concept of an operating system, as a network of computer programs stored within the computer system, or which are capable of being stored within the computer system, that operate on a perpetual basis and handle a large volume of activity. Since the emphasis in an operating system is on being self-contained and closed, this type of system is typically not designed to permit change. Lack of features for implementing executive management decisions is one of the elements that differentiates an operating system from an information system. This latter point is described in more detail in a subsequent discussion.

In an operating system, we must have some type of coding manual to indicate the proper notation for each transaction. The coding manual for an operating system indicates how 92 percent of the volume is to be recorded or coded. Therefore, a coding clerk can perform this coding function without asking any management personnel for assistance. In a simple operating system, the 8 percent of the transactions that the coding clerk cannot handle are simply forwarded to a manager for his consideration.

In a more complex environment, and at higher organizational levels, these 8 percent of the transactions become extremely important. They provide the incentive for establishing a management information system which encompasses operating systems. Later, we will examine some characteristics that these 8 percent of the transactions must possess before we will formally recognize them as being exceptional items. Otherwise, we might establish ground rules that the 8 percent are not to be discriminated against and state that they should be handled as if they were really part of the other 92 percent. A good example of this type of generalization is followed in selected inventory cases. Frequently, we treat all perpetual items of inventory on the same basis, even though we know there are some unusual items in the inventory. In other cases, of course, we follow the ABCD system of inventory control,[1] where we take special note of these unique differences and relevant characteristics of the inventory item.

Scale. How do operating systems compare with computer programs and advanced management information systems? We can establish a continuum running from 1 to 10, and designate 1 as representing a computer program, and designate 10 as representing an advanced management information system. On such a continuum, an operating system has a value between $5\frac{1}{2}$ and $6\frac{1}{2}$.

Computer programs have a value between 1 and 2; the latter value designates a more complicated and integrated set of computer programs. As integrated computer programs in an area or in an activity are clustered together into one network, we refer to these programs as an "activity program." On our scale, the activity program has a value of 3, and the activity program can be more formally

---

[1] The ABCD system of inventory control is described subsequently in this book on pp. 233–48.

described as a network of integrated computer programs for handling the typical events or transactions with which a given activity must cope.

After the activity program, we have a functional program, which, on our scale, has an assigned value of 4. A functional program is a much larger network of computer activity which encompasses a major delegation of management's responsibility. If a network of computer programs is labeled "functional program," we would envision these computer programs as being very involved, highly integrated, and approaching the position of being closed and self-contained.

On our scale, the range of $5\frac{1}{2}$ to $6\frac{1}{2}$ is used to designate an operating system. The range $7\frac{1}{2}$ to 9 designates an information system, and the point of 10 designates an advanced information system. The overall continuum is presented in Figure 3.2.

FIGURE 3.2
A Continuum Showing Relative Positions of Programs and Systems

Computer Program	Activity Program	Functional Program	Operating System	Information System	Advanced Information System

1   5   10

Example. If we had a simple perpetual inventory system, this might be labeled a computer program with an assigned value of 2. If the perpetual inventory system were to be integrated with a procurement system, in which a requisition request is automatically prepared, then this might be called an "activity program" and designated by an assigned value of 3. If this integrated perpetual inventory system and procurement system were to be expanded so that it will not only initiate the requisition request but will designate who is to be the supplier and will scan recent purchase arrangements in the process of determining the pricing scale, then this might be called a "functional program" and designated by an assigned value of 4. If this network were an integrated perpetual inventory system, reorder system, and purchase status system, then this might be called an "operating system" and designated by an assigned value of 6.

Continuing with this example, if the network were to be expanded beyond the integrated perpetual inventory, purchase requisition, and order status system so that it also includes all inventory management, then this "integrated operating system," as we will refer to it, will have an assigned value of 6½. The next major step is to take the integrated operating systems and to build into these computer programs, vehicles or avenues for implementing management's decision. When this occurs, we are in the domain of a management information system which, on our scale, has a value between 8 and 9. As these planned systems become more complicated, we approach the advanced information systems position with an assigned value of 10.

Summary. An operating system is an integrated network of computer programs which have been specifically designed to handle approximately 92 percent of the activity. These integrated computer programs are self-contained, closed, and capable of responding to the same common inputs. These operating systems are not designed to quickly permit changes in parameters or variables. Instead, the operating systems are intended to service management through handling this major volume of activity and thereby releasing management's time for coping with the other 8 percent of the activity.

Management Information Systems

The terms information system and management information system are frequently used by management consultants to describe computer-based information networks that provide relevant, timely, and accurate information to management for decision-making purposes. Frequently, these networks do not possess the characteristics of an information system, but are really only operating systems. There are important technical distinctions between an operating system and an information system.

A management information system is a computer-based network containing one or more operating systems, which provides relevant data to management for decision-making purposes and also contains the necessary mechanism for implementing changes or responses made by management in this decision-making activity. It is not a sufficient condition that the management information system provides relevant data. The network must also be capable of responding to change. As an example, assume that we have three operating systems within one management information system. In the decision-making process, management may decide to change the parameters in each of these three operating systems, and this closed computer network will contain the appropriate mechanisms for accommodating this particular change. That is, the parameters can be quickly changed and these operating programs will be running in a response to a new set of parameters.

This feature of being able to respond to change is the dynamic element in a management information system. There is nothing more frustrating than providing an executive with timely, accurate, and relevant information and, at the same time, not giving the executive the capability of changing the situation. That is why this change element in the management information system is so powerful.

Relation to Operating Systems. Operating systems serve as the base or foundation for a management information system. We can depict a management information system as two or more operating systems that are linked together and provide relevant data to management or to a management team. Flows of information to management from the operating system are not the most significant features in the model. The role played by management is the most important feature in a management information system; and, secondly, connecting outputs from the management decision-making activities directly to the operating systems is the next most important feature in the management information system.

While an operating system is a closed network, the management information system may or may not be closed. In other words, the management decision makers, or management team, really serve as the connecting link in our diagram of a management information system, taking information generated by the operating systems and feeding back appropriate changes where necessary to the operating systems. In a given time period, management may elect to let the computer monitor these responses within certain guidelines. This latter situation is indicative of a management information system at a fairly low level within the organizational structure. Most of our attention is given to management information systems at higher organizational levels where the management team plays an active role in connecting the outputs from the operating system to new inputs to the operating system.

A generalized model of an information system containing three operating systems is presented in Figure 3.3. The diamond, denoting the decision-making process by management, is the key feature in the information system. Note that the three operating

FIGURE 3.3
A Generalized Model of an Information System
Containing Three Operating Systems

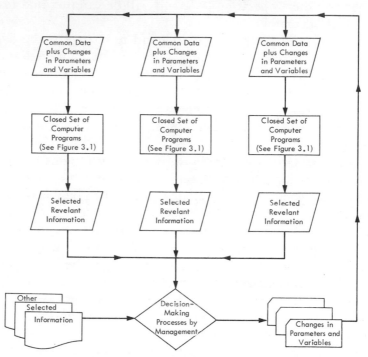

systems provide relevant information to management for decision-making processes. Management also uses other input locations for important planning information. The results of the management decision-making process are translated into changes into parameters and variables. These parameters and variables refer to the closed set of computer programs contained within each operating system. Note that the data flow for changes in parameters and variables is a closed loop, going from the decision-making process by management, and connecting with the input terminals to each operating system. In the subsequent paragraphs, we will see how difficult it is to design operating systems that permit changes in parameters and variables. The closed set of computer programs contains all the features that were present in the generalized model of an operating system presented in Figure 3.1.

Change Factors. The most difficult part in planning a management information system is determining the appropriate changes or critical elements that management may elect to establish, or modify, during a given period of time, and how these changes are to be directly incorporated into the existing ongoing operating systems. These anticipated changes must be planned for and described as variables or as parameters in the operating systems, which serve as the base for the management information system. If this is the case, management can then respond to the output from the operating system, establish new criteria, and determine that these parameters or variables will have new values for the subsequent time period. The management information system will contain the appropriate internal computer mechanism for taking the change in a variable or parameter and immediately establishing this change in the operating system. In this case, as the volume of transactions is being processed by the operating system, these data are immediately responding to this revised set of criteria.

As suggested by these comments, the systems analyst must possess a basic feel for the business organization and the decision-making processes associated with the major business activities before the systems analyst can even begin to identify feasible channels for responding to management's decision-making activities. This requires a thorough understanding of the organization. Thus, it is not surprising that the second phase in the five phases for designing and implementing an information system seeks to provide the team of systems analyst with this overview of the organization. This second phase is called the "organization review and administrative study phase," and this phase as well as the other four phases are discussed later in this chapter.

Special Problems in a Dynamic Setting. The establishment of management information system is not always an appropriate objective for a business organization. In fact, it may not even be a feasible objective. It was previously explained how a series of operating systems serve as a foundation for a management information system. The important elements in the management information system are the vehicles for responding to management's decision and these vehicles will connect to variables or parameters in the different operating systems.

If a business organization is located in an environment where there are significant changes in the mission of the organization during the short term, for example, during the next two years, then it may not be feasible to establish a management information system.

About the time the systems analyst and systems programmers have established channels for responding to executive management's decisions and incorporated these channels in the closed computer networks, then the change in mission of the organization will make the predicted channels inappropriate. If there are significant changes in mission, it might be necessary to compartmentalize this large computer network and to keep only a series of the operating systems for the subsequent period. The other operating systems will have to be replaced with new networks which are more appropriate to the new assigned mission.

When we have an extremely dynamic environment, then management's objectives can usually be better served through the establishment of a series of specific operating systems. In such a case, the management teams and management committees can serve to provide the linking of these different operating systems. So we have through management's action a "human" type of management information system. In the latter situation, the management team serves in place of the integrated computer programs that link operating systems together.

In summary, the systems analysts do not always work toward the establishment of an information system. Instead, they strive toward the design of appropriate sets of programmed decision rules for handling reoccurring types of transactions. Then, depending upon the environment, the organizational structure, the decision makers and their capabilities, and the anticipated short-term objectives of this organization, these systems analysts determine what type of network should be established.

Constraints on Moving to Information Systems. It was indicated that operating systems have evolved through time from the integration of activity or functional computer programs. It would seem logical that we could move one step further and progress from an operating system to an integrated set of operating systems which serve as the foundation or base for a management information system. Unfortunately, this is not the case.

A step-by-step or building block approach toward the design of an information system is not always possible. We cannot necessarily move to higher levels of computer application merely by adding additional computer personnel, expanding the systems department, or acquiring more computer or communication equipment. These additional investments may occur and we will still be at the operating systems level of computer application. Why is this the situation?

We may have noncompatible segments that are not capable of being merged. Each operating system has a defined time frame and cycle in which the overall systems processing is performed. These closed loop operations may be performed in a two-minute time interval. At the other extreme, they may occur in a monthly time interval. Most operating systems use a time interval between the two-minute and the monthly time cycle. If two operating systems' time periods are not identical, it is frequently not possible to merge the two systems unless one of the systems is reprogrammed. This type of situation is described in a case study at the end of this chapter.

Each operating system is designed to respond to or process a defined set of inputs. Two operating systems in the same general area will frequently require different types of inputs. The only way such systems can be merged is to reprogram one of the systems. Even if management desired to integrate these two systems, the systems analyst should not start at this point in designing an integrated system. Instead, an administrative type of organization review should be performed to gain an overview of the decision-making processes that are to be serviced by the integrated set of operating systems. This point is further developed in a subsequent discussion of the five phases in the design and implementation of an information system.

There are optimal locations for obtaining information from an operating system and there are limitations on the volume of data that can be transmitted by communication equipment. This may mean that a plant manager and a department manager at the home office cannot fully use the some operating system. The department manager may hourly use information provided by the operating system. The plant manager may be limited to daily reports that are mailed to him. Limitations on integrating operating systems, because of the location of the decision maker, are not restricted to the plant and home office arrangements. This same type of problem may apply to decision makers in different departments of the central office where the company does not have extensive online computer terminals.

Another reason that a building block approach cannot be followed is that two operating systems may have incomplete coding patterns. For example, a given inventory identification code may be excellent for use with the ABCD Method of Inventory Control; however, items of inventory that are classified by this system may not be appropriately identified for marketing management system. The latter system is more sensitive to varying markup rates than it is to dollar price and volume. If the systems analyst desires to integrate these two operating systems, each item of inventory may have to be recoded.

While an inventory identification code was used as an example, this type of problem is equally applicable to other coding structures. For instance, trying to combine an accounts receivable identification code with the requirements of customer profile data for marketing purposes is a similar type of problem.

A final reason for not employing building block approach is that the systems analyst, in working with one operating system, cannot have a "big picture" perspective for the overall area. In any computer program there are many optional values that must be specified. After these values are specified, they become constraints in the computer programs. If the systems analyst does not possess a broad perspective of the company's decision-making activities, then it is unlikely that many of these constraints in the computer programs will be compatible with the requirements of an expanded, integrated set of operating systems.

In summary we cannot always move step-by-step to higher levels of computer applications in a systems context. Noncompatible time frames and cycles may not permit the integration of two related operating systems. The content of the network and the input requirements may be such that two related operating systems are really totally different types of systems. The latter operating systems must be redesigned and reprogrammed if they are to be integrated. The organizational location of various decision makers may be such that an integrated set of operating systems cannot fully service these managers under existing facilities for online computer terminals. Finally, many optional values in a computer program later become constraints which may prohibit the integration of two existing operating systems.

The only way to avoid these latter types of constraints is for the systems analyst to gain a broad perspective of the decision-making activities before he specifies these optional values in a computer program. The second phase in the five phases for planning and implementing an information system is designed to provide for this type of perspective. The shortcomings of the building block approach are also resolved when the systems analyst employs the five phases in planning and designing an information system.

III

Five Phases in Planning and Implementing an Information System

Operating systems may evolve through the integration of functional computer programs. Information systems, on the other hand, cannot be created on an evolutionary basis or even by a building block approach. There is a lengthy planning phase in the *formal* program for any information system.

The concept of planning for an information system is intuitively more acceptable than the notion of a formal program. However, a *third-generation systems philosophy* (which is compatible with the capabilities of third-generation computer and transmission equipment) has been applied to planning, designing, and implementing information systems in various types of business corporations and organizations. While there are always unique organizational arrangements and different sets of plans for achieving similar objectives, there is an overall process or formal program that must be followed.

This formal program does not commence until executive management has approved the preliminary report from the systems analysts or management consultants which recommends that such a system study should be undertaken. In other words, the high-point review or quick study of the existing operations suggests that there are substantial tangible benefits from an information system or from an increased utilization of computer systems in a particular business or organization; moreover, these tangible benefits are of such a magnitude as to justify the expenditure of funds and the utilization of management's time in carrying out an information systems study.

In a given organization, executive management will frequently ask one or two management consulting firms, as well as the organization's information systems department, to perform a high-point review or quick study of selected existing operations from the standpoint of identifying profitable areas in which increased computer utilization might be employed. After these preliminary reports are submitted, executive management must perform a resource allocation and capital expenditure analysis including ranking of projects and determining the extent to which outside consultants should be used.

As previously indicated, the formal program for planning and implementing an information system begins with executive management's approval of the preliminary report recommending such a study. This formal program encompasses all of the operations through the full implementation of the information systems designed as part of this study. However, this formal program may not be followed to that point; instead, it may be terminated at an intermediate position where another cost-benefit analysis is performed. This intermediate evaluation is emphasized in the subsequent discussion of the formal program for planning and implementing an information system.

We have found the following five phases to be a useful compartmentalization of the formal program to plan and implement an information system: (1) planning, including commitment and orientation by executive management, (2) organization review and administrative study, (3) conceptual systems design, (4) equipment selection and program design, and (5) implementation.

Management consultants and systems analysts frequently do not separately recognize the first three phases in this formal program. Instead, some parts of the planning phase, the organization review and administrative study phase, and the conceptual systems design phase are integrated into one overall process called a "scoping study" phase. In these cases the conceptual systems design activities are generally not as thorough and complete as will be the situation where these activities are pursued as a separate phase. Therefore, when we have a scoping study phase, the equipment selection and program design phase usually includes more conceptual systems design activities than is the case in the framework used here.

The five phases in this formal program are separately examined in the following sections of this chapter. Since the equipment selection and program design phase and the implementation phase are highly procedural, only brief attention is given to these two phases. The major focus of this discussion is directed to the conceptual dimensions of this formal program embodied in the first three phases.

Planning Phase

The executive commitment part of phase one has received considerable attention. The monetary and personnel commitment for an information systems project are extensive undertakings and should be evaluated like any other long-term capital expenditure. As indicated earlier, the formal program for planning and implementing an information system does not begin until executive management approves the preliminary report recommending such a systems study. Therefore, a preliminary monetary and personnel commitment evaluation in reference to this proposed system has already been performed. A more extensive and rigorous analysis is not performed to more clearly indicate the range of benefits and costs for this project.

While the executive commitment part of the planning phase has been frequently examined in the professional literature, the orientation part of phase one has not received the attention it warrants. This brief discussion will, therefore, focus on this orientation part.

If management, particularly executive management, does not appreciate the "management by systems" concept and have some feel for what the company or organization might do with an advanced computer system, then there is really no reason to begin a management information systems study. Management is a key element in an information system. The network provides relevant and timely data to management for decision-making purposes and the network also contains the appropriate mechanism for responding to these decision-making activities. Members of management, therefore, must be oriented to the concept "management by systems," and they must have a feel for the types of decision-making activities which may be engaged in after the information system has been implemented.

There is a tendency for individuals to be more concerned with solving current problems than planning for future settings where today's problems will be handled by new techniques. Frequently, members of management must be given a formal orientation program before they are willing to accept the fact that the proposed information system will process most of today's problems by a series of programmed decision rules.

When a series of large-scale systems studies are being initiated, it is common for the company or organization to sponsor a 4- to 10-day orientation program for key executives. This formal education program usually covers the "management by systems" concept, the information systems approach, and orientation to computer equipment and communication equipment, management controls over computer operations, and the impact of information systems on organizational structure. Typically, the latter topic is not overemphasized because of the possible adverse repercussions that might result from this. In addition to these topics, considerable attention is given to discussing the business or organization as a system, and the sponsoring company is used as the example for these analyses.

After this orientation program is held for key executives, then specialized training sessions are conducted for other management and supervisory personnel. Some of the latter sessions will be scheduled to coincide with the implementation phase of the information systems study.

Organization Review and Administrative Study Phase

In a previous discussion it was explained *why* the team of systems analysts must obtain a basic feel for the nature of the company's business and for the types of major decision-making activities involved if the team is going to design an information system. The organization review or the rethinking phase is where this type of understanding is obtained.

After the basic understanding has been obtained, the team must perform detailed analyses of the major decision-making activities. From these thorough studies, the information requirements for the major decision-making activities can be ascertained. These information requirements will be matched with information sources in the process of establishing information flows, and these information flows will be integrated into information systems.

From these statements[2] we can see that the desired output from the organization review phase is *a specification of information requirements for the major decision-making activities throughout the business organization*. The attainment of this desired output does require that some degree of structure be superimposed upon the team of systems analysts' work. We have found it useful to classify this "structure" into three steps, which are separately explained in the following discussion.

Understanding the Business Process. The first step in the organization review and administrative study phase is to gain an understanding of the business process for the business organization under

---

[2] The following material in this section on "Organization Review and Administrative Study Phase" initially appeared as part of Chapter 11, "Information Systems for Planning and Control," in *Management Science in Planning and Control* (New York: Technical Association of the Pulp and Paper Industry, 1969), pp. 243–59. Permission of the Technical Association of the Pulp and Paper Industry was given to use this material in the current chapter.

study. This requires a familiarization with the unique industry characteristics and practices as well as an appreciation of the general environment in which the business organization is located. This appreciation will include a general insight into how the business organization reacts to its environment.

The accomplishment of this first step in the organization review process requires that the study team obtain a basic feel for the nature of the company's business. This demands that a general understanding be obtained of the following items:

1. What are the products and the product groups?
2. Who are the customers for each group of products?
3. What is the competitive situation with respect to each product group?
4. What is the demand forecast for the current products in each group?

   (It is surprising how many elaborate computer-based operating systems have been installed at about the same time that the major product group's demand was significantly reduced, and in some cases the product group was shortly discontinued.)
5. What is the nature of the company's products from the perspective of the customers?

   (What is the customer actually buying? Is the consumer's concept of the product compatible with management's concept?)
6. What is the environmental situation?

   (For instance, does some recent action by a governmental agency affect the future of some product line?)

Now, focusing more directly on the company:

7. What tangible and intangible resources does the company possess?
8. How are these resources being used?
9. How could they be used?
10. Are the resources being allocated in the most efficient manner?

    (The answering of this latter question will involve obtaining some rough marginal contributions by product groups, demand forecasts, and capacity requirements to produce a given product for lot size.)

After the above types of questions are resolved, the study team is beginning to obtain a feel for the nature of the company's business—

step one in the organization review process. The questions that are posed in this first step are common, basic business questions, and because the questions are of this type, study teams all too often merely give lip service to this type of organization review. "We have worked for the company for fifteen to twenty years; we know all aspects of this business." The facts are, of course, that management and even executive management may be too deeply involved in the day-to-day operations of the company to have an objective perspective of the company's business.

The following case study presents a situation where an organization review should have revealed some serious management problems. A family-owned industrial machine manufacturer with annual sales in excess of $25 million was recently sold because the president did not want to invest any more of the family funds in expanding the productive capacity of the 60-year-old company.

A representative of this machine manufacturing company approached an officer of a New York City-based investment group, and this investment group became interested in possibly purchasing the machine manufacturing company. A management consulting firm was engaged to perform a quick, high-point administrative review of the machine manufacturing company.

Three management consultants spent a week primarily performing an organization review of this reputable, industrial machine manufacturer. Incidentally, two of the consultants spent over half of their time at places other than the office or plant of the industrial machine manufacturer. They talked with old and new customers; they talked with the company's leading competitors; they went to a private business library and studied the economic forecast for this industry.

Based on the report of the three management consultants (which was supplemented by the investment group's staff studies), the industrial machine manufacturer was immediately purchased. Why? As part of the organization review, the consultants had attempted to answer the question: "Are the resources being allocated in the most efficient manner?" The engineering times required to produce the different types of machines were multiplied by the respective sales volumes for the different types of machines. This determined that there was not a shortage of capacity, but that there was a significant excess capacity. Obviously, there must be some scheduling problems. The talks with customers and with competitors had also suggested that there were some organization problems in production scheduling, plant operations, and marketing.

This case study does not end here or it would not have been cited as an information systems case. The investment group employed this same management consulting firm to design and implement a computer-based information system at this industrial machine manufacturing company. The consulting group already had some feel for the real nature of the industrial machine manufacturer's business, and these consultants worked with the new management group planning for this information system. Two years later this industrial machine manufacturing company is making the highest profits in the company's history and is using the identified excess capacity to produce new products.

In summary, the first step in the organization review process is to perform an organization type of administrative review of the company and to gain a basic understanding of the nature of the company's business. The formal recognition of this first step is not the author's original idea. Peter Drucker devoted the sixth chapter of a book[3] he wrote in 1954 to this first step; the chapter was entitled, "What Is Our Business—and What Should It Be?" Drucker[4, 5] and Watson[6] have continued to focus on the first step from an administrative position. Johnson, Kast, and Rosenzwieg[7] and Ackoff[8] have examined this step from a systems point of view.

Develop Conceptual Model of Major Decision-Making Activities. The second step in the organization review and administrative study phase includes the thorough examination of the major decision-making activities in the company and the construction of an all-encompassing conceptual model that will contain these major decision-making activities. While this detailed analysis is being made, the study team is comparing its findings with the descriptive overview of

[3] Peter F. Drucker, *The Practice of Management* (New York: Harper & Row, Publishers, Inc., 1954).

[4] Peter F. Drucker, "Managing for Business Effectiveness," *Harvard Business Review,* Vol. XLI (May–June, 1963), pp. 53–60.

[5] Peter F. Drucker, "The Effective Decision," *Harvard Business Review,* Vol. XLV (January–February, 1967), pp. 92–98.

[6] Edward T. P. Watson, "Diagnosis of Management Problems," *Harvard Business Review,* Vol. XXXVI (January–February, 1958).

[7] Richard A. Johnson, Fremont E. Kast, and James E. Rosenzwieg, "Systems Theory and Management," *Management Science,* Vol. X (1964), pp. 367–84.

[8] Russell L. Ackoff, "Management Misinformation Systems," *Management Science,* Vol. XIV (1967), pp. B-147 to B-156.

the company's business process and environment that was developed as the final part of step one. Where the findings and the dscriptive summary are not compatible, then further study is given to the activities involved.

The accomplishment of the second step in the organization review process requires that:

1. The major decision-making activities in the business must be identified.
2. The identified decision-making activities in the business must be matched against the overview of the business process to see if they appear to be reasonable and in harmony with this former understanding.
3. Each major decision-making activity is thoroughly examined with consideration given to such items as:
   A. What is the nature of the decision-making activity?
   B. What appears to be the company's policies or ground rules that relate to this decision-making activity?
4. The findings for each major decision-making activity are compared with the descriptive overview of the company's business process and where appropriate, further study is given to any items not in harmony.
5. Some type of model is developed for integrating all of these major decision-making activities into a large network with the interrelationships among major decision-making activities being clearly shown.

Another part of this second step in the organization review and administrative study phase is to examine the operating systems. For purposes of this discussion, let us assume that either the business organization has a series of operating systems or that a subgroup of this study team is designing such operating systems. These operating systems will handle most of the day-to-day transactions involved with a given set of major decision-making activities.

In summary, the second step in the organization review process is fairly easy for an individual to comprehend in terms of scope. It seems logical that if we are going to plan an information system, then we have to examine the major decision-making activities that are to be serviced by the proposed information system. If we are going to have one system or network, the creation of a model to represent all of these major decision-making activities and the relationships among activities appears to be a reasonable requirement. What is not so readily appreciated is the *time required* (1) to perform a thorough and comprehensive study of the decision-making activities, (2) to compare the findings of this study with the overview of the company's business, and (3) to examine the details surrounding the inconsistencies revealed by the latter comparisons.

Determine the Specific Information Requirements for System. The third step in the organization review and administrative study phase is to determine the specific information requirements for the proposed information system. This task is simplified by having a series of operating systems, such as integrated inventory control and production control system. These operating systems are closed data flows in a given time frame which match information requirements and information sources. Thus, the day-to-day, repetitive types of requirements have already been identified and matched with information sources in the existing set of operating systems.

Therefore, the specific information requirements that are determined by this third step will typically be one of four types:

1. The so-called "exceptional items" that are not handled by the series of operating systems.
2. Management activities that have previously been accomplished by a "seat of pants" type of information or by some informal information flow that is now being formally recognized.
3. Old decision-making activities that were part of the business process, in "name only." That is, these activities were recognized as being important, but management was so busy with other activities that management frequently did not consider these matters. Now, with the new computer-based information system, all decision-making activities that are part of the business process will be serviced.
4. New decision-making activities that were identified in the act of comparing the overall understanding of the business and its environment (based on the organization type of review) with the business organization's present way of doing business. The latter would be revealed by studying the existing major decision-making activities within the business organization.

The specific information requirements that are determined by this third step may be classified into two groupings: "tentative information requirements" and "information requirements." The organization type of review of the company and the study of the decision-making activities may reveal certain types of decisions that could be made. Data for these proposed types of decision-making activities may be cited as "tentative information requirements" for the purpose of evaluating if it is economically feasible to provide for that specific, tentative information requirement.

This evaluation is based on a comparison of the direct benefit obtained from using the "satisfied" tentative information requirement in a decision-making activity versus the cost of creating the data to be used in "satisfying" this tentative information requirement. Items that do not pass this test are excluded from the "information requirements" grouping.

In summary, the third and final step in the organization review and administrative study phase is the determination of the specific information requirements for the proposed information system that are not satisfied by the existing set of operating systems. From this examination of the three steps in the organization review phase, we have a better understanding of the objectives and operations of this administrative process.

The organization review and administrative study phase in an information systems program represents a formal effort to incorporate into the proposed system a feel for the business and the major decision-making activities to be serviced by the proposed system. Where this process is not applied, an operating system will be implemented rather than an information system.

Conceptual Systems Design Phase

As previously stated, many management consultants do not separately recognize the third phase in planning and implementing an information system. Instead, their "scoping study" phase will encompass most of the conceptual aspects of the first three phases. Other management consultants may follow a five-phase program, but they will use a different compartmentalization of the steps included in the second and third phases.

In the latter case, the second phase will only consist of a high-point organization review. The second and third steps in the organization review and administrative study phase—the development of a conceptual model of major decision-making activities and the determination of specific information requirements for the system—are encompassed in the conceptual systems design phase. When these steps are included in the third phase, of course, the conceptual systems design phase becomes the major time-consuming activity in planning and designing and information system.

If our above framework is followed and the organization review and administrative study phase is fully accomplished, then the conceptual systems design phase represents a period of intent thinking and cogitating over possible alternative networks for handling the information requirements identified in step three of the second phase. The team of systems analysts will spend considerable time in questioning, examining, dissecting, pondering, and grasping the information dimensions of the organizational unit under scrutiny.

From this period of detail analysis and intent thinking, many proposed conceptual arrangements of information flows will be discarded, and the study team will envision a network of information flows that satisfies the information requirements identified in the second phase of this formal program. The overall objective in the third phase is for the study team to reach a consensus as to the best conceptual arrangement of the information dimensions of the organizational unit under scrutiny. Once this agreement has been obtained, the study team will begin to explore in the fourth phase if any technological constraints limit the immediate implementation of the proposed system.

Frequently, there is a gap between the conceptual arrangement proposed in the third phase and the computer and systems programs designed in the fourth phase. If an advanced information system is being planned, the absence of a gap between the third and fourth phases of the formal program would bring into question the quality of the systems planning effort. Further attention is given to this point and to the technological constraints in the subsequent section of this chapter.

The study team may use the following approach in performing the conceptual systems design phase. Using the specification of information requirements for the major decision-making activities throughout the business organization as a beginning point, the study team commences to develop different arrangements of information networks which encompass these information requirements. In these proposed arrangements, the study team is intentionally not restricted to existing technology, such as the capabilities of current computer systems and transmission equipment. Instead, the study team's focus is on the development of logical arrangements for carrying out the organization's activities and for servicing these identified information requirements.

In focusing on these logical arrangements of information flows, the study team is really examining the information dimensions of the decision-making activities within the organizational unit under scrutiny. Since all "information dimensions" must relate to "decision-making activities," we can specify this operation as follows: the study team is really examining the information dimensions of the organizational unit and is proposing new arrangements for these dimensions.

Study teams frequently use various management science techniques in performing this analysis. Systems flowcharts, program flowcharts, lattice networks, matrix models, and communication charts are some of the typical techniques used for analyzing these information dimensions. Various types of coding and classification models have also been employed, and cluster analysis is currently being experimented with as another technique for assisting the study team in performing this analysis.

At the completion of the conceptual systems design phase, the study team will have reached a consensus as to the best, logical arrangement of the information dimensions in the organizational unit under scrutiny. Before this agreement can be obtained, the proposed arrangement must be fully described and thoroughly documented. Therefore, at the completion of the third phase, the study team will have produced a comprehensive report which summarizes the team's analysis and clearly presents the proposed arrangement of information flows. Descriptive models, diagrams, and flowcharts are integral parts of this documented report.

Equipment Selection and Program Design Phase

This fourth phase in planning and implementing an information system is a subject that has been extensively covered in the professional literature over the past decade. What is most important about the fourth phase is that *the equipment selection and program design phase should not begin until after a preliminary attempt has been made to complete the third phase.* Frequently, a study team's analysis is in the domain of the fourth phase when, in fact, the study team is supposed to be concentrating on the latter steps in the second phase.

In the fourth phase, the study team has to carefully consider the various technological constraints in computer systems, transmission equipment, "software packages," and other supporting facilities. In addition, some recent equipment capabilities may not currently be available at a reasonable price. For instance, online transmission of volumes of raw data from many remote locations into large computer systems coupled with a return transmission of relevant information in response to specific inquiries is a type of proposed arrangement that is frequently not economically feasible. Periodically, new transmission developments permit some companies to install such arrangements, and it is anticipated that this type of proposed arrangement may be economically feasible for many other companies in the near future.

We believe that there should be a significant gap between the proposed arrangement in the third phase and what can be operationally and economically planned for in the fourth phase. The existence of such gap tends to indicate the extent to which the study team in the third phase was really focusing upon proposed conceptual arrangements without thinking about technological constraints.

The major thrust of this argument can be viewed from another perspective. Specifically, what criteria are used in selecting members for the study team? It is believed that the majority of the team members should intentionally not be too deeply aware of the "state of art" in regard to computer systems, transmission equipment, and other supporting facilities. Instead, the team members should be predominately management-types with a strong orientation to the organization and to its environment. If the study team consists of six individuals, then one member might be the director or manager of the computer center. The other five members should be from other departments, and their actual departmental designation will vary depending upon the organizational units encompassed in the information systems study.

The study team in performing the fourth phase of this formal program will typically make extensive use of consultants. There are consultants who specialize in specific parts of the operations encompassed in the overall equipment selection and program design phase. Because of this degree of specialization by consultants, there is an additional reason why the study team needs a comprehensive report representing the team's thinking at the end of the third phase. Otherwise, the study team may select the group of specialists and may participate in the detail planning of an information system with a different set of characteristics than would have been the case if another group of specialists were the consultants.

There are several companies that sell general computer programs, and frequently these computer programs are fairly advanced. For example a computer program may contain a few subroutines that through experience have proven to be useful processors of data for a special class of decisions. While these decisions may not be important or critical enough to be planned for (in the sense of the special computer programming effort required for processing these data), the marginal cost in obtaining such general programs from a computer services company may be low when it is part of a "package."

In summary, the study team in performing the fourth phase in planning and implementing an information system primarily serves in a coordinating capacity. Specialists and computer systems personnel are assigned many of the tasks, and outside consultants and computer services companies are used in performing other tasks. The study team coordinates these efforts and questions the interface opportunities between assignments. In many companies the membership of the active study team may change during the fourth phase with only one or two members being retained who have participated in the first three phases of the formal program.

Implementation Phase

The scope of activities encompassed in the fifth phase of a formal program to plan and implement an information system is rather obvious. The project manager for the systems study must coordinate, administer, and supervise the full implementation of the planned system. Priorities must be established so that the appropriate sequence of activities is followed. The project manager must give special attention to those related subsystems that have common information flows; otherwise, noncompatible information flows may be established.

The fifth phase is an extremely important part of the formal program for planning and implementing an information system. There are many techniques and procedures that project managers successfully employ in carrying out this function. However, because of the orientation of this book, attention is not given in this text to these techniques and procedures.

Summary

The need for management to participate in planning for an information system is the overriding theme of this chapter. Management cannot participate in planning for a system unless management appreciates how the proposed system is going to be used. Thus, the "management by systems" concept is a perspective that management must possess before members of management can intelligently discuss how a proposed system might be used.

If an information system rather than an operating system is going to be established, then the systems analysts must examine management's decision-making activities so that selected responses to critical decisions can be anticipated and planned for in the design of computer programs. In the latter situation, these anticipated responses are identified as change factors, and they are represented in the designed computer programs as parameters and variables.

The five phases in a formal program for planning and implementing an information system were examined in the latter part of this chapter. These five phases are (1) planning, including commitment and orientation by executive management, (2) organization review and administrative study, (3) conceptual systems design, (4) equipment selection and program design, and (5) implementation. Because of the overall orientation of this book, only brief attention was given to the fourth and fifth phases of the formal program.

TOPICS FOR CLASS DISCUSSION

1. In a systems engagement at a commercial bank, the study team will frequently establish a simulation model to represent the proposed new system. Customers of a commercial bank expect a new system to operate with a minimum number of delays and errors. This is the reason that the commercial bank's management is willing to pay for the design of a special simulation model that represents the proposed system.

In this systems study, where does the simulation model fit in? Is it part of the third phase? The fourth phase? The fifth phase? Explain your answer.

2. In a governmental agency we may have a quarterly change in the assigned mission of the agency. Sometimes the mission may

change monthly. In this type of dynamic setting, is it possible to design and implement an information system? Explain your response.

3. Select some part of a business organization, describe the activities within this organization unit, and explain how these activities can be handled by a *functional program*. Next, modify the organizational unit and indicate what is necessary for an *operating system*. Finally, expand the context and explain what might be encompassed in an *information system* for this same area.

4. When a study team is analyzing a computer-based management system over a period of time, the comment is sometimes made that, "this cycle's information system will become an operating system in the future." What does this general expression mean from an information systems standpoint? Explain your answer.

5. As a management consultant you are confronted with the following situation: You have undertaken an information systems study in a company and you now discover that members of executive management are not willing to spend time in the organizational review and conceptual study phase of the study. Explain the philosophical problem confronting you.

6. Figure 3.2 in this chapter presented a continuum showing the relative positions of programs and systems. In determining the assigned value for a specific network, what attributes are being quantified?

CASE 3–1. BROOKFIELD LABORATORIES, INC.

Mr. Bruce Whitman is vice president, manufacturing, at Brookfield Laboratories, Inc. He has requested the management consulting firm with which you are employed to perform a high-point review of Brookfield's manufacturing operations and to recommend a specific program for improving the existing computer-based information system.

This is not the first time that Mr. Whitman has engaged the services of the management consulting firm with which you are employed. Recently a management science team from this firm completed the design and implementation of a special computer program that concurrently assigns (1) products to vats and equipment, (2) employees to vats and equipment, and (3) employees to

products. Mr. Whitman is especially interested in proposed extensions to this special program and in developing an information
system for the manufacturing operations around the new capabilities
provided by this computer program.

The Company

Brookfield Laboratories, a subsidiary of a large, diversified corporation, is a drug and chemical manufacturing company with annual
sales of $150,000,000. Brookfield is more indicative of a company in
the pharmaceutical industry than one in the chemical industry. For
example, Brookfield's return on invested capital last year was over 23
percent, and this return is comparable with that of companies in the
pharmaceutical industry.

Brookfield is organized along traditional lines. In addition to the
president and the executive vice president, the management committee consists of the following individuals: vice president, marketing;
vice president, manufacturing; treasurer and financial manager; vice
president, research and development; vice president, employee and
public relations; and secretary and general counsel.

Computer equipment was installed at Brookfield in 1955, and this
equipment has been updated when major technological developments have occurred. Currently an IBM 360/Model 50 computer
system is being used. While the Model 50 is located at Brookfield,
some of the computer applications are for other companies owned by
the parent corporation. However, a large segment of the computer
time and storage capacity on the Model 50 is devoted to Brookfield's
research and development activities, and these computer applications
include intensive testing of new products. The other major computer
applications are financial accounting, payroll, invoicing, product and
territory reports for marketing, and cost and performance reports.

The Manufacturing Division

Bruce Whitman, as vice president, manufacturing, has responsibility for the following daily decision-making activities. He must
daily assign employees to products; some employees cannot produce
all products. In fact, most employees can only create a limited
number of products, and each of these are produced at varying
degrees of efficiency. Second, he must assign vats and equipment to

products; different products can be manufactured by different combinations of vats and machinery. The cost of production varies by the combination of vats and machinery actually used in the creation of the product. Third, he must assign employees to vats and equipment. Most employees have varying degrees of efficiency with some vats and equipment, regardless of what product is being manufactured in that vat.

Bruce Whitman is an extremely conscientious executive and has tried to stay abreast of developments in management science that relate to his operations. For the past several years he has used linear programming in daily making a two-way assignment of products to vats and equipment, and he has combined this assignment with business experience in assigning employees to products. Because of the procedure used, 7 to 8 percent of Brookfield's employees will be unassigned for a given shift. In other words, the unassigned vats and equipment cannot be used by the unassigned employees to produce additional products.

Management Science Technique

Based on the potential savings from more efficient use of the unassigned employees, a management science team was engaged to develop some type of mathematical technique for handling this task. The team's initial approach was to use the classical assignment model as illustrated by Exhibit A. The cost data for the products to men matrix are based on the varying efficiencies that employees have in creating different products, regardless of which equipment is used in the manufacturing process. The cost data for the products to vats matrix represent the out-of-pocket cost for creating a product, exclusive of the varying efficiencies that employees have in manufacturing different products. The unused equipment row is necessary for this model so that the columns for vats and products equal the rows for men, products, and unassigned equipment.

The assignment model as presented in Exhibit A is not complete. Products are not manufactured in vats according to a one-to-one assignment; instead, certain products may require more than one vat for their creation. Moreover, selected products can be manufactured by different combinations of vats. In addition to these refinements of the problem, some employees have varying efficiencies with using

EXHIBIT A
Assignment of Products to Men to Vats
(for illustration purposes only)

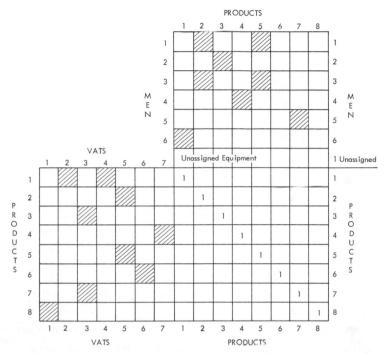

Note: The products to products matrix serves as a connection between the products to men matrix and the products to vats matrix. The total assignment for any row must equal one and the total assignment for any column must equal one. Therefore, as a man to product assignment occurs, the *one* on the diagonal in the products to products matrix is replaced by a zero. It is immediately necessary to assign a vat to a product for that row; otherwise, the total assignments for that row would not equal one.

The shaded areas in the products to men matrix and in the products to vats matrix indicates that certain assignments cannot occur. All vats cannot be used to produce all products; all workers cannot create all products.

selected equipment and vats, regardless of which products are being manufactured.

These other dimensions of the problem cannot be adequately handled by the assignment model. The management science team had to develop another algorithm for coping with the broader dimensions of this concurrent assignment problem. Using Alex Orden's transshipment problem (see *Management Science,* Vol. II (1956), (pp. 276–85) as a guide, the management science team developed an algorithm that linked a series of assignment models. A rough illustration of this approach is presented in Exhibit B; a more

EXHIBIT B
Concurrent Assignment of Products to Men to Vats
(for illustration purposes only)

PRODUCTS

	P1	P2	P3	P4
M1 (MEN)				
M2				
UE1				
P1 (PRODUCTS)	1			
P2		1		
P3			1	
P4				1

VATS

	V1	V2	V3
M1			
M2			
UE1			
P1			
P2			
P3			
P4 (MEN: M1 M2 UE1)			

VATS

	P1	P2	P3	P4
V1	1			
V2		1		
V3			1	

PRODUCTS

	M1	M2	UE1	P1	P2	P3	P4
M1 (MEN)	1						
M2		1					
UE1			1				

Note: The symbol "UE1" represents unassigned equipment. In the first matrix, a product is assigned to a man; the number one is removed from the diagonal in the products to products matrix, and a vat must be assigned to that product in the vats to products matrix. When the assignment occurs in the vats to products matrix, the number one is removed from the diagonal in the vats to vats matrix; therefore, a row assignment must occur in the men to vats matrix. As the assignment occurs in the men to vats matrix, the number one is removed from the diagonal in the men to men matrix; thus, a row assignment must occur in the products to men matrix. This products to men matrix is identical with the initial products to men matrix. The concurrent assignment process is complete.

precise description of the algorithm is not possible because of the proprietary nature of the model.

In Exhibit B, the products to products matrix, the vats to vats matrix, and the men to men matrix provide the linking capability. These matrices serve as the intermediate location in the transshipment. Beyond these similarities to the standard transshipment model, the actual algorithm developed was different for it had to cope with a combination of assignment of vats to a given product.

For purposes of this discussion, assume that a computer program was developed which would produce an optimum three-way assignment along the general lines suggested by Exhibit B. This computer program requires less than two minutes of computer time to determine the assignment of 150 products, 110 employees, and 130 vats. In this assignment, not all products are manufactured during any shift. In addition, there are constraints on the current assignment of vats to products, depending on which drugs and chemicals were produced in each particular vat during the previous shift. However, these variables and constraints are easily handled in the special computer program that was designed by the management science team.

Current Situation

Bruce Whitman initially had reservations about the management science team's proposed model. Eventually he was convinced that this three-way assignment model was acceptable and should be used at Brookfield. After a period of time Bruce Whitman was able to accept the fact that the new computer program could in less than two minutes perform a three-way assignment, a task which previously had taken all of his time. Moreover, the computer assignment was an optimum solution, while Whitman's manually derived assignment had only been a satisfactory approach to the problem.

Since *you* have been assigned to this engagement, you begin to ponder over how to plan an information system around this special computer program. Since all of Bruce Whitman's decision-making experience over the past 20 years has related to the three-way assignment, you cannot ask him to tell you his information requirements.

REQUIRED:

Indicate step-by-step how you will approach this consulting assignment. Be specific!

CHAPTER 4

Applications to Business
Organizations

MANY LARGE BUSINESS ORGANIZATIONS are using a series of operating systems to handle the required daily volume of transactions for administering, controlling, and planning their activities. In some business firms a series of information systems has been established in place of these operating systems. Where this has occurred, we will frequently find that the systems designers have followed a formal program for planning and implementing an information system, and this formal program will usually encompass the five phases in the program which we outlined in the previous chapter. These five phases are (1) planning, including commitment and orientation by executive management, (2) organization review and administrative study, (3) conceptual systems design, (4) equipment selection and program design, and (5) implementation.

While we may desire to apply these five phases in planning and implementing an information system, we may find it is difficult to fully apply these phases in an actual situation. Moreover, if we have only limited experience in designing such systems, we may have a special problem of not knowing when we have adequately accomplished each phase in the formal program. For example, how do we establish priorities in the conceptual systems design phase? How do we determine which of a series of related activities should be grouped together in a system?

In a small business organization with a typical set of business activities, the systems analyst soon discovers that there are numerous ways or arrangements for matching information requirements of decision makers with information sources. The team of systems analysts must select one set of arrangements over all other possible configurations. Unfortunately, after this selection process has occurred, there is no assurance that the selected set of networks is, in fact, the best of all possible configurations.

This latter point is really a reflection of the current "state of the art." We have only recently become aware that this problem exists, and a few doctoral candidates are currently studying some facets of this problem. It is hoped that as a result of these efforts some management science technique may be developed which will at least give the study team a handle to use in coping with this significant problem.

In this chapter we will examine some of the typical arrangements used in clustering information flows into a series of information systems. The general arrangements or general models that are presented in this chapter are based on business experience; these models do not necessarily reflect any optimum configuration. As indicated above, we do not have any management science technique that can be employed in scientifically selecting the best set of information networks.

Before we can fully appreciate these general models of information systems, we need some understanding of how a business firm's management organizes for a series of information systems. This overview will consist of four parts: (1) the organizational arrangement of the information systems function in a large corporation, (2) the organizational arrangement for planning and coordinating a series of information system studies, (3) an approach to vertical slicing of the organizational structure for purposes of identifying a chain of events for inclusion in a given information system, and (4) a conceptual model of the business firm. After this overview, attention is focused on four general models of information systems which have proven to be useful compartmentalizations of clusters of information flows.

Organizational Arrangements of Information Systems Function

There is no uniform location of the information systems function in corporate organizations. The centralization versus decentralization of this function varies somewhat by size of corporation (both in annual dollar volume of sales and the average dollar value per customer order), geographical dispersion of corporation, and the degree to which there are physical similarities among items in various product lines. The current location of this function is also influenced by which corporate officer was primarily responsible for initially introducing large-scale computer systems into the company during the 1950's or early 1960's.

In a few corporations the information systems function is organizationally located at the vice president level, and the corporate officer responsible for this division has one of the following five titles: vice president—operations, vice president—planning, vice president—administration, vice president—information services, and vice president—information systems. While there is an increasing number of corporations where the information systems function is organizationally located at the vice president level, such arrangements are still exceptional cases.

The latter statement requires some qualification. Where the information systems function is integrated with the corporate planning function, then this combined function, almost by tautology, must be at the vice president level. The highly diversified corporation with a strong central management will frequently have a vice president—information systems, and this individual will have corporate-wide (including all the merged companies) responsibility for planning, implementing, and monitoring all types of information systems. A 1968 American Management Association research study which included 16 companies and 9 industries indicated that there is some shift toward a vice president level organizational location of the information systems function.[1]

Regardless of our individual preferences as to where we think the information systems function should be organizationally located, it is frequently located as a department at the first level below the vice president's tier. The director, information systems department in many cases reports to the vice president—finance. For purposes of this discussion, we will assume, unless stated otherwise, that the information systems department has this organizational arrangement. In a later chapter we will examine how this function is being modified as advanced information systems are being planned and implemented.

Figure 4.1 presents a typical arrangement of the information systems department. In this department less than 40 percent of the regular work load relates to maintenance and housekeeping activ-

---

[1] Robert R. Reichenbach and Charles A. Tasso, *Organizing for Data Processing: AMA Research Study 92* (New York: American Management Association, Inc., 1968).

FIGURE 4.1
Information Systems Department

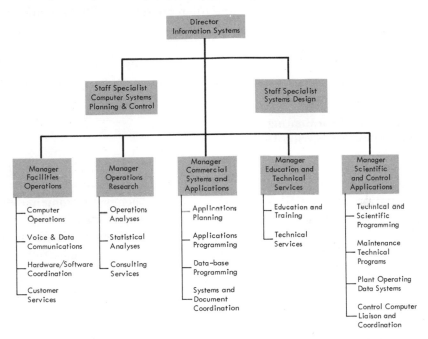

ities. The major portion of the department's activities pertains to planning and designing of new systems. The two staff assistants are barometers of this orientation: (1) staff specialist—systems design and (2) staff specialist—computer systems planning and control.

The organizational arrangement of the information systems department is primarily for identifying responsibilities and for administrative purposes. During the systems planning and designing efforts, it is unusual for a study team to be staffed by members from any one group or unit. Housekeeping and systems maintenance activities are, on the other hand, primarily performed by members of one group.

The study coordinator for each major information systems project (those projects that involve planning, designing, and implementing of new systems) is usually selected from the group of managers in the information systems department. Typically, the manager from one of the following three groups will be selected as study coordinator: commercial systems and applications, operations research, and scientific and control applications.

In some organizations, the two-staff specialists are also selected as study coordinators. In other companies one of these two-staff specialists will serve as an ex officio member on the study team for each major information systems project.

From this brief description we can see the expertise available in the information systems department. Now let us focus on the overall organizational arrangements for major information systems studies.

Planning and Coordinating for a Series of Information Systems Studies

As previously explained, management must participate in the planning and designing phase of an information system, or else an information system will not be created. This general statement pertains to all levels of management including the members of the management committee. In this section brief attention is given to one organizational arrangement that facilitates participation by management at all levels.

Any proposed large-scale information systems study should be approved by the management committee. The proposal setting forth this planned study should be sufficiently specific so that this group of executives fully appreciates what it is that they are being asked to approve. The preliminary study proposal should at least call for the establishment of an information systems coordinating group, a committee that has responsibility for handling all policy issues that arise in planning and coordinating an information system.

The typical arrangement is for each member of the management committee to have a representative on the information systems coordinating group. Since each member of the management committee selects his own representative for this group, any recommendations by this group would be expected to be approved by the management committee if necessary. The director, information systems department, generally serves as the chairman of this group.

Each representative on the information systems coordinating group serves in a dual capacity. First, he is the designee of a member of the management committee to serve in this group. Second, he is the representative of an individual department or group that will be using the services of the proposed information system. This representative is the user department's primary contact with the information systems study team, and all formal communications between the study team and operating and functional personnel in the department are channeled through this representative. This latter communication function encourages, at least, a minimum level of involvement and participation by each member of the information systems coordinating group.

Each member of the information systems coordinating group is not equally involved with a particular information systems project. Some user departments are primarily affected by the study; other departments are only indirectly affected. Those departments that are primarily involved are normally represented by a full-time systems analyst on the information systems study team. The other departments will have a part-time representative on the study team who will participate when the study team is exploring these indirect activities.

Someone must have primary responsibility for pushing and directing the study team. It is typical for the study team coordinator to be a manager or staff specialist in the information systems department. For the duration of the project, the coordination of this study team and the successful completion of the undertaking are his primary responsibilities. Where a user department's representative has been selected as study team coordinator, the project frequently becomes sidetracked when more pressing departmental activities take precedence over the proposed study.

The full-time members of the information systems study team will consist of the study coordinator (who is from the information systems department) and the representatives from those user departments that are primarily affected by the study. In addition, technical and staff personnel may be assigned to the project, and these individuals are selected because of their expertise and areas of competence rather than because of the department in which they are currently located.

The part-time members of the information systems study team should include a representative from the certified public accounting firm that annually audits the company's information systems and reports. This representative may desire to establish within the proposed information system certain checks and balances as well as other types of internal control features. The monitoring role performed by this external accountant is discussed in a later chapter.

Other part-time members of the information systems study team will include external consultants. It is unusual for an information systems study team not to include, at least, one consultant. In fact, the typical business problem is one of making too much use of consultants. Management cannot depend entirely on external consultants to design an information system; instead, management should participate in planning and designing the proposed system so that it appropriately satisfies the unique information requirements of the business firm. Moreover, if management has participated in planning a new information system, knowledge about how the system operates resides with the management group and this understanding does not immediately disappear when the consultants depart.

The Operating Cycle Concept

How does the study team determine which sets of information flows should be incorporated in a given information system? As previously indicated this is a difficult problem for which the current "state of the art" does not provide any one solution or even a management science technique that gives a handle for coping with the problem. Third-generation systems philosophy does offer a concept or approach for attacking the problem.

This approach is a reinterpretation of the operating cycle concept that has traditionally been used in accounting. This approach has been redefined for coping with the diversified business firm, and the concept has been given a new label as it is used in grouping a sequence of information flows. The new label that is assigned to the operating cycle concept varies by management consulting groups and teams of systems analysts. Some call it a "management systems approach"; others label it a "management analysis approach." A few individuals use other unusual labels to refer to the operating cycle concept as applied to the design of information systems. For purposes of this discussion, we will continue to use the terms "operating cycle concept."

The operating cycle concept was selected for use in slicing through the organizational structure because a trained observer using this perspective will focus on *chains of events* that begin outside the company, encompasses a mainstream of events within the company, and terminates at a point external to the organization. One of the benefits of this concept is that it identifies a beginning point and an ending point (both of which are external to the business firm) which are connected by these chains of events. Having the beginning and ending points so clearly specified gives the team of systems analysts two concrete locations to anchor their mainstream of events. Where these beginning and ending points are so clearly specified, the team of systems analysts does not run the risk of designing an information system for only a portion of the information flows. These omitted flows later become apparent when other information dimensions of the decision-making process that is serviced by the system are brought into focus.

In accounting we refer to the operating cycle concept as the chain of events beginning with the purchase of raw materials, incorporating all of the activities within the business firm to manufacture and distribute products using these raw materials, and finally collecting for the sale of the products so that these funds can be used to purchase new raw materials. Where we have a diversified company, different product groups will have their own operating cycle.

As the terms operating cycle concept are applied to the design of information systems, we see a close analogy to the physical movement of economic goods in the accounting concept. In the case of information systems, the relevant dimensions included in this mainstream of events has been expanded to include all types of information flows that will assist in the company's decision-making processes.

How does the operating cycle concept differ from a functional approach to the design of information systems? In a functional study we may design an ideal operating system for manufacturing a group of products, while we ignore the special problems encountered in distributing the products. In other words, a functional approach frequently gives an ad hoc solution to a specific problem without addressing itself to a balanced approach to a related set of issues.

In following the operating cycle concept, we are concerned with examining all of those activities in a functional area that relate to the identified chain of events. Above all, we desire a mainstream of events that connects all of these activities so that there are no delays or bottlenecks in our information flows.

The study team in applying the operating cycle concept encounters another type of problem. The identified chain of events may be too narrowly perceived, and the proposed "mainstream" may not encompass all of the information dimensions that are needed by the decision-making process. In other words, the study team should not abandon the information systems approach that was explained in Chapter 2.

Attention is now focused on an overall reexamination of the business process from the perspective of emphasizing differences in information flows. Using this discussion as a base, a set of criteria is presented for grouping related major information flows into a series of information systems. In this examination we will assume the role of the systems analyst rather than the perspective of different members of the study team.

Searching for a Set of Criteria

As previously stated, the systems analyst's perspective of a business organization is significantly influenced by organization theory. He recognizes that a business enterprise is a group of individuals united by some common objectives or goals and directed by management toward the production and distribution of goods and services. What are these common objectives and goals? There is difference of opinion regarding the identification of the order of these common objectives for the business enterprise,[2] and the following viewpoint is presented as our opinion.[3]

Assuming that the business organization is united by the common objective of maximization of "long-term income," then business management has the responsibility of relating day-to-day events and problems to this long-term objective. It is difficult for management to simultaneously focus on immediate events and forecasted events, particularly from the standpoint of having the proper relation between the numerous events. Therefore, business management usually specifies intermediate measures of this long-term goal. These intermediate measures include:

1. Profitability
2. Market standing
3. Technological developments
4. Innovations
5. Research and development

---

[2] Three interpretations of the "profit motive" are presented in the following paper by Thomas R. Prince, "The Motivational Assumption for Accounting Theory," *Accounting Review,* Vol. XXXIX (July, 1964), pp. 553–62.

[3] This book presents the justification for Thomas R. Prince's viewpoint and cites numerous references for the more concerned reader: *Extension of the Boundaries of Accounting Theory* (Cincinnati, Ohio: South-Western Publishing Co., Inc., 1963).

6. Market position
7. Productivity
8. Physical and financial resources
9. Worker performance and attitude
10. Manager performance and attitude
11. Business climate
12. Public responsibility
13. Preservation of industrial peace
14. Price leadership (peace and harmony)
15. Image of corporation (no price fixing, etc.)
16. Others
17. Balance between short-term and long-term objectives[4]

The significance of the various intermediate measures of the long-term concept of income will vary by business enterprise within each industry and by industry. Business management implicitly or explicitly specifies the relative importance of each of these intermediate measures and frequently states in numerical values the levels of aspiration for the various intermediate measures. These stated levels of aspiration may be short-term, annual, two-year, three-year or for a longer period of time.

Business management's role, then, is to coordinate the business organization's efforts (including people, resources, properties, and activities) in such a manner that it is possible to realize the organization's long-term goal. This management process can be divided into four functions— (1) acquisition, (2) production, (3) distribution, and (4) administration. Each function can be divided into four steps—(1) organization, (2) planning, (3) control, and (4) evaluation.

Business management is involved in decision-making activities in the performance of each of these steps applied to each of the functions which may be directed toward various intermediate measures of this long-term goal—the maximization of "long-term income." Thus, the four steps multiplied by the four functions equal 16 separate decision-making activities for each intermediate measure. Depending on the degree of complexity, there will be several information flows associated with each of these separate decision-making activities.

While the management process may be schematically divided into four functions, the organizational structure of a given business enter-

---

[4] *Ibid.*, p. 175.

prise may not be compatible with this arrangement. For example, the production function might be organizationally represented by three manufacturing departments, and engineering services department, and a research and development department. Instead of having a single group of homogeneous products, the business enterprise may have several heterogeneous groups of products. In this latter situation, different groups of products may be sold in different markets. Furthermore, the production process may vary completely between different groups of products.

In addition to the above modifications from the standpoint of the organizational structure, the steps performed by business management in a given business organization for the purpose of accomplishing a series of related activities may vary significantly between different groups of products. For example, in the performance of the production function, business management may be able to complete all aspects of the planning process for a group of products before any activity commences in the period covered by the plan. With another group of products, business management may continuously be involved in the planning process as activity occurs.

Other factors assist in further complicating the situation. The environmental setting may vary between different groups of products. The advertising strategy may vary not only between markets, but between different products within the same market. Finally, the time frames of different decision activities may vary completely.

In summary, the reader may now envision a business organization as being represented by a more complicated network of information flows than was envisioned before this current discussion was undertaken. In *searching for a set of criteria*, attention has been given to the differences rather than to the similarities between different aspects of the business process within a given business organization. These distinctions serve as the bases for the general models of information systems presented in the next section.

Models of Information Systems

The systems analyst repeatedly applies three primary factors to the task of grouping and integrating general information flows (or systems at a higher level of analysis) into more compact units. These three factors are (1) the general business activity to which an information flow relates, (2) the general nature or characteristic of the information being processed and transmitted, and (3) the time frame of the information flow.

If the systems analyst is able to repeatedly apply these three factors to successively higher levels of study, eventually he will have a single information system that will encompass the essential aspects of all of the known, major information flows within the business organization. When this is possible, the resulting system is labeled a "traditional information system."

However, in the majority of situations, conflicting time frames or dissimilar information prohibits the general integration of all information flows into a single system. We have arbitrarily selected two states of these latter conditions and have labeled the two states based on the primary types of variables. These two states are "production and operation information system" and "marketing information system."

If the state of conditions for the production and operation information system or the marketing information system were specially selected, either system could in a special situation represent an organization-wide single information system encompassing all of the known major information flows within the organization. However, this is not the normal setting in which these two types of systems occur. Therefore, the production and operation information system or the marketing information system is presented as an organization-wide single information system encompassing a selected group of known major information flows within the organization.

Frequently, when it is not possible to have a "traditional information system" for all known major information flows within the business organization, a type of "traditional information system" will be used on an organization-wide basis for the accumulation, processing, and transmission of certain groups of information.

Thus, in a complicated business organization with conflicting time frames and dissimilar information characteristics for different information flows, the systems analyst may reach the point where the business organization under study has three concurrent major information systems. A type of traditional information system operating on a one-month cycle may contain a certain group of information flows. A production and operation information system operating on a daily cycle may contain another group of information flows. A marketing information system operating on a weekly cycle may contain a third group of information flows. (The time frame of these three systems was entirely illustrative and will vary significantly between business organizations.)

Some systems analysts, upon approaching the point of having these three concurrent major information systems, have accepted the challenge of trying to develop connecting links between each of the information systems. If these connecting links can be developed, then it may be possible to have a unique type of "total information system" for each large, complex business organization. The process by which systems analysts attempt to achieve some versions of this objective is labeled "movement toward a total information system."

Before attention is given to citing some of the differentiating characteristics of these general models of information systems, the following qualification should be noted. In the process of grouping and integrating related major information flows into an information system, the systems analyst is cautioned to give proper attention to the matter of exceptions. For example, in 95 percent of the time, this is what happens; in 5 percent of the time, something else happens. The designed information system must be able to accommodate these latter, exceptional items, or, else, the system will not function according to the plan. In other words, a general information system may contain a subsystem that specifies the flow of activity for all exceptional items that can be predicted, and an individual is assigned to handle all exceptional, nonpredictable occurrences. In the following discussion of general models of information systems, it is assumed that any general system may contain one or more such subsystems for coping with these exceptional items.

Traditional Information System

The general model for a traditional information system is a *closed* system encompassing all of the major information flows within a business organization. The network supporting this closed system contains both vertical and horizontal flows. The characteristic of a closed system suggests that the business organization under study must be situated in a given type of environment and that the business process can be conducted in a specified manner. Each of these differentiating characteristics is examined.

Environment. Within the time frame of the cycle contained in the traditional information system, business management does not plan on either responding or reacting to changes in the raw materials market, the finished goods market, or actions by competitors. This latter remark, of course, is a generalization; within the time frame of the cycle, business management may be forced to change its procurement plans or its marketing plans (including price of finished goods). However, what is important is that the overall system does not react or respond to these external changes. (In the production and operation information system this overall system response does occur.) This matter of degree of response by the system to changes in the environment is clarified in the following examination of the business process.

Business Process.   The nature of the business activity is such that all phases of the planning process can be completed *before* any of the activity in the time period covered by the plan begins. Thus, the control process begins after the planning process has been completed, and this control process seeks conformance of activity to the "plan."

This planning process consists of (1) identifying the tasks to be performed, (2) coordinating these tasks to be sure there are no conflicts, (3) specifying the extent to which each task is to be performed (expressed in some unit of measure), (4) assigning personnel to tasks, and (5) allocating the resources and materials for the accomplishment of each task.

After all the assignment and coordinating activities have occurred, then action commences on the work toward the achievement of each task. As this work is performed, it is monitored by the control process, which seeks conformance or adherence to plans.

As far as the time frame of the cycle, it may be a year, a month, a week, a day, or a shorter specified period of time. For example, in one business organization, a four-hour frame is used. Every four hours the business organization decides (1) which raw materials will be used in the manufacture of (2) which finished goods employing (3) which groups of machines handled by (4) which employees. This overall planning process is accomplished in a matter of minutes by the use of a complicated, sophisticated operations research model that is stored in the memory of the computer system.

What is important from the standpoint of this discussion is that all aspects of the planning process must be performed within the time frame of the cycle. Furthermore, once the complete planning process has been performed, the process cannot be repeated during the time frame of the cycle. In other words, based on changes in the environment under the conditions of a traditional information system, it is not possible to quickly change the assignment of resources, materials, or personnel for purposes of accomplishing a new order of identified tasks.

The general model of a traditional information system is further examined in Chapter 5. In this latter examination, special attention is given to the matter of how the system connects various requirements for information in decision-making activities with sources of data.

Production and Operation Information System

The general model for a production and operation information system is a *partially open* system encompassing certain types of major information flows within a business organization. The environment and the business process in which the production and operation information system is located are such that business management must be able to respond and react quickly to changes in the raw materials or finished goods markets or actions by competitors.

If this degree of sensitivity is to be achieved, then the general model for a production and operation information system cannot contain the same planning and control steps that were specified for the traditional information system. Instead, the planning process must be redivided, and two new groupings formed: planning process and coordinating process.

Inputs to the production and operation information system may ask that certain tasks be performed (part of the planning process— identifying the proposed tasks to be performed). However, the performance of these proposed tasks may conflict with other scheduled tasks in the use of either personnel, resources, or materials. Therefore, the coordinating process must assign priorities and determine how these conflicts will be handled. In other words, these conflicts occur so frequently in a production and operation information system that the general model must specifically provide for them, rather than letting these conflicts be handled on an exception basis.

In a production and operation information system, many information flows may be specifically excluded. A set of decision rules or programmed responses is substituted in place of some decision processes; therefore, the system contains business management's response to a set of questions. Many day-to-day, routine types of questions are handled by these predetermined responses; thus, the information flows that would otherwise be required for coping with these types of issues are eliminated.

This matter of decision rules or programmed responses to a set of questions adds another dimension to the systems analyst's work. What are the primary assumptions underlying each set of decision rules? Are these primary assumptions compatible between different sets of decision rules? Are these primary assumptions compatible with executive management's current beliefs?

From another perspective, if the systems analyst is to evaluate an existing production and operation information system, he must pass judgment on the appropriateness and general accuracy of the management science tools and techniques that are currently being used within the overall system. These sets of decision rules or programmed responses to a series of questions usually take the format of different management science tools and techniques.

The systems analyst must have a general understanding of how a given management science tool or technique is being used. This general understanding should be of sufficient depth so that the systems analyst knows the critical business assumptions and the simplifying assumptions upon which the tool or technique is based. The systems analyst must have this degree of insight into management science tools and techniques *before* he can intelligently evaluate the overall system. Thus, the education and background of a systems analyst who is going to cope with production and operation information systems must include this type of knowledge.

This matter of evaluating an overall production and operation information system is complicated by another factor. Recently, there have been significant changes in business technology, computer equipment, and communication facilities. With all of these changes and advances, there has been a gradual reduction in the cost of most types of mechanized operations. Furthermore, items that were previously unknown or nonquantifiable can now be measured by new measurement devices.

Therefore, the systems analyst may frequently face a basic question that is outside his area of expertise: Are the existing mechanized operations the most efficient and economical way of handling the situation? The systems analyst should have enough familiarization with the current state of the art so that from his thorough understanding of the business process of the organization under scrutiny, he would be able to specify the relevant factors that would suggest that the above question should be reexamined by management scientists.

In summary, the typical production and operation information system represents a situation where management, out of necessity, has forced some unlike information flows into the same system for purposes of achieving stability in dynamic or fluid setting. Although unlike information flows are forced into a mold, the resulting overall system gives management an extremely powerful management control system. This latter point is further examined in Chapter 8.

Marketing Information System

The general model for a marketing information system is an *open* system encompassing certain types of major information flows within a business organization and between a business organization and its environment. The network for a marketing information system in a complex business organization contains many diverse information flows. In fact, there are so many different types of information with dissimilar characteristics and in diverse time frames that the marketing information system can be described as a multidimensional system. For example, information within the marketing information system may be expressed by four measurement methods: (1) complete enumeration, (2) sample, (3) management by exception based on complete enumeration, and (4) management by exception based on sample.

From another standpoint, the time dimensions of the requirements for information vary completely. At the one extreme, information may be required continuously, as it is happening on a real-time basis (or instantaneously, as is the case of airline reservations). At the other extreme, information may be required periodically, such as monthly statistical data on the Consumer Price Index, quarterly forecasts of general business conditions, or annual statistical data on the gross national product. Information required periodically also includes weekly, daily, hourly, and other time frames. For example, when a new record is released by a recording studio, the response by the general public to the record in selected localities during the first 24 hours after the record has been released is used to make the decision of how many records will be initially manufactured and distributed.

The construction of a total marketing information system for a complex business organization with diverse products in a competitive environment is almost an impossibility. From a conceptual standpoint, not only are there six different levels of reference for making major distinctions about information,[5] but there is an inconsistent set of objectives or missions for the marketing department. At any point in time, business management is attempting to plan, select among alternatives, coordinate actions, and control performance. At this same point in time, business management is also attempting to destroy or at least alter the environment that currently exists by its marketing operations, such as advertising, promotions, and so forth.

Of course, management science techniques currently exist for coping with this type of complex system, and it is theoretically possible to construct a total marketing information system in the above described complex environment. For example, a combination of simulation techniques along with gaming might be used. However, from a practical standpoint, there may not be much payoff in the current time frame from integrating all of the diverse marketing subsystems into a single marketing information system. With the changes in business technology, computer equipment, and communication facilities in a *future* time frame, more practical importance may be attached to the formal integration of all marketing subsystems into a total marketing information system.

Movement toward a Total Information System

The general model has not been specified for a total information system in a complex business environment with diverse information flows of dissimilar characteristics regarding the nature of the information and possessing conflicting time dimensions. Special consideration is given in Chapter 13 to citing the approach that some systems analysts have followed in attempting to design such a total information system in the previously described setting.

---

[5] These multidimensions are (1) sources of information, (2) types of information, (3) measurement methods applied to the information, (4) the time dimensions of the requirements for information, (5) the location of the decision maker requiring such information, and (6) the use of the information by the decision maker.

Other Levels of Application

The discussion thus far in this chapter has emphasized how the systems analyst can group related major information flows into more compact networks. Consistent application òf this approach will result, at least, in the development of major information systems, where each major information systems would encompass all of the information flows related to some major business activity.

The systems analyst may be applying the information systems approach to the study of only a part or segment of the overall business organization. For example, the systems analyst's study may be restricted to a division, a department, a major operation within a given department, or to a given problem area.

Whenever the systems analyst is studying the information dimension of decision-making activities in only a part or segment of the overall business organization, he will encounter many partial major information flows. These partial major information flows occur when the information source is outside the parameters of the current area of study. Here, the systems analyst should prepare a list of such partial major information flows and should identify the general question that would be resolved by the complete major information flow and the location of the information source for resolving said question.

What the systems analyst does with this list of partial major information flows depends on the scope of the systems analyst's study. In a narrowly defined study this list would serve as a basis for specifying the parameters or qualifying assumptions to the recommendations of the current study. In a more generally defined study, the systems analyst would evaluate the overall appropriateness of each of these qualifying assumptions.

Summary

We examined how a business firm's management organizes for a series of information systems. Our analysis consisted of three parts: (1) the organizational arrangement of the information systems function in a large corporation, (2) the organizational arrangment for planning and coordinating a series of information systems studies, and (3) an approach to vertical slicing of the organizational structure for purposes of identifying events for inclusion in a given information system.

After this overview, we presented our interpretation of the basic objectives of a business organization and our interpretation of the steps within the management process. Any basic reference book in economics will cite some of the other recognized views regarding the basic objectives of a business organization. As far as the management process, there are almost as many classification schemes as there are basic reference books in management. No value judgment is assigned to any of these views.

Any attempt on the part of the systems analyst to group information flows into sets must be based on the systems analyst's overall understanding of the nature of a business organization. Practitioners with different education, training, and background will possess different understandings of a business organization. The interpretation presented in this chapter is our view that has been used both in practice and in research.

Using this interpretation as a base, we presented three general factors that can be used in grouping and integrating major information flows into more compact networks: (1) the general business activity to which an information flow relates, (2) the general nature or characteristic of the information being processed and transmitted and (3) the time frame of the information flow. These three factors combined with variations in the environment and in the nature of the business process were used to form a brief sketch of the general models of information systems: (1) traditional information systems, (2) production and operation information systems, (3) marketing information systems, and (4) the movement toward a total information system.

In subsequent chapters, each of these general models is examined in detail. However, the reader is encouraged to reexamine periodically the contents of Chapter 4 so that he will have an overview of the different general models of information systems.

TOPICS FOR CLASS DISCUSSION

1. Explain the relation between the information systems coordination group and the management committee.

2. Explain the meaning of the "operating cycle concept" as applied to information systems. Indicate in your explanation how the

operating cycle concept differs from the functional approach to the design of information systems.

3. Differentiate between a traditional information system and a production and operation information system.

4. Differentiate between a traditional information system and a marketing information system.

5. Is it possible to have three major information systems concurrently in a given business organization—specifically, a traditional information system, a production and operation information system, and a marketing information system? Explain.

6. In a production and operation information system, many routine decisions are monitored by the computer system using predetermined programmed responses. Therefore, business executives will respond only to the unprogrammed decision problems. Explain how a systems analyst evaluates this type of advanced information system.

7. The scope of the systems analyst's study may be restricted to a given department or a given activity within a department. Explain how the systems analyst's general "plan of attack" would vary under such restrictions.

CASE 4–1.   AMOCO CHEMICALS CORPORATION

The manager—information services department at Amoco Chemicals Corporation is currently reviewing the recently completed planning study report for the overall corporation. This report, dated May 1, 1969, represents a company-wide study of information systems requirements by systems analysts and user department personnel. The coordinated planning study included eight study teams that examined the major activities within the company.

The management committee at Amoco Chemicals had initially approved the planning study project, and this committee appointed an information systems coordination group to handle interdepartmental problem areas and to make recommendations on policy issues. The 178-page planning study report reflects the overall summary of these coordinating efforts during the past 12 months. The report has just been approved by the information systems coordination group and has been forwarded to the management committee with a recommendation for approval.

At this point in time, the manager—information services department is reflecting upon the activities over the past 12 months. In his reflection, he recalls the creation of the information services department, the planning for the scoping study, and the coordination activities that were required during the scoping phase. While these events were occurring, the company (Amoco Chemicals) was growing at a rapid rate., This growth was partially attributed to internal activities and was partially attributed to the acquisition of 11 small- and medium-size corporations.

The Company

Amoco Chemicals Corporation is a wholly owned subsidiary of Standard Oil Company (Indiana). The letters "AMOCO" are used under a license from The American Oil Company, which is also a subsidiary of Standard Oil Company (Indiana). Since Amoco Chemicals is a wholly-owned subsidiary, annual financial statements on Amoco Chemicals' activities are not made available to the general public. (For purposes of this case study, a stand alone company equalling Amoco's 1968 sales would rank in the lower half of the *Fortune* list of 500 U.S. corporations.) Some operations of AMOCO are conducted by subsidiary companies. To simplify this case study, references to AMOCO include its subsidiaries.

Between 1961 and 1968, Amoco Chemicals annual sales tripled. With the recent diversification into plastic fabricators and polypropylene, it is expected that the annual sales will be at least double the present level by 1972.

Until 1965 Standard Oil Company (Indiana) operated about 40 computers in 30 locations. That year the decision was made to modernize and consolidate computing capacity into two major centers which would serve all elements of the total company. These two centers are located in Chicago, Illinois, and Tulsa, Oklahoma. Each center has an IBM 360 Model 65 and an IBM 360 Model 75 as its major computers. The centers are linked by broad-band lines, and outlying facilities and terminal devices are tied into one center or the other through a communications network. Amoco Chemicals currently has an IBM 360 Model 20 that is located in Chicago, Illinois, and is online with the Chicago center. An IBM 360 Model 30 is scheduled to replace the Model 20 during the early 1970's.

Prior to 1962, Amoco Chemicals was engaged almost exclusively in the manufacture and marketing of intermediate chemicals. The organization chart for that period showed a vice president—manufacturing and a vice president—marketing reporting to the president. In recent years the company has expanded into other product lines such as plastics and fabricated plastic products. This has been accomplished through a program of acquisition and internal expansion. As a result, changes in the organizational structure have taken place. Exhibit A presents the organization chart as of April 1, 1969. It reflects one phase of the transition from a chemical company to a chemicals, plastics and plastics products company.

The position of vice president—plastics has primary responsibility for plastics, polymers (polypropylene, polystyrene and polyethylene) and fabricated products. As of April 1, 1969, the vice president—plastics had five members of management reporting to him:

President—Polymer Subsidiary
General manager—Fabricated Products
General manager—Commercial Development and Planning
Manager—Plastics Laboratory
Manager—Propellants Division

EXHIBIT A
Organization Chart
(April 1, 1969)

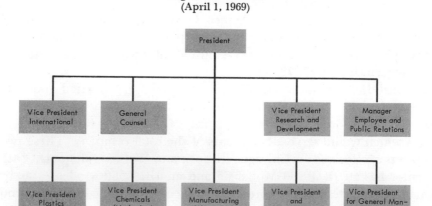

Information Services Department

The information services department at Amoco Chemicals was formed in October, 1967, by bringing together 22 individuals in

Amoco's financial department, manufacturing department, and the parent company—Standard Oil Company (Indiana)—who had been working on computer applications of interest to Amoco. Additional staffing was accomplished by selective outside recruitment of experienced analysts and programmers. Exhibit B presents the organization chart for the information services department. The manager —information services department reports to the vice president and treasurer.

Planning Study Project

On July 1, 1968, the Information Systems Planning Study was formally begun after being approved by Amoco's management committee. The resources requested by the information services department to cover the cost of the study were approved. Each major project recommended in the study was subsequently separately presented to the user department management for authorization of funds. In short, management is interested in and informed about the study, its objectives, risks, costs, and incentives.

The specific assignment of the study is to make a preliminary analysis of the operations and principal support, staff and administrative functions, and to draw initial conclusions concerning feasible information systems required to conduct these functions efficiently within the framework of corporate goals and policy. In addition, it is required that the study be fully coordinated and documented in final form on or before May 1, 1969.

The objective of the study is to provide for Amoco's management a statement of estimated incentives and costs associated with the development of computer-oriented information systems. Of necessity, these will be gross estimates because the time constraint does not allow the detailed study required to produce more refined estimates. Accuracy, per se, is not the critical issue in evaluating the estimates. What is needed is a measure of the ratio of incentives to costs, and an approximate measure of the resources which would have to be committed to information systems projects in order to achieve the benefits.

Management's immediate problem was one of determining how to allocate time and manpower so that Amoco maximized the likelihood that high-incentive applications will be found and confirmed during the study. This philosophy means allocating the major effort to those activities which directly impact profits and costs: sales,

EXHIBIT B
Organization Chart
Information Services Department
(April 1, 1969)

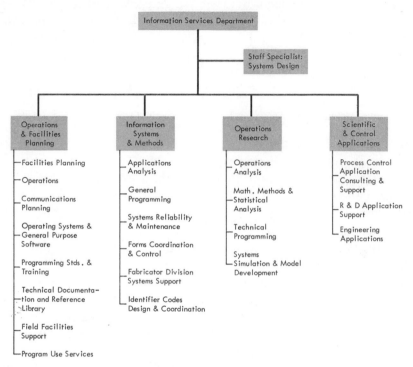

manufacturing, supply and transportation. In addition, there are activities in the "operating necessity" category—such as accounting—which inherently are focal points for the accumulation and dissemination of certain data. The study will include the information systems requirements of such activities.

The unique approach that Amoco took with this planning study reflects the realities and constraints associated with Amoco's rapid growth. Full-time participation in the study by user department key people was not feasible under existing conditions. On the other hand, the study would be worthless unless user department needs were properly identified and systems were designed which meet those needs. The way in which Amoco attempted to resolve this apparent conflict is explained in the following material.

Several organizations—e.g., international division; employee and public relations; legal department—were not specifically included in the planning study, although exploratory interviews were held with each organization. Information requirements of international division for its domestic offices will initially be covered by sales report extracts from chemicals marketing applications, and by other reports generated from the financial system. The foreign operations will be reviewed during the year ahead to determine what support and coordination of computing activities may be required. Employee and public relations needs are thought to be covered adequately for the present by the Standard Oil Employee Information System (EIS). No specific needs were identified in the legal department, although some interest was expressed in an information retrieval capability and a special-purpose simulation model. These leads will be pursued as time and user interest warrants.

As previously indicated, there are eight major study teams included in the overall planning study report. These study teams are (1) polymers, (2) chemicals, (3) financial, (4) supply and transportation, (5) fabricated products, (6) research and development and sales technical services, (7) economics, and (8) general engineering. Amoco's unique approach for handling the interface among these eight teams is explained in the following section.

Organizational Structure for the Study

Amoco's management committee established an Information Systems Coordination Group (ISCG) that would have overall responsibility for coordinating the company-wide study and for resolving problem areas. The ISCG was formed to represent user organization interests in the performance, progress and findings of the study. Each major department is represented on the ISCG by at least one member. Plastics division currently has three members; international has two. The manager—information services department serves as chairman, Information Systems Coordination Group.

ISCG members were the primary contacts in their respective organizations for study team analysts and assisted in steering analysts to key sources of information regarding detailed operations. They reviewed preliminary findings, evaluated the adequacy of proposed systems, and verified estimated benefits developed jointly by the study team and operating department personnel. For systems which cross departmental lines, ISCG representatives worked together to resolve questions affecting the departments involved. And finally, the ISCG members reviewed this report for accuracy, appropriateness and readability.

The general organizational structure within which the study was performed, coordinated and reviewed is shown in Exhibit C. Study teams included people specifically assigned by user departments to contribute factual knowledge about their functions and to evaluate proposed alternative ways of supporting those functions via information flow. Systems analysts representing ISD were responsible for the fact-finding and initial analysis of information requirements leading to a preliminary body of documented systems proposals.

Composition of the study teams varied depending upon the functional area under investigation and the stage of the study. But in general, the skills represented within any given team included expertise in general business systems (order processing, finance and accounting, materials management (sales forecasting, inventory control, and production planning and scheduling) , computer hardware facilities, and communications. User department personnel were chosen on the basis of their key positions within the operating and management structure of the respective organization.

The primary user groups provided the pertinent information to the ISD study team and developed information system requirements. They also determined if their requirements had been met in the conceptual design of the systems, and assisted the ISD study team in developing related economic justifications.

The ISD functions were to perform (with the assistance of the user group) a detailed analysis of the operations planning and decision-making functions at all levels of designated organizations, and to design systems which would support these functions and meet user group requirements.

Although the fact-finding begins in a given division or department, most systems of interest affect more than one department and must be defined in a way that recognizes the requirements of everyone concerned.

To avoid the confusion and duplication of effort that could arise if each study team covered every organization, a study team coordinator was assigned to each major organization.

The job of each coordinator was to keep the corresponding ISCG member informed regarding the status, progress and findings of the study team. He arranged initial briefings of the key departmental

EXHIBIT C
Information Systems Planning Study
Study Team Structure

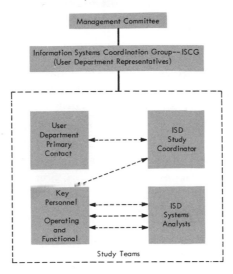

representatives, maintained liaison with other coordinators, arranged internal ISD reviews of interdepartmental systems developments and set up meetings with the ISCG representative and other user department personnel, and coordinated visits to outlying facilities.

Information Systems Principles

Like every company, Amoco Chemicals has an information system. It has served the company well. However, key operating department personnel are vocal in their demands for more timely, accurate information concerning the current status of orders, inventories, shipments and other aspects of the physical system. Likewise, management has requested improved systems for strategic planning, decision analysis and operations control, and a more efficient way to cope with the flood of data, paper work and internal coordination problems which accompany industrial growth.

As a matter of policy, information services department statements contain no reference to "total" or "integrated" management information systems. It is the view of the manager—ISD that such phrases tend to mislead the user groups and raise their expectations to unrealistic or impractical levels. As a result, the Planning Study Report does not consider or address the problem of building a *total* man-machine system encompassing every facet of Amoco's business. Rather, it is concerned with efficient manual and computer-oriented systems designed to support specific, profit-generating operations and essential control functions.

To emphasize the practical flavor of the study, the following working definition of an information system has been applied to each system proposed in the Planning Study Report: "An information system is any efficient arrangement of people, procedures, equipment and technology assembled for the purpose of providing the timely, reliable information required to manage an enterprise for profit."

Many factors influence the design and content of an information system which satisfies the above definition. Some of the more significant factors are:

Management's intermediate and long-range plans.

The organizational structure which the system must support.

Size and growth rate of the business.

Nature of the operations (integrated from raw materials through marketing; single phase; service only; etc.).

Technical complexity of the business.

Geographic dispersion of the business.

Volume and size of transactions.

Time value of information flow.

Volume of information required to describe transactions, events or conditions.

These factors represent the major areas of investigation pursued by the ISD study team.

The Line of Profit Generation Concept

An adequately designed information system must distinguish between the changing organizational structure and the relatively stable operations mechanism inherent to the ongoing physical system of Amoco Chemicals Corporation. This underlying mechanism consists of many interlocking actions and events:

a) Products must be sold at a profit.

b) Raw materials must be purchased and transported to the plants.

c) Manufactured products must be stored, packaged and shipped.

d) Someone must administer inventories and costs, pay bills and invoice customers, pay the staff and the taxes.

This chain of logical events, beginning with a sale and ending with an invoice is, in the manager—information services department's terminology, *a Line of Profit Generation.*

This rather simple concept provides a rational starting point for system design and is fully consistent with the earlier definition of an information system. Once a Line of Profit Generation has been identified and analyzed, implementation can proceed by phases and produce subsystems which, upon completion, are immediately useful as stand alone components. Other system components can later be added under a priority sequence dictated by need without losing compatibility or system integrity.

Alternative Design Concepts

Alternatives to the Line of Profit Generation concept fall into two categories. One is the *nonsystem* or piecemeal application approach which limits the scope of work to generating a single report or set of reports. Such applications, viewed in perspective, tend to simulate exactly the procedures formerly carried out by clerks. Frequent manual intervention in the computer processing of such reports, with resulting vulnerability to error, is characteristic of this approach. And, finally, because user requirements and interests are seldom explored beyond the primary user level, such applications are subject to constant change in content and output and thus absorb excessive amounts of manpower for program modification and maintenance.

The second category contains information systems designed to support a single major department or division: for example, a manufacturing department information system. This approach is equivalent to the Line of Profit Generation concept *only* where the function of the department is self-contained. An example of a self-contained function is the engineering department. In day-to-day operations engineering is not affected by, nor does it directly affect, the processing of orders, product inventories or shipments to customers.

This is not the case in activities such as sales, manufacturing, or supply and transportation. These are mainline operations, interlocked in complex fashion. Any event, condition or transaction occurring in one mainline department creates a chain of interactions affecting operations in the other departments. As a result, efforts to define an information system for a single major department are

EXHIBIT D

Information Systems Planning Study—Line of Profit Generation Concept

PRODUCT	MAINLINE FUNCTIONS				FINANCIAL
	SALES	MANUFACTURING	SUPPLY & TRANSP.	OTHER	
POLYMERS					P & L
					TAX
					PAYROLL
CHEMICALS					INVOICING
					CREDIT
FABRICATED PRODUCTS					PAYABLES
					PROPERTY ACCOUNTING
OTHERS					CONTROL BUDGET
					GENERAL LEDGER

usually self-defeating. The interactions among departments imply so many required in-and-out paths of information flow that it is impossible to know when the system is completely defined.

Exhibit D illustrates the Line of Profit Generation (LOPG) concept in the context of information systems definition and development. Using polymers as an example, the analysis of information requirements to support management planning, control and evaluation of operations is accomplished by defining the sequence of events affecting polymers through all departments which have a direct impact on the physical system. In other words, the system requirements are defined in relation to the underlying mechanism which must operate as long as Amoco competes in the polymers business. As a result, LOPG systems reflect a corporate view of operations rather than a department view.

Note that information systems designed to support the physical system can readily provide reports and special studies using current operating data required to:

Analyze sales.
Manage inventories.
Schedule plants.
Trigger purchases of raw materials.
Operate the distribution system.

Forecast demands, production and material requirements.

Schedule preventive maintenance.

Gather data needed by the financial system and by other departments.

Systems designed under the Line of Profit Generation concept are capable of responding to the needs of operating departments for current information about the status of all sensitive phases of operation.

Designing the LOPG Information System

Accounting systems, being geared to month-end reports, are not designed to meet requirements for real-time information. Until quite recently, in fact, it was not possible to gather, edit, analyze and distribute operations data on a real-time basis. Consequently, large companies often pay the cost of maintaining two information systems. One is an accounting system which issues operations control reports describing the status of operations as of four to six weeks ago, and the other is a *sub rosa* manual system maintained within the individual operating departments in an effort to stay abreast of day-to-day events.

A prime characteristic of the LOPG concept is that the need for two systems is eliminated. Operating departments can capture and retrieve the information they need to schedule, flex and control current operations on whatever level of time response they can justify, and the financial people are relieved of the burden of clerical work to produce reports having nothing to do with their primary functional responsibility.

However, the financial department has a need for a certain accounting data which, while not of immediate interest to operations personnel, may easily be acquired in the plant or district sales office through an LOPG system. The systems design task is to recognize such requirements and satisfy them in the most efficient manner.

A fundamental principle of systems design is to develop a statement of requirements which is independent of the present means by which any requirement is met; and then proceed to examine all feasible alternative ways (including the existing way) by which each requirement *could* be met. This principle of uncoupling the statement of requirements from the means by which they are satisfied is applied in the design of LOPG systems and permits design alternatives to be subjected to cost/performance analysis.

To summarize, it is proposed to design and implement manual and computer-oriented systems which support specific product groups, or which meet the requirements of self-contained functions. Where desirable, appropriate linkage or interface capability between LOPG systems will be provided. LOPG systems lend themselves to implementation by phases so that useful system components can be installed without waiting for the entire system to be completed. These systems are complete within themselves, incorporating interfacing modules for data input, retrieval, analysis and output of operating data under whatever response-time requirement is justified.

REQUIRED:

1. From a conceptual standpoint, briefly indicate the advantages and disadvantages of the organizational approach that was followed for the planning study.
2. Compare and contrast the Line of Profit Generation (LOPG) concept with the information systems approach.
3. The organization chart (Exhibit A) indicates separate vice presidents of manufacturing and marketing for chemicals. There is one vice president—plastics who has five managers reporting to him. How may the conceptual arrangement of information flows be different between the chemicals and plastics divisions because of this organizational structure?
4. As indicated in the case, 11 companies have been acquired in the past three years. Several of these companies continue to operate with their former accounting and information systems; however, they will soon begin to implement new systems as suggested by this planning study.

   Most of these companies are under the vice president—plastics. All of the activities under the general manager—fabricated products are the results of these acquisitions. Some of the acquired companies are under the president—polymer subsidiary.

   At the present time two large-scale planning and control *operating systems* are being planned, respectively, for fabricated products and polymers. After these planning and control operating systems become fully implemented, what types of informations systems developments do you envision for the plastics division?

CASE 4–2. BARKER AUTOMATIC TRANSMISSION SERVICE

Ralph Barker, president of Barker Automatic Transmission Service, is confronting a situation that is typical of many small business firms. His firm's sales have increased at a rapid rate during the past six years, while the profit margin per dollar of sales has not only decreased, but the actual total dollar profit for the current year's increased volume of sales was less than the total dollar profit for a much smaller volume of sales in a former year. Furthermore, during the same period of time, Barker had expanded his operations from a one-location business to one main shop with three other outlets.

As a result of these developments and the keen competition that he is encountering, Ralph Barker has engaged the management consulting firm with which you are associated to perform a review of his operations. Your objective is to determine the type of information system that would best meet his requirements. Following are some of the data you ascertained in your review.

The Company

The Barker Automatic Transmission Service's operations are conducted through a main shop and three branch outlets in the metropolitan area of a large midwestern city. As indicated by the name, the principal activities of the firm are rebuilding and installing automatic transmissions in automobiles. In addition, general automotive repairs are performed during slack periods.

At the main shop, there are three different work areas. The automatic transmission rebuilding section maintains the inventory of parts and the inventory of rebuilt automatic transmissions. The supervisor, two mechanics, and a laborer work full time rebuilding automatic transmissions for inventory and for current installation requirements. The automatic transmission installation and general repairs section is the dominant work area. The shop manager and seven mechanics rotate between installing rebuilt automatic transmissions and performing general automotive repairs, depending on the hour-by-hour requirements. The third section is the central office for the company. In addition to Ralph Barker, there is a sales manager, a purchasing agent, and a combination cashier-bookkeeper-secretary. There is also a laborer at the main shop who makes deliveries to the outlets.

The first outlet (Outlet A) has a shop manager and three mechanics; the second outlet (Outlet B) has a shop manager and two mechanics; and the third outlet (Outlet C) has a shop manager. Outlet B and Outlet C receive all of their rebuilt automatic transmissions from the main shop. Whenever a customer comes to Outlet B or Outlet C for replacement of an automatic transmission in an automobile, if the appropriate type of automatic transmission is not on hand in inventory at the location, the shop manager will telephone the main shop. The desired automatic transmission is delivered by truck to the outlet. When there is a slack period at Outlet B or Outlet C, the mechanics and shop managers will perform general automotive repairs.

Previously, Outlet A operated on the same basis as the other two outlets. However, the shop manager at Outlet A recently received permission from Ralph Barker for the Outlet A mechanics to rebuild automatic transmissions during slack periods. This change occurred because of recent complaints over the performance of the automatic transmissions that were rebuilt at the main shop. Eventually, Ralph Barker fired the individual responsible for the poorly rebuilt transmissions and hired a qualified machinist. (The latter individual is the supervisor of the automatic transmission rebuilding section.) During this period, the manager of Outlet A felt that his volume of business had declined because of this poor performance and, therefore, he desired to have his own mechanics perform the rebuilding function.

The mechanics at Outlet A rebuild transmissions only during slack periods. If the volume of business is high and the type of automatic transmission required for installation is not in inventory, the manager of Outlet A will secure the desired automatic transmission from the main shop by the same procedure as was followed by the managers of Outlets B and C. Because Outlet A mechanics do rebuild transmissions, the shop manager must maintain an inventory of parts for use in rebuilding.

This discussion of "the company" would not be complete without some consideration being given to the president. Ralph Barker is a self-educated, aggressive entrepreneur, who through his own efforts has created a growing business enterprise. His office desk always contains several library books on business, which Barker reads at night. From books, periodicals, and discussions with bank officials and other businessmen, Barker gains ideas regarding new business procedures. For example, last year he decided to install an incentive system for shop foremen. But shortly after the incentive system was established, it was terminated because Barker Automatic Transmission Service was paying large incentives to shop foremen in the same months in which the bookkeeper reported that the firm had incurred some of its largest losses.

Periodically, Barker has tried other new procedures, but eventually has discontinued each new procedure because of other competing requirements for his time and energy. During rush periods, Barker will assist the main shop foreman. When business slacks off, Barker will assist the sales manager or will review the financial report for the previous month.

Accounting Records and Reports

All journals and the general ledger are maintained on a cash basis. The bookkeeper at the main shop maintains all records. The shop managers of the other three outlets send daily reports to the bookkeeper of their cash transactions and their ending cash positions. The shop managers are permitted to make small cash purchases as required by operations, and at the end of the day the shop manager will make a night deposit in the bank of all cash on hand, except a small reserve for cash purchases during the next day.

Previously, perpetual inventory records were maintained of parts in inventory and rebuilt transmissions. However, because of the cost involved, these records were discontinued several years ago. At present, no inventory records are maintained on a regular basis, and cost data on rebuilt automatic transmissions are not accumulated. An annual physical inventory count is performed, and an external accountant prepares the income tax return and the appropriate annual financial statements.

Ralph Barker complained to his bookkeeper that he needed timely information for controlling expenditures and managing operations. In response, the bookkeeper started preparing an accrual type of monthly operating report (see Exhibit A). From your analysis, you determine that the 12 monthly reports do not compare with the data reported on the annual report after adjusting for the difference between the cash and the accrual bases of accounting.

EXHIBIT A
Operating Statement for Month of February

	Total	Main Shop	Outlet A	Outlet B	Outlet C
Gross sales:					
Cash	$20,120	$4,990	$6,430	$6,100	$2,600
Charge	1,840	820	620	400	–
Transfers to outlets	4,600	4,600	–	–	–
	$26,560	$10,410	$7,050	$6,500	$2,600
Cost of sales:					
Purchases	$ 4,040	$3,110	$ 820	$ 60	$ 50
Transfers from main shop	4,600	–	1,400	2,400	800
Labor	10,200	6,350	1,950	1,400	500
Subcontractor	430	250	80	60	40
Supplies	80	35	15	10	20
Sales refund	200	200	–	–	–
	19,550	9,945	4,265	3,930	1,410
Gross profit	$ 7,010	$ 465	$2,785	$2,570	$1,190

Expenses:

	Total	Main shop	Outlet A	Outlet B	Outlet C
Accounting*	$ —	$ —	$ —	$ —	$ —
Advertising*	1,540	770	385	231	154
Auto and truck†	90	50	30	10	—
Commission†	30	30	—	—	—
Depreciation†	325	150	75	60	40
Donations*	15	7	4	2	2
Dues and subscriptions*	—	—	—	—	—
Insurance—fire*	460	230	115	69	46
Interest expense*	180	90	45	27	18
Laundry*	140	70	35	21	14
Maintenance and repair†	882	400	198	265	19
Miscellaneous†	10	10	—	—	—
Postage†	5	5	—	—	—
Rent†	1,520	970	300	150	100
Supplies—office†	20	20	—	—	—
Taxes—general†	18	18	—	—	—
Taxes—payroll‡	382	244	73	50	15
Tools†	20	6	12	—	2
Utilities†	540	230	135	130	45
Wages*	400	200	100	60	40
Welfare—employees‡	240	154	46	31	9
	6,817	3,654	1,553	1,106	504
Net profit	$ 193	(—$3,189)	$1,232	$1,464	$ 686

* Prorated between locations on a 50, 25, 15, 10 basis, respectively, for the main shop and Outlets A, B, and C.
† Actual by location.
‡ Prorated between locations on a 64, 19, 13, 4 basis, respectively.

Competitive Situation

Ralph Barker informs you that his three primary competitors finance their own accounts receivable. He is wondering how much profit his competitors are making from financial charges. For example, one competitor advertised in a daily newspaper that he would install a rebuilt automatic transmission in a specified group (make and year) of automobiles for $56 and that the prospective customer did not have to make any down payment.

Since unit cost data are not maintained on a regular basis, Ralph Barker designed a record for accumulating the number of automatic transmissions rebuilt during February and the labor and parts costs associated with this production. During the month of February, 145 automatic transmissions were rebuilt. At this level of operation, the average direct labor cost for rebuilding a transmission was $17, and the average parts cost was $16. In addition to these two costs, there is the labor cost of installing the rebuilt transmission and the overhead cost; however, special data were not accumulated on these latter two elements of cost.

At present, Barker has a working relation with a small loan firm where the latter firm will finance most of Barker Automatic Transmission Service's prospective customers. Barker directs his efforts toward getting a prospective customer to telephone or visit one of his four locations. If the prospective customer does not have sufficient funds (and the typical customer having an automatic transmission replaced in an automboile does not have said funds), then one of Barker's employees will have the prospective customer prepare an application for credit statement. This latter information is telephoned to the manager of the local small loan firm, and a credit investigation is performed. This investigation is performed the same day the prospective customer applies for credit. If the loan is approved, the prospective customer is telephoned and asked to bring his automobile in for service. Sometimes on nonapproved loans (especially during slack periods), Ralph Barker will agree to carry these accounts, if the customer has some down payment.

Barker asks you if he should start financing his own accounts receivable. He says that for less than $2 per application, a metropolitan credit screening service will perform the credit investigation and will provide quick service. Within three hours after the agency is contacted, the results of the credit investigation will have been telephoned to Barker Automatic Transmission Service. Furthermore, Barker says that he can borrow sufficient funds at 6 percent from a commercial bank to finance the accounts receivable.

The automatic transmission business experiences seasonal fluctuations. Snow and ice as well as vacation trips significantly influence the volume of business. Barker is wondering if he should not try to level off his volume of operations by entering into long-term contracts with two or three of the major automotive repair shops in the metropolitan area. Barker felt that he could secure enough business from two or three major automotive repair shops to finance a base of operations. In other words, these contracted sales would approximate the cost of operating the automatic transmission rebuilding section. Thus, there would only be variable cost associated with the rebuilt automatic transmissions for the regular customers of the Barker Automatic Transmission Service.

Ralph Barker also discussed with you the matter of slack time. Should Outlet A be permitted to rebuild automatic transmissions or should all transmissions be centrally rebuilt? What is a reasonable transfer cost for the centrally rebuilt automatic transmissions? What type of incentive system could be established so that Barker Automatic Transmission Service would actually experience an increase in profit when the employees receive an incentive payment? Should the Barker Automatic Transmission Service only rebuild and install automatic transmissions and not perform general automotive repairs? If so, during the slack periods the mechanics might work on rebuilding old automobiles. When some customer comes in with an old automobile needing a rebuilt automatic transmission, then a salesman might sell the customer another old automobile in excellent mechanical condition instead of selling the customer on reworking his present automobile.

REQUIRED:

1. Following the information systems approach, analyze the present operations.
2. Present in outline form the steps you would take in designing and installing a modified information system. Be specific.

PART II

TRADITIONAL INFORMATION SYSTEMS

CHAPTER 5

Responsibility Accounting Systems

PART I PRESENTED an overview of the information systems approach with special emphasis on the systems analyst's perspective for observing the information dimensions of decision-making activities and how these various identified information flows are grouped into information systems. Finally, a sketch was made of the general models of information systems, and distinctions were drawn between traditional information systems, production and operation information systems, and marketing information systems.

Now, these three models along with the movement toward a total information system are separately examined in this and the next three parts of this book for the purpose of clarifying distinctions and emphasizing the degree of variation and flexibility that is encompassed within each of these general models.

This part on traditional information systems contains chapters on responsibility accounting systems, profitability accounting systems, and critical path planning and scheduling information systems.

This chapter reexamines the general model for a traditional information system and reiterates the approach that the systems analyst follows in grouping information flows into larger information networks. Next, the general model for a responsibility accounting system is differentiated from the general model for traditional information systems. Then, attention is given to explaining how a responsibility accounting system is used in matching information requirements with information sources throughout the business organization. This matching process is dependent upon a resorting operation which utilizes a predetermined coding pattern for initially coding all inputs to the responsibility accounting system. This resorting operation and the coding pattern are examined and illustrated in the later sections of this chapter.

The General Model

The general model of a traditional information system is a closed network that permeates the entire business organization and serves as a vehicle for connecting information requirements with information sources within this business organization. This network may encompass *all* major information flows or may encompass only *certain types* of major information flows. In the latter situation, the traditional information system is typically used in conjunction with a production and operation information system and frequently also with a marketing information system. Traditional information systems representing each of these situations are presented in the various case studies at the end of this and subsequent chapters.

When a systems analyst can say that a given business organization's major information flows are indicative of a traditional information system, then this comment suggests that the systems analyst has almost completed the initial phases of his analysis of the given business organization. As previously stated, in this initial phase the systems analyst is concerned with the nature of the environment in which the business organization operates and the characteristics of the business process.

The systems analyst, in following the information systems approach, begins by specifying the major information requirements of decision makers throughout the business organization. Next, the systems analyst desires to group these major information requirements into more inclusive units. He could use the three criteria cited in Chapter 4 for this grouping process: (1) the general business activity to which an information flow relates, (2) the general nature or characteristic of the information being processed and transmitted, and (3) the time frame of the information flow.

However, the systems analyst does not follow this step-by-step approach of identifying all major information flows and then systematically grouping all major information flows into larger and larger units of analysis until, finally, the traditional information system is developed. Instead, the systems analyst builds upon his experience and employs some shortcuts.

He still begins by specifying the major information requirements of decision makers throughout the business organization. Next, he examines the general nature of the business process in this business organization. Using some minimum time frame (such as a week, a day, or other time unit) as an arbitrary point of departure, the systems analyst makes simplifying assumptions and attempts to force the time dimension of the specified information requirements for the various decision-making processes into his arbitrary time frame.

Specifically, is there some minimum point in time for which the general model of a traditional information system is applicable? This means that within this minimum time frame, all phases of the planning process must be completed before any of the activity in the time period covered by the plan commences. There may be numerous information inputs to decision makers collectively engaged in the planning process; however, all of the action by decision makers collectively engaged in the planning process must occur before the time period covered by the plan starts.

These decision makers collectively engaged in the planning process must complete the following steps: (1) identifying the tasks to be performed within the time frame of the plan, (2) coordinating these identified tasks to be sure that there are no conflicts, (3) specifying the extent to which each task is to be performed (expressed in some unit of measure), (4) assigning personnel to tasks, and (5) allocating the resources and materials for the accomplishment of each task.

If the planning process can be completed before action commences in the period covered by the plan, then the systems analyst will compare this diagnosis of the business process with the general environment in which the given business organization is located. If his diagnosis of the business process is valid and appropriate for the business organization, then the business environment must be such that during the time frame of each cycle of the traditional information system no attempt is made to permit the business organization to react or completely respond to changes in the business environment. In other words, within the time frame of each cycle, the traditional information system does not contain any networks that accept new inputs regarding the conditions and characteristics of the environment.

From the previous statements we can perceive the specific characteristics for a general model of a traditional information system. This general model is becoming more widely used, and it is now possible to present a flow chart representing this model which has some degree of acceptance in business firms. In other words, the above-defined set of characteristics for a traditional information system are beginning to become generally accepted; however, some systems analysts prefer not to have the word "traditional" as the primary descriptive adjective for such a system. Because of the negative connotations of the word "traditional," we will not label our general model with this descriptive adjective.

TYPE 1 Information System

Figure 5.1 presents a generalized model of a TYPE 1 information system, which will be our label for a traditional information system.

FIGURE 5.1
A Generalized Model of a TYPE 1 Information System

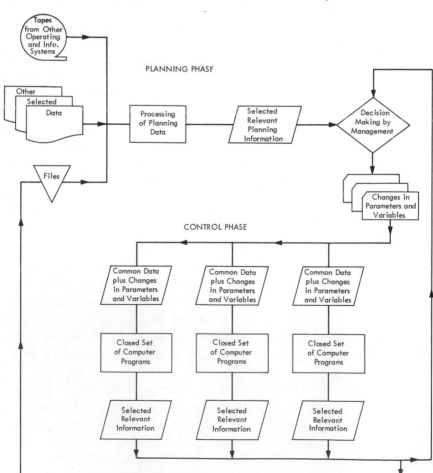

The separation of the planning phase from the control phase is clearly indicated in this model. The decision-making group concludes the planning phase by specifying changes in the parameters and variables. The closed sets of computer programs in the three operating systems are designed so that they can respond to these specified changes in parameters and variables.

The sets of generalized inputs for the three operating systems can handle both the common data as well as the specified changes in parameters and variables. These input terminals accept common data all during the control phase; the specified changes in parameters and variables are only accepted at the beginning of the cycle for the control phase.

The reports and documents from the three operating systems are transmitted to the decision-making group; another set of reports and documents is placed in the general files for the planning phase. Note that the planning phase is not restricted to reports and documents generated by the three operating systems. Instead, the generalized model includes tapes from other operating and information systems as well as selected data from other information sources. Thus, the decision-making group in the TYPE 1 information system is not restricted to a closed system for providing data for use during the planning phase.

After the systems analyst has determined that the business process and the environment of the business organization under scrutiny are compatible with the general model of a TYPE 1 information system, the systems analyst must decide which of the three prototypes of this model most appropriately fits the specific requirements of this business organization. This chapter presents the special characteristics of the responsibility accounting system; Chapter 6 presents the special characteristics of the profitability accounting system. Extensions from these two types of traditional information systems are presented in Chapter 7 as critical path planning and scheduling information system.

Special Characteristics of the Responsibility Accounting System

The general model for a responsibility accounting system contains two refinements over the general model for a traditional information system. First, the general characteristic of the information within all of the major information flows included in this analysis is such that the information can be precisely expressed as either accounting financial data or as accounting statistical data (such as performance data). Second, there is a hierarchy of decision makers which is compatible with the organization chart, and the activities of decision makers at one level of the organization structure are monitored by decision makers at the next level of the organization structure.

If the general model contains these two refinements, then several generalizations can be made. First, all information used in the planning phase and in the control phase (the monitoring of activity during the period covered by the "plan") of the business process within each cycle of the information system can be adequately expressed either as accounting financial data or as accounting statistical data. This first generalization is applicable to three different conditions: all information *requirements,* all *sources* of information, and all information *uses* can be adequately expressed as either accounting financial data or as accounting statistical data.

Second, the financial and cost accounting systems must serve as the framework for *all* information flows within a responsibility accounting model. In other words, the financial and cost accounting procedures used must be modified so that they are compatible with the information requirements of the various decision makers within the business organization.

Third, the time frame of each cycle is the minimum time span within which there is a requirement for accounting information. Thus, an accounting reporting period that corresponds with the time frame of each cycle will meet the time dimensions of all information requirements of the various decision makers within the business organization.

Fourth, the business organization under scrutiny contains a clearly defined organization chart with well established lines of authority for the conduct of the operations of the organization. Following these lines of authority, the supervisory and administrative functions for the various groups of operations must be delegated to the various supervisory personnel. Concurrently with this delegation of responsibility to the various supervisory personnel, there is an accountability requirement which flows in reverse order. This, from the standpoint of supervisory personnel, requires that the individual who has made the delegation of responsibility must be informed by supervisory management as to what *was* and *was not* accomplished. In other words, there is feedback from supervisory management to

FIGURE 5.2
The Loop Relation

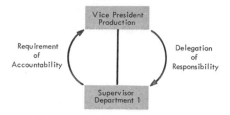

department management. Figure 5.2 reflects this feedback relationship.

This loop of delegation of responsibility with an accounting requirement incumbent upon the recipient exists between departmental management and the chief executive officer of the company. The chief executive officer has been delegated authority from the stockholders, the board of directors, governmental bodies and agencies, and the general public (social society as a whole). Likewise, there is a reporting requirement incumbent upon this chief executive officer of accountability. The external loop relation of the chief executive officer with (1) board of directors, (2) stockholders, (3) governmental bodies and agencies, and (4) the general public would differ from Figure 5.2 only in terms of the titles of individuals, number of loops, and the substitution of the word "authority" for "delegation of responsibility."

This feedback relationship between the chief executive officer and individuals external to the business organization can be viewed from another perspective that is more compatible with the information systems approach. These individuals external to the business organization can be described as decision makers outside the business organization who impose requirements for information upon the business organization's accounting system. These external requirements for information are specified by legal institutions, by custom or by tradition; and these external decision makers include stockholders, governmental tax authorities, Security and Exchange Commission personnel, members of governmental regulatory agencies, and the general public.

For purposes of comparison, several distinctions can be made between the information requirements of internal and external decision makers. First, the time dimensions of the information flow for the typical internal decision maker is substantially different from that of the typical external decision maker. Internal decision makers desire information weekly, daily, or more frequently; external decision makers normally require information on either a quarterly or an annual basis.

Second, the specific information requirements of external decision makers are normally presented in a formal, written document, and there is a high degree of homogeneity between the specified information requirements of the different external decision makers. On the other hand, the specific information requirements of internal decision makers have typically not been completely reduced to writing, and there is a high degree of heterogeneity between the specified information requirements of the various internal decision makers.

Finally, the characteristic of the information within the information flows is significantly different for the external decision maker versus the internal decision maker. Information that is being transmitted to an external decision maker must be objectively measured by a financial accountant according to some prescribed set of procedures and rules. Frequently this measurement process has also been attested by a certified public accountant. On the other hand, information transmitted to internal decision makers may be based on several different levels of measurement or scales of measurement.

In summary, the internal requirements for information are much more demanding in terms of time dimension, range of requirements, scope, and measurement characteristics. In fact, the typical set of external requirements for accounting information regarding a business organization's activities is normally completely contained within the set of internal requirements for information.

Based on this latter fact, the systems analyst can design an internal information system for coping with the information requirements by decision makers within the business organization and simultaneously satisfy all the information requirements of external decision makers. Since the time frame of the network of information flows for external decision makers is substantially longer than the cycle for internal flows, the systems analyst will design his information system so that it is initially compatible with the internal requirements.

Consideration is now focused upon the development of a coding pattern that permits the responsibility accounting system to satisfy fully all internal and external requirements for information. For pedagogical purposes, the internal and external reports that are generated by the application of this coding pattern for a given business organization are illustrated and described before the coding pattern is discussed.

Responsibility Accounting Reports

This section presents the responsibility accounting reports for the United Manufacturing Company. Since the organization structure is the backbone of a responsibility accounting reporting system, Figure 5.3 presents the organization chart for the United Manufacturing Company.

FIGURE 5.3
Responsibility System for Internal Reports*

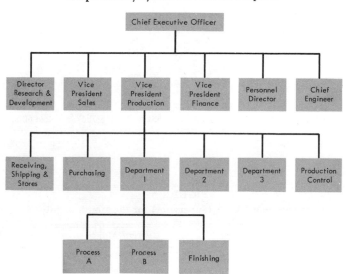

° Only selected segments of the organization chart are included, and between each segment of the organization chart it is assumed that the internal loop relation of delegation of responsibility with a requirement of accountability exists as illustrated in Figure 5.2.

The time dimensions or time frame of each cycle in the United Manufacturing Company's responsibility accounting system is one month. The responsibility reports covering the July cycle of the current year for Process A (see Figure 5.4), Department 1 (see Figure 5.5), vice president—production (see Figure 5.6) and chief executive officer (see Figure 5.7) are illustrated on the following pages. The reader should trace the cost data from one report to the next and

FIGURE 5.4

Process A Costs (Foreman) for the Month of July

	Current Month		Year to Date	
	Actual	(Over) Under Budget	Actual	(Over) Under Budget
Direct materials	$24,800	$(600)	$176,400	$(3,500)
Direct labor	3,850	(25)	27,000	(150)
Factory overhead—foreman's responsibility:				
Supplies	200	—	1,500	(100)
Power & utilities	100	—	700	—
Maintenance & repairs	200	(100)	1,500	(200)
Salaries—staff	700	—	4,900	—
Depreciation—equipment	700	—	4,900	—
Total foreman's responsibility	$30,550	$(725)	$216,900	$(3,950)
Factory overhead—others' responsibilities:				
Depreciation—plant	300	—	2,100	—
Insurance	100	—	700	—
Taxes—real estate & personal property	200	—	1,400	—
Payroll taxes & employee benefit programs	500	—	3,500	—
Total Process A costs	$31,650	$(725)	$224,600	$(3,950)

FIGURE 5.5

Department 1 Costs (Supervisor) for the Month of July

	Current Month		Year to Date	
	Actual	(Over) Under Budget	Actual	(Over) Under Budget
Supervisor's office	$ 1,800	$ (100)	$ 12,200	$ (300)
Process A foreman's cost	30,550	(725)	216,900	(3,950)
Process B foreman's cost	6,375	(115)	44,725	(800)
Finishing foreman's cost	3,875	(75)	26,150	(550)
Total supervisor's responsibility ...	$42,600	$(1,015)	$299,975	$(5,600)
Factory overhead—others' responsibilities:				
Depreciation—plant	900	—	6,300	—
Insurance	300	—	2,100	—
Taxes—real estate & personal property ..	600	—	4,200	—
Payroll taxes & employee benefit programs	1,100	—	7,700	—
Total Department 1 costs	$45,500	$(1,015)	$320,275	$(5,600)

FIGURE 5.6

Factory Cost Summary (Vice President of Production) for the Month of July

	Current Month		Year to Date	
	Actual	(Over) Under Budget	Actual	(Over) Under Budget
Vice president's office*	$ 10,400	$ 200	$ 74,500	$ 1,200
Dept. 1 supervisor's cost	42,600	(1,015)	299,975	(5,600)
Dept. 2 supervisor's cost	35,600	(1,275)	245,625	(5,350)
Dept. 3 supervisor's cost	38,100	(825)	264,700	(3,775)
Production control manager's cost	1,800	(100)	12,200	(300)
Purchasing manager's cost†	2,500	(800)	13,900	(2,000)
Receiving, shipping, and stores manager's cost	1,600	400	13,000	1,000
Total vice president's responsibility	$132,600	$(3,415)	$923,900	$(14,825)
Factory overhead—others' responsibilities:				
Depreciation—plant	3,100	—	21,700	—
Insurance	800	—	5,600	—
Taxes—real estate and personal property	1,900	—	13,300	—
Total factory cost summary ...	$138,400	$(3,415)	$964,500	$(14,825)
Other items:				
Materials purchased at standard (material records are maintained at standard)	$ 63,400	$ —	$484,100	$ —
Material price variance	800	(800)	1,900	(1,900)

* Payroll taxes and employee benefit programs for all factory-related employees are considered to be under the responsibility of the vice president of production. Since the charges vary significantly depending on the length of service by each worker, management at United Manufacturing Company feels that it would be inappropriate to hold foremen or supervisors responsible for such charges. (Note: it is acknowledged that some accountants would argue that it is not proper to hold the vice president of production accountable for such costs, but that the management labor relations committee should be held accountable for the cost of employee benefit programs. If a standard cost system for direct labor were employed, the costs of payroll taxes and employee benefit programs would be part of the standard cost hourly rate and thus would be included in the costs chargeable to the lowest level of accountability. Thus, the payroll taxes and employee benefit programs are special items demanding consideration at the United Manufacturing Company because direct labor is not charged at standard.)

† The purchasing manager's cost includes the material price variance.

note that a responsibility accounting system is like a group of building blocks or steps with each higher level indicating the source of data. At the United Manufacturing Company, the head of each responsibility unit participates in the planning of the budget for his responsibility unit and subsequently is held accountable for the expenditures charged to his unit. The budget columns in these reports present accounting data on a management-by-exception basis which

FIGURE 5.7

Departmental Cost Summary (Chief Executive Officer) for the Month of July

	Current Month		Year to Date	
	Actual	*(Over) Under Budget*	*Actual*	*(Over) Under Budget*
Chief executive officer's office (for purposes of emphasis, certain items charged to this office are identified as follows):				
Depreciation—plant	$ 4,000	$ —	$ 28,000	$ —
Insurance	1,100	—	7,700	—
Taxes—real estate and personal property	2,400	—	16,800	—
All other items	9,600	(100)	66,700	(200)
Total chief executive officer's office	$ 17,100	(100)	$ 119,200	$ (200)
Vice president production's cost	132,600	(3,415)	923,900	(14,825)
Director of R & D's cost	3,400	100	24,200	300
Personnel director's cost	4,200	—	29,800	(200)
Vice president—sales' cost	37,200	(400)	267,600	(900)
Vice president—finance's cost	15,600	(100)	108,000	500
Chief engineer's cost	8,200	—	57,200	200
Total chief executive officer's responsibility	$218,300	$(3,915)	$1,529,900	$(15,125)
Other items:				
Materials purchased at standard	$ 63,400	$ —	$ 484,100	$ —
Material price variance	800	(800)	1,900	(1,900)
Sales, net	274,200	100*	1,910,200	(1,200)†
Other income less other expense	9,100	(200)†	64,800	(300)†

* Indicates favorable variance, actual revenue higher than budgeted revenue.
† Indicates unfavorable variance, actual revenue less than budgeted revenue.

are expressed in terms of standard cost data (in other words, only variations from standard are printed).

After the responsibility reports have been prepared, it is necessary to resort the data for purposes of preparation of traditional reports. This resorting process can be performed in as much detail as desired by management. The extreme position would be to resort all the data until each type of cost is ascertained, such as determining the aggregate cost for supplies by totaling the supply cost by department or other responsible unit. At the other end of the gamut, no attempt would be made to specify the detailed cost below the vice president level. Under the latter position, a detailed resorting of cost data would occur when special cost studies were undertaken. Figure 5.8

FIGURE 5.8

Resorting of Departmental Costs to Product Costs for the Month of July

	Current Month		Year to Date		
	Actual	*(Over) Under Budget*	*Actual*	*(Over) Under Budget*	
Total chief executive officer's responsibility	$218,300	$(3,915)	$1,529,900	$(15,125)	
Other items:					
Materials purchased at standard	63,400	—	484,100	—	
Material price variance	800	(800)	1,900	(1,900)	
Sales, net	274,200	100	1,910,200	(1,200)	
Other income less other expense	9,100	(200)	64,800	(300)	

THE RESORTING PROCESS

Net sales	$274,200	$ 100	$1,910,200	$ (1,200)	Figure 5.7
Cost of production:					
Direct materials at standard					
Dept. 1:					
Process A	$ 24,800	$ (600)	$ 176,400	$ (3,500)	Figure 5.4
Process B	1,800	(100)	12,700	(700)	not shown
Total Dept. 1	$ 26,600	$ (700)	$ 189,100	$ (4,200)	
Dept. 2 (details omitted)	23,800	(1,100)	163,200	(4,300)	not shown
Dept. 3 (details omitted)	24,800	(700)	171,700	(3,000)	not shown
Total direct materials at standard cost	$ 75,200	$(2,500)	$ 524,000	$(11,500)	
Direct labor					
Dept. 1:					
Process A	$ 3,850	$ (25)	$ 27,000	$ (150)	Figure 5.4
Process B	3,375	(15)	23,625	(100)	not shown
Finishing unit	2,075	25	14,750	(50)	not shown
Total Dept. 1	$ 9,300	$ (15)	$ 65,375	$ (300)	
Dept. 2 (details omitted)	7,800	(75)	54,425	(350)	not shown
Dept. 3 (details omitted)	9,100	(25)	63,600	(75)	not shown
Total direct labor	$ 26,200	$ (115)	$ 183,400	$ (725)	
Factory overhead*					
Aggregate value included in vice president—production's factory cost summary†	$ 30,400	$ —	$ 214,600	$ (700)	not shown
Chief engineer's cost	8,200	—	57,200	200	Figure 5.7
Expenses not charged to department	8,200	—	57,400	—	not shown
Transfers	(700)	—	(4,900)	—	not shown
Total factory overhead .	$ 46,100	$ —	$ 324,300	$ (500)	

FIGURE 5.8 (*Continued*)

	Current Month		Year to Date		
	Actual	*(Over) Under Budget*	Actual	*(Over) Under Budget*	
Total cost of production with materials at standard	$147,500	$(2,615)	$1,031,700	$(12,725)	
Material price variance†	800	(800)	1,900	(1,900)	Figure 5.6
Total actual cost of production	$148,300	$(3,415)	$1,033,600	$(14,625)	
Cost of goods sold:					
Total actual cost of production	$148,300	$(3,415)	$1,033,600	$(14,625)	
Change in finished goods inventory (increase)	(4,300)	—	18,000	—	not shown
Total cost of goods sold .	$144,000	$(3,415)	$1,051,600	$(14,625)	
Operating expenses:‡					
Director of R & D's cost	$ 3,400	$ 100	$ 24,200	$ 300	Figure 5.7
Personnel Director's cost	4,200	—	29,800	(200)	Figure 5.7
Vice president—sales' cost	37,200	(400)	267,600	(900)	Figure 5.7
Vice president—finance's cost ..	15,600	(100)	108,000	500	Figure 5.7
Chief executive officer's office cost	17,100	(100)	119,200	(200)	Figure 5.7
Expenses not charged to department	700	—	4,900	—	not shown
Transfers	(8,200)	—	(57,400)	—	not shown
Total operating expenses	$ 70,000	$ (500)	$ 496,300	$ (500)	
Other income less other expense	$ 9,100	$ (200)	$ 64,800	$ (300)	Figure 5.7

° Each element of factory overhead can be shown and each instance of the element reported as indicated for direct materials and direct labor; however, for purposes of illustration, only aggregate values are presented.

† The material price variance which was originally charged to the purchasing manager is not included in the computed value under "factory overhead," but (as indicated) is presented on a separate line.

‡ For purposes of illustration, only aggregate values are presented.

presents United Manufacturing Company's resorting of departmental costs to product costs. For purposes of illustration, the extreme right-hand column of this exhibit indicates the source of data by line.

Now that the data have been resorted according to product costs, it is possible to prepare a traditional income statement (see Figure 5.9) .

FIGURE 5.9

Income Statement for the Month of July

	Current Month		Year to Date	
	Actual	*(Over) Under Budget*	*Actual*	*(Over) Under Budget*
Net sales*	$274,200	$ 100	$1,910,200	$ (1,200)
Cost of sales at budget†	140,585	—	1,036,975	—
Gross profit at budget	$133,615	$ 100	$ 873,225	$ (1,200)
Manufacturing variances:				
Material price variance	$ 800	$ (800)	$ 1,900	$ (1,900)
Material usage variance	2,500	(2,500)	11,500	(11,500)
Labor time variance	115	(115)	725	(725)
Overhead variance	—	—	500	(500)
Total manufacturing variance	$ 3,415	$(3,415)	$ 14,625	$(14,625)
Gross profit	$130,200	$ 3,515	$ 858,600	$ 13,425
Operating expenses	70,000	(500)	496,300	(500)
Profit from operation	$ 60,200	$ 4,015	$ 362,300	$ 13,925
Other income less other expense	9,100	(200)	64,800	(300)
Earnings before taxes	$ 69,300	$ 3,815	$ 427,100	$ 13,625
Provision for income taxes	34,600	1,900	213,000	6,800
Net income for period	$ 34,700	$ 1,915	$ 214,100	$ 6,825

* Competitive conditions forced a reduction in the sales price per unit during the first quarter of the year; however, normal prices were reestablished during the second quarter. Extremely severe winter storms of ice and snow forced the production plants to be closed for 10 working days. When operations were resumed, management decided against working overtime to restore the inventory to its previous level.

† The data for "cost of sales at budget" and for each of the variances are presented in Figure 5.8. The former values are computed as follows:

	Current Month	Year to Date
Total cost of goods sold (actual)	$144,000	$1,051,600
Less unfavorable variance	3,415	14,625
Cost of goods sold at budget	$140,585	$1,036,975

Coding Pattern

The responsibility accounting reports for the United Manufacturing Company were illustrated in the previous section, and special attention was given to the resorting process. This resorting process is based upon a coding pattern. When financial accounting and cost accounting data are initially recognized as inputs to the responsibility accounting system, these sources of accounting data must be coded in such a manner that they can be easily processed and transmitted in the appropriate format to the many decision makers that require information.

This coding pattern draws heavily upon the two refinements that the general model for a responsibility accounting system has over other traditional information systems. Specifically, the general ledger chart of accounts and the organization chart are used as the two sides of a large matrix in which the coding pattern is developed for a given business organization.

Figure 5.10 illustrates a segment of the matrix used by the United Manufacturing Company in the development of a coding pattern. Based upon this exhibit, it would appear that a seven-digit code would satisfy all requirements for information. These seven digits are illustrated as follows:

> 1234567   Seven-digit code.
>
> 123xxxx   The first three digits would designate the general ledger account number.
>
> xxx456x   Digits four, five, and six would designate the organization unit to which an expenditure relates or the organization unit that benefits from the expenditure or the organization unit to which an amortization charge relates or benefits.
>
> xxxxxx7   The seventh digit would designate the characteristic of the cost or amortization charge per the key presented in Figure 5.10.

Example:

> 6414311 Direct Labor (#641xxxx) that relates to or benefits Process A in Department 1 (#xxx431x) and for which the Foreman of Process A was responsible for incurring said expenditure (#xxxxxx1).

Illustration:

Assume that a payroll voucher was processed for the exact amount of direct labor for the month of July per Figure 5.8. The total direct labor voucher of $26,200 would be coded as follows:

code 6414311 for $3,850   Direct Labor, Department 1, Process A, Foreman of Process A responsible for incurring expenditure.

code 6414321 for $3,375   Direct Labor, Department 1, Process B, Foreman of Process B responsible for incurring expenditure.

code 6414331 for $2,075   Direct Labor, Department 1, Finishing, Foreman of Finishing responsible for incurring expenditure.

$9,300 (total)   The total direct labor for Department 1 is *not coded* 6414305; in fact, at the United Manu-

FIGURE 5.10

Coding Pattern Matrix

	Foreman Process A	Foreman Process B	Foreman Finishing	Supervisor, Department 1	Manager, Receiving, Shipping and Stores	Manager, Purchasing	Supervisor, Department 2	Supervisor, Department 3	Manager, Production and Control	Vice President—Production	Director, Research and Development	Vice President Sales	Vice President—Finance	Personnel Director	Chief Engineer	Chief Executive Officer
CODE	431	432	433	430	410	420	440	450	460	400	200	300	500	600	700	100
Direct materials 631	1	1		5			5	5		5						5
Direct labor 641	1	1	1	5			5	5		5						5
Factory supplies 651	1	1	1	1,5	1	1	1,5	1,5	1	1,5						5
Factory power and utilities 652	1	1	1	1,5	1	1	1,5	1,5	1	1,5						5
Factory maintenance and repairs .. 653	1	1	1	5	1		5	5	5	5						5
Factory salaries—staff 654	1	1	1	1,5	1	1	1,5	1,5	1	1,5						5

Key:
1 = Cost for which decision maker is responsible for incurring expenditure.
2 = Amortization charges for which decision maker was initially responsible for incurring expenditure.
3 = Cost that benefit decision maker's activities but for which other decision makers currently have responsibility for incurring expenditure.
4 = Amortization charges that benefit decision maker's activities but for which other decision makers were initially responsible for incurring expenditure.
5 = Summary information on cost and amortization charges for which decision maker has an administrative responsibility for monitoring the activities of sub-ordinates.

facturing Company it is not necessary to code
this amount.

$7,800   The total direct labor for Department 2 is not
coded 6414405; instead, the sections (which are
not shown) within the Department are coded in
the same way as that followed for Department 1.

$9,100   The total direct labor for Department 3 is like-
wise not coded 6414505.

At the United Manufacturing Company the lines of authority
have been clearly specified and are compatible with the organization
chart. Therefore, it is not necessary to use the code xxx4305, for
this specified code can always be determined by adding the
xxx43xx's for that general ledger account.

In other business organizations, the specified lines of authority
may not be completely compatible with the organization chart. For
example, the foreman of the finishing section in Department 1 may
report to the supervisor of Department 1 except for matters relating
to marketing, in which case he reports to the marketing manager.
Furthermore, the foreman of this finishing section in Department 1
may have the responsibility for initially incurring certain types of
expenditures that relate to marketing.

Whenever the specified lines of authority are not completely
compatible with the organization chart, the coding pattern will have
to contain extra digits to provide for these additional information
requirements. When this situation does occur, it represents a variation in the general model for a responsibility accounting system.
(It is suggested that the reader reexamine the first paragraph under
the heading "Special Characteristics of the Responsibility Accounting System" which was presented earlier in this chapter.)

Accounting Statistical Data

The first refinement that the general model for a responsibility
accounting system contains over the general model for a traditional
information system is that the general characteristic of the information within all of the major information flows included in this analysis is such that the information can be precisely expressed as either
accounting financial data or as accounting statistical data (such as
performance data) .[1]

---

[1] See above, p. 115.

Attention thus far in this chapter has focused exclusively on accounting financial data. However, the previous discussions, including the development of a coding pattern, are equally applicable to accounting statistical data.

When the various decision makers throughout the business organization are collectively engaged in the planning phase of the information systems cycle, these decision makers may express the plan in more than dollar objectives. As previously stated, the general model for a responsibility accounting system will accept certain nonfinancial accounting data.

All of the significant information used in developing the formal plan may be included as yardsticks or criteria for measurement of performance. This, in turn, means that the responsibility accounting system has to provide for the accumulation and reporting of the degree of achievement toward each of these criteria for measurement of performance. Following are some typical yardsticks:

1. Units of material
2. Hours of labor
3. Amount of spoilage
4. Number of purchase orders processed
5. Number of invoices processed
6. Line items on invoices
7. Letters written
8. Customers called on
9. Miles traveled by salesmen
10. Days subsistence by salesmen
11. Sales orders received
12. Others[2]

There are almost an unlimited number of yardsticks that may be used, and each possible yardstick must be evaluated in terms of the anticipated benefit derived from the accumulation of these data. Sometimes these data are used in special management studies that may be performed a year later; however, the cost of accumulating such information cannot be justified on the basis of its possible future use in unplanned, special management studies. In other words, the systems analyst may determine after evaluating the current in-

---

[2] For a discussion of other yardsticks, see Cecil Gillespie, *Standard and Direct Costing* (Englewood Cliffs, N.J.: Prentice-Hall, Inc., 1962).

formation system that additional information should currently be accumulated for use by decision makers in a planned study that will commence three months from now.

Reporting Guidelines

The primary guidelines followed in designing effective internal reports in a responsibility accounting system are to comply with the desires of the users of said reports (the decision makers) as to format, content, and frequency. Monetary factors regarding the cost of preparing such accountability reports are secondary considerations.

While the primary and secondary considerations may appear to be simple, difficulties are encountered in the practical implementation of an effective internal reporting system. First, many decision makers are unfamiliar with alternative reporting systems and are capable of requesting only those types of information presentations with which they are familiar. Second, some decision makers are conversant with alternative reporting systems; however, they do not desire to make any change from traditional procedures (regardless of the monetary considerations) because of the organization aspects of any change.

Sometimes, in those situations where a decision maker is familiar with other reporting systems but does not request a change because of organization factors or other considerations, the decision maker may periodically ask for other information from the individual to whom he has delegated responsibility. These information data requests are as much a part of the reporting system as the prescribed traditional reports.

Summary

This chapter reexamined the general model for a traditional information system and considered the practical steps that the systems analyst employs in grouping information flows and forming information systems. Next, the special characteristics of the general model for a responsibility accounting system were examined in detail. Then, responsibility accounting reports were illustrated in detail for the purpose of emphasizing the resorting process that occurs at each step of the way in the responsibility accounting system. After seeing the application of the resorting process, attention was given to the development of a coding pattern for accomplishing this resorting process.

TOPICS FOR CLASS DISCUSSION

1. Cost accounting reporting procedures as followed by many accountants in numerous business organizations are designed to provide historical cost data encompassing several kinds of information: (1) the results of operation, (2) unit costs for pricing inventory, (3) cost accumulation to be used in pricing products for sales, and (4) cost data to be used for evaluating alternatives in capital expenditure decisions. While the typical accounting system may provide historical cost data for these information requirements, the system does not provide cost data in a manner that is most effective for cost control. In order to be effective in the area of cost control, the accounting and reporting system should permit control of expenditures by directly relating the reports of expenditures to the individuals within the business enterprise who are responsible for their control.

Do you agree with this statement? Evaluate this statement from the perspective of the information systems approach. Be specific.

2. After completing his study, a systems analyst describes a given business organization's information network as a "typical responsibility accounting system in which the information cycle is one week." Based on this study, what would you expect to be the nature and general condition of the environment in which this business organization is located? What would you expect to be the nature of the business process in this business organization? Be specific and explain each generalization in detail.

3. "In a very small business organization, a formal responsibility accounting system may not be necessary. Frequently, most of the benefits that would be derived from such a system can be achieved by establishing a monthly cost reporting system that features planned versus actual contribution to margin for each product. In addition, a system of control over direct labor and materials will satisfy most of the other benefits that would be derived from a responsibility accounting system." From the standpoint of a systems analyst, evaluate the above statement.

4. Why is the time frame of each cycle in a responsibility accounting system so important to the systems analyst? Explain the impact that the time dimensions have upon design of a responsibility accounting system.

CASE 5–1.   CENTRAL NATURAL GAS COMPANY

The Central Natural Gas Company serves 484,000 gas customers in five states. Organizationally, each state's operations are under the management of a general superintendent. In four of the five states, the area is divided into two divisions. The remaining state is not divided; thus, the Central Natural Gas Company has a total of nine divisions. Each division is headed by a division manager.

Each division is partitioned into three districts, and each district is headed by a district manager. The town is the next organization unit below the district level, and each town's operations are under the direction of a supervisor. In summary, the Central Natural Gas Company has 5 general superintendents, 9 division managers, 27 district managers, and 353 town supervisors.

The public accounting firm with which you are associated has been engaged by the Central Natural Gas Company to develop a responsibility accounting system. In addition to responsibility statements for the various responsibility units within the company and an annual detailed operating statement for the Federal Power Commission, the Central Natural Gas Company's controller requested detailed operating statements by town, by district, by division, and by state. These latter detailed operating statements will be based on full-absorption costing, and *a given general ledger account may contain elements of both direct and amortization charges.*

You are assigned to this engagement and begin to review the company's operations. You note that the 353 town supervisors are not all of equal status. In fact, some of the supervisors might more appropriately be called "foremen," since the supervisor in a given town may be over the supervisors in two or three of the surrounding towns.

After further study of the organization chart and the business process, you conclude that there are 286 area heads for responsibility accounting purposes. The controller also clarified what he meant by "responsibility accounting reports." The contents of a "responsibility accounting report" should be restricted to those costs for which the manager of a given reponsibility unit has responsibility for incurring the related expenditure. Furthermore, company-wide responsibility for the procurement of certain items of supply and material has been assigned as an additional task to be performed by selected responsibility area heads.

REQUIRED:

Design a coding pattern which will produce operating statements on a responsibility basis and consolidate into one top management report while, at the same time, it will contain the appropriate designation of expenditures for preparing detailed operating statements on a full-absorption cost basis for the various geographical and political units: by town, by district, by division, and by state. The attached appendix presents the *Uniform System of Accounts* as prescribed by the Federal Power Commission for natural gas companies subject to the provisions of the Natural Gas Act. The Central Natural Gas Company is subject to these regulations.

APPENDIX TO CASE 5–1

UNIFORM SYSTEM OF ACCOUNTS
Prescribed for Natural Gas Companies (Class A and Class B)
Subject to the Provisions of the Natural Gas Act
Federal Power Commission
In Effect on February 1, 1964

Balance Sheet Accounts
Omitted for purposes of this case study

Gas Plant Accounts
Omitted for purposes of this case study

Income Accounts

1. Utility Operating Income
400   Operating revenues.

Operating Expenses.
401   Operation expense.
402   Maintenance expense.
403   Depreciation expense.
404.1   Amortization and depletion of producing natural gas land and land rights.
404.2   Amortization of underground storage land and land rights.
404.3   Amortization of other limited-term gas plant.
405   Amortization of other gas plant.
406   Amortization of gas plant acquisition adjustments.
407.1   Amortization of property losses.
407.2   Amortization of conversion expenses.
408   Taxes other than income taxes.

409   Income taxes.
410   Provision for deferred income taxes.
411   Income taxes deferred in prior years—Cr.
          Total Operating Expenses

          Operating income.
412–413 Income from gas plant leased to others.
414   Other utility operating income.
          Total Operating Income

2. Other Income

415–416 Income from merchandising, jobbing, and contract work.
417   Income from nonutility operations.
418   Nonoperating rental income.
419   Interest and dividend income.
421   Miscellaneous nonoperating income.

3. Miscellaneous Income Deductions

425   Miscellaneous amortization.
426   Other income deductions.
          Total income deductions.
          Income before Interest Charges

4. Interest Charges

427   Interest on long-term debt.
428   Amortization of debt discount and expense.
429   Amortization of premium on debt—Cr.
430   Interest on debt to associated companies.
431   Other interest expense.
432   Interest charged to construction—Cr.
          Total interest charges.
          Net Income

5. Earned Surplus

216   Unappropriated earned surplus (at beginning of period) .
433   Balance transferred from income.
434   Miscellaneous credits to surplus.
435   Miscellaneous debits to surplus.
436   Appropriations of surplus.

          Net Addition to Earned Surplus
437   Dividends declared—preferred stock.
438   Dividends declared—common stock.
216   Unappropriated earned surplus (at end of period) .

Operating Revenue Accounts

1. Sales of Gas

480	Residential sales.
481	Commercial and industrial sales.
482	Other sales to public authorities.
483	Sales for resale.
484	Interdepartmental sales.

2. Other Operating Revenues

487	Forfeited discounts.
488	Miscellaneous service revenues.
489	Revenues from transportation of gas of others.
490	Sales of products extracted from natural gas.
491	Revenues from natural gas processed by others.
492	Incidental gasoline and oil sales.
493	Rent from gas property.
494	Interdepartmental rents.
495	Other gas revenues.

Operation and Maintenance Expense Accounts

1. Production Expenses

A. Manufactured Gas Production Expenses Omitted for purposes of this case study

B. Natural Gas Production Expenses Omitted for purposes of this case study

C. Exploration and Development Expenses Omitted for purposes of this case study

D. Other Gas Supply Expenses

Operation

800	Natural gas well head purchases.
801	Natural gas field line purchases.
802	Natural gas gasoline plant outlet purchases.
803	Natural gas transmission line purchases.
804	Natural gas city gate purchases.
805	Other gas purchases.
806	Exchange gas.
807	Purchased gas expense.
808	Gas withdrawn from underground storage—Cr.
809	Gas delivered to underground storage—Cr.
810	Gas used for compressor station fuel—Cr.
811	Gas used for products extraction—Cr.
812	Gas used for other utility operations—Cr.
813	Other gas supply expenses.

2. Underground Storage Expenses

Operation

814	Operation supervision and engineering.
815	Maps and records.
816	Wells expenses.
817	Lines expenses.
818	Compressor station expenses.
819	Compressor station fuel and power.
820	Measuring and regulating station expenses.
821	Purification expenses.
822	Exploration and development.
823	Gas losses.
824	Other expenses.
825	Storage well royalties.
826	Rents.

Maintenance

830	Maintenance supervision and engineering.
831	Maintenance of structures and improvements.
832	Maintenance of wells.
833	Maintenance of lines.
834	Maintenance of compressor station equipment.
835	Maintenance of measuring and regulating station equipment.
836	Maintenance of purification equipment.
837	Maintenance of other equipment.

3. Local Storage Expenses

Operation

840	Operation supervision and engineering.
841	Operation labor and expenses.
842	Rents.

Maintenance

843	Maintenance supervision and engineering.
844	Maintenance of structures and improvements.
845	Maintenance of gas holders.
846	Maintenance of other equipment.

4. Transmission Expenses

Operation

850	Operation supervision and engineering.
851	System control and load dispatching.
852	Communication system expenses.
853	Compressor station labor expenses.
854	Gas for compressor station fuel.
855	Other fuel and power for compressor stations.

856	Mains expenses.
857	Measuring and regulating station expenses.
858	Transmission and compression of gas by others.
859	Other expenses.
860	Rents.

Maintenance

861	Maintenance supervision and engineering.
862	Maintenance of structures and improvements.
863	Maintenance of mains.
864	Maintenance of compressor station equipment.
865	Maintenance of measuring and regulating station equipment.
866	Maintenance of communication equipment.
867	Maintenance of other equipment.

5. Distribution Expenses

Operation

870	Operation supervision and engineering.
871	Distribution load dispatching.
872	Compressor station labor and expenses.
873	Compressor station fuel and power.
874	Mains and services expenses.
875	Measuring and regulating station expenses—general.
876	Measuring and regulating station expenses—industrial.
877	Measuring and regulating station expenses—city gate check stations.
878	Meter and house regulator expenses.
879	Customer installations expenses.
880	Other expenses.
881	Rents.

Maintenance

885	Maintenance supervision and engineering.
886	Maintenance of structures and improvements.
887	Maintenance of mains.
888	Maintenance of compressor station equipment.
889	Maintenance of measuring and regulating station equipment—general.
890	Maintenance of measuring and regulating station equipment—industrial.
891	Maintenance of measuring and regulating station equipment—city gate check stations.
892	Maintenance of services.
893	Maintenance of meters and house regulators.
894	Maintenance of other equipment.

6. Customer Accounts Expenses

Operation

901   Supervision.
902   Meter reading expenses.
903   Customer records and collection expenses.
904   Uncollectible accounts.
905   Miscellaneous customer accounts expenses.

7. Sales Expenses

Operation

911   Supervision.
912   Demonstrating and selling expenses.
913   Advertising expenses.
914   Revenues from merchandising, jobbing, and contract work.
915   Costs and expenses of merchandising, jobbing, and contract work.
916   Miscellaneous sales expenses.

8. Administrative and General Expenses

Operation

920   Administrative and general salaries.
921   Office supplies and expenses.
922   Administrative expenses transferred—Cr.
923   Outside services employed.
924   Property insurance.
925   Injuries and damages.
926   Employee pensions and benefits.
927   Franchise requirements.
928   Regulatory commission expenses.
929   Duplicate charges—Cr.
930   Miscellaneous general expenses.
931   Rents.

Maintenance

932   Maintenance of general plants.

SOURCE: As indicated by the title of this appendix, the above data are reproduced verbatim from a Federal Power Commission's manual entitled *Uniform System of Accounts Prescribed for Natural Gas Companies (Class A and Class B) Subject to the Provisions of the Natural Gas Act: FPC A–12* (Washington, D.C.: U.S. Government Printing Office, n.d.).

CHAPTER **6**

Profitability Accounting Systems

THE GENERAL MODEL for traditional information systems contains a high degree of freedom and a substantial amount of flexibility. The previous chapter described the additional characteristics that are possessed by the typical responsibility accounting system. This chapter will emphasize those additional characteristics that are possessed by the typical profitability accounting system.

The discussion is divided into three parts: basic concept of profitability accounting system, general model for profitability accounting system, and differentiation between responsibility accounting system and profitability accounting system.

Basic Concept

Robert Beyer, one of the earliest writers to use the terms "profitability accounting," recently stated that profitability accounting is essentially three things: "It is the integration of all modern, accounting-oriented, managerial control tools into a single, decision-compelling management information system which contains throughout the common threads of incremental costing and marginal income contribution."[1]

A close scrutiny of the above statement indicates that profitability accounting and responsibility accounting are related concepts. In fact, professional accountants who are adherents to each of these concepts have designed comparable integrated management information and control systems in similar business situations. The only

[1] Robert Beyer, "Managerial Control through Profitability Accounting," *Proceedings 1964 Chicago Systems Conference* (Systems & Procedures Association, 1964), p. 53.

difference is that one professional accountant would call his system a "responsibility accounting system," while the other professional accountant would call his system a "profitability accounting system." Since the use of these two concepts overlap in accounting practice, another frame of reference must be used in drawing a distinction between them.

From a historical perspective, responsibility accounting was a product of the integrated standard cost and financial accounting era which emphasized the relating of expenditures to the individual who has responsibility for the occurrence of said expenditures. This identification of the individual responsible along with the expenditures for which a given individual is accountable assisted all echelons of management in the control of expenditures.[2]

Profitability accounting has a later vintage in a business environment that included many responsibility accounting systems. At the risk of being criticized by advocates of each concept, we will describe the profitability accounting system as a *third-generation* integrated management accounting system.

This historical origin is depicted by the following three generalizations. The first generation consisted of the integration of standard cost data with financial accounting data in the single accounting system. During the second generation the idea of resorting data was introduced into the integrated standard cost and financial accounting system, with the resulting development being called "responsibility accounting."

Subsequently, there was a change in emphasis in the management process with management planning assuming an increasingly more important position. Management planning was an integral part of the responsibility accounting system in that the "plan" provided the criteria or yardsticks against which to "control." But this responsi-

---

[2] Cf. John A. Higgins, "Responsibility Accounting," *The Arthur Andersen Chronicle,* Vol. XII (April, 1952), p. 17: "Responsibility accounting does not involve a drastic change in accounting theory or principles. It is for the most part a change in emphasis from product cost to the cost control aspects of accounting wherein the statements to management emphasize the control of costs by reporting and summarizing them on the basis of 'who did it' before they are adjusted and blended for product cost purposes to obtain the conventional financial statements. To say it another way, it is a system which emphasizes the information that is useful to operating management and de-emphasizes the accounting and bookkeeping aspects that clutter up so many of our financial statements today." (This paper by Higgins is one of the earliest papers on the subject of "responsibility accounting.")

bility accounting system did not provide the marginal analysis types of planning data as an essential part of the accounting system. In response to this increasing emphasis on management planning, a management information system was developed which highlighted deviations from planned performance on a management-by-exception basis as well as presented appropriate marginal analysis for short-term planning. This latter development of profitability accounting was accompanied by other changes in the business environment, including the wide-scale use of computers and communication equipment in the processing and transmission of business data. Of course, these latter environmental changes permitted more extensive use being made of mathematical tools and techniques in all phases of the management process.

In summary, while responsibility accounting emphasized the relating of expenditures to the individual who has responsibility for the occurrence of said expenditures, profitability accounting is focused on *planned profits.* This emphasis on planned profits requires that certain modifications must be made in the general model for traditional information systems before a representative model for profitability accounting systems can be specified.

General Model

We have found it useful and convenient to label a given type of general model for traditional information systems as a "profitability accounting system." The model so labeled does not contain all of the attributes of Robert Beyer's previously cited description of profitability accounting.[3] The label "profitability accounting system" is restricted to those information networks in which there is one, and only one, cycle of information flows within the time frame of the overall profitability accounting system. The term "profitability accounting" refers to a wide range of management planning and control operations, where different operations are performed in substantially different time frames. Therefore, all of the management planning and control operations generally associated with the term "profitability accounting" cannot be incorporated in a single information system in which there is one and only one cycle of infor-

---

[3] For a more detailed discussion of Beyer's views on the concept of profitability accounting, see Robert Beyer, *Profitability Accounting for Planning and Control* (New York: Ronald Press Co., 1963).

mation flow within a specified time frame. Other aspects of the difference between the concept of profitability accounting and the general model for a profitability accounting system are discussed in the subsequent section, where profitability accounting systems are differentiated from responsibility accounting systems.

The general model for a profitability accounting system is a closed model encompassing most (not all) of a certain type of the major information flows within a business organization. Specifically, major information flows that are not compatible with the time frame of the profitability accounting system's cycle are excluded. The general model for profitability accounting systems incorporates one of the two special characteristics of the responsibility accounting system: the general characteristic of the major information flows included in this analysis (the profitability accounting system) is such that the information can be precisely expressed as either accounting financial data or as accounting statistical data (such as performance data) .[4]

The general model for profitability accounting systems contains three additional refinements not present in the general model for traditional information systems. First, the business organization must be situated in a business environment where marketing management can respond to periodic (such as hour-to-hour, day-to-day, or week-to-week) changes in the demand and supply for products. Sometimes the changes in the demand and supply for products may be attributable to fluctuations in the prices of various raw materials which permit the marketing management to modify the short-term price for certain finished goods.

There are two essential aspects of this first refinement. First, the condition of the business environment must be such that it is appropriate to respond to short-term changes in price, volume, and mix. Second, the response from the business organization is characterized by the "marketing management function." This latter point does not mean that it must be by a marketing executive; the executive vice president may be performing this function. Thus, the test is not *who* performs the function, but that the "marketing management function" is performed where the business organization responds to changes in the marketplace on a day-to-day, hour-to-hour, or some other unit of time basis.

The second refinement in the general model for a profitability

---

[4] See Chapter 5, p. 115.

accounting system is that the "management information system" must permit the business organization to make a *complete response,* when appropriate, to changes in the business environment. In other words, the "management information system" will monitor the data being received regarding the business environment. On a management-by-exception basis, when the data being received exceed some predetermined limits, management will evaluate these exceptional data. These latter data may be a freak occurrence, and management may elect not to respond to it. On the other hand, these exceptional data may be evaluated to be worthy of further consideration, in which case, some type of sensitivity analysis is performed to see if the magnitude of the change is such that a new planning cycle should be performed. If this is affirmative, then the business organization makes a *complete response* to the change in the environment, and all relevant steps of the planning phase are repeated.

The third refinement focuses on another dimension of *planned profits.* On a day-to-day, hour-to-hour, or some other short time frame, management evaluates changes in the environment which are expressed as either financial accounting data or as statistical data. Because of the speed with which management must respond and the time frame determined by management's response, only marginal types of information are provided to management. Thus, managerial reports are prepared containing incremental cost data rather than absorption cost data, because marginal types of analyses are more meaningful for short-term operations than are traditional cost reports based on full costing.

Responsibility versus Profitability Accounting Systems

The general models for responsibility accounting systems and for profitability accounting systems have been sketched, and from the refinements in each model, the major distinctions between these two general models can be cited. The responsibility accounting system is closely identified with the organization structure and features a network in which there is a periodic resorting of the information inputs for purposes of providing relevant information to decision makers in meeting information requirements. The profitability accounting system is for an organization in a business environment where the business organization must react quickly to changes in the environment. The general model for a profitability accounting system does not include all information flows within the organization, but only accepts into the network certain types of selected information. The information so selected is typically of a marginal analysis type.

While the general models for responsibility accounting systems and for profitability accounting systems have been described and contrasted, the pedagogical objective is not to emphasize the differences between these two general models. Instead, the objective in studying these two types of traditional information systems has been to emphasize that (1) organization considerations can be recognized in the design and operation of successful management information systems, (2) the powerful technique of resorting information permits a single information accumulation process to be successfully used in diverse information-reporting situations, and (3) management needs critical information in the day-to-day administrative process. The nature of the critical information will vary to some extent by the personal preferences of each manager along with the restraint of the monetary cost of such special information.

Since these three points are the underlying emphasis of this discussion, the systems analyst should ponder the implications of these points. For example, the technique of resorting information as used under responsibility accounting systems is a powerful device which has become even more potent by the widespread use and availability of computer facilities. This powerful technique has almost unlimited applications when it is coupled with an information system where information is processed into the computer network at almost the point of inception. It behooves the systems analyst to stretch his imagination and ask what other resorts of information would be meaningful to management. The thorough consideration of this latter question would include the measurement of the cost versus the estimated benefit derived from the new information created by the resorting process.

Frequently, the systems analyst will study the overall business process and the environment in which the business organization is situated and then conclude that the major information flows appear to be representative of the general model for a traditional information system. However, as the systems analyst attempts to group information flows into larger information networks, he encounters some problems in selecting the period of time for the information cycle.

After further study, the systems analyst finally perceives two general time frames with some overlapping of information flows. The shorter time frame will probably be indicative of some type of profitability accounting system, and the longer time frame will be indicative of some type of responsibility accounting system. The information accumulated for marginal analysis (the profitability accounting system) is resorted and used in the historical cost reports (the responsibility accounting system).

There are numerous business organizations that have both responsibility accounting systems and profitability accounting systems. Both systems use the same inputs of information, but each system has its own screening system and resorting process. When a given business organization possesses both types of traditional information systems, normally the time frame of the responsibility accounting system is a month. On the other hand, the profitability accounting system can be extremely selective in terms of which information flows are included within the network and can operate on a daily, an hourly, or a shorter time frame.

When a business organization has a responsibility accounting system operating on a monthly information cycle and a profitability accounting system operating on a daily information cycle, there will probably be another information cycle. Specifically, when the planning phase of the monthly responsibility accounting system is being performed, management must also establish guidelines for the profitability accounting system. In other words, while the profitability accounting system is referred to as a daily information cycle, there is also a monthly information cycle associated with the profitability accounting system in which management establishes the critical control guidelines around which the day-to-day activities are evaluated. Typically, some type of "direct costing" report is frequently used in establishing these sensitivity points.

There are a sufficient number of business organizations possessing both a responsibility accounting system and a profitability accounting system that the following distinction is frequently made between these two types of systems by practitioners. The profitability accounting system is an instrument for *short-term planning*. The responsibility accounting system is an instrument for *control*.

In more complex business organizations, responsibility accounting systems and profitability accounting systems may be used in conjunction with production and operation information systems and marketing information systems. These separate systems maintain their individual uniqueness (the integrity of the general models for these information systems is not questioned), but, at the same time, they are integrated into an overall network of information systems. This type of integrated network of information systems will be examined in Part V of this book, under the heading, "Movement toward a Total Information System."

Summary

The systems analyst is concerned with the identification of the major information flows within a business organization and with the systematic and orderly grouping of these major information flows into larger information networks. Chapters 5 and 6 have emphasized two general types of information networks that the systems analyst may elect to use. Both of these were traditional information systems, which means that the systems analyst envisions the business process occurring so that at some point in time all steps of the planning operation are completed before activity for the period covered by the plan commences.

Within the category of traditional information systems, the systems analyst has ample room for developing the type of information system that best meets the unique information requirements (both as to timing, type of information, and the degree of relevance of said information) of the decision-making processes throughout the business organization under scrutiny. The systems analyst may install a type of responsibility accounting system, a type of profitability accounting system, or he may concurrently install both types of information systems in the given business organization.

TOPICS FOR CLASS DISCUSSION

1. Differentiate between the concept of "profitability accounting" and the characteristics of the general model for a profitability accounting system.

2. Explain the difference between a responsibility accounting system and a profitability accounting system.

3. The Ward Manufacturing Company has a "business informa-

tion system." During the past few years, there has been a systematic conversion of the manual cost accounting and financial accounting records to a data processing system. Recently, the perpetual inventory records for each item of inventory were transferred to the data processing system. A management consultant performed a high-point review of the business information system, and he described the system in his report as an "after the fact, irrelevant reporting system."

REQUIRED:

Explain the conditions that must be present before the Ward Manufacturing Company's business information system can be classified as a "management information system." Be specific.

4. The Murphy Engineering Company is the manufacturer of precision parts which are sold exclusively to two of the large automotive companies. Currently, the Murphy Engineering Company is producing 27 different parts for these two consumers per the terms of 30 different contracts (three parts are purchased by both automotive companies). These contracts specify the minimum volume of parts that the automotive company will purchase during the annual production season at a fixed price; the contract also includes a clause that the Murphy Engineering Company may be asked to supply a higher volume of parts at this same fixed price, depending on the production volume experienced by the respective automotive company. You, as a systems analyst, are asked by Richard Murphy, the president of Murphy Engineering Company, to evaluate the company's operations and to design a profitability accounting system. Mr. Murphy states that he wants an information system that permits him and his associates to respond daily to changes in the company's operations.

REQUIRED:

Explain the type of information system that you would probably design and install at the Murphy Engineering Company. Be specific.

A NOTE ON THE INDUSTRIAL CHEMICAL INDUSTRY

Prof. Jules Backman introduces a monograph on *Chemicals in the National Economy* with this comment: "*Test tube* competition has been the vital stimulating and driving force in the industrial chemical industry. Such competition is so intensive and so widespread that it has become indispensable to competitive success. The industry is constantly obsoleting its own products and processes. It is marked by intensive struggles for product leadership."[5]

The industrial chemical industry is a major investor in research and development. Many large chemical companies take pride in emphasizing that the majority of the products that they currently sell were unknown five years previously.

The Vogt Chemical Company, Inc., is not representative of a large industrial chemical company. For example, it is not included among the 100 largest chemical companies in the United States. Instead, the Vogt Chemical Company is a small company that manufactures four industrial chemicals which it sells in this highly competitive environment.

The raw materials that the Vogt Chemical Company uses are subject to day-to-day major fluctuations in price. The various crushed ores and the basic chemicals that are raw materials to the Vogt Chemical Company contain many short-run imperfections in price. In fact, a given required raw material may be obtained in several different ways, each from basic materials with different degrees of concentration of the desired substance. Therefore, the purchasing manager must frequently redetermine which raw materials in what form will be purchased from whom.

Since Vogt Chemical Company sells its products to other industrial companies including chemical companies, the demand and supply for Vogt Chemical Company's four products fluctuates on a day-to-day basis in the same manner as the day-to-day fluctuations in the raw materials to Vogt Chemical Company. In other words, Vogt Chemical Company's four products are raw materials to other chemical companies and are subject to the same short-run fluctuations in price that are experienced by Vogt Chemical Company's raw materials.

Vogt Chemical Company sells some of its products to nonchemical companies, and these sales are on a regular order basis. These nonchemical company sales provide a certain amount of stability to Vogt Chemical Company's price system and volume of operations.

The physical plant of a chemical company is unique. Since some type of chemical is being manufactured (in either a solid, liquid, or gas state) under a set of prescribed conditions (such as temperature, humidity, and time), some type of physical network is typically re-

---

[5] Jules Backman, *Chemicals in the National Economy* (Washington, D.C.: Manufacturing Chemists' Association, Inc., 1964), p. 1.

quired for controlling, processing, and transmitting the substance during the various phases of the manufacturing process.

This physical network might be described as an enormous series of pipes that connect the storage containers of raw materials with the finished goods supply area. It is not unusual for this series of pipes to be a closed system from the raw materials point to the finished goods point. Within the pipes and conveyor system, periodically there are pumps, control and regulatory equipment, processing equipment, storage tanks for chemicals being used in the manufacturing process and retrieval tanks for capturing these chemicals as they are used, purifying equipment for converting the used chemicals into their formal state so that these chemicals can be used again in the next cycle of the manufacturing process, and transmission equipment.

In summary, each manufacturing plant in a typical chemical company (such as the Vogt Chemical Company, Inc.) will have the physical appearance of being a single pipeline of connected vats, pots, processing equipment, transmission equipment, and control and regulatory equipment which spans the distance from the raw materials receiving point to the finished goods shipping point.

CASE 6–1. VOGT CHEMICAL COMPANY, INC.

Frederick Vogt, president of Vogt Chemical Company, Inc., has contacted the certified public accounting firm with which you are associated and asked for assistance in the area of administrative services. You are the manager assigned to perform this high-point review of the present system. The stated purpose of this general accounting and financial review is to determine (1) the nature of financial accounting information that would be useful to management and (2) the accounting procedures required to obtain this information.

In performing this task you discover the following information about the client.

The Company

George Vogt came to the United States from Europe immediately prior to World War I and was employed by a relative of the family in a family-owned chemical company. Within several years George Vogt discovered a new process for extracting the industrial chemicals.

When his relatives would not use the new process, he left the company, moved to Pennsylvania, and started his own chemical company—the Vogt Chemical Company, Inc.

Later, Ernest Vogt came to the United States from Europe and joined his brother George in the management of the new company. Both men were well-educated in the sciences; George with a Ph.D. in chemistry and Ernest with a Ph.D. in physics. With the two brothers occupying the top positions in the firm, the history of the firm is a story of extensive scientific research and development with only minor considerations of financial management. As a result of this emphasis on scientific research, the firm had unique processes and employed specially constructed equipment which gave the company a significant competitive advantage over other firms. Some of its former competitors shifted to the manufacture of other chemical products, and Vogt Chemical Company, Inc., became one of the few producers in the United States of four different industrial chemicals. These four products have a current annual sales of approximately $4,500,000.

The company's major product has a wide variety of uses in several industries. Recently, this product was offered on the market for use in the metal fabricating industry as the "ideal wash solution." Scientists at Vogt Chemical Company, Inc., had been aware for some time that the company's major product was the ideal solution for the metal fabricating industry's problems. However, in the past it was not financially feasible to manufacture the chemical for this purpose. Recent inventions of new equipment and the discovery of a new manufacturing process by scientists at Vogt Chemical have permitted this chemical to be sold in the competitive market. Thus, in this sense, it is a new product on the market for sale in the metal fabricating industry.

At present, the market outlook for Vogt Chemical Company, Inc., is extremely favorable. Frederick Vogt, George Vogt's son, is the current president of the company, and Frederick Vogt recently stated that the company was on the verge of expanding its annual sales of $4,500,000 to $9 or $10 million. With this expansion in mind, Frederick Vogt and his associates desired a general review to determine the type of information which would be useful in making management decisions, controlling costs, and obtaining outside financing.

Frederick Vogt stated that the present accounting system was useful primarily in generating historical data for income tax purposes, but the system provided very little financial information for the company's management to use in making operating decisions. Frederick Vogt had heard his friends in other manufacturing firms speak of the managerial information their controllers periodically provided them, and Frederick Vogt had frequently brought this matter up with his own controller. Each time the subject was discussed, the controller of Vogt Chemical Company, Inc. (who was employed 20 years ago as a bookkeeper immediately following graduation from high school) would comment about the unique aspects of company operations. The controller had stated that because of this unique condition, the accounting system for Vogt Chemical Company, Inc., could not provide the type of information which Frederick Vogt had heard friends speak of obtaining from their accounting systems. Furthermore, the controller stated that he was already using 24-column paper to accumulate detailed cost data, and there were not any more columns for additional breakdowns of cost data. The controller's typical comment was, "If any additional data are needed, it will be necessary to have a complete system's review."

Frederick Vogt had accepted the situation of not having timely financial information for managerial decisions, particularly since the firm was currently making a substantial profit. Like his father and uncle, he was more concerned with scientific research than with financial management. However, as he envisioned a doubling of the sales volume within a matter of months, he thought that now was the appropriate time to have the company's accounting system examined.

At a social gathering in a friend's home, Frederick Vogt mentioned his predicament regarding his lack of information for current managerial purposes. His friends advised him to obtain the services of a particular public accounting firm. One of the individuals making this recommendation stated that this public accounting firm had recently performed some administrative service work for his company.

The next day Frederick Vogt went to a city bank and talked with a bank officer regarding a possible loan to finance the anticipated increased volume of sales. After Frederick Vogt had explained his problem, the banker advised him to seek the administrative service assistance of a particular public accounting firm (which happened to be the same firm his friends had advised him to consult the previous night).

* * *

This background information explains why you are currently engaged in performing a general review of operations. Following is a summary of your findings regarding the current reporting system.

The Current Situation

In performing your general review you find the following statements have been prepared for the current period:

1. Balance sheet (annually)
2. Income statement (annually)
3. Cost of goods manufactured (annually)
4. Departmental profit and loss statement (annually)
5. Departmental profit and loss statement (for the fourth quarter)
6. Departmental cost of goods sold statement (annually)
7. Departmental cost of goods sold statement (for the fourth quarter)
8. Analysis statement reflecting unit cost data (annually)
9. Analysis statement reflecting unit cost data (for the fourth quarter)
10. Source and application of funds statement (annually)

As indicated, with the exception of the fourth quarter reports, all reports are prepared on an annual basis. Furthermore, your general review of operations and procedures suggests that the small certified public accounting firm which has performed the annual audit in the past did a thorough job of examining and testing financial procedures.

From an examination of these reports, you prepare a complete chart of accounts (see Exhibit A).

After preparing the chart of accounts, you make a detailed examination of the manufacturing process employed in the production of each of the four chemicals. Because of considerations of time and space, a detailed discussion is not included on the manufacturing processes involved in the production of the four products. However, it should be noted that Vogt Chemical Company, Inc. has three separate physical plants. Product A is manufactured in Plant 1; Product B is manufactured in Plant 2; and Product C and Product D are manufactured in Plant 3.

Some of the initial costs incurred with Product C and Product D are joint cost; however, the major portion of the processing cost is individual cost. Because of frequent measurements taken by the technicians working in the processing operations, reliable statistics are available for distribution of joint cost. Furthermore, the sales volume of Product C is four to five times as large as that experienced for Product D, and the profit margin per unit of Product C is also greater than that achieved for Product D. (Incidentally, Product D is manufactured out of what was formerly waste created in the manufacture of Product C.)

Each plant contains a network of specially designed equipment (on which the Vogt brothers have patents) that is used throughout the manufacturing process. Since this manufacturing process is highly mechanized, the employees are technicians and the direct labor cost tends toward being a fixed cost. Of course, with a significant change in volume, the direct labor cost is increased because of overtime work. However, for small changes in volume, the direct labor cost is constant. On the other hand, raw materials and containers are variable manufacturing costs. Within certain limits, the factory overhead cost tends toward being a fixed cost (see chart of accounts for suggestions of items that might vary with a change in volume).

Suggestions for New System

After you have carefully examined the current reports, chart of accounts, and manufacturing processes, Frederick Vogt says that he would like to have current financial information on the following areas:

1. Company management (the total company)
2. Engineering*
3. Process*
4. Accounting
5. Marketing

---

* Manufacturing cost would include both engineering and process items. The separation between the two areas would be based on the nature of the work, that is, some direct labor costs for technicians would be classified as "engineering" and other similar cost as "process." However, the majority of the "engineering" cost is overhead cost.

Chart of Accounts, Current Date

ASSETS

CURRENT ASSETS

Cash
Accounts receivable—trade
Accounts receivable—other
Inventories:
    Raw materials
    Materials in process
    Finished goods
    Shipping containers
Accrued interest on tax-exempt bonds
Accrued interest on XYZ Company notes
Prepaid insurance premiums
Unused factory supplies

INVESTMENTS

Stocks—First National Bank in Metropolis
Bonds—Tax exempt (at amortized cost)

LOANS

Notes receivable—XYZ Company
Notes receivable—officers and employees
Executive life insurance (cash value)

FIXED ASSETS

Land
Buildings
Allowance for depreciation—buildings
Machinery and equipment
Allowance for depreciation—machinery and equipment
Equipment under construction
Motor truck and locomotives
Allowance for depreciation—motor truck and locomotives
Office equipment
Allowance for depreciation—office equipment
Miscellaneous equipment
Allowance for depreciation—miscellaneous equipment

LIABILITIES

CURRENT LIABILITIES

Accounts payable—trade
Accrued payroll
Accrued taxes:
    State and local
    Social Security and unemployment
    Federal withholding
    Federal income tax

STOCKHOLDERS' EQUITY

CAPITAL STOCK

Capital stock (authorized and issued 2,000 shares, par value $100)

RETAINED EARNINGS

Retained earnings
Profit and loss summary

SALES*

Sales
Freight allowances
Dealers' discounts

COST OF GOODS SOLD*

COST OF GOODS MANUFACTURED

Purchases—raw materials
Purchases—shipping containers
Direct labor
Factory overhead:
  Repairs to equipment
  Repairs to buildings
  Depreciation—machinery and equipment
  Depreciation—motor truck and locomotives
  Depreciation—buildings
  Depreciation—miscellaneous equipment
  Insurance
  Taxes
  Indirect labor
  Indirect supplies and miscellaneous expenses
  Coal, fuel oil, and gas
  Purchased electric power
  Purchased steam

SELLING, ADMINISTRATIVE, and GENERAL EXPENSE

Officer's salaries
Office salaries
Office expenses
Professional fees—legal, audit, and surveys
Depreciation—office equipment
Publications, photostats, etc.
Taxes—sales, use, and franchise
Bad debts
Dues and miscellaneous expenses
Contributions
Traveling expense
Employee's pensions
Advertising
Sales commissions

NONOPERATING INCOME

Dividends received
Interest received—tax exempt
Interest received
Discounts earned
Miscellaneous income

NONOPERATING EXPENSE

Expense of real estate held for future use
Discounts allowed
Executive life insurance premium
Cost of junking equipment
Experimental expense—current
Pilot plant expense
End use research (marketing research)

FEDERAL TAXES

Federal taxes on income

* The departmental profit and loss statement and the departmental cost of goods sold statement have five column headings: Total, Product A, Product B, Product C, and Product D. However, separate general ledger accounts are not maintained for the departmental breakdown of information, but this information is obtained from the detailed data reflected on the 24-column paper. Moreover, the departmental reports reflect detailed data only for the "sales" and "costs of goods sold" groupings of accounts; "selling, administration, and general expense" are allocated in total between the four departments. In other words, the departmental report would reflect, in *one amount,* the total "selling, administrative, and general expense" for the period, and this departmental report would not contain any individual extensions by item.

6. Process research and control
7. Administration

Furthermore, Frederick Vogt says that the following individuals are responsible for the various sections within the firm:

1. Company management   Frederick Vogt and Edward Vogt
2. Engineering   Edward Vogt
   a) Maintenance   Irving Howard
   b) Pilot plant   Henry Day
   c) Engineering services   Edward Vogt
3. Process   John Snyder
   a) Product A (Plant 1)   John Snyder
   b) Product B (Plant 2)   George Rickard
   c) Product C (Plant 3)   Charles Simon
   d) Product D (Plant 3)   Charles Simon
4. Accounting   Robert Jones
5. Marketing and Sales   Bruce Williams
   a) End use research (mar-
        keting research)   Maurice Weber
6. Process research and control Arthur Bell
7. Administration   Frederick Vogt

REQUIRED:

Prepare a report reflecting the findings and recommendations gained from your high-point review of the present system. Incorporate in your recommendations the suggestions made by Frederick Vogt regarding areas of responsibility and type of information desired: ". . . information which would be useful in making management decisions, controlling costs, and obtaining outside financing."

CHAPTER 7

Critical Path Planning and Scheduling Information Systems

DURING THE PAST DECADE, there has been a significant change in the fundamental nature of the business organization. In addition to expansion and diversification, many business organizations have had an important segment of their resources applied to activities which have varying or uncertain life-spans. These latter activities are called "projects." Management has exerted considerable time and effort toward developing adequate management tools for these projects.

In addition to research and development activities which are classified as "projects," many business organizations have participated in space and defense contracts which are also of this project classification. Management in other business organizations has found that the "project" perspective is appropriate and compatible with recent changes in management techniques and tools (such as operations research). These latter indiviuals have applied the "project" approach to the various segments of the business organization, even where the activities would not normally be classified as "projects" but would generally be classified as permanent activities of the business organization.

There has also been a change in the business environment regarding the speed and quality of performance expected from a project chairman. Today, the manager of a project must be able and willing to answer questions concerning progress, changes, deliveries, costs, and revenues. These questions must be answered more quickly and with much greater accuracy than was previously the case. The stakes are high, and corporate management cannot afford to allow project managers to rely on opinion and subjective guidance. Instead, an arsenal of tools and techniques is available for the modern professional manager to use in planning and scheduling activities, in selecting among various alternatives, and in controlling and monitoring activities according to the plan.

Two basic methods have emerged as the more powerful management techniques for planning, scheduling, and controlling larger projects. This chapter examines these two methods from the perspective of the information systems approach. Since both methods require the planning phase to occur before the activity for the period covered by the plan commences, this business process is analogous to traditional information systems. We have found it meaningful to approach major segments of the organization or major "projects" as though they were traditional information systems.

Benefits from This Approach

The previous study of traditional information systems has emphasized that (1) organization considerations can be recognized in the design and operation of successful management information systems, (2) the powerful technique of resorting information permits a single information accumulation process to be successfully used in diverse information-reporting situations, and (3) management needs critical information in the day-to-day administrative process.

These three insights can be directly applied to those business processes that are classified as "projects." First, while the responsibility accounting system paralleled the organization structure, the critical path planning and scheduling information system will parallel the time sequence of jobs or activities to be performed. Second, the jobs or activities in the arrow or network diagrams of the critical path planning and scheduling information system are analogous to the responsibility units in a typical integrated standard cost and responsibility accounting system. Third, like the responsibility accounting system, the critical path planning and scheduling information system can serve as the backbone for the application of the bundle of management tools and techniques, such as cost determination, cost control, cash flow analysis, return on investment, and make or buy analysis. As is the case with all "information systems," the systems analyst will match the information requirements with the information sources. If the decision maker needs marginal analysis within a given time frame, then this is what will be provided.

Now that the perspective for viewing these "projects" has been established, attention is focused on different aspects of these two basic methods for planning, scheduling, and controlling larger projects. The remaining discussion consists of seven parts: (1) the history of these two methods: the *Critical Path Method* (CPM) and *Program Evaluation and Review Technique* (PERT), (2) a comparison of the two methods, (3) a list of the basic terminology for the CPM method, (4) illustrations of the CPM method applied to two situations, (5) advantages of both methods, (6) other considerations, and (7) examination of the two methods from the perspective of the systems analyst.

History

The critical path method (CPM) had its inception in January, 1957, on a job that the Remington Rand Division of the Sperry Rand Corporation performed for E. I. du Pont de Nemours & Company. The basic development was accomplished by Morgan R. Walker, who was with the Engineering Service Division of Du Pont, and James E. Kelly, who was with Remington Rand–UNIVAC.

While the CPM technique was being developed, a parallel development was in progress at the Special Projects Office of the United States Navy's Bureau of Ordnance. Members of the management consulting firm of Booz, Allen, and Hamilton developed this system for the United States Navy. The latter system was christened PERT—Program Evaluation and Review Technique—and was initially used in scheduling the numerous contractors engaged in the Polaris Missile Project.

Comparison

There are significant differences between these two methods of planning, scheduling, and controlling large projects. While PERT has been used almost exclusively on military projects, the CPM method has been applied to projects where enterprise survival is based more strongly on profit making. This points to one of the original differences between the two methods: namely, that as a planning tool, CPM includes consideration of dollar resources while PERT does not. PERT, being developed for military requirements, is primarily concerned with *time;* cost information does not enter into the analysis. Once the PERT network has been constructed, cost considerations are given to questions such as: "Should more dollars be applied to a given activity so that it will be completed on a 'crash basis' in order that the total time for the project is reduced?" "What is the minimum dollar cost required to complete the total project within a specified number of days?"

In contrast, management in business organizations uses the CPM method in the initial steps of the decision project regarding whether or not a particular project should be undertaken. Thus, CPM networks are prepared for many proposed projects which are eventually rejected on grounds of insufficient return on investment or insufficient return for the risk involved.

The matter of time estimates is another significant difference between the CPM method and the PERT technique. Because of the difference in the manner in which the time estimates are specified, there is an important difference in the underlying mathematical support for the CPM and PERT methods. The CPM method has much stronger mathematical support.

PERT technique uses three time estimates for each activity—optimistic, most likely, and pessimistic. The "expected time" required to complete the activity is determined from these three estimates based on an assumed probability distribution. Following are the typical symbols used for these three time estimates:

$$a = \text{optimistic time}$$
$$m = \text{most likely time}$$
$$b = \text{pessimistic time}$$

The PERT formula for computing the expected time (t_e) is as follows:

$$t_e = \frac{a + 4m + b}{6}$$

While an individual may question the assumed probability distribution associated with these three time estimates, at least the PERT approach suggests that there may be some illusion regarding expected time required to perform some activity where the activity involved has no precedent. From a planning standpoint, it is easier to obtain three estimates of time from individuals responsible for a particular activity than to obtain only one time estimate. However, where the activities have been performed previously, a "standard time" may be used and reports prepared on a management-by-exception basis for major deviations from standard.

Because of the assumed probability distribution for PERT networks, it is possible to make inferences based upon the mathematical laws of probability regarding the expected completion date. For example, an individual might state that there is a 50 percent probability that the project will be completed within a specified number of days; there is a 60 percent probability of completion within a longer number of days; and so forth. On the other hand, the CPM technique uses only one time estimate and is completely deterministic.

Since CPM method (1957) and PERT technique (1958) were separate developments, each method has its own notations as indicated by the following chart:

CPM and PERT Notations Compared[1]

CPM	*PERT*
Arrow diagram	Network
Node	Event
Job	Activity
Duration	Scheduled time
Total float	Slack (primary)
Free float	Slack (secondary)
Earliest start	T_E
Latest start	T_L

For purposes of this discussion, the CPM notations are discussed with the PERT notations (where appropriate) indicated in parentheses.

CPM Terminology

The basic terminology for the CPM method is presented in the following statement and contains an explanation of these terms: *arrow diagram, activity, activity-oriented network, node, event-oriented network, critical path, dummy activity, duration, earliest start, earliest finish, latest finish, latest start, total float, free float, independent float, normal cost, normal time, crash time, crash cost,* and *cost slope.*

---

[1] A similar chart is presented in Robert W. Miller, *Schedule, Cost, and Profit Control with PERT* (New York: McGraw-Hill Book Co., Inc., 1963), p. 28.

The *arrow diagram* (network) is a model or pictorial description of how a project is planned including an identification of the inter-relationships between all required activities.

An *activity* is a time-consuming element of a network which has a definite beginning and end. Each activity is represented by an arrow; the tail is the start and the head is the finish. The length of the arrow means nothing. An activity cannot start until all preceding activities have been completed; no following activity can start until this activity is completed.

The *activity-oriented network* uses the activity as the basic building block. The activity arrow is titled with the name of the job or task, and this system is representative of the CPM approach.

A *node* (event) marks the beginning and end of each activity. The node occurs at a specific point in time; *it cannot consume time.*

The *event-oriented network* uses the event as the basic building block of the network in lieu of an activity. The event-oriented network originates from the PERT method. "Milestone" events in the project are the focal point of the PERT network, and "milestone" dates may be set before the network is developed.

The *critical path* is that particular sequence of activities, connecting the starting event with the ending (objective) event, which requires the greatest elapsed time to complete. A network will have one or more critical paths all equal to the project duration.

A *dummy activity* is used to maintain proper relationships between functional activities. The dummy activity requires no time and involves no direct cost. The dummy activity is usually shown as a broken-line arrow.

Duration is the time required by a job (activity) or project.

Earliest start (T_E) is the earliest time a given event takes place represented by the longest path between the project start (beginning event) and the given event. The earliest start for an activity is the latest, earliest finish of all preceding activities, or the earliest occurrence of all activities leading to the given event.

Earliest finish is the earliest time an activity can finish as determined by the earliest start (T_E) plus the estimated activity elapsed time.

Latest finish is the latest time an activity can finish without affecting completion of the project or terminal event.

Latest start is the latest time an activity can start without affecting completion of the project (terminal event). The latest start is determined by subtracting the estimated activity elapsed time from the latest finish.

Total float (primary slack) is the maximum time that can be made available for an activity minus the time required for the activity. The total float is the difference between latest finish and earliest finish; thus, it is the amount of flexibility an activity can have without affecting the critical path. (Computer programs have been designed to allocate float based upon a priority rating assigned by the planning engineer.)

Free float (secondary slack) is the float available to an activity if all activities are started as early as possible.

Independent float is the float available to an activity when all preceding activities are started as late as possible and all following activities are started as early as possible.

Normal cost is the cost associated with each activity if it is carried out in the *normal time*.

Crash time is the minimum possible time in which an activity can be carried out. *Crash cost* is the minimum cost to complete an activity in crash time.

Cost slope is the increase in cost units for each decrease in time unit of an activity: (crash cost minus normal cost) divided by (normal time minus crash time). Figure 7.1 illustrates this relationship.

In Figure 7.1, point D,C_1 is assumed to be, or is in the region of, the minimum cost at which this job can be performed. This would be considered as the *normal time* in which to accomplish this job. Point d,C_2 is, or is in the region of, the maximum cost at which this job can be accomplished under *crash conditions*. Furthermore, linearity is assumed between point d,C_2 and point D,C_1. The slope of this line is negative, since there is a decrease in cost for each increase in time unit. The slope of the line is indicated as follows:

$$m = \frac{C_2 - C_1}{d - D} \qquad m = \frac{\text{crash cost} - \text{normal cost}}{\text{crash time} - \text{normal time}}$$

Since an inverse relationship exists between the crash point and the normal point and a positive answer is desired from the formula, the signs of the demonimator are reversed and the revised formula (which is the *cost slope formula*) is as follows:

$$\text{cost slope} = \frac{C_2 - C_1}{D - d} \qquad \text{cost slope} = \frac{\text{crash cost} - \text{normal cost}}{\text{normal time} - \text{crash time}}$$

FIGURE 7.1

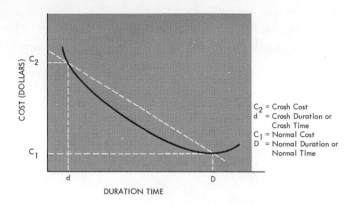

| | Normal | | Crash | | Cost |
Activity	Time	Cost	Time	Cost	Slope
A (1,2)........	6 days	$140	3 days	$500	$120
B (1,3)........	3	90	3	90	—*
C (2,3)........	4	160	2	360	100
D (3,4)........	5	110	3	410	150
E (2,5)........	2	80	1	120	40
F (4,5)........	4	100	2	260	80
G (5,6)........	3	130	1	410	140
H (4,6)........	5	120	2	390	90
		$930		$2,540	

° This activity cannot be expedited.

Illustrative Examples of CPM Technique

Figure 7.2 is an arrow diagram (network) of a project.

FIGURE 7.2

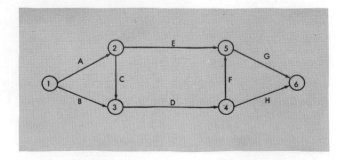

First, it is necessary to identify all the paths within the arrow diagram. Each path is identified by the combined letters that indicate the activities interrelated to form the path. Following are the paths within the previous arrow diagram:

Path	Normal Time
A,E,G	$6 + 2 + 3 = 11$
A,C,D,F,G	$6 + 4 + 5 + 4 + 3 = 22$
A,C,D,H	$6 + 4 + 5 + 5 = 20$
B,D,F,G	$3 + 5 + 4 + 3 = 15$
B,D,H	$3 + 5 + 5 = 13$

Path *A,C,D,F,G* is the critical path under normal conditions, and for a cost of $930 the project can be completed within 22 days. If the project is to be completed in less than 22 days, activity along this critical path must be expedited under crash conditions. However, if the project is to be completed within 21 days, which of the five activities along the critical path should be reduced? The cost slope provides the answer to this question. Activity *F* (4,5) has a $80 cost slope; thus, for an additional penalty of $80 (total of $930 + $80 = $1,010) the project can be completed in 21 days (22 days normal less 1 day saved by crash procedures).

If the duration of the project is 20 days, path *A,C,D,F,G* must be reduced one day. Activity *F* (4,5) can be reduced one additional day by using crash procedures at a cost of $80. Thus, the total project can be completed in 20 days for a cost of $1,090 (total of $930 normal cost + $80 + $80 = $1,090).

Following is a summary of all paths when activity *F* (4,5) has been completed on a crash basis:

Path	Time
A,E,G	$6 + 2 + 3 = 11$
A,C,D,F*,G	$6 + 4 + 5 + 2* + 3 = 20$†
A,C,D,H	$6 + 4 + 5 + 5 = 20$†
B,D,F*,G	$3 + 5 + 2* + 3 = 13$
B,D,H	$3 + 5 + 5 = 13$

Path *A,C,D,F*,G* and path *A,C,D,H* are critical paths. On path *A,C,D,F*,G* the cost slope for activity *C* (2,3) is the minimum ($100 per day); the duration time of the project can be reduced by two

---

* Indicates that activities are reduced to their limits by being completed on a crash basis.

† Indicates a critical path.

days (20 days $- 2 = 18$) if activity C is completed on a crash basis for an additional cost of \$200 (total of \$930 normal cost $+$ \$80 $+$ \$80 $+$ \$100 $+$ \$100 $=$ \$1,290). Since activity C is also on the critical path A,C^*,D,H, this path is likewise reduced to 18 days.

Note in the above example that if path A,C,D,H was considered before path A,C,D,F^*,G, the cost slope for activity H (4,6) would be the minimum. However, if activity H is completed on a crash basis, it is still necessary to complete activity C of path A,C,D,F^*,G on a crash basis if the total project time is to be reduced below 20 days. Since activity C is an activity common to both paths, the total cost is minimized by reducing only the time element on activity C and leaving the time for activity H at normal time. This type of consideration is possible where a simple arrow diagram is manually computed and there are only a limited number of activities and events. With an increase in the number of activities and events, it would be a time-consuming process to check common activities to various critical paths and to determine which common activities would minimize total cost. Therefore, a simple rule has been established: *Reduce that activity along the critical path that has the lowest cost slope.* The above example will be modified according to this rule; thus, two days are saved at an additional cost of \$180 by completing activity H on a near-crash basis. The total cost for the project being completed within 18 days would be increased from \$1,290 to \$1,470 (\$1,290 $+$ \$180 $=$ \$1,470). The revised paths are indicated as follows:

Path	Time
A,E,G	$6 + 2 + 3 = 11$
A,C^*,D,F^*,G	$6 + 2^* + 5 + 2^* + 3 = 18$†
A,C^*,D,H‡	$6 + 2^* + 5 + 3$‡ $= 16$
B,D,F^*,G	$3 + 5 + 2^* + 3 = 13$
B,D,H‡	$3 + 5 + 3$‡ $= 11$

The next objective is to reduce the total time to 15 days. Path A,C^*,D,F^*,G and path A,C^*,D,H‡ are over 15 days and must be reduced. Activity A (1,2) has the lowest remaining cost slope on the first path (\$120), and the time can be reduced by three days if the activity is completed on a crash basis (total additional cost $3 \times$ \$120

---

* Indicates that activities are reduced to their limits by being completed on a crash basis.

† Indicates a critical path.

‡ Indicates some expediting is being performed but activity has not been performed on an all-crash basis.

= $360). A three-day reduction in time on path A,C^*,D,F^*,G would mean the project would be completed in 15 days (18 days − 3 = 15). Activity H on path A,C^*,D,H‡ can be completed on an all-crash basis and the total time reduced by one day, which would mean the project would be completed within 15 days. Additional cost for activity H would be $90 (total cost would be $930 normal cost + $80 + $80 for activity F + $100 + $100 for activity C + $90 + $90 + $90 for activity H + $120 + $120 + $120 for activity A = $1,920). Following are the revised paths:

Path	Time
A^*,E,G	$3^* + 2 + 3 = 8$
A^*,C^*,D,F^*,G	$3^* + 2^* + 5 + 2^* + 3 = 15$†
A^*,C^*,D,H^*	$3^* + 2^* + 5 + 2^* = 12$
B,D,F^*,G	$3 + 5 + 2^* + 3 = 13$
B,D,H^*	$3 + 5 + 2^* = 10$

Note that path A^*,C^*,D,H^* was reduced by an additional three days because activity A was common to both paths (paths A^*,C^*,D, F^*,G and path A^*,C^*,D,H^*); however, the rule of applying the lowest cost slope to each critical path was applied—any path having over 15 days is a critical path if 15 days is the desired goal.

This procedure of completing activities on a crash basis can be continued until the project is completed within 11 days for a cost of $2,500. The latter amount is $40 less than the maximum cost; the reason is that no time is saved by completing activity E on a crash basis. The final listing of paths is as follows:

Path	Time
A^*,E,G^*	$3^* + 2 + 1^* = 6$
A^*,C^*,D^*,F^*,G^*	$3^* + 2^* + 3^* + 2^* + 1^* = 11$†
A^*,C^*,D^*,H^*	$3^* + 2^* + 3^* + 2^* = 10$
B^*,D^*,F^*,G^*	$3^* + 3^* + 2^* + 1^* = 9$
B^*,D^*,H^*	$3^* + 3^* + 2^* = 8$

The previous example of an arrow diagram for a project presented the simplest type of situation. Another example is cited in Figure 7.3 for purposes of illustrating some other important considerations.

Activity G, activity K, and activity L are dummy activities; although they do not require any time for being completed, they are essential coordinating activities that must be recognized in the ac-

---

* Indicates that activities are reduced to their limits by being completed on a crash basis.

† Indicates a critical path.

FIGURE 7.3

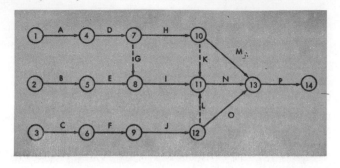

Activity	Normal Time	Activity	Normal Time
A (1,4)	10 days	I (8,11)	5 days
B (2,5)	3	J (9,12)	7
C (3,6)	2	K (10,11)	0 (dummy)
D (4,7)	4	L (11,12)	0 (dummy)
E (5,8)	6	M (10,13)	7
F (6,9)	3	N (11,13)	7
G (7,8)	0 (dummy)	O (12,13)	6
H (7,10)	3	P (13,14)	4

complishment of the overall project. For example, path *A,D,G* and path *B,E* must both be completed before activity *I* (8,11) can be started.

The systems analyst approaches an arrow diagram for a project in much the same manner as he approaches a network diagram of the major information flows for a given business organization. These various major information flows must be grouped into larger units of analysis, for purposes of getting a "handle" on the mass of information. Likewise, all activities must be carefully examined and all separate paths of activities indicated. Each path of activities is a *unique* ordering of events to be performed through time; therefore, each possible path must be ascertained and separately considered if the overall project is to be managed. Following are the paths within the previous arrow diagram:

Path	Normal Time
A,D,H,M,P	$10 + 4 + 3 + 7 + 4 = 28$ days
A,D,G,I,N,P	$10 + 4 + 0 + 5 + 7 + 4 = 30$ days
A,D,H,K,N,P	$10 + 4 + 3 + 0 + 7 + 4 = 28$ days
B,E,I,N,P	$3 + 6 + 5 + 7 + 4 = 25$ days
C,F,J,O,P	$2 + 3 + 7 + 6 + 4 = 22$ days
C,F,J,L,N,P	$2 + 3 + 7 + 0 + 7 + 4 = 23$ days

Close scrutiny of the arrow diagram shows there are only six paths, and path *A,D,G,I,N,P* is the critical path under normal conditions. In this situation, management could delay activity *C* (3,6) for 7 days (not 8 days; note that activity *C* is a part of two paths and both paths must be considered) and still complete the overall project in the same number of days—specifically, 30 days under normal conditions.

Advantages of the Method

The previous illustrations of the CPM method have emphasized the mechanical and procedural aspects of the method without giving proper attention to the other aspects of the method. These non-mechanical aspects are briefly mentioned in the following discussion of advantages gained by employing the CPM method.

First, a Foundation for Other Analyses. In order to prepare a CPM or PERT network, the systems analyst must identify in detail all the essential steps required for the accomplishment of a given operation. After these steps are listed, then time and cost estimates are made for each step. These time and cost estimates may include the appropriate information for (1) cost sensitivity analysis, (2) cost control, (3) direct costing type of analysis, (4) contribution to margin analysis, (5) cash flow analysis, and (6) other analyses. Thus, the CPM or PERT method serves as a foundation from which the arsenal of management tools and techniques may be employed.

Second, Effect on Management. The power of the critical path method is not the identification of those items that determine the minimum time period within which the total project can be accomplished (the critical path) but is the effect or influence that the application of this method has on management's thinking. The controller of a large corporation listed on the New York Stock Exchange recently spoke of the impact on his associates that a company training program on CPM method had made:

It is surprising what effect this program has had on management's behavior. They are requiring their subordinates to submit CPM networks in support of any new project. It is not as if we did not plan before, for we did. We were just never so specific in relating both the steps to be accomplished and the time required for the attainment of each step.[2]

---

[2] From notes of private interview by Thomas R. Prince with the controller whose name is withheld at his request.

Third, Statement of Problem.   The CPM method is a practical example of the application of the principles of the scientific method. The most difficult and the most important task confronting the management scientist is "the determination of the problem." Once the problem has been identified and precisely stated, the management scientist has an easier task of selecting, from the available alternatives, the particular procedure that will be employed in either the minimization or elimination of the identified problem. Likewise, the CPM method includes the identification and specification of the problem area—the critical path which encompasses these activities . . . with a cost of . . . and a time of. . . .

Fourth, Stimulation for New Alternatives.   Once the critical activities have been ascertained, then management's attention is focused on the most important activities. Not only are these "critical" activities identified by the application of the CPM method, but the approach also expresses the degree of criticalness and sensitiveness in terms of time and cost measures. As a result, management has often formulated a new alternative for the accomplishment of a critical activity. For example, the plans may be modified to provide for more expensive equipment or construction which can be economically substituted for existing proposed equipment or construction. In one company several thousand dollars was saved by having a furnace shipped in sections and assembled on the construction site. The additional cost of assembly was more than offset by being able to erect the steel beams and pour the concrete for the main floor before the furnace was installed, thus making it possible to complete the construction project three months earlier.

Other Considerations

Although many critical paths are manually solved, there are practical restrictions regarding the size of such a network that can be manually solved in a reasonable length of time. On the other hand, the procedural aspects of the critical path method make it an ideal application for the computer. The combination of a large storage capacity coupled with a tremendous speed for processing information enables an enormous critical path schedule to be solved in a matter of minutes.

Strange as it may seem, there are many major construction projects where the combination of activities and events exceeds the capacity of existing CPM computer program packages. Economically, it is not financially feasible to prepare a special CPM computer program which is going to be used only once. Therefore, different approaches have been followed in coping with this situation.

One approach is to reduce the CPM network to a size that can be handled by existing CPM computer program packages. This is accomplished by taking groups of activities and expressing them as though the group was only one activity. Of course, the solution as determined by the computer under such conditions would probably not be optimum, if there were significant differences in the time requirements of the collection of activities handled as one activity.

Another approach in coping with this problem of the "oversize" CPM network is to divide the total network into segments which can be handled on the computer. The computer outputs for each of the segments are the inputs for another computer program which determines a practical (in all situations it may not be optimal) solution to the total CPM network.

Regardless of whether the CPM schedule is going to be solved manually or by the computer, it is not always desirable to prepare the CPM schedule at the activity level. For example, it may not be economically feasible to identify the activities at the lowest level and to determine the time and cost estimates for each activity. Instead, groups of activities may be scheduled as though they were one activity.

At this point, a warning note is inserted. The CPM method cannot provide any better answer than the quality of the input information. It is well to remember that as far as improvement is concerned, there is usually a higher degree of probability associated with the questioning of the input information than there is with the preparation of CPM schedules at a lower level.

From a practical standpoint, it may be desirable to sketch cost curves for each of the critical activities under normal and overtime conditions before categorically stating which crash procedures will be employed. In other words, the suggested solution by the CPM method may be analogous to the suggested solution of alternative financial investments measured by return on investment formula. The real advantage of both the CPM method and the return on investment formula is not in solving a problem, but in focusing attention on the problem area which management should evaluate. Thus, the benefit is more in terms of *eliminating* areas and activities that should not be evaluated, than in the *selection* of the area or activity to be evaluated.

As far as applications are concerned, the CPM or PERT method may be used in coping with any scheduling assignment. For example, a certified public accounting firm can use the method in determining the staffing requirements of employees by grade or in the assignment of existing personnel to jobs. The CPM method has frequently been used in expediting the preparation of the end-of-the-month statement. The planning and supervision of the audit program for a large corporation has also frequently been achieved through the use of the CPM method. Another type of application is the case of a maintenance problem for a multiplant operation where the CPM method is used in identifying the significant factors (such as the idle and travel time of mechanics, the lost time of machine operators, production delays, the size of the maintenance parts inventory, and the location of the inventory).

The Method from the Perspective of the Systems Analyst

The systems analyst views the critical path method as an extension of the control features of responsibility accounting systems (each activity is a "responsibility unit") which is combined with the short-term planning features of profitability accounting (the time and cost estimates for each planned activity are core ingredients in the CPM system, and this information is accumulated in such a manner as to permit marginal analyses). For example, as time passes and activities are performed, the CPM network can be reused, with actual information substituted in place of planned data; thus, the periodic application of the method to the same project will provide management with revised, up-to-date, critical information.

The systems analyst also sees this extension from traditional information systems as a practical example of the implementation of the scientific method, particularly from the standpoint of the emphasis given to the identification and statement of the problem.

Summary

The CPM method is a powerful tool which can be employed in diverse situations, limited only by the imagination of the systems analyst to employ the method. On the other hand, the systems analyst sees the method as a technique which is ideally employed in conjunction with other management tools and techniques. Furthermore, the systems analyst perceives the method as a connecting network which permits the matching of information requirements and sources of data for all decision makers associated with the project under scrutiny.

If it were not for the information dimensions associated with the critical path method, this chapter would not have been included in this book. These information flows must be considered in the same manner as the evaluation made by the systems analyst in the previous traditional information systems. The systems analyst must measure and evaluate the expected benefit derived from the application of the CPM method versus the cost of implementing the method. In addition, there are practical restrictions from the standpoint of available computer capacity and from the standpoint of the level at which the CPM network should be prepared.

TOPICS FOR CLASS DISCUSSION

1. Why are critical path planning and scheduling information systems presented as an extension from traditional information systems? Explain.

2. Explain the similarities between a responsibility accounting system and a critical path planning and scheduling information system. Be specific.

CASE 7–1. JAEGER MANUFACTURING COMPANY

CPM Exercise

The Jaeger Manufacturing Company is a small tool and die company which operates strictly on a job order basis. Currently, Carl Jaeger, who is president of the company, is evaluating a customer's request regarding the construction of a proposed project.

This project (which is a job order type of special item) is normally completed within 17 days at a selling price of $1,350. The customer stated that he urgently needed this particular item and would pay a premium of $150 a day for the completion of the project by an earlier time (for example, $1,350 + $150 = $1,500 is the selling price if the project is completed in 16 days; the price for 15 days is $1,350 + $150 + $150 = $1,650; and so forth).

EXHIBIT A

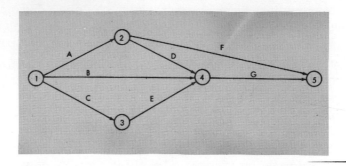

EXHIBIT B
Cost Table

Activity	Normal Time	Normal Cost	Crash Time	Crash Cost	Cost Slope
A (1,2)........	4 days	$100	2 days	$ 200	$ 50
B (1,4)........	7	160	5	300	70
C (1,3)........	3	50	1	110	30
D (2,4)........	7	120	2	620	100
E (3,4)........	3	90	3	90	—*
F (2,5)........	8	130	4	210	20
G (4,5)........	5	120	2	360	80
		$770		$1,890	

* This activity cannot be expedited.

Although this offer of a premium for "crash" construction sounds inviting, Carl Jaeger is concerned with the efficient employment of all of the resources of the company during the current "busy" season. In evaluating the customer's offer, an arrow diagram (see Exhibit A) was prepared to show the sequence of activities, and a cost table (see Exhibit B) was developed showing the normal and crash time and cost for each activity.

REQUIRED:

1. Assuming that Carl Jaeger desires to maximize income by having the *highest return per dollar of cost incurred,* determine which schedule of operations should be followed if the project is undertaken. Include quantitative computations in support of your answer.
2. What assumption is made regarding the nature of the cost slope in the above question?

3. Using the additional information revealed by Exhibit C, redetermine the schedule of operations that should be undertaken.

4. With the following additional information, prepare a daily cash forecast for the schedule of operations that was selected to be undertaken in the above step (3):

   a) Assume that all purchases are for cash. Except for activities *A*, *B*, and *C*, all material for each activity must be purchased the day *before* work on that activity can begin. In the case of activities *A*,

EXHIBIT C

Cost Data

Activity	Basis	Material	Labor	Other Expense	Total Cost
A (1,2)........	Normal	$ 20	$ 70	$10	$100
	Crash	150*	40	10	200
B (1,4)........	Normal	20	130	10	160
	Crash	190*	100	10	300
C (1,3)........	Normal	10	35	5	50
	Crash	10	95	5	110
D (2,4)........	Normal	10	100	10	120
	Crash	10	600	10	620
E (3,4)........	Normal	5	80	5	90
F (2,5)........	Normal	10	115	5	130
	Crash	10	195	5	210
G (4,5)........	Normal	10	100	10	120
	Crash	10	340	10	360

* The material cost includes a purchased part which is partially finished, and this "partially finished part" can only be purchased in this given state. (There are two such partially finished parts: one for activity *A* and another for activity *B*.)

B, and *C*, assume that the materials are purchased in the morning of the first scheduled work day for each activity.

b) Assume that each activity's labor and other expenses are incurred on a proportional basis and must be paid for on a daily basis.

CASE 7–2.   WOODRUFF GROCERY COMPANY

CPM EXERCISE

The management consulting firm with which you are associated was engaged by the Woodruff Grocery Company, a regional wholesaler for frozen foods, to (1) perform an overall review of the data processing operations for inventory control, sales management, and

EXHIBIT A

Description of Work to Be Performed in Developing an
Integrated Information System for Inventory Control, Sales
Management, and Accounts Receivable Collection Procedures

Step No.	Description	Assigned to	Estimated Time
1.	Inventory Control System:		
1.1	Obtain copies of monthly stock status report for the past 36 months	Woodruff Grocery Co.	
1.2	Obtain copy of current month's monthly stock status report in punched-card form	Woodruff Grocery Co.	
1.3	Develop projected sales quantities for each item by month for the next twelve months, which would include identifying seasonal demand patterns for certain items	Information Systems Specialists, Inc.	50 man-hours
1.4	Review projected sales quantities developed in previous step with sales manager	Information Systems Specialists, Inc.	7 man-hours (7 consecutive hours, only)
1.5	Develop reorder quantities for each item, which would include giving consideration to sources of supply, shipping time, price breaks, storage and handling costs, and total storage capacity (Step 1.5 cannot begin until after Step 1.4 is completed)	Information Systems Specialists, Inc.	120 man-hours
1.6	Review reorder quantities developed in previous step with Inventory Manager and Purchasing Manager	Information Systems Specialists, Inc.	7 man-hours (7 consecutive hours, only)
1.7	Develop reorder points for each item (Step 1.7 cannot begin until after Step 1.6 is completed)	Information Systems Specialists, Inc.	50 man-hours
1.8	Review reorder points developed in previous step with sales manager, inventory manager, and purchasing manager (a comparative report of monthly forecasted sales, reorder quantity, and reorder point by item)	Information Systems Specialists, Inc.	5 man-hours (5 consecutive hours, only)
1.9	Assist in designing a computer program so that when the existing perpetual inventory system indicates that the balance of a given item has reached the reorder point, a purchase request for the reorder quantity of the desired item is initiated (Step 1.9 cannot begin until after Step 1.8 is completed)	Information Systems Specialists, Inc.	30 man-hours (minimum of 14 consecutive hours)
1.10	Monitor the installation, testing, and operation of designed system, including the monitoring of input cards (punched cards) for transmitting the computed reorder points and reorder quantities onto magnetic tape (the perpetual inventory system is maintained on magnetic tape) (Step 1.10 may be partially performed concurrently with Step 1.9; however, 10 man-hours and a minimum of 7 consecutive hours must be performed *after* Step 1.9 is completed)	Information Systems Specialists, Inc.	45 man-hours (minimum of 14 consecutive hours)

EXHIBIT A (*Continued*)

Step No.	Description	Assigned to	Estimated Time
2.	Sales Management System:		
2.1	Obtain copy of the current month's monthly stock status report	Woodruff Grocery Co.	
2.2	Obtain a list of the per unit cost data for each item included in the monthly stock status report	Woodruff Grocery Co.	
2.3	Assist in the design of computer program for sales management system which would include: 2.31 Master tape file of cost data for each item of inventory 2.32 Program routine and report format for comparing and extending cost data against item sales data per sales invoice 2.33 Program routine and report format for computing monthly gross margin by invoice for each customer 2.34 Program routine and report format for computing monthly gross margin by customer for each salesman	Information Systems Specialists, Inc.	80 man-hours (minimum of 21 consecutive hours)
2.4	Monitor the installation, testing, and operation of the designed sales management system (Step 2.4 cannot begin until after Step 2.3 has been completed)	Information Systems Specialists, Inc.	24 man-hours (minimum of 14 consecutive hours)
3.	Accounts receivable collection procedures:		
3.1	Obtain a print out from the master tape file of the identification code, name, and address of each customer	Woodruff Grocery Co.	
3.2	Obtain a list of approved credit limit per order and in total for each customer	Woodruff Grocery Co.	
3.3	Assist in the design of a computer program for exceptional reporting, where each salesman will receive weekly a list of his customers whose current accounts receivable balance *plus* the approved credit limit per order will exceed the maximum approved credit limit for that customer	Information Systems Specialists, Inc.	40 man-hours (minimum of 20 consecutive hours)
3.4	Monitor the installation, testing, and operation of designed system (Step 3.4 cannot begin until after Step 3.3 is completed)	Information Systems Specialists, Inc.	10 man-hours (10 consecutive hours, only)
3.5	Assist in the design of computer program routine and report format for an exceptional reporting system to the credit manager of all overdue accounts. This report will be prepared on the first and the fifteenth days of each month, or at any other time based on request.	Information Systems Specialists, Inc.	14 man-hours (minimum of 7 consecutive hours)
3.6	Monitor the installation, testing, and operation of designed system (Step 3.6 cannot begin until after Step 3.5 is completed)	Information Systems Specialists, Inc.	7 man-hours (7 consecutive hours, only)

accounts receivable collection procedures and to (2) design an improved integrated information system for these operations.

You have accompanied your immediate superior, a manager, on a high-point review of the above specified data processing operations at the Woodruff Grocery Company. After you completed your preliminary examination of the company's operations, your manager decided that:

1. A scientific inventory system should be established in place of the existing inventory system which uses last period's sales as the minimum inventory level for the current period.

2. Unit cost data should be available for each line item on a sales invoice, and gross margin type of reports should be prepared for each line item and each invoice and on a monthly basis for each customer and each salesman.

3. The accounts receivable collection procedures should be modified to include an information system for monitoring cumulative balances in customer accounts versus approved credit limits.

Your manager outlined the work to be performed (see Exhibit A) and indicated the estimated number of man-hours that members of the management consulting firm (Information Systems Specialists, Inc.) would spend in accomplishing each step.

REQUIRED:

1. Prepare a critical path schedule of the steps to be performed.
2. The Woodruff Grocery Company is an out-of-town client, and the manager is wondering if there should be *three* or *four* men assigned to this job. Because of high transportation cost, the minimum assignment of a man to the job is on a weekly basis (35 man-hours, consisting of five 7-man-hour days). Quantitatively determine the number of men *by week* that should be assigned to this project.
3. If six men were assigned to this project on a full-time basis, how many days would be required to complete the project? Determine the number of idle man-hours under this assignment of six men.

CASE 7–3. WEBSTER CONSTRUCTION COMPANY, INC.

The construction firm with which you are associated, the Webster Construction Company, Inc., has a contract to erect a $10 million educational complex at a leading midwestern university. Because of labor difficulties climaxing in an eight-week strike, the construction project was two to three months behind the contract completion date, according to the project manager.

The contract provided for $500 a day liquidating damages for noncompletion of the project by the specified date.

You have just been transferred by the home office management of the Webster Construction Company from a Massachusetts construction project (which was ahead of schedule) to this critical construction project at the midwestern university.

Ralph Worthington, the project manager, was desperate for some way to expedite the construction operations and agreed to your suggestion of using the critical path method. Worthington stated that he had seen articles in trade publications on the CPM method but that he had never actually supervised a project where the CPM method was employed. Worthington also said that most of his associates were in the same predicament as himself regarding CPM. However, Worthington said he was sure the various foremen would cooperate with you.

You devoted the next several days to the task of reading blueprints, scheduling the operations, and preparing network diagrams. Considerable time was spent with different foremen asking for "estimated time" to complete the different jobs (activities or operations) and also in verifying that the sequence of activities per the network diagrams was correct.

Eventually, the CPM network was completed and reviewed with Ralph Worthington. According to the network, there was a 110-day period between the contract completion date and the earliest actual completion time, which, at $500 per day, totaled $55,000 penalty.

Worthington said that he would discuss the jobs along the critical path with the various foremen and see if they were not too pessimistic in stating their "estimated time."

The above talks resulted in several revised critical path schedules, which eventually reflected a shift in the critical path and a 90-day delay (rather than a 110-day delay). The forecasted penalty was $45,000. However, the delay would probably mean that the Webster Construction Company would not be selected for another proposed construction project for which this midwestern university was currently seeking financial assistance from alumni and friends of the university.

Worthington summarized his predicament:

I have 210 days remaining before the contract completion date and your CPM schedule tells me that it will really be 90 days beyond the contract completion date before we finish the project. Of the more than 1,500 activities that I have to supervise, the CPM network tells me where to focus my attention. However, there are still too many activities on the critical path involving too many dollars for me to efficiently and economically manage by mere observation. Frankly, this CPM approach has been overrated; it just tells the project manager "how bad off he really is."

REQUIRED:

Design an information control system that will assist Worthington in his management activities and yet not upset the normal accounting routines. In accomplishing this task, you review the current accounting routines:

1. The Webster Construction Company's management requires that a bill of materials (units and prices) and a schedule of labor (hours and average wage per hour for groups of workers) be prepared as a basis for determining the *bid price*. Then, on all projects, actual material and labor costs are compared with the estimated costs.
2. Ralph Worthington has a manager of materials and supplies who is responsible for seeing that such items are on hand as required. Furthermore, the manager of materials and supplies is responsible for maintaining a record of the actual materials and supplies used.
3. As a control device, each foreman maintains the payroll records for his employees and submits a weekly report to the accounting payroll clerk.
4. In addition to these procedures for materials, supplies, and labor costs, a special bank account is established for each construction project. All expenditures, including general and administrative overhead, are charged against this special bank account.

CASE 7–4. LEVI CONSTRUCTION COMPANY, INC.

The management consulting firm with which you are associated has been engaged by the Levi Construction Company, Inc., to assist management in the construction of a $2,000,000 public school building. George Bradford has been assigned by the Levi Construction Company as the project manager for this school building.

Based on the architectural drawings and the General Superintendent's narrative of the major steps in construction of the school, you prepare an arrow diagram consisting of approximately 300 events and 550 activities. When the proper dependencies among activities are recorded, time estimates were assigned to each activity and the earliest possible completion times were calculated. Next, the activities were placed on a time scale and the dependencies were appropriately identified. In addition to the scale drawing, a working day calendar and delivery schedule for major outside purchased equipment were prepared.

Bradford, in reviewing your drawings with you, made the following comment:

Although the specifications on the contract indicate a delivery date of the school building by September 1, 1970, we would like to avoid incurring heating and maintenance costs during January–September, 1970. Is it possible that the school building can be completed by December, 1969? If it can be completed by the earlier date, we are sure that the school board will accept the building and use the facilities during the second semester of the 1969–70 school year.

Your critical path diagrams for the planned project indicate a normal completion date on June 10, 1970. Therefore, you tell Bradford that you will reexamine the plans and see if some alternative types of construction might be followed in shortening the construction period.

The delivery time for the boiler was previously believed to be the governing factor in the completion time for the basement of one of the wings. As a result of your reexamination and thorough analysis of the specifications for the boiler, it was revealed that the boiler could be delivered in sections and lowered through the stairwells at a later date. Your reexamination indicated other alternative procedures including a different plan for excavation and other sources for selective purchase items whereby the planned project could be completed by December 30, 1969.

After preparing revised arrow diagrams, working day calendars, and a schedule for major outside purchased equipment, Bradford discusses with you his other requirements:

Since the project has not begun, I would like to have a suggested information system that would not only aid me in completing the school building by December 30, 1969, but would also assist me in (1) controlling costs and (2) forecasting cash requirements. As the construction proceeds and unexpected events occur, this suggested information system must permit the easy rescheduling and recomputation of (1) the earliest completion date for each step in the project, (2) the planned and actual costs, and (3) the cash requirements.

REQUIRED:

1. Reply to Bradford's request.
2. As a systems analyst, what are some of the practical problems involved in the design of such an information system? (Your comments should include such considerations as data restrictions, time restrictions, and the out-of-pocket costs in designing and monitoring such a system versus the estimated benefit to be derived from the system.)

PART **III**

PRODUCTION AND
OPERATION INFORMATION
SYSTEMS

CHAPTER **8**

Production Information Systems

PART II DESCRIBED the general types of traditional information systems where the systems analyst was able to design an information network that encompassed most of the major information flows associated with decision-making activities throughout the business organization. In Part III the systems analyst is not trying to simultaneously handle all of the major information flows within the business organization; instead, he is focusing only on a selected group of major information flows.

The general models of information systems were described and contrasted in Chapter 4. The traditional information system was categorized by a given type of environment and nature of the business process. Specifically, in a traditional information system, the systems analyst must be able to select arbitrarily a time frame for the "information cycle" in which all steps of the planning process can be completed before activity for the planned period begins. On the other hand, in the production and operation information system, aspects of the planning process are occurring as activity occurs.

Other characteristics of this latter model are subsequently reexamined. This chapter also gives a detailed description of the steps that the systems analyst follows in studying and evaluating the production function within a given business organization. This lengthy description is followed by a brief examination of some special concerns which the systems analyst encounters in designing and evaluating production and operation information systems.

The General Model

The general model for a production and operation information system is a *partially open* system which incorporates all of the major information flows within the business organization that are associated with the production function. The general model is partially open in the sense that the network permits new inputs from production management, marketing management, or financial management *after* the previous inputs to the model are evaluated, for example.

The environment surrounding the typical business organization in which a production and operation information system is employed is such that a quick response and reaction to certain types of events must be permitted within the information network. Business management needs an information network that (1) not only informs them of a significant change in certain business events, but (2) also contains the necessary, direct communication link within the information network so that business management's reaction to the situation can be immediately implemented in the form of modified operating criteria within the information network.

In this type of environment, the nature of the business process cannot be grouped into the planning phase and control phase as described for the traditional information system. Within the time frame of an "information cycle," business management must be able to respond and react to the actions of competitors, indications of a possible change in customer preferences, changing level of customer demand, and to special requirements of certain customers, such as priority sales orders or rush service in all phases of the production function.

Therefore, in the production and operation information system the business process is grouped into three parts: the planning phase, the coordination phase, and the control phase. Of the three, the coordination phase is the most distinctive characteristic of the production and operation information network.

The coordination phase of the business process permits inputs to the information network at any time. These inputs may ask that certain tasks be performed which would require the use of personnel, machines, or raw materials that are already assigned to previous tasks that are currently scheduled for production. The information system must be able to handle these conflicting requirements for assigned personnel, machines, or raw materials.

The crux of the coordination phase is the establishment of a set of criteria and the assignment of priorities that will be followed in coping with future events. Thus, these predetermined responses are used in managing conflicts in assignment of personnel, machines, or raw materials. The predetermined response may span the gamut from taking "no action" (in the sense of not modifying the previous assignment of raw materials, machines, or personnel and holding the conflicting customer request for the next "information cycle") to a total response (in which case there might be a complete reassignment of tasks to be performed within a given period of time using specified personnel, machines, and raw materials).

TYPE 2 Information System

In the last few years, production and operation information systems have been designed and implemented in several business organizations. The primary attributes of this type of system have been encompassed in new information systems that were unrelated to production or operation activities. For example, some of these information systems have been designed to handle the information flows in a marketing division. In which case it is awkward to refer to the information system in the marketing division as a production and operation information system. Therefore, we will use the label TYPE 2 information system to refer to an information system encompassing these specific attributes.

Figure 8.1 presents a generalized model of a TYPE 2 information system. From this flo. chart we can see more clearly the unique characteristics of the coordination phase in this type of system. We note that the coordination phase has a separate input terminal from that used in the planning phase or in the control phase. This separate terminal permits inputs to be accepted into the coordination phase of the system at any time during the operating cycle. Or, from an alternative perspective, the coordination phase is what differentiates a TYPE 1 information system from a TYPE 2 information system and is the mechanism that permits the latter system to be *partially* open.

If the coordination phase is going to continuously accept inputs of selected data into the system, then we must design some type of screening device for sorting these selected data. Otherwise, the continuous flow of selected data into the system might exceed the storage and processing capabilities of the system; in which case this excessive volume of data would bring the system to a halt.

The generalized model shows the screening process in the coordination phase as consisting of two steps. First, the selected data are

FIGURE 8.1

A Generalized Model of a TYPE 2 Information System

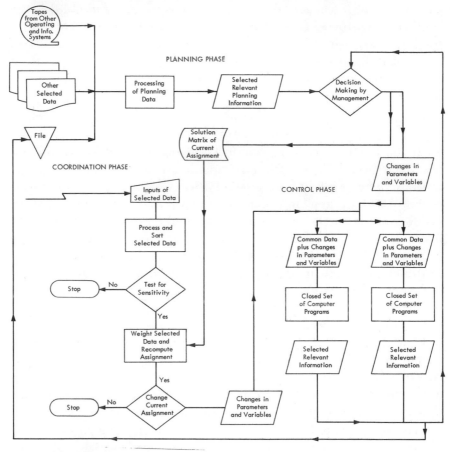

processed, sorted, and tested for sensitivity. If these selected data are determined to be critical, then these data are filtered by the second step in the screening process. In the second step the critical data are weighted by a time factor, and these adjusted selected data are used in a recomputation of the assignment for the current cycle. A computer analysis is made of the new computations to determine if a change in the current assignment is required. If so, changes in parameters and variables are made in the closed sets of computer programs contained within the operating systems.

The time factor used in weighting these selected data is the critical element in this overall process. For example, the price of raw material no. 1874 is defined as critical (step one in the screening process) if it is less than \$21.18 per unit, or if it is more than \$22.37. Assume that an input of new data is accepted into the system that specifies the price as \$22.41 per unit. Since \$22.41 is more than \$22.37, this price change is determined to be sensitive. If the overall operating cycle is eight hours and this new data on price of raw material no. 1874 occurs during the first hour of the cycle, then it is highly likely that a revised assignment will occur for the remaining seven plus hours in the cycle. On the other hand, if the new data on raw material price occurs late in the sixth hour of the cycle, then it is highly unlikely that a revised assignment will occur.

The flowchart of the coordination phase in Figure 8.1 shows a closed set of integrated computer programs from the input terminals through the outputs in the form of changes in parameters and variables. Therefore, this time factor that is used in weighting the critical data must be computed within the system. The online storage of the "solution matrix of current assignment" will also include the time at which the control phase (or the operating cycle) began for the current cycle.

The control phase in the TYPE 2 information system is similar to the control phase in the TYPE 1 information system. The difference, of course, is that the control phase must be capable of accepting during the cycle, changes in parameters and variables as specified by the coordination phase. The closed sets of computer programs in the operating systems must be specially designed so as to accommodate those identified changes.

The planning phase in the TYPE 2 information system is similar to the planning phase in the TYPE 1 information system. The only difference is that the "solution matrix of current assignment" from the decision-making process in the planning phase is stored online in the computer system. This solution matrix is required in the coordination phase for recomputation of the current assignment.

The Production Function as Viewed by the Systems Analyst

If the systems analyst desires to study and evaluate the production function in a given business organization, he would begin by first looking at the general, overall environment in which the business organization is located. Until he has an overall appreciation of the general nature of the business process of a given business organization, the systems analyst cannot appropriately design and evaluate the production and operation information system.

The same point can be seen from another perspective. Any reasonably competent practitioner can design a data processing system which will handle 90 percent of all the transactions that occur in the area of production for a given business organization. However, it is the other 10 percent of the transactions that "kill" most data processing systems.

The systems analyst is equally concerned with the 10 percent of the transactions as with the major group, and he manifests this concern by his sincere attempt to *understand the unique environment and the unique nature of the business process for the given business organization under scrutiny.*

Many of the so-called "exceptional transactions" are merely indications of the "unique nature of the business process as performed by this business organization." For example, if among the 200-plus customers, there are six customers who are given special consideration over any of their requests, then this is just part of the environment as viewed by the systems analyst. Or, the systems analyst would view this business organization's "way of doing business" as incorporating a priority system where six customers are given special consideration. Any information system that the systems analyst designs must be sufficiently flexible to permit these six customers to continue to receive special consideration.

On the other hand, the systems analyst must use discretion in providing for the "exceptional events." He has a professional obligation to inform business management what it costs the business organization in terms of time and effort in order for the information network to accommodate these "exceptional events."

More specifically, when the systems analyst views the production function within a given business organization, he is looking at the day-to-day set of operations being performed by certain decision makers which relates to the production function. He views this set of operations, the decision makers, and the general environmental setting in which this occurs. Next, the systems analyst attempts to specify the information requirements for these various decision makers. The procedures that the systems analyst follows in (1) studying the environment, the nature of the business process, the functions being performed, and the special characteristics of each decision maker and in (2) specifying information requirements are comparable with those procedures described in Chapters 2 and 4. It is suggested that the reader review the general frame of reference used in specifying and identifying information flows and in grouping information flows into more inclusive information networks which were presented previously in these chapters.

Relation of Production Function to Other Operations

Today, it is not sufficient to have just the necessary technological abilities and appropriate plant facilities to manufacture a given product. Accordingly, the production function in "mature industries" has shifted to a subordinate position following that of the marketing function.[1] Thus, many of the critical information flows associated with the production function will have their origin in the activities of the marketing function. Other critical information flows will originate in the financial management activities.

When the systems analyst is studying the production function and designing a production and operation information system, he must obtain some policy type of decision from business management regarding those issues that do not completely follow within the boundaries of the production function. Or, from another position, one of the important insights provided by the systems analyst's study is the identification of the "broken line" types of major information flows that are associated with the production function.

Marketing Management and Production Management. In a business organization within a mature industry, marketing management provides production management with information regarding what items should be manufactured during a given period of time. Periodically, marketing management can give production management some estimate of the general volume of units that is predicted to be sold during the coming period. The general accuracy or degree of confidence of these estimates may be so low that corporate management desires to operate on a system where the production department responds to actual sales rather than to estimated sales.

---

[1] See Philip Kotler, "Diagnosing the Marketing Takeover," *Harvard Business Review,* Vol. XLIII (November–December, 1965), p. 70: "Today it is almost axiomatic that a *marketing orientation* should pervade the way a company thinks about itself and the accomplishment of its goals."

There is a close relation between the production department and the marketing department in terms of product design and market research. But in the area of customer service, there are frequently conflicting priorities assigned to customer orders as viewed by members of these two departments. For example, the number of stockouts for regular stocked items and the number of nonshipments by promised date for job order items are two negative measures of customer service. Both of these measures bridge the gap between the production department and the marketing department, and these measures are interpreted as indicators of the cooperation between these departments (especially where the level of customer service is not compatible with the overall corporate policy) .

Financial Management and Production Management. The production department is given financial restrictions within which production management must manage the inventory investment. Production management also receives financial guidance in terms of payroll expenditures, investment in plant facilities, and investment in operating facilities. Production management has the responsibility of operating within these financial restrictions and providing the maximum degree of customer service.

Predetermined Decision Rules

In a production and operation information system, corporate management desires to establish a set of decision rules that can be used in the day-to-day operations of the business. The reason for this is one of practical necessity. There is insufficient time for production management to daily reexamine all major production questions; furthermore, this is a waste of manpower.

Once business management has established a set of decision rules which adequately covers all combinations of business events, then business management can delegate the monitoring or administering of this set of rules to clerical employees and to some computer program system. Typically there will be two sets of rules. The first set will be for the normal, ordinary transactions that occur 90 percent of the time. The second set will be for those predicted, special transactions which will be given special consideration. In other words, if six customers are to be given special consideration, the set of rules would tell a clerical employee how these requests are to be expedited (there might be a control procedure where a production manager would have to approve special considerations involving certain types of actions) .

Special Concerns

In studying and evaluating production and operation information systems, the systems analyst has three special concerns. First, he must be able to specify the implicit corporate management assumptions that are contained in each set of decision rules. The systems analyst is concerned with the degree of comparability between these implicit corporate management assumptions for the different sets of decision rules.

Second, the systems analyst is concerned with the appropriateness of some implicit corporate management assumptions in view of the current environment. For example, there may be a rather significant change in the environment in which the business organization is located. Consequently, some rather heterogeneous business events are "forced into a mold" by these predetermined decision rules.

Third, has corporate policy changed since these sets of decision rules were established? The systems analyst is concerned that his understanding of overall corporate policy is consistent with the implicit corporate management assumption upon which these various sets of decision rules are based.

TOPICS FOR CLASS DISCUSSION

1. In the critical path scheduling and control information systems, the coordination process preceded the construction of a critical path network. Explain how the coordination process is different from this in the general case of production and operation information systems.

2. Explain why corporate management desires to substitute a set of decision rules in place of day-to-day production management decisions.

3. Explain the function performed by the coordination phase in a TYPE 2 information system.

4. Explain how changes in the current assignment are introduced into the system during the control phase in a TYPE 2 information system.

CASE 8–1. WALKER MILL COMPANY

The Walker Mill Company manufactures sash, doors, windows, trim, molding, and custom cabinets. The company is located in a large mid-western city and provides delivery service within a 100-mile radius of the plant. Sales are made through representatives to general contractors, industrial contractors, lumber companies, and selected retail stores.

Company management is concerned with recent complaints regarding customer service. A 90 percent level of customer service has been the goal, and the president of the company asks you to investigate the situation and to see if the company's goal is being achieved.

You spend the next two days reviewing the operations of the plant and talking with foremen, supervisors, managers, administrative personnel, and the plant superintendent. From the latter individual you are told that the company tries to provide three-day delivery service on all stocked items and three-week delivery service on all custom-built cabinets and millwork. Furthermore, you are told that all rush orders must be personally approved by the plant superintendent and that these orders are expedited as fast as possible.

Sales orders are prepared by the various representatives whose salaries are primarily on a commission basis. Many of these representatives are part-time employees in the sense that they are also representatives of several different manufacturers, concurrently.

As part of your study, you have selected 68 delivery orders for custom-built cabinets and millwork which were completed during the first three weeks in March. Exhibit A presents the order date, promise date, and delivery date for these selected sales orders.

REQUIRED:

1. Specify the appropriate assumptions under which the selected 68 items may be used in further statistical analyses.
2. Compute the level of customer service that appears to be currently provided by the Walker Mill Company based upon this sample.
3. Prepare a letter to the president of the company containing any insights that you have gained from your study.

EXHIBIT A

Data on 68 Selected Orders

Order Date	Promise Date	Shipment Date	Order Date	Promise Date	Shipment Date
2/5	2/26	3/1	2/16	3/2	3/11
2/8	3/1	3/1	2/9	3/2	3/11
2/8	2/24	3/1	2/8	3/1	3/11
2/3	2/22	3/1	2/15	3/2	3/11
2/2	2/19	3/1	2/15	3/3	3/11
2/5	2/24	3/1	2/16	3/2	3/12
2/8	2/26	3/2	2/9	3/2	3/12
2/10	3/3	3/2	2/15	3/8	3/12
2/4	2/25	3/2	2/15	3/8	3/12
2/2	2/23	3/2	2/16	3/9	3/12
2/1	2/22	3/2	3/5	3/12	3/12
2/4	2/25	3/3	2/16	3/9	3/15
2/3	2/24	3/3	2/17	3/10	3/15
2/5	2/26	3/3	2/18	3/11	3/15
2/8	3/1	3/4	2/18	3/4	3/16
2/9	3/2	3/4	2/19	3/12	3/16
2/9	3/2	3/4	2/18	3/11	3/16
2/25	3/5	3/4	2/17	3/10	3/16
2/10	2/26	3/5	2/22	3/11	3/16
2/5	2/26	3/5	2/19	3/12	3/17
2/11	3/4	3/5	2/22	3/15	3/17
2/12	3/5	3/8	2/23	3/16	3/17
2/12	3/1	3/8	2/22	3/15	3/17
2/9	3/1	3/8	2/19	3/12	3/17
3/3	3/9	3/8	2/18	3/11	3/18
2/11	3/4	3/9	2/17	3/10	3/18
2/12	3/5	3/9	2/22	3/15	3/18
2/11	3/3	3/9	2/24	3/10	3/18
2/8	3/1	3/9	2/23	3/5	3/19
2/12	3/3	3/9	2/25	3/18	3/19
2/11	3/3	3/10	2/24	3/17	3/19
2/15	3/8	3/10	3/11	3/18	3/19
2/9	3/1	3/10	2/23	3/9	3/19
2/8	3/1	3/10	2/25	3/18	3/19

CHAPTER 9

Inventory Management
Information Systems

IT IS RECOGNIZED that the design and structure of production and operation information systems vary not only by business organization, but by division and department within a given business organization. Whether the information system is an inventory management information system for raw materials, subassemblies, or finished goods, or an integrated inventory management and production scheduling and control information system, there are certain common features in each of these networks. Each network is designed to make a procedural decision through some optimization technique for allocating funds, equipment, facilities, materials, and personnel.

Although the allocation of these resources as related to inventory management activities has been selected as the primary focus of the production and operation discussion in this book, we believe that the systems analyst's approach toward evaluating other types of activities within the production and operation area is similar to the approach followed for inventory-related systems. Thus, this analysis of inventory-related information systems should be considered as a frame of reference for analyzing other production and operation information systems.

This examination of inventory-related activities follows the information systems approach toward studying any business process. The systems analyst first attempts to understand the diverse objectives served by the inventory activities, because these diverse objectives are indicative of the basic requirements for information that the inventory management information system must satisfy. After the information requirements are identified, then the systems analyst can focus on matching the data sources with the information requirements through the use of processing procedures. This chapter, therefore, consists of two parts: (1) requirements and (2) processing procedures.

REQUIREMENTS

An effective inventory management information system is an operational system designed to provide the maximum inventory "service" to all users of inventory at the minimum cost to company management. The attainment of such a system within a large, complex business organization is difficult because of the conflicting objectives as to the use of inventory stock. For example, production management desires inventory stock to absorb the short-term demand variations and resultant fluctuations in production requirements. Such inventory stocks permit economical production runs and production balancing which will result in the least number of line changeovers consistent with effective leveling of the labor force.

Marketing management desires inventory stock at a level which will minimize the chance of a stockout condition. In the case of stocked items, marketing management will argue for a level of inventory that will almost eliminate the risk of insufficient stock to provide immediate delivery on customer orders. On the other hand, financial management is concerned with reducing the investment in inventory in order to release funds for investment in other company operations.

Without elaborating any further, it is obvious that an effective inventory management information system must be compatible with corporate managerial policy. This requires that corporate policy in various areas must have been previously specified before the inventory management information system can operate within the boundaries established by corporate policy. Following are some of the critical areas that corporate inventory policy must encompass:

1. Customer service
2. Back orders
3. Model and engineering changes
4. Facilities
5. Personnel policy (including labor leveling)
6. Crash programs

Quantitatively, this corporate inventory policy can be expressed as the relation between the following two costs: (1) the cost of carrying inventory versus (2) the cost of not carrying inventory or the cost of a stockout.

The Cost of Carrying Inventory

Many of the costs associated with carrying inventory are obvious, others are less apparent. These costs include interest on investment, storage and handling, obsolescence, deterioration, pilferage, personal property tax, and insurance. As long as the focus is on *all* inventory versus *no* inventory, it is easy to identify and measure in dollars the cost of carrying inventory. However, this is not the normal situation.

Typically, each item in inventory is assumed to have been selected by the criterion that the anticipated benefit of having the item in stock exceeds the cost of not having the item on hand. Thus, in analyzing inventory, the systems analyst is not speaking of *all* inventory, but only of the stock on hand for a given item.

The inventory analysis, therefore, becomes much more difficult. Which of the total inventory related costs are relevant or applicable to a given item of inventory? A frame of reference must be developed for coping with this question which would include expressions regarding the time and extent of change as well as an assumption regarding the independence of each item in inventory. In other words, the condition of having costs that would vary only with changes in two or more items in inventory is not considered in the analysis. Instead, a marginal approach is followed where relevant costs are identified in relation to changes in a selected item of inventory out of the total mass of inventory.

Most of the relevant costs associated with carrying inventory are available or easily determined from the formal accounting records. However, one significant item is not available: the investment cost of carrying inventory. This latter component may be as large as the aggregate value of the remaining components of the total cost of carrying inventory. Most of the professional literature on this subject argues that the marginal rate of capital of about 6 percent should be used as the investment cost. A recent paper presents an excellent rejection of the marginal rate of capital in favor of using the long-run average cost of capital.[1]

Our preferences are to identify all of the risk elements of inventory by type of risk, such as the risk of obsolescence, the risk of

---

[1] Robert H. Bock, "Measuring Cost Parameters in Inventory Models," *Management Technology,* Vol. IV (June, 1964), pp. 59–66.

deterioration, and the risk of pilferage. Then, the matter of interest on investment for this analysis can be separately expressed as the marginal rate of interest. Actually, more often than not, the critical cost is going to be the "negative stockout cost." In other words, management cannot afford to fail to carry the item in inventory. Thus, in the choice between carrying and not carrying an item of inventory, the marginal rate of interest is believed to be an appropriate item for use in the analysis *provided* that the risks of obsolescence, deterioration, and pilferage are separately considered along with the relevant cost of storing and handling the inventory.

In the matter of determining whether the business organization should invest in inventory or in other aspects of the business organization's operations (such as investment in plant expansion, new products, or research and development), then it might be more appropriate to use the long-run average cost of capital in these analyses. However, as previously suggested, we believe that even in this type of study, the negative stockout cost is probably the most appropriate measure to use in decisions regarding investment in inventory. After the decision has been made that a given item is to be stocked in inventory, then another order of questions arises: How much to buy? When to buy? In the subsequent discussion of these latter questions, the matter of interest on investment will be re-examined.

The Cost of Not Carrying Inventory

There are different aspects of this measurement. Is there sufficient demand for a given item to justify carrying that item in inventory? In those situations where the answer to the previous question is negative, then, are there other factors which would suggest that the item should be stocked anyway? For example, customers may expect your business organization to have a full stock of inventory, including slow-moving items. If the business organization does not have a full stock, then the company might be expected to lose some customers.

In the latter case, the systems analyst would like to quantify this belief. How many customers would be lost if slow-moving items were not stocked but were sold on an "order basis"? What are the expected, average annual sales for each of these customers? With answers to these two questions, the systems analyst has the appropriate information with which to begin an analysis of the situation.

Frequently, where company management has systematically faced these questions regarding inventory, it has reached its own conclusion before even responding to the systems analyst's second question. In other words, after company management has estimated the number of customers that would be lost from a change in inventory policy, then members of management have often not answered the second question. Instead, company management has stated that a given item should be eliminated from the list of regular stocked items. However, there are shortcomings to this latter situation. Company management should delay making a decision on the matter until after the systems analyst has completed his analysis, which encompasses all dimensions of the problem.

In many business organizations, company management views its sales activities and customer relations in a mystic manner, and management will not permit even a management scientist to question the business organization's customers in hopes of understanding what it is that presently attracts customers. Company management is afraid that in the process of resolving this question or other related questions on the matter of customer services, some customers may be offended and, therefore, terminate their relation with the business organization.

In some of the previously described business organizations, there may be a subsequent change in management or else current management has to cope unexpectedly with a tight money situation. In either of these cases, management may, for the first time, systematically examine its inventory policy. When this has occurred, a substantial change in all facets of inventory management has usually resulted. Some items are eliminated from inventory; faster service is provided for other items; special expediting procedures are designed for those critical situations; reduction in price of items is announced because of economies from the new inventory policy; and so forth.

In summary, the relevant items included in the computation of the cost of not carrying inventory is a matter that varies not only by business organization, but by division and department within a business organization. While there are many items, some within and some outside the formal accounting records, we believe that the estimated loss of customers from the stockout condition is the dominant factor in most situations. Furthermore, the contribution to margin from these estimated lost customer sales is probably the best practical measure of the stockout cost.

PROCESSING PROCEDURES

Frequently, the systems analyst assumes away the necessity for performing the first step in this study. Specifically, he does not measure the cost of carrying inventory versus the stockout cost. Instead, the systems analyst says: "I am not going to question company management. I assume that they believe that each item currently included in inventory was selected for inclusion because the anticipated benefit from carrying the item in inventory was greater than the cost of carrying inventory." From a practical standpoint, it is obvious that the short-term returns from effort expended are greater in most situations from starting with the second step than with the first step. After the systematic inventory management information system has been designed and installed and is operating, then the systems analyst can effectively question why certain inactive items in inventory are included. However, the active items that would fail the requirements test (step one) will probably continue to be maintained because there is no reason why these active items in inventory would be selected by the systems analyst for evaluation on a management-by-exception basis.

Not only is it advantageous to begin with the second step from the practical standpoint of marginal benefit to be derived from the efforts expended by the systems analyst but there are also considerations of organization that would suggest beginning with the second step. The systems analyst runs the risk of having his efforts misinterpreted when he is trying to evaluate the stockout cost. Middle management might and will accuse him of questioning the past decisions of top management when, in fact, the systems analyst is probably questioning the past actions by an inventory clerk.

It has been repeatedly revealed in the process of evaluating existing operation systems for inventory that a $500- to $600-a-month inventory clerk has the responsibility for managing a $200,000 or more inventory stock. This clerk will decide which items shall be stocked, how much shall be stocked, and when the items will be reordered.

From another perspective, the systems analyst has to ask management for information as part of the measurement of the cost of not carrying inventory (which is the critical question in the first step). Securing the full cooperation of management is an unusual accomplishment on the part of the systems analyst. This degree of cooperation is essential if the first step is really to be accomplished.

Therefore, in conclusion, while admitting the disadvantages from a nonoptimal condition, we tend toward favoring, from a practical viewpoint, commencing the inventory management information system with the second step and calling all of the first step, "the corporate inventory policy which is taken as a given." This conclusion is based upon the following considerations: (1) a recognition of the organization problems involved in beginning with the first step, (2) the imputed cost for management's time in providing the information for step one, and (3) the high marginal return from the systems analyst's efforts when beginning with the second step.

One major shortcoming of this latter approach is that conflicting objectives and inconsistencies on the part of management's diverse understanding of the corporate inventory policy are not immediately obvious. These situations become apparent primarily when trying to resolve problems in the existing operating inventory system.

Regardless of whether the systems analyst began with step one or step two, the focus is now upon the processing procedures. Assuming that the items to be included in inventory have been determined by one means or other, the systems analyst must determine the two critical factors in each of these information networks: the reorder quantity and the reorder point. After these two factors have been examined, attention is subsequently given to the other aspects of these information networks.

Reorder Quantity

One of the basic decisions in an inventory management information system is how much to order from suppliers or from the production department. Economic Order Quantity (EOQ) formulas are used in coping with this decision. The reorder quantity (the economic order quantity, standard order quantity, or economic lot size) is that quantity which produces a balance between the cost of ordering and setup on the one hand, and the cost of holding and storing inventory on the other hand.

Following is a simple EOQ formula.

$$Q = \sqrt{\frac{2AS}{UI}}$$

where

$Q =$ Economic order quantity, the amount to order for least total annual cost

$A =$ Annual quantity used in units

$S =$ Setup cost for production or the cost of placing an order from suppliers

$U =$ Unit cost

$I =$ Inventory carrying charges expressed as a percent of cost

Given the terms Q, A, S, U, and I as specified, the above formula is derived as follows:

$\dfrac{A}{Q} =$ Number of orders placed annually

$\dfrac{AS}{Q} =$ Annual setup costs for production or the annual cost of placing orders with suppliers

$\dfrac{Q}{2} =$ Average number of units in inventory at any given point in time

$\dfrac{UIQ}{2} =$ Annual inventory carrying cost

$\dfrac{AS}{Q} + \dfrac{UIQ}{2} =$ Total annual cost of inventory which is designated by C

This latter equation is solved as follows:

(1) $C = \dfrac{AS}{Q} + \dfrac{UIQ}{2}$

(2) $\dfrac{dC}{dQ} = \dfrac{-AS}{Q^2} + \dfrac{UI}{2}$

(3) Set $\dfrac{dC}{dQ} = 0$; $\dfrac{-AS}{Q^2} + \dfrac{UI}{2} = 0$

(4) $\dfrac{UI}{2} = \dfrac{AS}{Q^2}$

(5) $Q^2 UI = 2AS$

(6) $Q = \sqrt{\dfrac{2AS}{UI}}$

Example

If the annual requirements are 400,000 units, the cost of ordering is \$15, the unit cost is \$20, and the investment carrying charge is 19 percent, then the economic order quantity is computed as follows:

$$Q = \sqrt{\dfrac{2AS}{UI}} \qquad\qquad Q = \sqrt{\dfrac{2\,(400,000)\quad (\$15)}{\$20\quad (19\%)}}$$

$$Q = \sqrt{3,157,895} \qquad\qquad Q = 1,777.047 \text{ units}$$

As is indicated by the above example, it is easy to determine the reorder quantity if the relevant cost and statistical information are known. However, this task of determining and collecting relevant cost information for the EOQ formulas is difficult. In performing this task, there are two conflicting objectives. On the one hand, the task should be given enough scrutiny so that all relevant costs are considered and properly measured. At the same time, the task of determining and collecting relevant information does not have to become a cost accounting study.

The EOQ formulas are used as management techniques and tools for planning and control, and these formulas are not considered as rigorous and inflexible methods. Furthermore, some of the relevant information possesses the unusual characteristic that it must be considered for any valid measure of the economic order quantity, while at the same time being the type of information where precise measurement is not required. In other words, some of this latter relevant information may be approximate value (for example, plus and minus 15 to 20 percent) without significantly changing the value derived by the EOQ formula.

Thus, the systems analyst views the collection of data for the EOQ formulas in much the same way as he views the process of determining which measures of performance will be employed in a given standard cost system. The anticipated benefit from using the new information should at least equal (if not exceed) the expenditures required for collecting and processing the information. Although this matter of measuring the anticipated benefit from using the new information is not emphasized in the following discussion of information for the EOQ formulas, the reader is encouraged to maintain this questioning perspective regarding this discussion, particularly when applying this discussion to a real situation.

Relevant Data for Formulas

In the search of relevant data for the EOQ formulas, sensitivity analyses are used in identifying which costs are influenced by changes in the reorder quantity or in the number of orders processed. When the inventory is provided by an outside supplier, the following questions are asked: Which costs increase (or vary) with changes in the number of orders placed? Which costs increase (or vary) with changes in the size of the reorder quantity?

The response to the first question is included in the S factor in the illustrated EOQ formula and includes such items as clerical costs, data processing costs, paper and stationary costs, postage, and telephone. The response to the second question is included in the I factor in this formula and includes such items as investment cost, storage and handling cost, obsolescence, deterioration, pilferage, insurance, and personal property taxes.

When the inventory is not being provided by outside suppliers but is being provided by the production department, a different set of basic questions is asked: Which costs increase (or vary) with changes in the number of lots of a part manufactured? Which costs increase (or vary) with changes in the average lot size used in the production process? The responses to these questions are included in the S and I factors, respectively, in the given EOQ formula.

Costs Varying with the Number of Lots Processed. The S factor is expressed in terms of *dollars per order* and encompasses the following items:[2]

1. Machine setup costs
   a) Setup personnel hours
   b) Maintenance or materials used with each machine setup
   c) Raw material "preparation labor costs" for an order
2. Paperwork costs
   a) Setup documents
   b) Dispatching documents
   c) Shop order documents
   d) Payroll documents
   e) Inspection and quality control documents
   f) Purchase order and records
3. Indirect order preparation costs
   a) Production time lost per lot if not used (for example, lost time)
   b) Production control costs per order processed (Of the total production control costs, which costs vary with the number of orders processed? From a practical standpoint, an average cost per order will generally suffice.)

---

[2] This list of costs varying with the number of lots processed draws heavily from a paper used by the staff at Arthur Andersen & Co. in a production control training course. Used by permission.

c) Inspection or quality control time varying with the number of lots processed

d) Tabulating and data processing costs associated with the volume of orders processed (Generally, an average of variable costs is appropriate for this component.)

e) Accounting and related processing costs generated as a result of handling production orders or lots (For example, pricing, scrap recording)

f) Material handling costs that vary with the number of orders processed (In many cases, material handling activities—outside of the storeroom—are somewhat independent of the order quantity or lot size and are more dependent on the overall level of activity of the plant.)

g) Purchasing effort resulting from the ordering of an item as a part

Costs Varying with the Size of an Order Quantity. The *I* factor is expressed as a *percent of unit cost* and includes the following items:[3]

1. Cost of investment
   a) The cost of funds invested in inventory (This is a subject that is frequently discussed in the professional literature, and a subject for which there is no single conclusion. Each position on the subject varies depending on the company's management and situation. Many approach the subject and immediately say that the current cost of funds for working capital should be used. Therefore, the prime loan rate of about 6 percent is frequently used. Generally, management should make this decision based upon company policy, company conditions, and the general economic conditions.)
   b) Insurance cost of inventory (Many companies have insurance costs based upon a percent of the investment in inventory or other assets. Normally, this cost is not large and may be less than 1 percent of the unit cost for the items included in inventory.)
   c) Tax cost of inventory (Local, state, or national taxes may be based upon a percent of the investment in inventory, for example, the Illinois state personal property tax.)

---

[3] This list of costs varying with the size of an order quantity draws heavily from a paper used by the staff at Arthur Andersen & Co. in a production control training course. Used by permission.

d) Storage costs (The first consideration in determining storage costs is to identify the *variable costs.* Heating, depreciation, maintenance, supplies, and so forth are generally variable as more or less space is used. However, the cost of storage space may not be variable if there is no alternative use for this space. If the storage space has an alternative use, then the costs associated with maintaining or providing the work space-storage space are variable with the inventory size. This cost can generally be expressed as a percent of inventory invested in stores. The second consideration in determining storage costs is to ascertain the relevant stores administration and operating costs which vary with the size of an order quantity. This is a difficult task because stores administration and operating costs tend to follow the total investment in inventory and the total inventory stock level. It is unusual for the stores administration and operating costs to significantly vary based on a change for a single item of inventory. Instead, stores administration and operating costs tend to vary based on changes for groups of items. In the latter case, these costs may vary with the number of orders processed as well as the size of the inventory. When this situation does exist, these two costs should be measured separately; costs varying with the orders processed should be included in that category and costs varying with inventory size should be accumulated and expressed as a percent of inventory in stock.)

2. Other costs
   a) The risk of obsolescence (When there are many different items that are sold to only a few customers, the imputed cost for obsolescence may be high and may be the dominant factor in determining the size of the order quantity. Case 9–1, Precision Screw Company, at the end of this chapter illustrates this situation.)
   b) Deterioration, pilferage, and other similar types of cost.

Note that in many industries the cost of inventory and investment (the *I* factor) is in the range of 15 to 20 percent of cost.

Reorder Point

The second basic decision in an inventory management information system is when to order the EOQ determined quantity. If the items to be included in inventory have previously been decided upon based on a systematic examination of each item in inventory as suggested by the first step or based on the corporate inventory policy which is taken as a given, then the question of when to order each selected item can be resolved as follows:

1. What is the annual forecasted demand for the selected item?
2. Is there an expected seasonal variation in this forecasted demand?
3. What degree of confidence does management desire with respect to the nonoccurrence of a stockout condition?
4. How much lead time is required for initiating and placing an order, shipment of the items ordered, and receiving and storing the items ordered?
5. How much minimum stock of inventory is required for use during this reorder period?
6. How much stock should be on hand to provide a cushion for those unexpected events that occur during the reorder period?

Each of the above questions is examined in the following discussion. The first three questions are covered under the heading, forecasting demand, and the remaining three questions are covered respectively under the headings: Lead-time Demand, Safety Stock, and Cushion.

Forecasting Demand.   Estimating the demand for each item in inventory is a critical step in any inventory planning and control operation and is a prerequisite for determining either the reorder quantity or the reorder point. The forecasted demand is a significant factor in each of these latter computations, and this discussion will focus on the general statistical approaches followed for forecasting demand.

Under the "pure," traditional statistical approach the systems analyst would thoroughly consider the past demand pattern of an item in conjunction with a study of the general economic forces. Based on the insights gained from these studies, the annual forecasted demand is determined using three variances: trend, cyclical, and random. After the annual forecasted demand is determined, then the seasonal variation is considered in estimating the demand within the year.

If there are many items in inventory where each item has its own unique demand pattern, then the pure, traditional statistical approach would require the services of several professional statisticians.

Thus, this approach is not generally followed in most business organizations. Instead, some practical technique is used as a substitute for the professional statistician's insight. The least squares technique or the moving average method can easily be programmed for the computer so that the estimated demand trend for each item is quickly determined. The computer program can include adjusting this estimated demand trend by some adjustment factor to compensate for the cyclical and random forces. Finally, the computer program can contain an adjustment factor for the seasonal variation which is applied to the previously adjusted demand in determining the forecasted actual demand for a given quarter.

An alternative procedure for coping with trend, cyclical, and random variation is to apply the 12-month centered moving average method. Seasonal indexes can be used in adjusting the 12-month centered moving average to the actual forecast for a given period. This alternative procedure is widely used in inventory forecasting because of its simplicity, which permits the complete procedure to be encompassed in a simple computer program.

Another alternative procedure that is used by several firms is exponential smoothing. This particular procedure is especially suitable for the company with a highly fluctuating short-term demand pattern that is not attributable to seasonal forces. From a practical standpoint, the exponential smoothing technique is frequently used in the initial establishment of a systematic inventory management information system by those companies that do not have historical information on demand for each item in inventory that can be readily and easily retrievable.[4]

Each of the above procedures is a variation in the traditional, statistical forecasting technique for time series analysis wherein the actual activity for an item is the result of the interaction of four forces: trend, seasonal, cyclical, and residual. There is another statistical approach toward forecasting that is based on probability models. Estimates are assigned to each of the possible levels of activity for an item, and an expected value is computed. This probability approach is especially useful when dealing with a new product for which there

---

[4] It is assumed that the reader is familiar with these statistical techniques, and no attention is given in this book to explaining these techniques. If the reader is unfamiliar with these techniques, then he should consult a basic reference in statistics, such as Samuel B. Richmond, *Statistical Analysis* (2d ed.; New York: Ronald Press Co., 1964) .

is no historical experience nor any other product whose experience might be assumed to be comparable.

After the actual demand has been forecast by some statistical technique, then the systems analyst's attention focuses on the question: What degree of confidence does management desire with respect to the nonoccurrence of a stockout condition? This question can be rephrased in a positive manner: What level of service does management desire for the inventory item in question?

In coping with these questions, the statistical formula, "the standard error of the arithmetic mean," can be used in certain circumstances to indicate the probability of the occurrence of a stockout condition for a given item of inventory under consideration. These "certain circumstances" under which the formula may be used do not often exist in inventory management information systems. As previously indicated, the traditional, statistical approach for time series analysis is most frequently employed by business companies. Unfortunately, the assumptions regarding the distribution of data upon which the traditional forecasting techniques are based do not coincide with the assumptions associated with the use of the formula, the standard error of the arithmetic mean.

On the other hand, the forecasting approach based on probability models is compatible with these latter assumptions. Thus, in those companies where probability models are used for forecasting demand, estimates can be made regarding the likelihood of a stockout condition, and the amount of the shortage for different average levels of inventory stock can be ascertained.

Since the traditional forecasting approach is based on assumptions that are not compatible with the previous statistical formula, alternative techniques based on other data must be employed to quantify the level of customer service. One such alternative procedure is to compute an index of customer service based on the promised date of delivery compared to the actual shipment date. This particular index is frequently used in job order shops and in those companies where special items are manufactured on a "per customer request" basis. The appropriate information for computing the index is available on the sales order document and the shipping report.

In other companies, present and former customers have been interviewed by professional statisticians in an effort to quantify the level of customer service that has been provided. In other extreme cases, statisticians have interviewed the competitors of the company in question in an effort to quantify the level of customer service.

In summary, the procedures to be employed in attempting to quantify the level of customer service vary not only by company, but by division and department within a company and also by the product lines within a department. Each item in a product line may have its own unique demand pattern which is not compatible with any of the well-known distributions: the binominal distribution, the normal curve distribution, and the Poisson distribution. Therefore, the statistician will have to select some *ad hoc* set of procedures for measuring customer service in this situation, even though this set of procedures may not be completely applicable to all products.

Lead-Time Demand. This is the average demand for the lead-time period, which is the time required for replenishment of the stock. This will be the summation of the time required to order an item (the reorder quantity), to receive delivery, to handle and store the order (place the inventory on the shelves, in the bins, and so forth), plus the period of time that elapses between the actual reduction of the physical inventory stock to the reorder point and the time at which this event is known by the reorder clerk.

Under a real-time computer system, the occurrence of a reorder condition and knowledge of such a condition are simultaneous events. Under a perpetual inventory system that is daily processed by the computer or that is daily, manually processed by a clerk, the maximum time delay between the occurrence of a reorder condition and knowledge of such a condition is one day, with one-half day being the average time delay. Under a nonperpetual inventory control system where each item in inventory is checked once a month, for example, the maximum time delay between the occurrence of a reorder condition and knowledge of such a condition is one month, with one-half month being the average time delay.

The lead-time demand represents a required investment in inventory which must be controlled if management is to maximize the use of the company's resources. The primary method for controlling the size of this investment is to reduce the lead-time period by installing a perpetual inventory system. Another approach is to try to reduce the administrative time required for processing orders. For example, a prepunched data processing card containing the identification and description of the item under question along with the reorder quantity and the supplier's identification number might be the input document to the computer which has in storage the name and address of the supplier by identification number. Thus, the computer program can match the supplier's identification number, retrieve the name and address of the supplier, and process the complete purchase order. In a more advanced computer system, the input document is not necessary; the perpetual inventory system is maintained by the computer, and the computer program can encompass all phases of the reorder process.

Safety Stock. Regardless of the statistical procedures employed in forecasting demand, there will be a variance between the actual and forecasted demand. The safety stock is supposed to provide for these unplanned variances between actual and forecasted demand.

One of the major variances is associated with the lead-time demand. The lead-time demand is an *average* and is subject to the limitations of any statistical average. The *actual* demand during the lead-time period will probably not exactly equal the *average* demand. Instead, a frequency distribution can be constructed of the actual demands during the lead-time period for several years, and this frequency distribution will probably represent a normal curve where the average demand is the arithmetic mean of the frequency distribution. Thus, the safety stock should provide for this predictable variance between actual and average demand during the lead time.

Some inventory management systems employ a moving average technique where the lead-time demand is not an "average" demand (measured in terms of past experience) but is the forecasted actual demand based on an analysis of the time series data. Even in these situations, the forecasted demand will differ from the actual demand, and this variance must be provided for if a nonstockout condition is desired. On the other hand, the amount of this variance is statistically predictable for various levels of confidence, and these statistical tools should be employed in controlling the size of the safety stock.

Cushion. If the safety stock is restricted to the variance between actual and forecasted demand under conditions of certainty, then the remaining variance because of conditions of uncertainty can be called the cushion. Specifically, the cushion provides the allowance for this latter type of variance.

Some writers differentiate between safety stock and cushion in another manner. The safety stock is designed to provide for that predictable variance that occurs between actual and forecasted demand because of unusual action (or behavior) on the part of customers. The cushion is designed to provide for the unusual action on the part of management and personnel of the company in question.

For example, the cushion is supposed to provide for a clerk temporarily misplacing a purchase order.

Another approach toward differentiating between safety stock and cushion is to define safety stock as that value determined by a statistical formula containing two factors: (1) degree of customer service desired and (2) the standard deviation of the lead-time demand. Of course, these latter two factors must be expressed in terms of units of the product in question. All variances not associated with this formula are assumed to be represented by the cushion.

Summary

The inventory management information system is more than just a perpetual inventory system that has been modified to include reorder points and reorder quantities for each item in inventory where the system automatically handles the purchasing process. The systems analyst must first understand the nature of the business activity represented by this system before he can design and evaluate an information system for said activity.

For example, from a procedural standpoint, the reorder point is a predetermined value that signals that another reorder quantity should be requested. From the standpoint of the company, the reorder point represents the minimum inventory stock for an item that is required for providing a specified level of customer service during the reorder period.

Therefore, the purpose of this chapter has been to focus on some of the underlying assumptions and conflicts encountered in inventory management operations and to point out some of the significant statistical assumptions that are at the base of the systematic inventory operations. Through this type of understanding, the systems analyst is able to design an effective inventory management information system that appropriately copes with the real business activity handled by this system.

TOPICS FOR CLASS DISCUSSION

1. Some members of management say that in inventory control they are attempting to match the cost of ordering versus the cost of maintaining inventory. What is the basic question for which this previous statement is the answer? What is the order of this question?

If applicable, cite other general inventory questions that both pre-cede and follow this question.

2. When a systems analyst follows the information systems ap-proach, questions in inventory management are frequently pushed to a higher echelon, and the questions are restated in an effort to specify the basic problems. Why? Be specific.

CASE 9–1. PRECISION SCREW COMPANY

Obsolete inventory has been an annual problem confronting the management of the Precision Screw Company. The amount of obso-lete inventory has decreased during the past five years, and last year's amount was reduced by a greater amount than any previous year because automobile screws were daily monitored toward the end of the automobile production period. However, as management reviews the operations for the past year,[5] the perennial question remains, "How can we further reduce the annual loss from obsolete inventory without jeopardizing customer relations or restricting our expanded volume of sales within the framework of an integrated inventory control and production control system?"

Historical Development

Thirteen years ago the management of the Precision Screw Com-pany, a midwest manufacturing firm, partially changed to automatic data processing equipment as a means of coping with problem areas in the timely flow of information. The transition to ADPS (Auto-matic Data Processing System) was started with punched card equip-ment and has gradually been developed with the eventual goal of a total computer system. The processing of factory orders for shipment to customers was the first item programmed for the ADPS unit. Next, billing operations were programmed which, on a resorting basis, provide statistical sales data.[6] Inventory control and production control were the third and fourth areas to be programmed.

---

[5] Following are pertinent data on the operations for the past year. Inventories (at cost on the last-in, first-out basis) represent 35 percent of the assets of the firm (total assets $5,250,000), and cost of goods sold represents 75 percent of net sales (net sales $8,500,000). Raw materials are a minor element of cost; labor and machine time being the primary elements. For example, setup cost for the production of a screw averages $20 to $25.

[6] Statistical sales data, by groups of items, are continuously accumulated by the computer and stored in the IBM 1405 disk storage unit. These data are

Today the assistant controller, who is the director of the data processing operations, envisions a total information system using the present computer system. This system would encompass the other accounting operations—specifically, cost accounting data for internal information requirements, payroll processing, accounts receivable collection and other cash receipts, voucher processing and cash payments, and financial statement preparation. He plans to program these other operations in the order cited because of the interrelations between steps.[7] This ordering of phases or steps has been determined on a priority system of trying to maximize the benefit derived from each additional hour employing the computer facilities.

Integrated System

The integrated inventory control and production control system has been in full operation for over a year and is automatically administered by the computer. For each of the 8,000 items of finished goods inventory,[8] a 200-character record is continuously maintained giving the following information: (1) description of the item, (2) stock on hand, (3) unshipped sales, (4) reorder point (minimum level of inventory), (5) reorder quantity, (6) items in process (that is, items being manufactured in the production department), and (7) identification of the week of the year in which the last sales order was processed. Again, this 200-character record is maintained on a perpetual basis, which means that it is up-to-date; however, the 200-character record does not contain the historical details of how the present position was achieved. This latter informa-

---

reported in four ways: today, week to date, period to date, and year to date. In addition to the statistical sales data stored in the computer, by-product cards are prepared when orders and shipments are processed, and these by-product cards are fed into the IBM 1401 system whenever detailed statistical sales data are desired.

[7] For example, cost data can be applied to the present integrated inventory control and production control system, and from this extension, standard cost data can be obtained. With the addition of the payroll records being programmed, actual cost data will be available in the computer system. Phase two of the proposed total information system commences with the total programming of payroll operations, which, for example, would include the maintenance and reporting of all payroll tax data. In other words, each proposed phase is an extension of the data requirements achieved in the previous phase plus the addition of the minimum of new data.

[8] Thirteen years ago there were over 12,000 items, but close inventory supervision has reduced the number of different items to 8,000. The long-range goal is 6,000 items.

tion can be obtained in detail from the by-product cards or on a group basis from the data stored in other sectors of the computer.

As stated, 200-character records are maintained by the computer for each of the items of finished goods inventory. For this purpose, an IBM 1405 disk storage unit is used which contains 25 disks (Model 1). The total capacity of the 25 disks is 50,000 200-character sectors.[9] An indelible 7-digit record address precedes each 200-character sector. Daily, punched cards are processed by the IBM 1401 data processing system, and simultaneously with the preparation of the billing or production orders, the 200-character inventory records are updated.[10]

The integrated aspects of inventory control are as follows: when a given item of finished goods inventory reaches the reorder point, the computer is programmed in such a manner that a production request is initiated. The appropriate raw materials are ordered, a production order is processed, and the particular machines that will be used in the production process are identified. (This system permits the manual initiation of a production order whenever desired; this may be for a new item or a rush order of an existing item or when seasonal sales demands are relatively low and it is necessary to manufacture some items for stock that would not be ordered on an automatic basis.) Thus, when the finished goods inventory reaches the critical

---

[9] Each 200-character record is called a "track sector," and each track of a disk contains 10 track sectors. Furthermore, each disk has 200 concentric tracks on which information is recorded. Thus, the capacity of each disk is 2,000 track sectors or 2,000 200-character records. Since Model 1 contains 25 disks, the capacity of this unit is 50,000 200-character records.

[10] In this particular industry it is highly advantageous to know continuously the position of the finished goods inventory. The 200-character records provide this type of data. For example, it is an industrial practice to provide a weekly list of finished goods inventory for which there is an overstockage, and such lists are supplied to various users of screws. It is not management's objective to have items included on the overstockage list; however, if overstockage exists, then it is desirable that this information be made available to individuals needing such finished goods. (This is one of the reasons that in the initial phases of ADPS the programmers at Precision Screw Company concentrated on perpetual inventory data and statistical sales data rather than upon the usual payroll processing and cost data accumulation programs.) Another example of the use of the 200-character records is as follows: during the closeout phase of automobile production, daily records (if desired) can be provided on the status of the special screws that are used only by the automobile industry. This permits close monitoring of both production and inventory so as to meet the demands of the automobile industry and at the same time minimize the amount of obsolete inventory.

level, the computer takes the initial action required for the production of a new reorder quantity. As previously mentioned, the 200-character inventory record reflects that the production order is in process for a new reorder quantity (unless some other quantity is manually requested). This information is recorded on the disk simultaneously with the preparation of the production order.

The integrated inventory control and production control system may appear to be a logical, ideal system; however, in spite of this automatic system, one major problem remains: obsolescence of finished goods inventory. This problem is compounded by several factors. First, approximately 60 percent of the finished goods inventory is special items which may be sold to only *one customer*.[11] A large volume of a given item may be sold to a particular customer over an extended period of time, and then, abruptly, the customer does not make any additional orders. The remaining quantity of specially engineered screws becomes obsolete.

Second, 15 to 20 percent of the 8,000 items of finished goods inventory (approximately 1,400 items) are special items for the same collective customer: the automobile industry. Usually every three years this major group of items is completely changed by the new automobile designs. Since the automobile replacement parts market frequently uses different types of screws than used on the original equipment, any remaining finished goods inventory at the time of the automobile style change becomes obsolete inventory.

Third, management's policy is for increased emphasis on special screws rather than upon general screws. Wood screws sold in hardware stores are prime examples of standard or general screws. Since they are standard, price is the major factor. There is little room for product differentiation. In fact, if there is an imperfect screw, the customer does not usually bother to complain to the hardware store manager. On the other hand, engineered screws for production lines in manufacturing and assembling plants must be "perfect." This is particularly true where workers are paid on a "production basis" and where automatic equipment is employed. In the latter instances, a uniform, "perfect," durable screw is desired rather than a less "perfect" screw at a substantially lower price. As previously stated, 60

---

[11] In fact, the common situation for *special screws* is to have one salesman selling to one customer or to two customers. If there are several customers, the item will be classified as a "regular stock item" instead of a "special sales stock item."

percent of the 8,000 items of finished goods are special items, and management desires to increase this percentage.[12]

Fourth, this factor is really the summation of the previous factors: how do you establish the reorder point on a special screw that is sold *only to one customer?* (This reorder point is the critical factor that permits the inventory control and production control systems to be integrated.) Management established a task group to study the various quantitative models for determining economic lot size measures. After a thorough study, the mathematical-formula approach was abandoned because none of the formulas applied to the unique situation of Precision Screw Company, since they had only one customer for a special screw.

Sales Stock Committee

Recognizing that the establishment of the reorder point (the point at which a new reorder quantity is requested from the production department) is the critical element in the automatic system, management decided that the primary point of control would be the initial level of evaluating negotiations over a proposed contract for the production of a new screw. A standing committee, called "sales stock committee," was established with seven representatives: (1) sales manager, (2) controller, (3) production control manager, (4) tool manager, (5) inventory control manager, (6) assistant controller, and (7) "junk manager" (the individual who has responsibility for disposal of obsolete inventory and scrap).

This committee operates as follows: a salesman must formally request that a special item be manufactured and stocked. The salesman's request is evaluated by the Sales Stock Committee, and there may be formal and informal transmissions of information between

---

[12] Management's preference for special screws rather than general screws can be viewed from another standpoint. The tool cost for a new screw may range from $10 to $500 depending on the mix of standard versus new, specially engineered tools. Any competitor will have to incur these same tool costs if the competitor successfully obtains a contract for the production of any screw Precision Screw Company is currently manufacturing. Since the screw market is highly competitive, there is a slight advantage to the company that is presently manufacturing a special screw because the latter firm has already absorbed the initial expenditures. (Some competitors follow the "average cost" basis rather than "direct costing." These individuals average tool cost over the total volume of all types of production rather than charge such cost to the particular screw to which it is related. Competitors following this "average cost" practice may outbid a firm for the continuation of an existing order.)

the committee and the salesman. For example, the salesman may be requested to negotiate for a larger order at a lower price (the salesman initially had rough guidelines to follow in quoting prices for different size orders). At the conclusion of the action by the sales stock committee, the reorder point and the reorder quantity are established for the new item of inventory, and a 200-character record is opened in the IBM 1405 disk storage unit.

This system may sound as if it would be a simple system to administer; however, there are unusual industrial practices that aggravate the situation. For example, Precision Screw Company officials may negotiate to provide 15 units of a given type of screw for each automobile manufactured by a given firm. It is an open-end contract, and the automobile firm does not desire to maintain an inventory of screws at the assembly plants. Thus, Precision Screw Company officials must always have the items in finished goods inventory, available for immediate shipment whenever the automobile firm decides to manufacture more automobiles.[13]

Even though the previous examples highlighted the automobile industry, the same problem exists in other industries. For example, a television, radio, or electrical appliance manufacturer might order six screws of a given type for each unit the firm manufacturers over a stated period of time, with a minimum commitment for 100,000 screws. Furthermore, the screws must always be available with the possibility of a penalty clause covering shortages. To complicate the situation even more, the special customer (for example, an automobile manufacturer or electrical appliance manufacturer) under an open-end contract will not provide a monthly projected production report which could be used to administer the required volume of screws for the coming period. The Precision Screw Company officials must estimate the customer's production which, in turn, establishes the estimated volume of special screws that will be required.

---

[13] The dilemma that faces Precision Screw Company officials is to calculate the moment at which the automobile manufacturer will stop production. Usually, because of shipping time, there is a three-week supply of screws in the "pipeline." As an illustration, assume that 25 screws of a given type may be used in the same automobile. Multiply the expected production of automobiles during a three-week period times 25 in order to determine the obsolete inventory at the end of the year for this particular screw if the closeout date is not "properly" estimated. Now to get the total magnitude of the situation, multiply the previous answer by 1,400. There are 1,400 special items of inventory for the automobile industry.

Sales Stock Report

The obsolescence problem has continued to plague management; therefore, it was decided to establish an additional control feature: a "Sales Stock Report." (See the appendix for an illustration and detailed description of the report.) Each month a salesman was notified regarding any special items of inventory that he had requested to be manufactured. The report for each item contained a "print out" of the data in the 200-character perpetual inventory record, and for each sales stock item (special screws) there was a report of the total sales in units for each of the accounting periods (see appendix to this case study for discussion of this).

The salesman that requested the production of a special screw is held responsible for the continuous stock of that type of screw, and he can be relieved of this responsibility in one of two ways. First, he can cancel his special request and complete the sale of the present stock. (Another variation of this same approach would be the situation where the salesman requested that 50,000 screws be manufactured on a one-shot basis with the total production being sold to one customer; after this is sold, the salesman is relieved of his responsibility.) Second, the salesman can cancel his order and state that he cannot finish selling all the screws on hand. In the latter case, the "junk manager" is asked to try to find some alternative market for the screws, with authority to lower the price. If the junk manager is successful, then the salesman is notified by the computer on the next sales stock report that he has satisfied his responsibility. If the junk manager cannot sell the screws under adjusted price conditions, then the salesman must wait until the obsolete stock committee formally declares the screws obsolete. In the latter case, the junk manager is asked to sell the obsolete screws for scrap.

In addition to notifying each salesman of the particular items (special screws) that he has personally requested to be manufactured, a summary containing a detailed listing of all salesmen's reports is also prepared with copies for the (1) production control manager, (2) inventory control manager, (3) sales manager, and (4) assistant sales managers. This latter group receives three copies of the report.

With these facts in mind, management seeks additional ways of reducing the annual loss from obsolete inventory.

APPENDIX *TO* CASE *9–1*

PRECISION SCREW COMPANY SALES STOCK REPORT

Following is a detailed explanation of the sales stock report (Exhibit A) which is illustrated on a subsequent page. The description is in the same order as the block captions on the report.

YEAR: Fiscal year is July 1 to June 30.

DATE 1,   The fiscal year is divided into twelve periods, consist-
DATE 2,   ing of 10 four-week periods and 2 six-week periods.
ETC.:   The periods found in boxes captioned "Date 2" through "Date 11" are the ending dates of the 10 four-week periods. During the latter part of June and the first part of July there is a two-week vacation, and most of the vacation usually occurs during the first period, which in effect reduces the first period to a four-week period. The 12th period is the longest period, encompassing all the time remaining in the fiscal year.

SS NO.:   Sales stock number. This number is assigned to the salesman's request for the manufacture of a special screw. Production and control keeps the log of numbers.

Example: SS No. 950070

9   refers to the year: 1969

.50 ... refers to the 50th week in the year of 1969

...070 refers to the sequential requisition number within the 50th week

GROSS: All gross amounts are expressed in terms of 144 pieces. For example, GROSS 2083 means (2083) (144 pieces) = 299,952 pieces. The numerical amount that appears under "Gross" indicates the salesman's estimated cumulative sales for the specified sales stock number.

Example: GROSS 2083 means that 299,952 pieces of this item are expected to be sold over the life of this sales order number to the customer indicated.

C: Code. Normally this block is blank. Following are some letters that may appear in this block:

C This indicates that the salesman requesting this item has *canceled* his request for the item; however, the quantity on hand must still be disposed of before the salesman's responsibility is terminated.

R The salesman requesting this special item now feels that conditions have changed and the reorder point and reorder quantity must be *reduced*. An "R" will appear in this block of the report until the stock level comes down to the new desired level.

X This means that the salesman requesting the item says he cannot sell it. The "junk manager" attempts to find alternative markets in which to sell the items. The "X" will appear until either (1) the junk manager sells all the inventory or (2) the obsolete stock committee declares the items obsolete, and they are dropped from the inventory.

O This indicates that the customer has telephoned us that the paperwork is on the way but asks that we begin production. The "O" is removed when the written contract arrives. With some customers it is common to have a two-week delay between the telephone call and the receipt of the written order.

MAN: This refers to the salesman's payroll number. It is a way of identifying the salesman who requested the particular screw to be manufactured.

DESCRIPTION, CUSTOMER, PART NO.:   The description refers to our identification of the item. The name of the customer and the customer's part number are included in the remainder of this block. (The customer's part number is for the benefit of our salesman; he can keep up with his customers' catalogs for parts.)

ON HAND: Stock on hand. This amount (like all other figures in this report) is expressed in terms of 144 pieces (gross). The stock on hand includes the items sold but unshipped.

UNSHIP: Unshipped. This refers to items sold but unshipped.

IN PROC: In process. This refers to items that are currently being manufactured in the production department.

EXHIBIT A
Sales Stock Report

Date column headers (with date-sequence markers 1–12 printed in each row): DATE 1 (8-1), DATE 2 (8-29), DATE 3 (9-26), DATE 4 (10-24), DATE 5 (11-21), DATE 6 (12-19), DATE 7 (1-16), DATE 8 (2-13), DATE 9 (3-13), DATE 10 (4-10), DATE 11 (5-8), DATE 12 (6-30).

Row-field labels: DESCRIPTION, CUSTOMER, PART NO., ON HAND, UNSHIP, IN PROC, REOR PT, RE QUAN, LAST WK#.

1969 SS#	YEAR 1970 GROSS	Code	MAN	DESCRIPTION	CUSTOMER	PART NO.	ON HAND (1-16)	UNSHIP (2-13)	IN PROC (3-13)	REOR PT (4-10)	RE QUAN (5-8)	LAST WK# (6-30)
950070	2500	C C	15	QMT - 916A	General Motors	1945723	184		9	142	426	022
940083	1821	C C	15	POMI - 1041A	Ford	9763441	263	8	9	134	397	021
002017	2083	C	15	5/16 X 16/32	FLAT IMS	United Co.	627	45	9	50	300	021
001046	14044	C	15	1 3/4 X 10 PH	FLT WD New England Sales		481		694	347	694	020
SS				374	1459	694		3100		21	366	406
049018	1642	C	16	X1 - 4314-C	Auto Repl		247	51	9	114	342	022
003094	900	C	16	D1 - 1116-A	Western Electric		350	8	9	50	350	022
002040	2300	C X	16	POMI - 1038-A	Chrysler	8429362	372	8	9	120	365	008
024013	2500	C O	16	HSP 65 2X8	R/W RCA		130	8	520	200	450	
951014	1300	C	16	X1 - 4217 - B	Auto Repl		375	8	9	60	340	021
001024	1471	C C	16	PX1 - B2 - A	Western Electric		50	8	9	10	11	024 ☐
024036	800	G	16	PMS - 1832 - A	Frigidaire		50	8	750	10	11	

REOR PT: Reorder point. This is the minimum level of inventory. When this minimum level is reached, the computer will initiate the action for the production of the reorder quantity.

RE QUAN: Reorder quantity. This amount and the reorder point are established by the sales stock committee.

LAST WK NO.:   Last week number. This refers to the last week in which a sales order for the particular item was processed.

Example: LAST WK NO. 022

0.. refers to the year 1970

.22 refers to the 22nd week in 1970

The second line of the two-line report is filled in only for sales stock items (symbol "SS") which are sold on a continuous basis. If the second line is blank, it means one of two things: (1) either it is a special order for a specific amount with no inventory or (2) it is a regular stock item for which there is an abnormal, large request that is superimposed upon the normal reorder level. In the latter situation, there might be a large order of a normal, standard item. For example, in the past we have used a reorder point of 50 and a reorder quantity of 300. The special order requires a reorder point of 500 and a reorder quantity of 1500; therefore, the new reorder point for this item is 550 and the reorder quantity is 1800 (300 + 1500 = 1800).

The remainder of line two of the report is used to present the sales in gross during each of the 12 accounting periods. By-product cards are fed in the computer to provide the data for this line of the report. Again, the second line is filled in only for sales stock items, that is, special, engineered screws. Open-end contracts with an automobile, television, radio, appliance, or small electrical appliance manufacturer are prime examples of sales stock items.

When a salesman has completed his responsibility with regard to a particular screw, the computer prints a small rectangular box □ in the column headed "Last Wk#." Of course, this would be the last time this item is reported on the sales stock report.

CASE 9–2.   TAYLOR MANUFACTURING COMPANY

The Taylor Manufacturing Company, a subsidiary of a diversified corporation, is one of the country's major manufacturers and distributors of high-quality kitchen utensils and appliances with annual sales of approximately $25,000,000. The company does not engage in retail sales but sells exclusively to selected retail outlets. Furthermore, the company has approximately 1,700 items in its product line.

The company's manufacturing plant is centrally located in Ohio and the plant employs about 1,000 people. In addition to the main warehouse that is located near the manufacturing plant in Cleveland, Ohio, the company also maintains 20 branch warehouses plus a sales force of 70 men throughout the country.

Recently, company management decided to install an IBM 1410 system for inventory control and sales analysis, even though this would probably increase their current operating costs. Company management felt that the increases in reporting effectiveness in both the sales and inventory functions, plus the anticipated benefits from future applications, justified the added expense. These future applications included production control and payroll accounting.

Each of the 20 branches does its own billing; however, the accounts receivable and inventory functions are centralized in Ohio. Branch inventories are replenished automatically from the Cleveland warehouse stocks based upon computer-generated orders.

Former System

Prior to conversion, inventory replenishment was handled on a manual decentralized basis. Monthly, each branch manager would take a physical inventory and would then place orders equal to 30-day usage (the branch's reorder quantity) for any item in inventory falling below a predetermined level. This predetermined level or order point was based upon each branch manager's own estimate of his sales for the next 90-day period. With this 90-day base figure for each item, the branch manager would place a new order if *quantity on hand plus quantity on order but not received is less than the next 90-day sales.* Under this procedure, the Taylor Manufacturing Company was consistently carrying a 45- to 60-day inventory of finished goods.

New System

Under the new system, the inventory control function has been centralized at the main office and converted to computer processing.

All branch inventory transactions are analyzed weekly by the computer system. Any items requiring replenishment as well as the quantities needed are determined automatically by the computer system.

The formula used by the computer program for inventory replenishment is basically the same method used by the branch managers under the previous system. However, because the inventory levels are being reviewed weekly instead of monthly, the reorder point has been lowered to 75-day usage (from the original 90-day level), and the reorder quantity has been reduced to a 15-day supply for many of the items in the product line (from the original 30-day level). Using this new system, company management feels that inventory levels have been reduced from 15 to 20 percent.

Management decided against adopting any of the "sophisticated" inventory control formulas for determining reorder points and for forecasting future sales initially because (1) there was a lack of sales history data upon which to base such forecasts and (2) management felt that a new purchasing concept would aggravate any centralization problems which might arise during the conversion of the branch inventory functions. A master file, however, has been established in the computer system to record the high month's sales and the low month's sales quantity in addition to total sales and number of months included in total sales. These statistics can be used in the future to determine average sales and deviations. With these latter data plus seasonal trends, management plans on developing more sophisticated formulas in the near future.

With the conversion to automatic data processing, management now obtains more effective and timely sales analysis reports as well as information which will permit reductions in inventory investment without increasing the number of stockout conditions. Now that the sales analysis and branch inventory functions have been converted to electronic equipment, management is proceeding into the production control application. Following this, the plans are to program the complete payroll function and to integrate this system with the other computer programming systems.

REQUIRED:

1. Evaluate the centralized inventory control and sales analysis system.
2. Your brief study of the Taylor Manufacturing Company's opera-

tions indicates that the company is extremely profitable. From your review of the new centralized inventory control and sales analysis system, what would you expect to be the general nature of the company's environment? What type of cost-selling price relation would you expect to exist?

3. Do you agree with company management's movement toward a "total computer system" (integrated inventory control and sales analysis system; next, integrated inventory control, production control and sales analysis system; then, mechanized payroll operations with integrated inventory control . . .)? Be specific and include illustrations and examples in support of your comments.

4. Assume that company management is reconsidering the question of maintaining the reorder point at 75 days and the reorder quantity at 15 days. Indicate the format of a report that you might prepare for management which would provide guidelines for making a decision on this question. Even though the format of the report may be sketchy, please be specific as to *where* and *how* the information on the report would be *obtained* and *processed*.

CASE 9–3. GUYTON CHEMICAL COMPANY

Recently, the controller of Guyton Chemical Company engaged a management consulting firm to review Guyton's inventory operations and to suggest the type of inventory control system that should be employed, as well as the general implementing instructions for the recommended system. As part of this latter requirement, the management consultants submitted two schedules which supported the recommended cost factors for the EOQ formula (see Exhibit A and Exhibit B).

The controller is reviewing this tentative report from the management consulting firm and is wondering if it is proper to use a single

EXHIBIT A

Ordering Costs for EOQ Formula

	Per Order
Inventory control—administration	$1.184
IBM data processing	.741
Purchasing	.620
General accounting	.192
Cost accounting	.615
Receiving costs	3.152
Total ordering costs	$6.504

EXHIBIT B
Inventory Carrying Costs for EOQ Formula

	Percent of Inventory Cost
Cost of invested capital	4.95
Estimated costs for taxes, insurance, building, tanks, bins, utilities, supplies, labor, and supervision	5.60
Obsolescence, deterioration, pilferage, and shrinkage	6.95
Total inventory carrying costs	17.50

set of cost factors for all items in inventory. "After all," he thinks to himself, "each item that Guyton Chemical Company produces is independent and has its own unique demand."

Subsequently, the controller went to the local bank on other matters. He told one of the bank officers that he was considering establishing a systematic inventory control system at Guyton Chemical Company and asked the bank officer for assistance in determining the appropriate cost data in the EOQ formula. The bank officer suggested that the controller should use the long-run average cost of capital in his EOQ formula.

On his return trip to the plant from the bank, the controller pondered the bank officer's suggestion. He thought: "The long-run average cost of capital at Guyton Chemical Company has been in the range of 22 to 26 percent during the past few years. We have a competitive advantage over other chemical companies because we use our own specially constructed equipment and secret processes in production operations."

Finally, the controller decided to call another management consulting firm for assistance. You are associated with the latter firm.

REQUIRED:

1. Should Guyton Chemical Company use the long-run average cost of capital (ranging from 22 to 26 percent) in place of the cost of working capital (which the previous management consulting firm had determined to be 4.95 percent) as part of the inventory carrying costs? Explain your opinion.
2. Submit a report to the controller in which you clarify the various issues that he has raised regarding the determination of appropriate cost data for the EOQ formula at the Guyton Chemical Company.

CASE 9–4. ANDERSON COMPANY

A STATISTICAL EXERCISE

Management of the Anderson Company desires a uniform 95 per-cent level of customer service. Based on recent complaints, management is questioning if this level of customer service is being provided. You are asked to determine the extent to which the Anderson Company should increase its inventory stock in order to achieve this uniform level of customer service.

You begin your study by selecting four products at random. The inventory records show an average weekly demand of 250, 245, 230, and 255 units for Product No. 1, 2, 3, and 4, respectively. This average demand was computed 18 months previously, when the inventory control system was installed by another management consulting firm. Exhibit A indicates the weekly demand for the four selected products during the past eight weeks.

After studying the variations in demand indicated by Exhibit A, you decided to make a thorough analysis of each of the four product's demand. Exhibit B presents a frequency distribution indicating how often a given level of weekly demand occurred.

Next, you determine each product's average demand and standard deviation of demand (see Exhibit C).

Finally, you are given a copy of the report made by the previous

EXHIBIT A
Schedule of Demand for Past Eight Weeks

	Product No. 1	Product No. 2	Product No. 3	Product No. 4
*Average weekly demand** ..	250	245	230	255
Week:				
1	248	270	195	260
2	225	240	265	263
3	264	230	230	259
4	253	255	235	275
5	249	240	240	265
6	252	235	230	260
7	245	260	210	257
8	252	243	255	270

* Per inventory records based on computations performed 18 months previously by another management consulting firm.

EXHIBIT B
Frequency Distribution of Product Demand
(events expressed as percents)

Midpoint of Class Interval	Product No. 1	Product No. 2	Product No. 3	Product No. 4
175	0	0	0	0
180	0	0	1	0
185	0	0	2	0
190	0	0	2	0
195	0	0	3	0
200	0	1	4	0
205	0	2	4	0
210	0	3	5	0
215	0	5	5	0
220	1	6	6	0
225	4	7	6	0
230	6	8	7	0
235	9	10	8	1
240	10	14	8	2
245	13	11	8	3
250	15	9	7	5
255	12	9	6	8
260	10	5	6	9
265	8	4	4	11
270	7	3	3	12
275	4	2	3	12
280	1	1	1	11
285	0	0	1	8
290	0	0	0	7
295	0	0	0	6
300	0	0	0	4
305	0	0	0	1
310	0	0	0	0

EXHIBIT C
Statistical Computations

	Product No. 1	Product No. 2	Product No. 3	Product No. 4
Average Demand	250	240	234	272
Standard Deviation	13.58	17.13	23.20	15.64

management consulting firm. The report stated that the following formula was used in establishing the reorder point for each item in inventory:

$$\text{Reorder point} = \overline{LTD} + K \sqrt{\overline{LTD}\,(\overline{AD} + 1)}$$

where

$K =$ Number of standard deviations of lead-time demand

$\overline{LTD} =$ Average lead-time demand

$\overline{AD} =$ Average demand

$\sqrt{\overline{LTD}\,(\overline{AD} + 1)} =$ Estimate of "standard deviation" of lead-time demand

The management consulting firm's report recommended that a K factor of two should be used for purposes of providing the desired level of customer service.

Although you have never encountered a reorder point formula like the one given above, you begin to study this formula. You compute the reorder point quantity for a hypothetical product.

REQUIRED:

1. Assuming that the average lead-time demand was four weeks for each of the four products, compute the reorder point quantity using the previous consultants' formula and the previous consultants' computed "average demand" for each product.
2. Using the information that you have ascertained (especially that reflected by Exhibit B and Exhibit C), determine what level of customer service is currently being provided for each product. Quantitatively support your answer. (If necessary, refer to a basic reference in statistics for appropriate formula.)
3. Determine if the company must increase the inventory stock in order to achieve the 95 percent level of customer service. Quantitatively support your answer.

CHAPTER 10

Inventory Control Information Systems

THE PREVIOUS CHAPTER explained the general model for an inventory management information system. It contained a perpetual inventory control system which was modified to include reorder points and reorder quantities for each item in inventory.

This chapter presents the general model for a more advanced inventory control information system. This advanced information system builds upon (1) a thorough knowledge of the business environment in which the business organization under scrutiny is located, (2) a comprehension of the business process in said organization and in the role of inventory in this business process, and (3) an understanding of the heterogeneity among the various items in inventory.

Control Procedures

What is the most efficient and economic method of controlling inventory in a given situation? While this question is demanding, it calls for a different type of ability and understanding on the part of the systems analyst than was required in specifying the requirements and processing procedures for inventory management information systems. Specifying the requirements and processing procedures involves several matters that cannot be precisely determined but which are based on the systems analyst's study and understanding of the situation. Thus, the topics of requirements and processing procedures might be classified as "scientific inventory management," while the topic of control procedures in advanced inventory systems might be classified as "systematic inventory control administration."

The practical task of evaluating and designing systematic inventory control procedures is predicated on two assumptions. First, there is a high degree of heterogeneity in the inventory. The systems analyst, therefore, begins by examining the characteristics of the inventory and seeks to identify the major differentiating attributes possessed by the various items in inventory. Those common attributes serve as a basis for classifying the inventory into groups.

Second, there is the belief that what is good control for one group of items in inventory may be poor control for another group. The general practice of establishing one control system for all items is good for the average part, but it usually leaves many items either with too little or too much control. Although most of the criticism is associated with those items for which there is too little control, the systems analyst is equally concerned with the elimination of excessive control procedures. It is not unusual for substantial financial savings to result from a change in the inventory control procedures without any significant change in the degree of control over inventory.

Selective Analysis and Inventory Control

This practical method for evaluating and designing systematic inventory control procedures is referred to as "selective analysis and inventory control" or simply as "selective inventory control." The object of selective inventory control is to establish the best possible control at the least possible cost for each item or group of items in the inventory.

As previously stated, generally there is a high degree of heterogeneity in the inventory. In fact, the items in inventory can be sorted and resorted in numerous ways based on various criteria that point out some of this heterogeneity. The three most common classification systems are as follows:

1. Dollar selectivity
   Criteria: unit cost and usage value in dollars for specified period of time (annual, quarter, month, and so forth)
2. Commodity selectivity
   Criteria: type of item, product on which item is used, and characteristics of item
3. Usage selectivity

Criteria: activity of item to determine obsolescence and slow moving items

No single classification system is best for all business organizations, but, as is the case with other matters, the systems analyst will select that coding pattern which most appropriately meets the unique requirements of the business situation. While this classification system is being examined from the standpoint of inventory control, the systems analyst's overall perspective would suggest that a coding pattern should be developed for classifying the items in inventory so that these groupings might be used not only in inventory control and inventory management, but also in marketing management. In a subsequent part of this chapter, suggested classification scheme is presented for purposes of stimulating the systems analyst (1) to examine closely this heterogeneity in the inventory and (2) to determine what the requirements are of different decision-making groups within the business organization for information regarding inventory.

The systems analyst is typically not developing an inventory classification code that will meet the information requirements of the overall company, but he is coping with a given problem in a business situation where there is an existing identification system for items in inventory. In many cases, it is a financial problem of relating the degree of inventory control to the relative dollar importance of the items in inventory. The inventory control information system which is based on *dollar selectivity* is especially suitable for coping with this general type of problem. In fact, the dollar selectivity method has been used so often that the terms "dollar selectivity" and "selective inventory control" are used by some practitioners as being almost synonyms. Since dollar selectivity is used so frequently, this method is examined in detail in the following discussion.

Dollar Selectivity

The systems analyst follows a two-step approach in establishing the best possible control at the least possible cost for each item or group of items in the inventory under the dollar selectivity method. First, the items in inventory are classified based on a composite evaluation of two criteria: unit cost and usage value in dollars. Second, the most efficient and economic control system is chosen for each class of items.

In implementing this latter step, the systems analyst reviews each item in inventory selected for a change in control procedures to determine if other factors (that is, factors other than unit cost and usage value in dollars) might suggest that the control procedures for the item in question should not be changed.

Classifying the Inventory. Simple statistical procedures are used in sorting the items in inventory by the stated criteria: unit cost and usage value in dollars. First, the items in inventory are sorted based on their unit cost. For example, assume that there are 3,000 different items in inventory (not *unit of* stock on hand, but *items in* inventory) and that the cost per unit ranges from one cent to $100. These 3,000 items would be sorted as follows:

Item Identification Number	Unit Cost	Number of Item
2896	$100.00	1
1021	98.00	2
1874	97.00	3
2472	50.00	297
2361	49.95	298
3487	49.95	299
3942	10.00	930
4072	9.98	931
3824	9.97	932
3358	1.00	2730
1431	.99	2731
1214	.98	2732
2986	.02	2999
1878	.01	3000

The above list of items is summarized as follows:

Range	Number of Items	Percent of Total	Cumulative, More than Lower Limit Number	Cumulative, More than Lower Limit Percent
$50.00 to $100.00	297	9.9	297	9.9
$10.00 to $ 49.99	633	21.1	930	31.0
$ 1.00 to $ 9.99	1,800	60.0	2,730	91.0
$ 0.01 to $ 0.99	270	9.0	3,000	100.0
	3,000	100.0		

Figure 10.1 presents this same relation on a cumulative basis.

This same general relation as depicted by the previous graph has been charted for the items in inventory for numerous business firms. There are only a few items with a relative high unit cost, while the vast majority of the items have a relative low unit cost.

Second, the items in inventory are resorted by usage value in dollars. The expression, "usage value," of course, means the forecasted demand for the item during a specified period of time (such as a year, quarter, or month), and the computation of this forecasted demand was discussed in the previous chapter. Continuing with the same example of 3,000 items, the list of resorted items would appear as follows:

Item Identification Number	Per Unit Cost	Forecasted Annual Usage Requirements	
		In Units	In Dollars
4116	$96.00	10,000	$960,000
1951	$85.00	11,000	$935,000
1874	$97.00	9,500	$921,500
1727	$95.00	9,500	$902,500
1534	$ .02	100,000	$ 2,000
1878	$ .01	100,000	$ 1,000
1460	$ .02	25,000	$ 500

This list of items is summarized as follows:

Range	Number of Items	Percent of Total	Cumulative, More than Lower Limit	
			Number	Percent
$500,000 to $960,000	420	14.0	420	14.0
$ 90,000 to $499,999	597	19.9	1,017	33.9
$ 20,000 to $ 89,999	1,683	56.1	2,700	90.0
$ 500 to $ 19,999	300	10.0	3,000	100.0
	3,000	100.0		

Figure 10.2 presents the same relation on a cumulative basis.

From numerous studies of many business firms' inventory positions, this same general relation has been indicated between the usage value in dollars and the number of items in inventory. It is

FIGURE 10.1

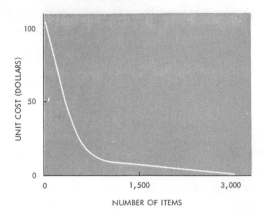

NUMBER OF ITEMS

FIGURE 10.2

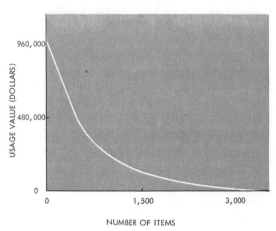

NUMBER OF ITEMS

common for 10 percent of the items in inventory to represent 65 percent of the total annual usage dollars, for 25 percent of the items in inventory to represent 25 percent of the total annual usage dollars, and for 65 percent of the items in inventory to represent 10 percent of the total annual usage dollars.

These three natural groupings of the items in inventory are labeled "Class A," "Class B," and "Class C," respectively. These natural groupings with these respective labels have been used so often that the dollar selectivity method of inventory control is frequently called the "ABC Method." The Class A item always refers to that small group of items which represents the majority of the total annual usage dollars, while the Class C item always designates that large group of items which represents a relatively minor part of the total annual usage dollars. Actually, there is another characteristic that varies by class which was presented in a previous graph: the range of unit cost for each class of items.

The simultaneous consideration of both criteria—unit cost and usage value in dollars—is the third step in the process of classifying the items in inventory according to the dollar selectivity method. Supplementing what was previously stated, the Class A grouping refers to that small group of high-unit-cost items which represents the majority of the total annual usage dollars. The Class B grouping refers to a larger group of medium unit cost items which represents a proportional share of the total annual usage dollars. The Class C grouping refers to that major group of low unit cost items which represents a relatively small share of the total annual usage dollars.

Continuing with the example, the following criteria are established for each class:

Class A

Unit cost: $50 to $100 (approximately 10 percent of items)
Annual usage value: $600,000 to $960,000 (approximately 11 percent of items)

Class B

Unit cost: $10 to $49.99 (approximately 21 percent of items)
Annual usage value: $90,000 to $599,999 (approximately 23 percent of items)

Class C

Unit cost: $0.01 to $9.99 (approximately 69 percent of items)
Annual usage value: $500 to $89,999 (approximately 66 percent of items)

Those items in inventory that meet only one of the two requirements for a class must be individually studied, and they are so examined in the following discussion of selecting control procedures for each class of inventory.

Selecting Control Procedures.   High unit cost and high usage dollar items (Class A items) deserve perpetual control and close record control and follow-up. On the other hand, low unit cost and low usage dollar items (Class C items) may be appropriately managed by physical control without record control. In other words, the high-cost items can be watched almost constantly, while letting the low-cost items "take care of themselves."

Before examining the selection of control procedures for each class of items, it might be appropriate to review the alternatives available. *Perpetual control* means there is a continuous control over the physical units of inventory. Generally, there is some type of inventory records that is kept up-to-date with an entry being made each time an item is issued or is received from a supplier. These daily records may be (1) manually recorded, (2) processed by EAM equipment on punched cards, or (3) processed by a computer for disk, paper tape, or magnetic tape storage. In summary, there are four common features of a perpetual control system: (1) an inventory clerk (who might also be a key punch operator under an online perpetual control system), (2) some type of daily records, (3) material issue and receiving slips, and (4) a guarded or locked storeroom.

Physical control is the opposite of perpetual control. Records are not maintained of the day-to-day changes in inventory stock, and the units of inventory are withdrawn by any worker on an open or "free" access basis. In other words, the inventory stock is available for any worker to use on a first-come basis. Generally, there is some type of physical indication that the stock level for a given item has reached the reorder point. Five common examples of this are as follows. First, the lead-time stock and the safety stock are stored in a locked storeroom. When all of the "free access units" in open stock are consumed, the supervisor must secure the additional units from the locked storeroom. When the supervisor does this, he is required to initiate a repeat requisition to replenish the stock.

Second, the lead-time stock and safety stock are tied in a bundle or bag, and a repeat requisition form is attached to the bundle or bag. When all of the units in the open stock have been used except those in the bundle or bag, the "bank is broken," the bag is opened or the bundle is untied. Concurrently, the repeat requisition form is processed.

Third, a "two-bin" procedure is followed. One bin is on an open stock basis, and the second bin triggers the repeat requisition form in the same manner as breaking the bank did in the previous example.

Fourth, a line is painted inside the storage bin or barrel. When the inventory stock reaches the painted mark, a repeat requisition is started into process by the worker who withdrew the units from stock at this critical point.

Fifth, the lead-time stock is controlled by any of the previously cited physical control procedures including having an attached repeat requisition. However, the safety stock is separately controlled, and the attached repeat requisition form is stamped EXPEDITE. This fifth type of physical control procedure is especially suitable for production operations where a shortage of any single item would stop the assembly line.

The task of selecting the control procedures for a given class of items is not an independent act, instead, there is a close relation between the inventory class of an item and the procedures followed in administering the reorder quantity and the reorder point. Furthermore, the amount of safety stock directly varies by the inventory class of an item. There is a natural relation, of course, between the high unit cost, high annual usage dollar items (Class A) and the frequency of ordering per EOQ formula.

Because of this nonindependent situation, practitioners do not begin the study of inventory with processing procedures and then subsequently study control procedures. Instead, the practitioner classifies items of inventory according to Class A, Class B, and Class C. (This grouping of items by class does require that the forecasted annual usage in dollars must be determined for each item in inventory; thus, this act overlaps the previously discussed processing procedures for forecasting demand.) If the practitioner labels an item of inventory as belonging to the Class A group, then this will limit the possible range of choice in which the processing procedures must be determined.

In other words, the practitioner establishes classes of inventory, and each class contains specified ranges in which the other variables must appear. Conversely, the degree of control applied to a class of items may be varied (1) by changing the frequency of ordering, (2) by varying the quantity of safety stock, and (3) by shifting from either a perpetual or physical record control to the other method. Thus, in selecting the control procedures for a given class of inventory items, it is necessary to specify what these other variables are. These other variables are cited in the following description of each of the groupings.

Class A items

Criteria: high unit cost, high annual usage value in dollars.

Frequency: low; generally, approximately 10 percent of the total items in inventory.

Reorder: frequently per EOQ formula, usually ranging from ordering on a weekly basis to ordering on a monthly basis.

Safety stock: none.

Type of control: perpetual records with weekly review. The item may be so critical (not only in terms of high unit cost and high annual usage dollars but also in terms of the production process) that two sets of records will be maintained, one set in the stockroom and one set in production control. Since no safety stock is going to be maintained, the Class A items require very close attention to keep from running out of stock and perhaps stopping a production line. Again, the Class A items represent only about 10 percent of the total number of items so that this close control is being given to only a small portion of the total number of items in inventory.

The reader may be surprised by the statement that no safety stock is maintained for Class A items while a double set of records is frequently recommended for controlling these Class A items. Using the EOQ formulas, the analyst can quickly determine the approximate break-even point between maintaining a safety stock of these high unit cost, high annual usage dollar items versus eliminating the safety stock and replacing this control measure with a duplicate set of records.

Class B items

Criteria: medium unit cost, medium annual usage value in dollars.

Frequency: more often that Class A items; typically, approximately 25 percent of the total items in inventory.

Reorder: less often than Class A items; per EOQ formula, usually ranging from ordering on a monthly to ordering on a quarterly basis.

Safety stock: small amount such as one to two weeks' supply.

Type of control: perpetual control with periodic review. The use of the EOQ formulas will result in Class B items having a higher average inventory stock level than for Class A items. In addition the carrying of protective stock (safety stock) will further increase the average stock level. However, there is less usage value and less dollar investment for the Class B items than for Class A, and the maintenance of safety stock decreases the necessity for close attention to the changes in stock level.

Class C items

Criteria: low unit cost, low annual usage value in dollars.

Frequency: high; generally, approximately 65 percent of the total items in inventory.

Reorder: seldom, usually ranging from ordering on a semiannual basis to ordering on an annual basis.

Safety stock: two weeks to a month's supply.

Type of control: physical control. Ordering on a semiannual or annual basis will mean larger quantities in inventory, but being low-cost, low-usage-value items, the dollar investment in inventory is relatively small.

In addition to the above-cited variables, there are other factors which are considered in classifying the items in inventory. These other factors include the consistency of rate of usage, lead time and procurement peculiarities, shelf life, likelihood of theft by employees, obsolescence risk, and the physical size of the bulk stock.

As is true of any classification system, there are those unusual items that tend to fall between class intervals. It goes without saying that the analyst must exercise considerable judgment in classifying the items in inventory. He may make mistakes in both directions: too much control as well as too little control. The nonpublicized condition of too much control may be of more financial importance to the business firm than the publicized condition of too little control.

It is difficult to offer any sure method for always identifying those items where there is too much control, aside from suggesting that a competent analyst should thoroughly examine each item of inventory for purposes of making this evaluation. On the other hand, there are several practical ways of reducing the possibility of the existence of a too little control situation. The most critical type of mistake would be to classify an item as Class C and to employ physical control when a different control system is really needed.

To guard against this occurring, a general procedure followed in installing an ABC inventory control system is to prepare a schedule of all items identified as Class C. The schedule will list each item so selected and will give the following data for each item: per-unit cost, forecasted annual usage value in dollars, reorder quantity, reorder point, and safety stock. This schedule will be distributed to different members of management for their close review and comment. As a result of this procedure, items that were originally labeled Class C may be redesignated Class B and subjected to Class B control and management procedures. Following are some of the reasons for not classifying an item for Class C control and management: (1) difficult procurement problem (such as long or erratic lead time), (2) susceptible to theft, (3) difficult forecasting problem (occasional usage in varying quantities), (4) shelf life too short for Class C control, and (5) too large a storage space requirement for bulk inventory under the Class C control procedures.

In summary, the overall selection of the appropriate control procedures for a business firm's inventory is a complex decision involving many factors and with implications on various activities throughout the organization. In addition to these considerations of organization, this selection process is even more complicated by the existence of numerous dissimilar items in inventory. The analyst sorts the items in inventory into arbitrary classes for purposes of establishing uniform control procedures for similar items. He attempts to determine for each class the most efficient and economic method of controlling the inventory in the given situation.

In this discussion, the different available methods were cited; however, most of the attention was given to only one method—the dollar selectivity method of inventory control—which is the method that is most frequently used.

The emphasis now shifts from the selection of control procedures to the systems analyst's evaluation of existing systems and suggestions of how to proceed in designing new systems. Before moving to this topic, however, an eight-digit coding pattern is suggested for identifying the items in inventory. This pattern encompasses a coding system that permits the retrieval of pertinent data regarding the inventory for the various decision-making groups throughout the organization.

12345678	There are eight digits in the inventory classification code.
12xxxxxx	The first two digits designate the product group.
xx345xxx	The third, fourth, and fifth digits designate the items within each product group.
xxxxx6xx	The sixth digit designates special characteristics of an item. For example, in the case of chemical inventory, a number one in this digit might indicate a perishable, flammable item; a number two, a perishable, nonflammable item; a number three, a nonperishable, flammable item; and so forth.
xxxxxx7x	The seventh digit designates a composite rating of two classification schemes: (1) price and degree of importance and (2) turnover frequency. The first classification scheme might include three alternatives:

> A—high unit cost
> B—critical item to the particular firm (excludes Group A)

C—bulk items (which would represent the majority of the items in inventory for most business firms)

The second classification scheme might include three alternatives:

F　—fast-moving
N　—normal
S　—slow-moving

The composite rating would include nine possibilities, and the appropriate number to designate the composite rating would appear as the seventh digit in this inventory classification code. These nine possibilities are as follows:

AF　—high unit price, fast-moving
AN　—high unit price, normal
AS　—high unit price, slow-moving
BF　—critical item (non-high unit price) , fast-moving
BN　—critical item, normal
BS　—critical item, slow-moving
CF　—bulk item, fast-moving
CN　—bulk item, normal
CS　—bulk item, slow-moving

This latter composite rating as expressed by the seventh digit in the inventory classification code might be an index based on different weights assigned to several classification schemes rather than just the two schemes cited.

xxxxxxx8　The eighth digit designates special data for marketing purposes. For example, a marketing composite rating might be developed based on two classification schemes: (1) average margin per dollar of sales and (2) approved marketing strategies for the item. Each of these classification schemes might have three alternatives with a composite rating determined in the same manner as stated for the seventh digit in this classification code.

Again, the above inventory classification code is presented only for purposes of encouraging the analyst to examine seriously the requirements for data regarding inventory by various decision-making groups throughout the business organization before the analyst specifies the inventory classification code. One can subsequently retrieve only what was previously coded in such a manner so that it can be retrieved.

Systems Analyst's Perspective

Following the information systems approach, the systems analyst views the production and operation activities, and he begins to specify the requirements for information and the sources of data. In determining the requirements for information, the systems analyst follows a three-step approach. First, he must understand the business process of the business organization in question and have an appreciation of those unique characteristics of this organization. Second, he must determine the goals and objectives of the production and operation activities at each level within the business organization. This second step, of course, draws heavily upon organization theory and might be described as a high-point organization review. Third, the systems analyst must specify the requirements for information that are incumbent upon the production and control information system in satisfying the previously determined goals and objectives.

After the systems analyst has specified the requirements for information, then he begins to ascertain the sources of data. Next, he has the practical task of matching requirements for information with sources of data. In the process of performing this matching process, the systems analyst will select from those tools and techniques (reorder point, reorder quantity, EOQ formulas, safety stock, cushion, perpetual control, physical control, repeat requisitions, and so forth) available to the systems analyst, the tools and techniques which seem appropriate for the business situation in question.

In the process of bridging the gap between the information requirements and the data sources, the systems analyst is governed by the practical guidelines of desire for simplicity, speed, economy, and accuracy. The management control system must function *through people;* therefore, it must be simple if it is to be effective, is to provide accurate information, and is to be processed in the minimum time. The management control system must be capable of coping with the exceptional item or event. While all regular items can be handled on a predetermined or automatic basis, the system must be capable of coping with the exceptional item without upsetting normal operations. There should be sufficient flexibility in the system to permit growth and expansion or internal change without upsetting the system. Furthermore, the system should be capable of being integrated with other information systems, possibly serving as the building block for the integrated inventory control, production control, and marketing information system.

Other types of problems are encountered in the installation process. First, as problems arise in the operation of an inventory management information system (such as described in the previous chapter), it becomes apparent that some of the statements which were previously made by corporate management regarding management inventory policy were incorrect. In addition, it is discovered that some of these statements regarding management inventory policy are in conflict. The experienced systems analyst can reduce the possibility of these types of situations from occurring by more thoroughly questioning management when the requirements are being originally specified. For example, the executive vice president of a manufacturing company stated that it was management policy to provide 95 percent level of customer service. After he was quickly told how much buildup in inventory must occur before the company could offer this level of customer service, the executive vice president said this was only an "advertised goal." Eventually, after considerable study, the uniform level of customer service idea was abandoned; instead, each of the Class A items in inventory (high unit cost and high annual usage value in dollars) was individually examined, and a management group decided the level of customer service that should be provided for that item in inventory.

Second, after the decision has been made to install an inventory management information system, for example, it may be a long time before the information system is in operation. For example, the production control manager for a large manufacturing company commented that his division had been in the process of implementing reorder quantities and reorder points for over 12 months. The executive vice president for this latter company would not approve the uneven production schedule which would be required for the company to install quickly the suggested inventory management information system.

Furthermore, in order to build up banks of inventory at points above the reorder level so that the inventory management information system can have a fresh start, production employees would have to work overtime in the short run. Later, after the inventory banks are established and during the initial phase of operating under the inventory system, production workers would have idle time until enough activity occurred to activate the reorder quantity (in other words, until the reorder point was reached) .

Faced with this situation, the production control manager weekly schedules a new group of items in inventory for conversion to the new inventory management information system. The production manager believes that within a few months all of the items in inventory will be under the new system.

Third, case after case can be cited where the workers and some of the supervisors have opposed the installation of an inventory management information system, which eventually resulted in a poor operating system that was subsequently discarded. This type of organizational problem is not unique with the installation of production and operation information systems, but is analogous to the situation encountered in installing a budgetary control and standard cost system in other business organizations.

In conclusion, the information flows in production and operation activities are much more extensive than what was cited in this discussion. For example, complete textbooks and several university courses are concerned exclusively with this general problem area. The information flows cited in this discussion were selected based on their general application to numerous business organizations.

TOPICS FOR CLASS DISCUSSION

1. The procedures required to design and install an ABC selective inventory management control system have been described in detail in this chapter. This classification code also contains valuable information for noninventory control decision makers. Indicate how this classification code might be used by various decision makers throughout the business organization. Be specific.

2. An analyst at the Bixby Company estimated the annual sales dollar volume for each item in inventory based on an examination of sales invoices for selected periods. After entering this information on each perpetual inventory card, the cards were arranged in a long box in the relative order of sales volume. Next, the analyst measured the length of the box. The group of items whose perpetual inventory cards were in the initial one fifth of the length of the box was classi-

fied Group A. The group of items representing the next 20 percent of the box's length was classified Group B. The remaining group, consisting of 60 percent of the box's length, was classified Group C. After each perpetual inventory card contained the appropriate group designation, the cards were resorted into their traditional sequence and filed. The card classification system was now used for making production scheduling decisions when it was necessary to choose between products.

REQUIRED:

1. Evaluate the above system. How does it differ from the typical ABC selective inventory management control system? Are these latter differences important?
2. The Bixby Company is in a highly competitive industry where the per-unit cost and cost-selling price relation are significantly different for each item in inventory. In this environmental setting, indicate the types of management decisions in which the company's ABC grouping data would provide useful information. In what types of management decisions might this ABC grouping data tend to mislead management, if it were considered? Be specific.

CASE 10–1.   WALLACE TOOL INDUSTRIES, INC.

James Brock recently became the controller of Wallace Tool Industries, Inc., following the unexpected death of the former controller. Brock has been employed by a certified public accounting firm for the past five years, and he terminated his employment with this firm last month to accept the controller position. The president of Wallace Tool Industries, Inc., stated that Brock's diversified background and experience should bring needed, increased competence for coping with the firm's problems.

The president of the firm discussed with Brock the findings of the recent annual audit. Specifically, the audit manager of the certified public accounting firm performing the audit expressed concern over the increase in size of finished goods inventory. The president said that he had discussed this problem with the previous controller, and he (the former controller) had worked a few days in analyzing the inventory position based on a sample. The president said that he was sure Brock's secretary (who was also employed by the former controller) knew where the working papers were for the inventory study.

The president asked Brock to complete the inventory study and to take into consideration the question: "Would a reduction in inventory result in a reduction in customer services and extend delivery dates?"

The Company

Brock was already familiar with the history of the Wallace Tool Industries, Inc.—how the firm had grown from its small two-man shop to its present size of almost $3 million of sales in a period of less than 15 years. It seemed to be the consensus of opinion by top management that Wallace Tool Industries, Inc., had almost reached its "fair share of the market" in terms of new customers, and some of the key officers stated that emphasis should be shifted from the new customer area to trying to expand the volume of services to existing customers. Furthermore, recent changes in the financial market necessitated that accounts receivable and inventory levels be reduced to a minimum.

Wallace Tool Industries, Inc., designs, develops, manufactures, and sells industrial tools. Currently, there are 2,647 different stock items which on December 31, 1969, had a cost of $1,042,137. About 80 percent of the inventory is stored at the home office warehouse in Chicago, with the remainder of the inventory located in five regional warehouses: Boston, Cincinnati, Dallas, Denver, and San Francisco. Annual sales are $2,850,000.

Perpetual inventory records are maintained on a manual basis for each item of finished goods inventory including the identification of place of storage. Another set of records is manually maintained in production and control for the purpose of providing the appropriate information for manufacturing operations including the scheduling of production.

Previous Study

Brock's secretary located the former controller's working papers for the inventory study. These papers contained:

1. An analysis of finished goods inventory turnover for stocked tools (Exhibit A).

EXHIBIT A

**Finished Goods Inventory Turnover for Stocked Tools
for 1969**

Annual sales for stocked tools	$2,850,000
Cost of sales (40 percent)	× .40
	$1,140,000
Average finished goods inventory	
Beginning	$ 826,715
Ending	1,042,137
	$1,868,852
Average	$ 934,426

$$\frac{\text{Cost of Sales}}{\text{Average Inventory}} = \frac{\$1,140,000}{\$934,426} = 1.22$$

NOTE: The tool industry surveys indicate that the finished goods inventory turnover ranges from 2.0 to 5.0, with 3.4 being an average of these surveys.

2. An analysis of finished goods inventory for stocked tools based on the working papers for the December 31, 1969, physical inventory count with cost extensions (Exhibit B).

EXHIBIT B

**An Analysis of Finished Goods Inventory for Stocked
Tools for 1969**

Number of Items	Percent of Total	Percent of Total Inventory Value
662	25%	76%
397	15	15
1,588	60	9
2,647	100%	100%

Number of Items	Percent of Total	Unit Cost
318	12%	Over $.50
873	33	$.50–$.25
1,456	55	Under $.25
2,647	100%	

Exhibit B is based on the working papers for the December 31, 1969 physical inventory count with cost extensions.

3. A random sample of finished goods inventory with an identification of the number of units on hand at each of the six warehouses as of December 31, 1969, and an identification of the number of

units sold from each warehouse during the past six months (Exhibit C).

4. An analysis of the above random sample including the cost, sales, gross profit, and carrying cost for finished goods inventory (Exhibit D).

5. An analysis of 697 orders shipped from the home office directly to customers for the period November 1–10, 1969. This exhibit compares the cumulative percent of the number of items promised for delivery within varying number of days with the cumulative percent of deliveries on time (Exhibit E).

6. An analysis of the above orders indicating the number of days elapsing between the promised delivery date and the actual delivery date (Exhibit F).

7. An indication of the lead time on the above orders, in other words, the actual number of days from order day to delivery date (Exhibit G).

Brock's Insights

Organizationally, there are five departments at the Wallace Tool Industries, Inc.: administration department, inventory control department, production department, sales department, and research and development department. However, from Brock's inquiries during the past month and from his observations, he was aware that the separation by department was more "in name" than "in fact." From his analysis, he felt that the organization structure was extremely informal with most of the top members of management having been employed by the firm for at least 10 years. In other words, management had collectively participated in most of the dynamic growth that Wallace Tool Industries, Inc., had experienced during its 15-year history.

REQUIRED:

1. Analyze, compare, and interpret the exhibits and the descriptive material presented in this case.
2. Prepare a concise report highlighting your findings from the previous step with *specific* recommendations regarding your approach toward the solution of the problem confronting Brock.

EXHIBIT C
Inventory and Sales Information for a Random Sample of Units

Number	Cost	Chicago Inventory 12/31/69	Chicago Sales for 6 Mo.	Cincinnati Inventory 12/31/69	Cincinnati Sales for 6 Mo.	Denver Inventory 12/31/69	Denver Sales for 6 Mo.	San Francisco Inventory 12/31/69	San Francisco Sales for 6 Mo.	Dallas Inventory 12/31/69	Dallas Sales for 6 Mo.	Boston Inventory 12/31/69	Boston Sales for 6 Mo.
WTI—													
421610	24¢	120	65	140	—	210	—	—	—	—	—	—	—
622612	72	704	71	—	—	—	—	11	3	70	28	47	—
532621	38	320	460	198	—	40	—	65	—	48	—	54	—
422636	10	1,450	225	114	—	102	—	—	—	—	—	—	—
621621	24	6,520	12	510	62	230	—	104	—	65	—	100	—
846614	46	4,210	1,236	—	—	—	—	—	—	—	—	—	—
231617	46	2,620	4,172	450	310	250	—	120	—	96	23	47	—
429632	8	3,605	—	140	24	52	—	89	—	75	—	75	—
174612	98	1,850	1,630	350	278	131	—	100	—	75	—	—	—
842624	20	2,210	265	503	—	140	545	25	—	48	—	—	—
622642	16	93	62	110	—	195	—	—	—	—	—	—	—
533512	26	578	—	50	—	—	—	800	600	—	—	650	—
422721	30	1,742	78	259	—	—	—	52	—	25	—	55	—
544721	24	1,247	122	30	—	300	110	25	—	75	15	—	—
832738	20	806	218	—	—	—	—	74	25	—	—	—	—

EXHIBIT D

Analysis of Inventory and Sales Information for a Random Sample of Units

Number	Cost	Chicago Inventory 12/31/69	Chicago Sales for 6 Mo.	Cincinnati Inventory 12/31/69	Cincinnati Sales for 6 Mo.	Denver Inventory 12/31/69	Denver Sales for 6 Mo.	San Francisco Inventory 12/31/69	San Francisco Sales for 6 Mo.	Dallas Inventory 12/31/69	Dallas Sales for 6 Mo.	Boston Inventory 12/31/69	Boston Sales for 6 Mo.
WTI–421610	24¢	120	65	140	—	210	—	—	—	—	—	—	—
		a 28.80 d 39.00		a 33.60		a 50.40							
		b 1.44 e 23.40		b 1.68		b 2.52							
		c 2.88		c 3.36		c 5.04							
622612	72¢	704	71	—	—	—	—	11	3	70	28	47	—
		a 506.88 d 127.80						a 7.92 d 5.40		a 50.40 d 50.40		a 33.84	
		b 25.34 e 76.68						b .40 e 3.24		b 2.52 e 30.24		b 1.69	
		c 50.69						c .79		c 5.04		c 3.38	
532621	38¢	920	460	198	—	40	—	65	—	48	—	54	—
		a 121.60 d 437.00		a 75.24		a 15.20		a 24.70		a 18.24		a 20.52	
		b 6.08 e 262.20		b 3.76		b .76		b 1.24		b .91		b 1.03	
		c 12.16		c 7.52		c 1.52		c 2.47		c 1.82		c 2.05	
422686	10¢	1,450	225	114	—	102	—	104	—	—	—	—	—
		a 145.00 d 56.25		a 11.40		a 10.20							
		b 7.25 e 33.75		b .57		b .51							
		c 14.50		c 1.14		c 1.02							
621621	24¢	6,520	12	510	62	230	—	104	—	65	—	100	—
		a 1,564.80 d 7.20		a 122.40 d 37.20		a 55.20		a 24.96		a 15.60		a 24.00	
		b 78.24 e 4.32		b 6.12 e 22.32		b 2.76		b 1.25		b .78		b 1.20	
		c 156.48		c 12.24		c 5.52		c 2.50		c 1.56		c 2.40	

EXHIBIT D (*Continued*)

Number	Cost	Chicago Inventory 12/31/69	Chicago Sales for 6 Mo.	Cincinnati Inventory 12/31/69	Cincinnati Sales for 6 Mo.	Denver Inventory 12/31/69	Denver Sales for 6 Mo.	San Francisco Inventory 12/31/69	San Francisco Sales for 6 Mo.	Dallas Inventory 12/31/69	Dallas Sales for 6 Mo.	Boston Inventory 12/31/69	Boston Sales for 6 Mo.
846614	46¢	4,210	1,236	—	—	—	—	—	—	—	—	—	—
		a 1,936.60	d 1,421.40										
		b 96.83	e 852.84										
		c 193.66											
231617	46¢	2,620	4,172	450	310	250	—	120	—	96	23	47	—
		a 1,205.20	d 4,797.80	a 207.00	d 356.50	a 115.00	—	a 55.20	—	a 44.16	d 26.45	a 21.62	—
		b 60.26	e 2,878.68	b 10.35	e 213.90	b 5.75		b 2.76		b 2.21	e 15.87	b 1.08	
		c 120.52		c 20.70		c 11.50		c 5.52		c 4.42		c 2.16	
423682	8¢	3,605	—	140	24	52	—	89	—	—	—	75	—
		a 288.40	—	a 11.20	d 4.80	a 4.16	—	a 7.12	—		—	a 6.00	—
		b 14.42		b .56	e 2.88	b .21		b .36				b .30	
		c 28.84		c 1.12		c .42		c .71				c .60	
174612	98¢	1,850	1,630	350	278	131	—	100	—	75	—	—	—
		a 1,813.00	d 3,993.50	a 343.00	d 681.10	a 128.38	—	a 98.00	—	a 73.50	—	—	—
		b 90.65	e 2,396.10	b 17.15	e 408.66	b 6.42		b 4.90		b 3.68			
		c 181.30		c 34.30		c 12.84		c 9.80		c 7.35			
842624	20¢	2,210	265	503	—	140	545	25	—	48	—	—	—
		a 442.00	d 132.50	a 100.60	—	a 28.00	d 272.50	a 5.00	—	a 9.60	—	—	—
		b 22.10	e 79.50	b 5.03		b 1.40	e 163.50	b .25		b .48			
		c 44.20		c 10.06		c 2.80		c .50		c .96			
622642	16¢	93	62	110	—	195	—	—	—	—	—	—	—
		a 14.88	d 24.80	a 17.60	—	a 31.20	—	—	—	—	—	—	—
		b .74	e 14.88	b .88		b 1.56							
		c 1.49		c 1.76		c 3.12							

EXHIBIT D (Continued)

Number	Cost	Chicago Inventory 12/31/69	Chicago Sales for 6 Mo.	Cincinnati Inventory 12/31/69	Cincinnati Sales for 6 Mo.	Denver Inventory 12/31/69	Denver Sales for 6 Mo.	San Francisco Inventory 12/31/69	San Francisco Sales for 6 Mo.	Dallas Inventory 12/31/69	Dallas Sales for 6 Mo.	Boston Inventory 12/31/69	Boston Sales for 6 Mo.
533512	26¢	578	—	50	—	—	—	800	600	—	—	650	—
		a 150.28 d		a 13.00	—	—	—	a 208.00	d 390.00	—	—	a 169.00	—
		b 7.51 e	—	b .65	—	—	—	b 10.40	e 234.00	—	—	b 8.45	—
		c 15.03		c 1.30				c 20.80		—		c 16.90	
422721	30¢	1,742	78	259	—	—	—	52	—	25	—	55	—
		a 522.60 d	58.50	a 77.70	—	—	—	a 15.60	—	a 7.50	—	a 16.50	—
		b 26.13 e	35.10	b 3.89	—	—	—	b .78	—	b .38	—	b .83	—
		c 52.26		c 7.77				c 1.56		c .75		c 1.65	
544721	24¢	1,247	122	30	—	300	110	25	—	75	15	—	—
		a 299.28 d	73.20	a 7.20	—	a 72.00 d	66.00	a 6.00	—	a 18.00 d	9.00	—	—
		b 14.96 e	43.92	b .36	—	b 3.60 e	39.60	b .30	—	b .90 e	5.40	—	—
		c 29.93		c .72		c 7.20		c .60		c 1.80		—	
832738	20¢	806	218	—	—	—	—	74	25	—	—	—	—
		a 161.20 d	109.00	—	—	—	—	a 14.80 d	12.50	—	—	—	—
		b 8.06 e	65.40	—	—	—	—	b .74 e	7.50	—	—	—	—
		c 16.12		—				c 1.48		—		—	

Symbol *a* represents the cost of inventory (unit cost × number of units on hand).

Symbol *b* is an estimate of the carrying cost of inventory based on an estimated annual cost of 10 percent of cost (since this information is for six months, 5 percent of cost is used).

Symbol *c* is also an estimate of the carrying cost of inventory based on an estimated annual cost of 20 percent.

Symbol *d* represents sales (sales price × number of units sold) which was based on the assumption that cost of stocked tools was 40 percent of selling price.

Symbol *e* is the gross profit on sales.

Recap of Exhibit D

	Total Inventory Cost of Sample	Total Sales of Sample for 6 Mo.	Gross Profit on Sales of Sample for 6 Mo.	6-Mo. Carrying Cost of Inventory Based on Annual Estimate of Cost	
				10%	20%
Chicago	$ 9,200.52	$11,277.95	$6,766.77	$460.01	$ 920.06
Cincinnati	1,019.94	1,079.60	647.76	51.00	101.99
Denver	509.74	338.50	203.10	25.49	50.98
San Francisco ...	467.30	407.90	244.74	23.38	46.73
Dallas	237.00	85.85	51.51	11.86	23.70
Boston	291.48	—	—	14.58	29.14
Total	$11,725.98	$13,189.80	$7,913.88	$586.32	$1,172.60

EXHIBIT E
Customer Service—Promise Dates

Number of Days from Order Day That Shipping Date Is Promised	Cumulative Percent of Orders Promised for Shipment within Specified Days	Cumulative Percent of Orders Shipped on Time
1	30	19
2	36	24
3	55	36
4	60	40
5	62	41
6	64	42
7	69	46
8	72	48
9	74	49
10	80	54
11	82	55
12	84	56
13	86	57
14	100	69

Exhibit E is based on an analysis of 697 orders shipped from the home office directly to customers for the period November 1–10, 1969.

EXHIBIT F
Customer Service—Lateness of Orders

Number of Days after Promised Shipping Time	*Cumulative Percent of Orders Shipped within Specified Days from Promised Time*
0	69
1	75
2	82
3	85
4	88
5	90
6	92
7	94
8	95
9	96
10	97
11	98
12	99
Over 12	100

Exhibit F is based on an analysis of 697 orders shipped from the home office directly to customers for the period November 1–10, 1969.

EXHIBIT G
Customer Service—Lead-Time Analysis

Lead Time—Days from Order Date to Shipment Date	*Cumulative Percent of Total Orders That Were Shipped within Specified Days from Order Day*
1	28
2	33
3	51
4	58
5	60
6	62
7	67
8	70
9	73
10	78
11	80
12	83
13	85
14	95
Over 14	100

Exhibit G is based on an analysis of 697 orders shipped from the home office directly to customers for the period November 1–10, 1969.

MARKETING INFORMATION
SYSTEMS

CHAPTER 11

Marketing Management
Information Systems

THE GENERAL MODEL for a marketing information system was presented in Chapter 4 as a multidimensional, open system which encompassed certain types of major information flows within a business organization and between a business organization and its environment. Because of the extensive interface of this system with other operating and information systems, it is rare to find a major business organization that has a complete marketing information system.

Several large corporations are in the process of planning and designing a multidimensional, open system that will incorporate the major marketing information flows. Where we find such systems being designed, there is usually a series of information systems studies which include an upgrading of the production and operation information system, the distribution operating system, the sales analysis operating system, the marketing media and advertising operating system, and the cost and performance reporting system. These latter identified systems are only some of the operating systems that have to support a large-scale, multidimensional, marketing information system.

The above statement on the "state of the art" is based on our in-depth studies of 34 corporations. As of the beginning of 1969, none of these corporations had a complete marketing information system. Several were in the process of implementing such systems; others had a series of excellent operating systems which supported different facets of the marketing management's decision-making processes. This perspective of the "state of the art" is compatible with the preliminary report of Professor Cox and Mr. Good's studies of marketing information systems that was recently presented in the *Harvard Business Review*.[1] A few management consulting firms and the administrative services divisions of public accounting firms have conducted independent studies of this topic and their proprietary reports are also compatible with Cox and Good's conclusions.

In Chapter 3 we contrasted operating systems with information systems, and we saw that a minimum level of participation by management in planning and designing a system was essential if we were, in fact, going to create an *information* system. If management has not worked with a computer-based, operating system, then it is unlikely that management can be an effective participant in planning for an information system. This same philosophy is even more applicable in the case of a marketing information system because this type of model is an advanced *information* system. (The adjective "advanced" is used in the sense that a marketing information system is more complex and involved than a TYPE 2 information system.)

During the past three years, there has been a significant increase in computer applications in marketing. The scope of activities encompassed in the marketing research department has expanded from limited studies of products and customers into an integrated marketing intelligence, analysis, and administrative services department. It is not unusual for this new department chairman to be called director, marketing information services.

If we can project ourselves 18 months ahead, then several corporations will have fully implemented marketing information systems. What types of information systems are these corporations in the process of installing? How are these new systems different from the current "state of the art"? In this chapter we will examine two general models of the types of marketing information systems that are representative of these new systems that are currently being implemented.

However, before we examine these two general models, we need an increased awareness of the complexity of a multidimensional marketing information system. Therefore, the initial sections of the chapter emphasize how the systems analyst will study the marketing activities in a given business organization. Consideration is given to matching of information requirements with information sources. In

---

[1] Donald F. Cox and Robert E. Good, "How to Build a Marketing Information System," *Harvard Business Review*, Vol. XLV (May–June, 1967, pp. 145–54.

this latter discussion, special attention is given to the establishment of a common coding pattern for data within a business organization so that the same information sources may be used in satisfying many information requirements by decision makers.

INFORMATION SYSTEMS APPROACH

The systems analyst attempts to specify the information requirements, to determine the data sources and to match the information requirements with the appropriate data sources by employing some of the current management science tools and techniques. In applying this approach, the systems analyst encounters numerous problems because of the inherent nature of the multidimensional marketing information system. Some of these problems are examined in the following discussion.

Information Requirements

Specifying the information requirements is the last step in a three-step sequence. The first step is to understand the business process for the business organization under study. This requires a familiarization with the unique industry characteristics and practices as well as an appreciation of the general environment in which the business organization is located. This latter appreciation will include a general insight into how the business organization reacts to this environment.

In the second step, the systems analyst expands his understanding of the business process for that particular segment of the overall business organization's operations that has been selected for detailed study. This second step is completed when the systems analyst is able to determine the exact missions (goals or objectives) of that particular segment of the company's overall operations that is being studied. In the case of marketing activities, it is difficult to accomplish this second step because of the complexity of the situation.

This task can be accomplished if the systems analyst uses "general statements"; however, the task may not be precisely accomplished if complete mathematical statements are desired for a complex business organization. In this situation, simplifying assumptions are made in order that a mathematical model can be developed that is of a "reasonable" size.

For example, does executive management view itself as existing in an environment where the business organization can only quickly react to changes in the environment? Or, does executive management see its role as that of modifying the present environment through the stimulation of demand for the company's products? To what extent do these perspectives change between points in time? The systems analyst must make some assumptions in order to cope with this complex situation if he is to proceed to the third step— specifying the exact information requirements that are needed for achieving the determined missions.

Reacting Rather Than Planning. Executive management may be unwilling to accept forecasted demand for each product as a basis for scheduling day-to-day or week-to-week production and operation activities. Although the forecast is a good guideline, executive management may believe that the forecasted demand for each product is not an ideal target for actually scheduling production and procurement activities.

Instead, minimum and maximum forecasted demand for each product are used in the quarterly schedules of production and in the leveling of the labor force. However, for the day-to-day information flows in the production and operation information system, executive management may desire a system that reacts to actual daily changes (or weekly changes) in the finished goods inventory requirements.

Today, most of the computerized marketing information systems are really just integrated sales analysis, inventory control, and production control information systems where the computer equipment and communication facilities are used for quickly *reacting* to day-to-day or week-to-week changes in inventory stock or estimated sales. There are very few computerized marketing information systems that are integrated with production and operation activities in such a manner that the day-to-day or week-to-week production scheduling is based on forecasted sales activity.[2]

In some large business organizations with numerous diverse groups of products, there may be so many statistical problems associated with the raw data to be used in making a forecast that management is unwilling to currently employ the planned forecast approach. For

---

[2] For a special report on the use of computers and communication equipment in marketing, see "Computers Begin to Solve the Marketing Puzzle," *Business Week* (April 17, 1965), p. 114 ff.

example, the lack of historical data on each product's past sales will mean that a low degree of confidence will be ascribed to the forecasted demand. Executive management may require a high degree of confidence before they will adopt the planned forecast approach.

But in a few of these business organizations, the above situation is only a temporary arrangement. While some type of computerized information system may be installed where the production and operation activities react to day-to-day changes in sales activities, an information storage and retrieval system may have been installed for accumulating appropriate data so that in future years the business organization can respond to planned sales.

Practical Considerations.   The systems analyst should not reject too quickly this idea of using only planned sales for each product as guidelines. In a given business organization under existing computer facilities, communication equipment, and management science tools and techniques, the use of planning models as a basis for determining guidelines for production and operation activities may be the only current optimum use of these models. For example, while the day-to-day changes in the inventory stock do represent a substantial financial investment, the larger opportunities for savings were the identification of the seasonal fluctuations in inventory requirements and the determination of guidelines for each item in inventory.

Data Sources

Arbitrarily, we group the data sources for marketing information systems into three categories. First, from the cost accounting and financial accounting records, the systems analyst obtains the following types of information: marginal cost, contribution to margin, and contribution from each salesman or each territory. Second, from the sales invoices, accounts receivable file, and the financial accounting records, the systems analyst obtains information on customer characteristics. Third, there are many special sources of information that are used in satisfying information requirements of marketing activities.

These special sources include market surveys, market research, research and development activities, and secondary sources. The recently published input-output analysis for the United States has been widely used for external criteria to evaluate a given business organization's sales potential for a group of products.[3] Industry reports, governmental reports and studies, private research studies, and the professional literature are some of the major groupings of secondary sources which are frequently used as data sources for marketing information systems.

Matching Process

Frequently, the data that are needed by decision makers in marketing-related activities are available in the accounting records and accounting documents. However, these data are not readily available for retrieval. In other instances, these data are accumulated according to a classification system which is different from one needed for marketing information systems.

These raw data must be coded in an appropriate manner so that these accounting and statistical data can be resorted and used as a common source of data for many diverse information requirements. When the data are not coded so they can be easily retrieved, it may be more economical to accumulate the data all over again, rather than to retrieve these data from the existing records.

In other situations, the exact data needed for satisfying information requirements of decision makers in marketing-related activities have not been accumulated. Business events have occurred; business management is aware that these events have occurred; but no one has accumulated any experience regarding the occurrence of these events. This is the task of the systems analyst: to match all the major information requirements with the data sources, and when sources do not exist for satisfying some information requirements, he will design and establish the appropriate sources.

For example, the president of a small manufacturing company desired to evaluate the effectiveness of the company's advertising program. However, he was operating with limited financial resources, and could not afford to hire an independent market research group to make this determination. After thoroughly pondering this question, the president devised a procedure whereby certain information on the results of the advertising program was accumulated.

---

[3] For the preliminary results of the 1958 Interindustry Relations Study, see: "The Interindustry Structure of the Unitel States: A Report on the 1958 Input-Output Study," *Survey of Current Business,* Vol. XLIV (November, 1964), pp. 10–29.

The sales order form was changed to include space for the customer's answer to the question of why he had made this purchase from the company: was he influenced by advertising media (if so, where), personal reference, reputation, or other factors (please specify). As a result of analyzing the information provided by this procedure, the small manufacturing company's total advertising program was substantially changed.

INFORMATION ACCUMULATION AND TRANSMISSION

Recent developments in communication equipment have permitted many business organizations' decentralized operations to be integrated into a single network. Production facilities, warehouse and storage facilities, and regional marketing offices are integrated into a single management information system.

In such situations, the systems analyst is primarily concerned with the determination of the variable information that must be transmitted. For example, a large group of independent grocery stores throughout the state of Illinois uses a common coding pattern for transmitting purchase orders to a large, central wholesaler. This wholesale grocery company makes deliveries the following morning for all orders received daily from grocery stores located as far as 250 miles away.

A six-digit identification code has been established for each stock item in the wholesale grocer's inventory. A two-digit identification code has been assigned to each of the independent grocery stores. The remaining 2 digits in a 10-digit group of information are used for specifying the quantities requested by the identified independent grocery store. Thus, each 10-digit group of information represents a complete purchase order.

In another case, a large, diversified corporation has its major computer facilities in Chicago. Daily, each of the subsidiary corporations will transmit to Chicago the variable data on each sales invoice, including the identification of the customer's name. A predetermined coding pattern is used for transmitting this information in the minimum amount of digits. The major computer facilities in Chicago contain programs that accumulate and process information for all requirements throughout the diversified corporation and its subsidiaries (for example, the perpetual inventory records and accounts receivable files for each of the subsidiary corporations are centrally maintained in the Chicago computer facilities) .

In summary, there are many major information requirements from decision makers in marketing-related activities that the systems analyst can satisfy by the establishment of the appropriate predetermined coding pattern. From another perspective, whenever inventory identification codes, customer identification codes, cost accounting identification codes, and financial accounting identification codes are being designed or revised, the systems analyst should give special consideration to the marketing information possibilities of each of these codes.

TYPE 2.5 Information System

In several companies TYPE 2 information systems have been established, and these systems have been in operation long enough for management to begin to acquire a high degree of confidence in these systems. Once this level of confidence and reliability has been obtained in the system, then management has begun to explore other ways of utilizing the TYPE 2 system. Management in a few companies has established formal extensions on the TYPE 2 system, and these new developments usually involve information retrieval activities for planning and coordinating purposes.

While the extensions on the TYPE 2 system vary somewhat by company, there are some common features of these modified TYPE 2 systems. These common features have been incorporated in our generalized model of a TYPE 2.5 information system which is presented in Figure 11.1. This general model is more complicated than the TYPE 2 system in that it contains five phases instead of three. These five phases are: (1) systems processing phase, (2) coordination phase, (3) planning phase, (4) monitoring and inquiring phase, and (5) control phase.

The coordination phase, planning phase, and control phase are very similar to their counterpart in the TYPE 2 system. The differences between these three phases are (1) the connection of the systems processing phase and the coordination phase with "online storage of critical data" generated by the systems processing phase and (2) the connection of the monitoring and inquiring phase and the control phase with "common data from other systems."

Since the flowchart of the above three phases in the two systems are similar, we can conclude that the information flows and time cycles of these systems are comparable. While the TYPE 2.5 system is coping with a more complex environmental setting, the information flows in the overall systems are being forced into the same general type of network as present in the TYPE 2 system. The only significant differences are the activities encompassed in the two new phases —the systems processing phase and the monitoring and inquiring phase. Therefore, our attention will be focused on these two new phases.

Systems Processing Phase.   The systems processing phase refers to a sequence of operations that generate common data for two or more information systems. The information requirements for these common data in the two or more systems may not be in the same time frame, much less at the same precise moment that these data flow through the channel. Therefore, a typical feature of the systems processing phase is for these common data to be stored in a series of banks, files, and disks. The same set of data may be concurrently stored in more than one location, depending on the overall information requirements for these data.

There is a high degree of similarity in how the systems processing phase has been employed in various companies. Specifically, this sequence of operations is usually applied to the handling of all financial accounting and cost accounting activities. This set of transactions will include order entry, invoicing, shipment, accounts receivable, purchase order, receiving reports, issue slips, accounts payable, payroll, selling expenses, administrative expenses, general expenses, and others.

Therefore, when we find a TYPE 2.5 system being employed by marketing management, we see a mechanism for retrieving common data from the systems processing phase that are required in the marketing decision-making processes. For example, the financial and cost accounting system may be providing marketing management with sales analysis data by territory, by customer, by product, and by salesman.

If the sequence of operations in the systems processing phase is going to provide information for two or more information systems, then the reliability and proper coding of inputs become extremely crucial factors. Erroneously coded data in the latter case may trigger a series of responses in different information systems, and such occurrences may have severe economic consequences. Or, from an-

FIGURE 11.1
A Generalized Model of a TYPE 2.5 Information System

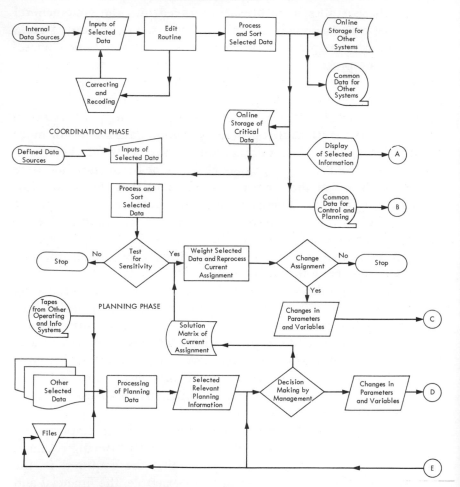

other perspective, if the same set of data is going to be used in two or more information systems, then it is economically feasible to give more attention to a screening of these inputs.

The *edit routine* is the name of an important computer program that screens all inputs into this system (the sequence of operations included in the systems processing phase). In Figure 11.1 we see that the process represented by the "edit routine" contains two flows. Those inputs that are successful in passing through the "screen" are forwarded to a subsequent location where these data are processed and sorted. Those inputs that are rejected by the screen are returned to another station where they are corrected and recoded before being resubmitted as inputs.

The mere existence of an edit routine indicates a high level of stability in the TYPE 2.5 information system. Specifically, the screen in the edit routine is based upon a prescribed coding of various combinations of inputs to the system. Each document for a particular

FIGURE 11.1 (*Continued*)

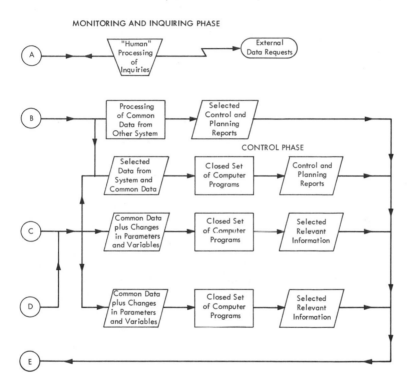

product, employee, account, or type of event will have a specified format for the descriptive data on that document, and the screen will test that the actual data are compatible with the specified format for these data.

In one company the edit routine contains 45 digits of data, exclusive of dollar amounts. The specified format of these 45 digits of data varies not only by document—such as sales invoice versus a purchase order—but also by the product that is being purchased or sold. In other words, the unique characteristics of each type of product are encompassed in the prescribed 45 digits used in coding this event.

From these comments, we can see that the edit routine cannot be established until after the team of systems analysts has completed their study of the types of documents and the types of transactions which are to be handled by the system. After this study has been completed, then the proposed screen can be programmed.

There is, however, a significant problem in using an edit routine. This screen may be so cumbersome that inputs are unnecessarily restricted to that set of transactions that were prescribed at a much earlier point in time. Fortunately, this limitation of the edit routine has been overcome. A computer program has been developed that updates the edit routine, and another program lets the edit routine print out a revised coding manual. These two programs permit the edit routine to respond to a dynamic setting.

Focusing again on Figure 11.1, we see that after the inputs have been screened by the edit routine, they are processed and sorted. Next, we see a series of files and banks for storing these common data. The same set of data may be concurrently stored in two or more of these locations. This general situation means that the computer program for sorting these data must incorporate a classification system that designates the locations to which these data will be stored.

The set of locations where these data are stored will depend, of course, upon the anticipated information uses of these data in different decision-making processes. The team of systems analysts must, therefore, study these different decision-making processes so that the team can determine the appropriate set of common data banks and the appropriate networks of information flows. In a subsequent chapter we will examine the classification system used in designating the locations where these data are to be stored and how this operation is related to information retrieval.

Monitoring and Inquiring Phase. The monitoring and inquiring phase is primarily an information retrieval service. A telephone inquiry is received from a customer, a salesman, a representative, or a decision maker, and information is obtained from the common data bank to answer this question. An individual serves as the "human processor" of these inquiries, and he gives a personalized response to the question. The "human" dimensions of this service are frequently extremely important from a marketing standpoint.

There is a second group of activities included in the monitoring and inquiring phase. This second series of operations pertain to the processing of common data (which were generated from the purposes of another information system) and preparing a set of reports for purposes of providing selected information for planning and control requirements. In this phase we are typically receiving periodic information rather than continuous information.

A sales order status system or a customer status system are examples of the first type of retrieval system in this phase. We might prepare a salesman profitability report at the end of the month, and all the data for this report might be provided by a financial and cost accounting data system. In the latter case we have an example of the second type of retrieval system in the monitoring and inquiring phase.

In Figure 11.1 we see a connecting line at the input location between the monitoring and inquiring phase and the control phase. This line is to represent those cases where data from the common data banks are merged with the data created within the operating system and these combined data are incorporated in control and planning reports. For example, we might desire a salesman profitability report that is combined with a performance report and with a sales potential report.

Extensions and Supporting Systems

In our general model of a TYPE 2.5 information system (see Figure 11.1) we depict three regular operating systems within the control phase. Each of these operating systems contain input, processing, and output capabilities. These input units can handle a regular source document as well as changes in parameters and variables that are generated by the planning phase and the coordination phase.

The first of these three operating systems is also connected by a data flow to the monitoring and inquiring phase, and we might think of this operating system as being a supporting system for sales force decision-making processes. Information for sales force administration will be obtained from the planning phase, and these data will be processed at the beginning of the cycle. Other changes in these assignments are made during the cycle with data flows from the coordination phase. Information sources for the salesman productivity report include common data from the monitoring and inquiring phase (as explained previously) as well as the ordinary data processed by the operating system for sales force decision-making processes.

The second operating system might be perceived as a supporting system for advertisement management and media selection. During the control phase we may be accumulating information on consumer-product behavior, consumer-media behavior, and consumer-advertising behavior. We may have a set of programmed decision rules that will change our short-term advertising expenditures and media selections based on these accumulated index and profile data. These programmed decision rules can be automatically handled by the computer system without going through a decision maker, and these programmed decision rules would be handled similarly to those for inventory management. During the control phase, this operating system will be responding to any "changes in parameters and variables" that may be instituted by the coordination phase. For example, new data from the external environment may suggest a revised weighting of various media selections.

The third operating system might be thought of as a support system for distribution management or for product planning management. In either case, the operating system will be handling a large volume of marketing-oriented data. If it is a supporting system for distribution management, then it is processing and accumulating relevant information on order processing, real-time inventory position, and status of orders or shipments. If it is a supporting system for product planning, then the information flows encompass research and development activities, product pricing data and pricing models, and marketing intelligence data.

From these descriptions of marketing-oriented applications, we can envision various flows of information being handled by these operating systems in the control phase. As previously indicated, the activities in the planning phase and the coordination phase are similar to those for a TYPE 2 system. In the explanation of the monitoring and inquiring phase, marketing-oriented examples were cited for purposes of illustration.

In addition to these regular features of a TYPE 2.5 system, we sometimes find another modification. Frequently, we will have a research group that is adding to the common data files throughout the operating cycle. We can depict such an arrangement as though it were part of our coordination phase, and from these new research findings, a revised assignment of resources might be generated. But in some cases the range of data examined by this research group is too broad to be encompassed within the coordination phase. That is, the sets of screens for selected data would not be extensive enough to include these research findings. Therefore, in some companies, we find this research team adding special data to the common data files on the environment, consumers, products, and competitors. Where these research efforts are broadly pursued, then we may find a more advanced type of information system being formulated. This is representative of the next type of information system.

TYPE 3 Information System

The TYPE 2.5 information system contained several features not present in previous information systems; the typical planning phase, coordination phase, and control phase were augmented with a systems processing phase and a monitoring and inquiring phase. While the latter two phases significantly changed the structure of this system over former systems, the TYPE 2.5 system continues to possess many of the attributes of the more primitive information systems.

This generalization is not valid for a TYPE 3 information system. In the TYPE 3 system, we have multidata flows and multitime frames all encompassed within one complex information system. With these multidimensions, we would expect the TYPE 3 system to contain a new array of phases not present in the TYPE 2.5 system. This logical deduction is only partially correct. There is one new phase in the TYPE 3 system over the five phases in the TYPE 2.5 system. This new phase is the information gathering, classifying, and storage phase which is interfaced with the coordination phase and with the planning phase.

Later we will examine the attributes of this new phase—the information gathering, classifying, and storage phase; however, the overall set of operations contained in this phase are not very complex. Therefore, the major differences between the TYPE 3 system and the TYPE 2.5 system must take the form of changes or modifications in the existing five phases. There are some changes in the coordination phase in a TYPE 3 system, and there are significant changes in the control phase over the characteristics of this phase in previous systems. The planning phase, the systems processing phase, and the monitoring and inquiring phase are identical in the TYPE 3 system with their respective counterparts in the TYPE 2.5 system.

In our generalized model of a TYPE 3 information system (see

FIGURE 11.2

A Generalized Model of a TYPE 3 Information System

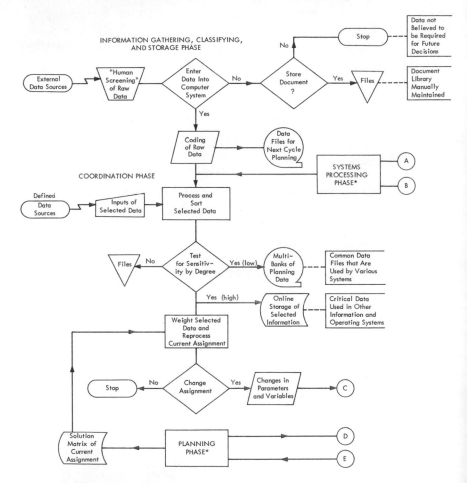

Figure 11.2) we have only shown in our flowchart of the major elements these three phases that are different in the TYPE 3 system from those in the TYPE 2.5 system. Specifically, we have presented the information gathering, classifying, and storage phase, the coordination phase, and the control phase. The other three phases—the planning phase, the systems processing phase, and the monitoring and inquiring phase—are represented by three large rectangles which are used for depicting the location of these phases for purposes of illustrating the information flows among all six phases in the TYPE 3 system.

FIGURE 11.2 *(Continued)*

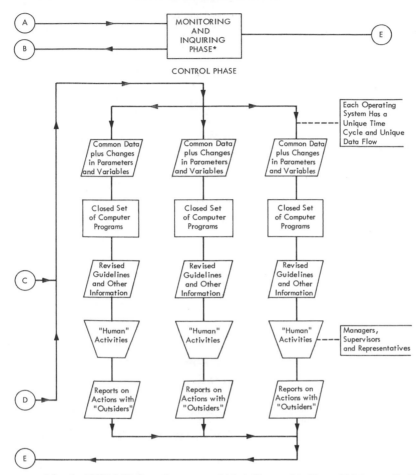

* See the TYPE 2.5 information system which is illustrated in Figure 11.1 for specific flow charts of the systems processing phase, the planning phase, and the monitoring and inquiring phase.

As suggested above, the major changes between the TYPE 3 system and the TYPE 2.5 system are contained in the modified control phase. Therefore, we will begin our examination of the TYPE 3 system with an analysis of this phase. Subsequently, we will briefly consider the other two phases that are presented in detail in our flow chart.

Control Phase.   Each operating system within the TYPE 3 system has a unique time cycle and a unique data flow. These character-istics—multidata flows and multitime frames—are based on the nature of the business process and the external environment. The management and administrative processes in a company containing a TYPE 3 system are such that there is a high degree of sensitivity to actions by competitors, customers, industry leaders, and governmental officials. Moreover, different segments of the operation respond in alternative ways to similar events.

In this type of setting, a new level of management is formally recognized in the information system. "Executive management" are terms that are used to refer to policy makers, and the policy makers are individuals who can specify the parameters in a decision model. Individuals who can specify variables in a decision model are called "decision makers." Thus far in our flowcharts of information systems, we have used the symbol of a diamond to represent the decision-making process by management, and we have indicated that this group can specify changes in parameters and variables.

In the TYPE 3 system within the control phase, management personnel immediately below the decision-making level serve as an integral part of each modified operating system. Technically, we can think of management personnel at this organization level as being "planners," for they are able to select among alternatives that are available within the guidelines set forth by the parameters and variables. These planners are represented in our generalized model by the symbol for manual operations that is labeled *"Human" Activities.*

These planners provide the necessary flexibility in the overall structure so that unique time cycles and unique data flows can be easily handled by the system. The manual operations performed by these individuals provide the mechanism for permitting multidata flows and multitime cycles within one overall system.

Or, from another perspective, this manual operation (Human Activities) and the inputs to the system by the planners (Reports on Actions with "Outsiders") can be viewed as extensions to a regular operating system. That is, the normal operating system contains an input unit, a processing unit, and an output unit. These extended operating systems contain two additional units.

These planners will have different titles, depending on the company. We may refer to these individuals, in general, as being managers, supervisors, and representatives, and we may describe their primary function as serving as connectors to customers, consumers, other division managers (as in the case of conglomerate companies), and the general public. It is important to note that the individuals serving in this "human interface" role are also capable of responding to revised guidelines and other instructions. This is where the management dimension of the "planner" comes into focus.

In the context of Figure 11.2, each planner will receive guidelines and other information from an output unit within his operating system. The information provided by these reports gives the planner a modified set of alternatives from which to select, and he responds to these alternatives and interacts with the external environment. His revised actions may be in the form of new prices for products, new distribution arrangements, "special deals" for the short-term, and so forth.

After the planner has interacted with the external environment, then he reports his actions to management. This is accomplished by some type of input unit, which we have labeled in our model as "Reports on Actions with 'Outsiders.' " The latter actions may be in the form of sales orders, advertisement agreements, transfer of salesmen, and so forth.

In summary the manual operations performed by planners serve as the vital connecting link in our network and provide the mechanism for a high degree of interaction with the external environment. If it were not for this conceptual arrangement, our model could not handle the multidimensions of a TYPE 3 system—specifically, the multidata flows and the multitime frames encompassed within one structure.

Information Gathering, Classifying, and Storage Phase. This new phase in a TYPE 3 system is necessary to satisfy the continuous requirement of revised intelligence on the external environment. These continuous information requirements include data on consumer behavior, customer product acceptance, actions by competitors, and actions by governmental officials.

A research team is continuously monitoring raw data on the external environment, and the actions by individual team members can be viewed as a "human screening" of raw data. As shown in Figure 11.2, this human screening is a manual operation, and the team members decide if the raw data should be processed into the system or if the data should be stored. If it is determined that the raw data should be entered into the system, then there are several different data banks in which these data may be stored.

If the raw data are to enter the computer system, then they are processed through an input unit, which is labeled "Coding of Raw Data." Note that one of the information flows from this input unit shows information being processed into "Data Files for Next Cycle Planning" and these latter files are offline. Obviously, this is an oversimplification of the process. After the data have been coded, they are processed and sorted; then some of these data are stored for use in next cycle's planning. In the TYPE 3 system, we will assume that the team members decide which raw data will be stored for next cycle's planning; in the TYPE 4 system, this decision will be handled by programmed decision rules incorporated within the computer system.

In summary, the title of this phase—information gathering, classifying, and storage phase—really expresses the scope of the operations encompassed in this phase. Selected data from this phase are processed and sorted by the computer programs used for screening data in the coordination phase.

Coordination Phase.   In general, the operations performed in this phase are similar to those performed by the respective counterpart in the TYPE 2.5 system. The new features in this phase include additional data flows from the actions of the research team in the information gathering, classifying, and storage phase. Since these additional data flows increase the range of types of data to be processed, the computer "screen" for filtering these raw data is much more complex in this setting.

Another feature of this modified coordination phase is that the testing for sensitivity is performed on a finer scale. Moreover, the sensitivity scale is integrated with a programmed set of decision rules that specify the information retrieval and storage dimensions of these data. Some data with a low degree of sensitivity are stored offline in multibanks of planning data; other data with a high degree of sensitivity are stored online. These storage and retrieval dimensions of the data are separate from weighting selected data and reprocessing the current assignment. Of course, the "solution matrix of current assignment" from the planning phase still serves as a framework in which to reconsider the assignment question.

Except for these two features, the modified coordination phase is very similar to its counterpart in the TYPE 2.5 system. As management gains more experience with this modified coordination phase, it is highly likely that extensions will be developed which may connect selected common data files from the coordination phase with the "Human Activities" of planners in the control phase. Such an extension may be the basis for the TYPE 3.5 system.

TOPICS FOR CLASS DISCUSSION

1. The TYPE 3 information system contains multidata flows and multitime frames. Explain from a conceptual standpoint how these multidimensions can be accommodated in the structure of a TYPE 3 system.

2. Assume that we have a corporation with $150,000,000 in annual sales which manufactures consumer goods in three major product areas. If a team of systems analysts were to appropriately install a TYPE 2.5 information system, then what would you expect to be the nature of the business environment in this company? Briefly describe what you would expect to find the management and administrative processes of this company to be like.

3. The same situation as Topic 2, except that a TYPE 3 information system is being installed. Respond to the same set of questions as above.

4. In Chapter 3 we examined five phases for planning and implementing an information system— (1) planning, including commitment and orientation by executive management, (2) organization review and administrative study, (3) conceptual systems design, (4) equipment selection and program design, and (5) implementation.

Within these five phases, when would the planning and implementation of an *edit routine* occur? Explain your answer.

5. Differentiate between the following: (a) responsibility accounting system, (b) profitability accounting system and (c) marketing information system.

6. From the standpoint of the business organization's internal marketing information system, explain the importance of establishing a coding pattern for each of the following items: (a) inventory identification codes, (b) customer identification codes, (c) cost accounting identification codes, and (d) financial accounting identification codes.

CASE 11–1. BEDFORD PUBLISHING COMPANY

A Coding Pattern Exercise

The Bedford Publishing Company, a division of a large, diversified corporation, is a major publisher and distributor of books for the adult education market. Many of these basic books are "programmed texts" in mathematics, statistics, quantitative methods, critical path method, data processing, computer programming, English, and bookkeeping. A second group of Bedford books are regular adult education books for the general market and include such topics as American history, English literature, business letter writing, principles of speech, composition, introduction to sociology, introduction to economics, introduction to psychology, introduction to anthropology, and the classics in philosophy and religion. The third group of Bedford books are designed for the trade market at the foreman level, and these books are applied descriptions with a "how to do it" slant.

Currently, the assistant controller is coordinating the establishment of a marketing information system which would encompass the sales analysis and accounts receivable activities. This marketing information system will be programmed and integrated with other computer programs on the Bedford Publishing Company's IBM 360 Model 30 computer system.

The current focal point of the assistant controller's work is on the development of a coding pattern for customer identification numbers. Based on the number of customers and the forecasted growth pattern by customer category, the assistant controller determines that an 11-digit identification code will be required.

Bedford's marketing manager would like to direct sales and marketing efforts by selective cities throughout the United States. Therefore, the assistant controller has agreed to assign the first 6 digits in an 11-digit customer account designation number to the IBM's state and city code. (An IBM manual contains a two-digit code encompassing each of the 50 states and the District of Columbia, and it contains a four-digit code which identifies within a state each city with a population of 2,500 and over.)

Thus, the assistant controller is wondering how to assign customer identification numbers within each city using the remaining 5 digits in the overall 11-digit code. Finally, the assistant controller began the long process of assigning a five-digit identification number to each customer. Numbers were arbitrarily assigned on a sequential basis.

The management consulting firm with which you are associated was asked to review the proposed marketing information system at the Bedford Publishing Company. You are assigned to this job.

You quickly determine that there are three major groups of

customers within each city: (1) educational institutions and public libraries, (2) governmental agencies and industrial companies (including both training programs and private libraries), and (3) individuals.

You also determine that although there are 99,999 digits available within each city for customer designation purposes, the total number of customers in a given city is less than 10,000. Thus, the five digits contain sufficient space for expansion, which would be especially applicable for individual customers.

REQUIRED:

1. Evaluate the present proposed marketing information system.
2. Design an 11-digit customer identification code for the Bedford Publishing Company. (Suggestion: review secondary sources of information on the publishing industry for purposes of obtaining a better understanding of how a typical publishing company does business.)

CASE 11–2. WICKER MANUFACTURING COMPANY

A CODING PATTERN EXERCISE

The systems analyst has completed the first part of his study, including (1) studying the business process and the environment of the business organization in question and (2) specifying the information requirements for the major decision activities. He believes that the financial accounting, cost accounting, and statistical information now being accumulated will be adequate data sources for all information requirements.

The systems analyst's attention is directed toward the establishment of a coding pattern that will assist in the matching of data sources with information requirements. While pursuing this task, he reviews his notes on the company and its operations.

The Company

The Wicker Manufacturing Company is a producer and distributor of industrial supplies and consumer goods, with a total annual sales volume of $22,000,000. Organizationally, the company has three major product lines, with a product marketing manager being assigned to each line. The company has extensive marketing activities throughout North America and has a sales force of 240 men.

The business environment is characterized by highly fluctuating prices. Marketing management does not have sufficient information with which to set short-term prices. Therefore, management has delegated this responsibility to the salesmen. Each salesman has the authority of negotiating the selling price with a certain group of industrial purchasers. The salesman may reduce the selling price by as much as 10 percent of the established selling price without seeking prior approval from the product marketing manager.

Prices tend to fluctuate on a regional basis. Thus, on a given day the Wicker Manufacturing Company may have 20 sales orders for a given item of industrial supply, and each sales order will be at a slightly different per-unit sales price.

In addition, marketing management does not have the appropriate information with which to supervise the marketing and sales effort. Monthly statistical sales reports are prepared that indicate the dollar volume of sales by customer, salesman, territory, and product. Monthly responsibility accounting reports show cumulative expenditures by individuals.

Thus, the total salesmen's salaries and commissions, travel and per diem expenses, delivery cost, sales supplies cost and advertising charges, for example, are known. However, the accounting reports do not relate the above monthly expenses to the product line.

Existing Information Reports

Monthly, a company income statement and balance sheet are prepared. In addition, 74 responsibility accounting reports are issued. These latter reports are representative of the strict responsibility accounting variety, and they do not contain any overhead and administrative items being allocated to other responsibility centers. The monthly sales statistical reports have been previously cited.

Major Concerns

There are significant differences in the contribution to margin of different products. While everyone is aware of this situation, marketing management feels that they need a better understanding on a more timely basis of the current market price and cost relationship.

For example, frequently they are surprised that a lower company profit results from a higher dollar volume of sales.

Marketing management would like an information system that would provide them with daily or weekly guidelines for reacting to sales price fluctuations. This proposed information system would really be two information systems. There would be a monthly information flow (a responsibility accounting type of traditional information system) that would encompass a planning phase in which marketing management would establish pertinent criteria for monitoring short-term changes in sales price of raw materials and finished goods. There would be a daily or weekly information flow (a profitability accounting type of traditional information system) containing the critical information to which marketing management will react.

Finally, marketing management would like an information system that would assist them in supervising and controlling the marketing and sales effort. The lack of gross margin and product line information has been previously discussed. One complicating factor in this issue is the problem that some expenditures chargeable to a distribution expense account cannot be easily identified with an individual sales effort for a particular product. For example, in the case of advertising expense, there are "programmed advertising expenditures" that are more closely related to a "period of time" than to the stimulation of demand for any product. On the other hand, major portions of the total advertising expenditures *can* be so identified with the stimulation of demand for a particular item of finished goods inventory.

REQUIRED:

1. Design a coding pattern for coping with the above situation.
2. Illustrate the application of your coding pattern by sketching major information flows in the Wicker Manufacturing Company's operations. Indicate the separate nature of the information in each flow and show how your coding pattern provides this information. Also, indicate the time frame of each information flow and the location of the decision makers.

CASE 11–3. SCHNEIDER FROZEN FOODS, INC.

Recently, all the capital stock of Schneider Frozen Foods, Inc., was acquired by R B D Diversified Enterprises, Inc., which has corporate offices in New York City. The parent corporation (R B D Diversified Enterprises, Inc.) has a data processing center to service all of its subsidiaries, and this center contains an IBM 360 Model 65 and an IBM 360 Model 67 computer system. A large communications network has been established so that all subsidiaries are connected to this center.

Executive management of the parent corporation is wondering which of the following two actions should be taken with respect to Schneider Frozen Foods: (1) keep its present data processing equipment and acquire a slow-speed remote terminal for access to the parent corporation's computing center or (2) sell its present data processing equipment and acquire a high-speed remote terminal for access to the parent corporation's computing center.

The management consulting firm with which you are associated was asked by executive management of the parent corporation to make a high-point review of Schneider Frozen Foods' operations and to recommend which of the above two courses of action should be taken. In addition, the management consulting firm was asked (1) to examine the present inventory control activities and sales analysis reporting procedures and (2) to design a new information system that will more effectively cope with these aspects of Schneider Frozen Foods' operations.

You were assigned to this engagement and have made the following notes on the company and its operations.

The Company

Schneider Frozen Foods, Inc., is a general wholesaler for frozen foods in the midsouth area and has an annual sales volume of approximately $14,000,000. The company's assets include major warehouse storage facilities, controlled zero temperature storage rooms, air-cooled storage rooms, and refrigerated trucks (at present, there are 20 such trucks). The company has 12 salesmen and employs 150 other personnel.

The inventory turnover rate at Schneider Frozen Foods has averaged 10 times a year, while the frozen food industry information would suggest that the inventory turnover rate should be between 13 and 23 times a year. According to the frozen food industry information a given frozen food wholesaler's inventory turnover rate would vary between these two representative points, based upon the retail-institutional relationship of the given wholesalers' customers. If most of the customers are classified as "retail," then a high inventory turnover rate would be expected. On the other hand, if there are many customers classified as "institutional," then a lower inventory turnover would be expected.

As suggested by the previous comments, a frozen food wholesaler has two types of customers. The retail grouping includes the typical grocery store as well as the chain grocery store. The retail grouping is the dominant grouping of customers and will generally include from 60 to 90 percent of the customers. The institutional grouping includes governmental agencies, military institutions, public and private schools, universities, hospitals, hotels, motels, restaurants, company cafeterias, and airline food operations.

Inventory Activities

Schneider Frozen Foods handles 940 different items. The reason for such a large number of line items is that the company has to maintain, for all practical purposes, two inventories. The 10-, 12-, and 16-ounce packages of vegetables are for the retail customer, while the 2-, 2.5-, and 3-pound packages of vegetables are for the institutional customer. This same situation exists for other items in inventory; the institutional customer always prefers the large, economy package with a plain wrapper. The retail customer prefers the small package with a highly decorative wrapper.

At Schneider Frozen Foods, the inventories for the two groups are physically separated in the respective storage facilities. In addition, the perpetual inventory records are separately maintained.

The company has an IBM 1440 system with additional storage facilities. The perpetual inventory records for both the retail and the institutional items are maintained in this data processing system. Quarterly, a physical inventory count is performed for all items in inventory. The results are compared with the perpetual inventory records, and significant deviations are rechecked. When necessary, the perpetual inventory records are adjusted to reflect the actual number of items on hand.

The data processing system provides a daily inventory stock status report for all retail items and a weekly inventory stock status report for all institutional items. In both cases, the inventory stock status report shows (1) identification code of inventory item, (2) description of item, (3) number of units on hand, (4) number of units on order, and (5) the "minimum" inventory level. This latter amount is computed monthly and represents the previous month's sales.

The purchasing manager uses the inventory stock status report as a guide in determining what items should be purchased. The resulting purchasing orders are not prepared by the data processing system but are manually typed by a clerk in the purchasing office.

From statistical information, you observe that there are significant differences in (1) the per-unit selling price of items in inventory, varying from a few cents per unit to $25 per unit, (2) the dollar volume of sales, (3) the frequency with which certain items are sold, and (4) the selling price-cost relationship. There are two aspects of this latter observation. First, the selling price-cost relationship varies not only between major groups of items in inventory, but also between the individual items within a group. (The frozen food wholesale operations are highly competitive, and the marketing strategy is to have loss leaders as well as to have varying markups on items within the same product group.) Second, in the case of institutional sales, the selling price for each item is at a negotiated price. Therefore, on a given day the actual sales price of an institutional item in inventory may vary completely between each customer.

Sales Activities

Ninety-five percent of all sales orders are telephoned by a salesman or customer to the home office of Schneider Frozen Foods. In the remaining cases the salesman brings the orders to the home office. The procedures followed in processing a sales order are different, depending on whether it is a retail customer or an institutional customer.

If the order is for a retail customer, a master preprinted form is used for recording the details of the sale. This form is immediately sent to data processing where a punched card is prepared for each item ordered by the customer. All customers and stock items have been previously assigned identification numbers. All inventory details are stored on magnetic disks in the IBM 1440 computer system. Thus, after the above punched card has been prepared for each item ordered, the cards are processed through the computer system and the inventory is reduced by the quantity of each ordered item.

The customers' names and addresses are also permanently carried on magnetic disks within the IBM 1440 computer system. In the case of retail customers, the selling price for each item is predetermined; thus, the magnetic disks also contain the product identification number and selling price for each item. With this combined information available, the computer system can prepare the complete sales invoice.

Today's retail sales orders are filled tonight and are shipped to the customer tomorrow. Therefore, while the data processing group is handling the daily retail sales orders, it is also accumulating the total number of each line item that is needed for filling that day's sales orders. At the appropriate cutoff point, a print out of these inventory items is prepared by the computer system, and copies of this report are sent to the order-filling department and to the control desk.

Schneider Frozen Foods' warehouse facilities are multistory, and different items in inventory must be maintained in different controlled-temperature rooms. During the early evening, workers will transfer the number of items requested by the above report to the order filling area. Here, each sales order is filled, and the designated items are loaded onto a specified refrigerated truck.

To complete the physical flow cycle, during the day, workers will unload the new shipments of stock and will place these units in the appropriate, predetermined storage locations.

As indicated previously, one copy of the sales invoice is used by the order-filling group. Other copies go to the control and shipping desk. Two copies of the sales invoice are given to the truck driver: one copy is to be signed by the customer as confirmation of delivery and returned to the home office, the second copy is given to the customer for his use as a receiving report. Another copy is used by the control group to notify a clerk in the data processing room that the sales invoice can be mailed to the retail customer. Some retail customers may purchase on a cash basis only; thus, the truck driver collects from these customers at the time of delivery.

If the sales order is for an institutional customer, a special sales order form is used which contains the necessary carbons for preparing five copies. Different copies of this handwritten sales order are used by the order-filling group, by the control desk, by the truck driver (two copies used in the same manner as specified for retail customers), and by the data processing group.

Frequently, there are substitutions of items on institutional sales. Therefore, the original handwritten sales order is marked up by the order-filling group. Subsequently, the other copies are also changed. The control group will send a corrected copy of the sales order to data processing. Here, a punched card is prepared for each item on the sales order.

Before the keypunch operator is given the marked-up copy of the sales order, a control manager has written on the document the appropriate price per unit *for this customer*.

Once this appropriate information has been processed into the computer system, sales invoices are prepared by the computer, and the accounts receivable balances are updated to reflect these new sales orders.

Reports

Separate reports are prepared for the retail customers and the institutional customers. The following three reports are prepared daily for both groups. First, the daily balance run is prepared as a control procedure which indicates each item per sales order. Second, the daily sales register shows, as a single line, the total information for each sales order. Third, the daily sales register recap lists, as a single line, the cumulative information for a given salesman. This information would be a summary of all the sales invoices identified with a given salesman. Since each salesman has an assigned territory, these two classifications are identical. This latter report, the daily sales register recap, contains totals for each sales district. The information included in these three reports are strictly sales statistics.

Twice a month, the credit manager is given a report of the overdue accounts receivable. The report presents an aging of such delinquent accounts.

The data processing system also provides inventory stock status reports, which have been previously discussed.

REQUIRED:

1. Evaluate the present information systems. Be specific in your comments.
2. Should Schneider Frozen Foods acquire a slow-speed remote terminal or a high-speed remote terminal? Indicate your overall recommendation on this point to the parent corporation's management.
3. Based on the information in this case, sketch a new information system that might be used at Schneider Frozen Foods. Explain in detail your proposed information system.

CHAPTER **12**

Sales Analysis and Credit Control Information System*

THE PREVIOUS CHAPTER emphasized the marketing information dimensions of customer identification numbers, inventory identification numbers, cost accounting classification systems, and financial accounting classification systems. In these areas, the systems analyst is designing a coding pattern so that these inputs into the management information system can be resorted and used in the most advantageous manner by marketing management.

The focus of the current chapter is different. Although the systems analyst is studying the information collection and processing activities within the organization, he is not limiting his recommendations to developing appropriate coding patterns for processing transactions. Instead, the systems analyst is advocating that other statistical information on sales invoices and documents as well as customer payment experience information in the accounts receivable files should be available for retrieval.

In other words, accounting records, documents, and files contain a substantial amount of information about a given business organization's customers. In fact, it is possible to construct a "profile" of the typical customer based on an analysis of these internal sources of data.

Certain large corporations in select markets have made extensive

---

* The author is indebted to William P. Boggess for many of the ideas presented in this chapter. Mr. Boggess did extensive basic research on the topic of scientific sales analysis and credit control, and he discussed his findings with the author. Mr. Boggess is currently an independent management consultant and was formerly a manager in administrative services at the Chicago office of Arthur Andersen & Co.

studies of customer characteristics based upon their internal accounting records, documents, and files. The possible benefits from understanding customer characteristics permeate all aspects of the business process from determining *which* products should be advertised in *what* manner to *which* groups of customers, to determining the actual payment behavior for each group of customers.

This chapter examines two applications based on knowledge regarding customer characteristics: (1) credit management and control and (2) product demand and advertising management. A special information network is presented for handling the information requirements associated with these business activities.

Although the general model that is described is for a hypothetical business organization in a given environment, modified versions of this general model have been successfully applied in several different types of market situations. In the interest of emphasizing the more extensive application of this general model, the first part of this discussion contains a brief description of two exogenous changes in the overall business environment. Following this discussion of environmental changes, the two applications cited above are examined— (1) credit management and control and (2) product demand and advertising management.

Environmental Changes

In addition to the four movements cited in the first chapter of this book—advancements in behavioral science, developments in electronic computers and communication equipment, developments in mathematical tools and techniques, and the application of scientific method to the study of business—two other significant changes have occurred in the business environment during recent years which have a direct influence on marketing operations. First, increases in productivity and technological changes have created an environment in which production costs represent a minor portion of the sales dollar, while distribution costs represents the dominant portion of the sales dollar. This change has not been static, but annually the distribution costs have assumed an increasingly important position.

Second, there has been a change in the nature of doing business. Credit and charge sales have become common practices, rather than being the exception. Throughout the economy, installment credit sales have rapidly expanded, and management of installment credit sales has become an important function of business management.

For example, since World War II, the total outstanding consumer credit grew from $5.1 billion as of December 31, 1944, to $113.2 billion as of December 31, 1968. This dynamic growth in consumer credit occurred in all types of operations, as indicated by the following schedule of selected data from the U.S. Department of Commerce, Office of Business Economics publications.

FIGURE 12.1
Selected Data on Consumer Credit

Consumer Credit	End of Year (Millions of Dollars)					
	1944	*1950*	*1960*	*1964*	*1967*	*1968*
Total outstanding	*5,111*	*21,471*	*56,028*	*76,810*	*102,132*	*113,191*
Total installment credit	*2,176*	*14,703*	*42,832*	*59,397*	*80,926*	*89,890*
Automobile paper	397	6,074	17,688	24,521	30,724	34,130
Other consumer goods paper ...	791	4,799	11,525	15,303	22,395	24,899
Repairs and modernizations	119	1,016	3,139	3,502	3,789	3,925
Personal loans	869	2,814	10,480	16,071	24,018	26,936
Total noninstallment credit	*2,935*	*6,768*	*13,196*	*17,413*	*21,206*	*23,301*
Single-payment loans	624	1,821	4,507	6,473	8,428	9,138
Charge accounts	1,517	3,367	5,329	6,300	6,968	7,755
Service credit	794	1,580	3,360	4,640	5,810	6,408

SOURCES: *Business Statistics 1963 Edition* (a supplement to the *Survey of Current Business*), pp. 91–92, *Survey of Current Business*, Vol. XLV (March, 1965), S–17 and S–18, and *Survey of Current Business*, Vol. XLIX (May, 1969), S–17.

For comparison purposes, the gross national product for 1944 was $211.4 billion, while the gross national product for 1968 was $860.6 billion.[1] If the total outstanding consumer credit had changed in the same proportion as the change in the gross national product, the 1968 consumer credit total would have been approximately $20.8 billion instead of $113.2 billion.

Part of this increase in consumer credit is attributable to the increase in population, but, of course, the primary increase is believed by us to represent a change in consumer buying habits.

Currently, the managements of many diverse business organizations are recognizing the fact that they are in an environment where most of the sales dollar is composed of distribution costs, rather than production costs. Therefore, in the maximum employment of distribution cost dollars, management is beginning to employ new marketing techniques.

------

[1] *Business Statistics 1963 Edition* (a supplement to the *Survey of Current Business*) , p. 3, and *Survey of Current Business,* Vol. XLIX (May, 1969) , S–1.

The extension of consumer credit is one of these marketing techniques that some business organizations have only recently begun to employ. This marketing technique has now been so widely used that the extension of consumer credit has become a major function of business, even for those business organizations not traditionally engaged in the "finance business."

For example, a small manufacturer of consumer goods was experiencing a declining net profit rate on a substantially increasing volume of sales. Currently, the manufacturing company was operating at about 80 percent of capacity. After studying the market situation and the cost picture, the president of this manufacturing company decided to operate at full capacity (thus spreading the fixed costs over more units of output) and to sell these additional consumer goods by increased advertising efforts and by installment credit sales.

The president decided that his company would sell to any purchaser who could make the down payment (which amounted to approximately 20 percent of the selling price), since this down payment almost equaled the total direct material and direct labor costs embodied in the finished goods. A year later, the president comments that his company has made a substantial profit from consumer sales, even though the noncollectible accounts have been approximately 10 percent of the total installment sales. The president continues: "To some extent, we have changed the nature of our business. Much of our profit has been made from consumer credit. It is almost as though the manufacturing facilities existed so that we could produce a product that we could sell on credit."

The above example is not an isolated case. Many small manufacturing companies with unused capacity are discovering that consumer installment sales can be a profitable method of expanding sales volume. The contribution to margin is high on these additional units, and the carrying charges will typically more than offset the normal loss from noncollectible accounts.

While the extension of consumer credit has only recently become a major function of business in numerous business organizations, it has always been a major function of business in a select group of large corporations. Furthermore, from recent studies of business operations, it would appear that credit management will be an increasingly important function in the future.

Credit Management and Control

Credit managers are generally aware of the nature of high-risk applicants. They have either analyzed or observed significant differences in several basic personal characteristics between "good" and "bad" risks. Such characteristics as marital status, home ownership, automobile ownership, age, occupation, and so forth may be more or less prevalent in the two basic classes of credit risk. One analysis of a sample of good and bad accounts revealed the magnitude of these differences, as indicated by Figure 12.2.

FIGURE 12.2

Profiles of Good and Bad Risks*

		Percent	
Characteristics of Applicant	*Good*	*Bad*	*Difference*
1. Married	91.2	87.0	4.2
2. Owns automobile	81.8	69.2	12.6
3. Owns home	81.6	43.8	37.8
4. Less than 4 children	85.1	80.2	4.9
5. Age 35 or over	96.9	89.4	7.5
6. At present address 3 years or more	91.9	71.2	20.7
7. Male employed with present company 3 years or more	74.3	58.6	15.7
8. Has bank reference	93.7	70.5	23.2
9. Has telephone	97.6	92.1	5.5
10. Has a business address	62.5	39.6	22.9

* These values are for illustration purposes only. The "real values" are the proprietary interest of the company performing this analysis and are not available for public disclosure.

There is a significant difference in the occurrence of each characteristic, as indicated by Figure 12.2. It is certainly reasonable to expect that the poorer risks would tend to possess these characteristics less frequently. However, experience has shown that the relative importance of each of these characteristics cannot be predicted accurately from this type of analysis.

Some characteristics tend to occur together or have a high degree of correlation, in which case these correlated characteristics should have the same relative importance. On the other hand, there are certain combinations of characteristics forming a unique set which is highly correlated with bad risks. If it were possible to evaluate all possible combinations of these characteristics, it might be possible to select those combinations which have the greatest accuracy in predicting poor risks.

Unfortunately, the statistical work required to test all potential combinations of these 10 characteristics would be substantial. Actually, there are many more than these 10 characteristics to be considered, and the number of combinations of characteristics would grow accordingly. Determining which of a hundred or so characteristics are the most significant and which combinations are best for predicting credit risks would be a staggering task if each potential combination of customer characteristics were tested separately.

If the above approach were followed, eventually all combinations of characteristics would be identified, and each combination would be assigned a value to indicate its relative position on a continuum between the two extreme positions: bad risk and good risk. With a hundred characteristics, the number of combinations would be unwieldy from the standpoint of a clerk comparing the combination of a given prospective customer with this tremendous list of combinations in order that the clerk can classify the applicant.

Establishing the Credit Rating System

Because of the unwieldy nature of the "combination approach," another statistical technique is followed for coping with the hundred or so characteristics. Stepwise multiple regression or, more specifically, stepwise discriminant analysis is used. The computer program covering this latter technique is designed so that the most important characteristics are selected in the order of their statistical significance, and the relative weight of each factor is determined by this computer program.

Multiple Regression Analysis. The concepts of multiple regression analysis are explained in several basic references, including any standard statistical reference.[2] This statistical technique has received notable use in many scientific and practical endeavors.

In the simplest application, multiple regression analysis is a method for developing a linear (first degree) equation relating a single dependent variable to two or more independent variables.

---

[2] For example, see Samuel B. Richmond, "Regression and Correlation Analysis," *Statistical Analysis* (2d ed.; New York: Ronald Press Co., 1964), pp. 424–72.

The following example illustrates a "regression equation" for the 10 characteristics presented in Figure 12.2.

$$Y = a + b_1X_1 + b_2X_2 + b_3X_3 + b_4X_4 \ldots + b_{10}X_{10}$$

where

$X_1 =$ Married or not (use "1" for "yes"; use "0" for "no")
$X_2 =$ Owns automobile or not (use "1" for "yes"; use "0" for "no")

. . .

$X_{10} =$ Has a business address or not (use "1" for "yes"; use "0" for "no")
$b_1 =$ Coefficient or multiplier for the first independent variable
$b_2 =$ Coefficient or multiplier for the second independent variable

. . .

$b_{10} =$ Coefficient or multiplier for the tenth independent variable

In the above example, the coefficients are the unknowns. The stepwise multiple regression program for the computer must determine the appropriate degree of emphasis that each independent variable should possess. This determination is accomplished by entering into the computer system numerous regression equations, where each equation represents the "yes" and "no" answers of a given customer or applicant to the 10 characteristics. The computer program will evaluate these numerous regression equations and will determine the coefficients that should be assigned to the general regression equation.

Discriminant Analysis. A special type of multiple regression analysis is called "discriminant analysis." In the simplest case, the objective of discriminant analysis is to compute weights as before (that is, to determine the coefficients) but only for purposes of distinguishing between the two types of accounts (or any finite number of classes of accounts), instead of predicting an individual general regression equation. This latter equation theoretically assumes an infinite number of values.

The discriminant analysis technique is useful because it is not always possible to have a very detailed breakdown by grades of actual credit ratings. Therefore, a "good" and "bad" breakdown is a simplification, although in theory it could be expanded to include more categories, such as "good," "fairly good," "medium," "fairly bad," and "bad." (Some business organizations using this technique for credit control have found it beneficial to use four to seven categories, rather than the simple "good" and "bad" groups.) However, for purposes of illustration, only the two classes are considered.

In summary, discriminant analysis is used not only for determining the most significant customer characteristics, but also for establishing the relative weight for each customer characteristic. The sum of the weights or the scores assigned to each prospective customer's application form (on the basis of the characteristics the applicant possesses) would determine the credit rating for the applicant. The higher the score, the higher the credit rating, and the better the risk.

Shifts in Weights of Characteristics. The coefficients assigned to each characteristic change by time period. For example, Figure 12.3

FIGURE 12.3
Monitoring the Change in Profiles

Characteristics of Applicant	Credit Rating Points Allowed				
	19x1	*19x2*	*19x3*	*19x4*	*19x5*
1. Married	6	7	7	9	?
2. Owns automobile	6	5	5	7	?
3. Owns home	19	21	18	20	?
4. Less than 4 children	11	9	10	9	?
5. Age 35 or over	8	8	9	8	?
6. At present address 3 years or more	12	14	13	14	?
7. Male employed with present company 3 years or more	7	6	8	5	?
8. Has bank reference.....................	26	24	25	23	?
9. Has telephone	5	6	5	5	?
10. Has a business address	16*	15*	16*	17*	?*
Total	100	100	100	100	100

* Bonus points, thus the maximum number of points equals 100 plus the points assigned for characteristic No. 10.

shows the shifting emphasis on coefficients that exist among the 10 characteristics presented in Figure 12.2. Because of these changing tendencies, it is necessary to periodically test and evaluate the credit rating system to see if a thorough study is required. In other words, should a large sample of applicants be subjected to stepwise discriminant analysis?

Selection of Relevant Characteristics. The previous discussion has omitted an important consideration. A prospective customer's application form may contain a hundred or so separate characteristics. However, many of these characteristics do not have any statistical significance in terms of predicting "good" and "bad" credit risk. In addition, there are many groupings of characteristics that have the same statistical significance, and these correlated characteristics can be indicated by a single factor.

Therefore, the stepwise discriminant analysis is really being used to select from the hundred or so characteristics that small group of characteristics (for example, a dozen) which will statistically differentiate between "good" and "bad" credit risks. Not only do the relative weights of these differentiating characteristics shift through time (as illustrated by Figure 12.3), but the characteristics selected based on their statistical significance also change through time.

Illustration of Credit Rating Procedures. Following is an example of applying the above technique. In a given business organization, sufficient studies have been conducted to give a high degree of reliance to the credit rating system, and a credit rating has been established for each applicant in a sample of 34,650 applicants. Figure 12.4 presents a schedule of the number of good and bad risks by each credit rating.

For purposes of illustration, assume that the profit from each good risk is $150 and that the loss from each bad risk is $100. Figure 12.5 compares the profit and loss from accepting all applicants within each credit rating class range. This exhibit indicates that the class range for which 50 is the midpoint (the interval from 45.0 to 54.9) has the highest cumulative return, if the minimum credit rating is

FIGURE 12.4
Good and Bad Risks by Credit Rating

Credit Rating (Midpoint of Class)	Good Risk Applicants		Bad Risk Applicants	
	Number	*Cumulative*	*Number*	*Cumulative*
10	0	0	1,250	1,250
20	0	0	2,500	3,750
30	700	700	3,000	6,750
40	1,700	2,400	2,900	9,650
50	4,300	6,700	1,800	11,450
60	6,000	12,700	700	12,150
70	5,800	18,500	0	12,150
80	3,100	21,600	0	12,150
90	900	22,500	0	12,150
100	0	22,500	0	12,150

FIGURE 12.5

Cumulative Profit by Minimum Credit Rating

Credit Rating (Midpoint of Class)	Good Risk Profit*	Bad Risk Loss†	Net Return	Cumulative Return if Minimum Credit Rating Is Lower Limit of Class‡
10	0	$125,000	($125,000)	$2,160,000
20	0	250,000	(250,000)	2,285,000
30	$105,000	300,000	(195,000)	2,535,000
40	255,000	290,000	(35,000)	2,730,000
50	645,000	180,000	465,000	2,765,000
60	900,000	70,000	830,000	2,300,000
70	870,000	0	870,000	1,470,000
80	465,000	0	465,000	600,000
90	135,000	0	135,000	135,000
100	0	0	0	0
	$3,375,000	$1,215,000	$2,160,000	

* $150 multiplied by the number of applicants in each class per Figure 12.4. The total of $3,375,000 equals 22,500 "good" applicants multiplied by $150 profit per applicant.
† $100 multiplied by the number of applicants in each class per Figure 12.4. The total of $1,215,000 equals 12,500 "bad" applicants multiplied by $100 loss per applicant.
‡ If the 34,650 applicants were accepted, the net return would be $2,160,000 ($3,375,000 profit less the $1,215,000 loss). If the minimum credit rating is set so that all applicants in Class 10 are eliminated, then the cumulative return would be increased by the amount of the net loss from Class 10 ($2,160,000 cumulative return plus $125,000 loss for Class 10 equals $2,285,000 cumulative return for Class 20). By repeating this procedure, the data for this column are determined.

the lower limit of this class. However, if this were a real situation, an analysis would be made of all items in Class 40 and Class 50 for the purpose of determining the slope of these lines. Since the "good risk" line is rising rapidly while the "bad risk" line is falling slowly, and since the profit is $150 per good risk while the loss is $100 per bad risk, the overall effect is that a minimum credit rating of approximately 43 will generate the highest return of $2,800,000.

The Credit Management and Control Screen. The previous discussion has explained the procedures involved in establishing a credit rating system. Once the credit rating points have been specified for a given time period and the minimum "acceptable" point has been determined, then the overall credit management and control procedure becomes a clerical task. As credit applications are received, each application is scored on the basis of the statistical point system. Next, each application score is examined, and if the score is above the minimum acceptable point, the application is accepted. If the score is below the minimum acceptable point, the application is rejected.

This process of scoring each credit application and comparing each application score with the minimum acceptable point is referred to as the "credit management and control screen." In other words, this is the practical extension of knowledge regarding customer characteristics to the task of selecting and rejecting credit applications.

The Basic Concept. Credit management and control is a systems concept designed to assist credit management in achieving maximum profits and is composed of four sequential and related management action phases: (1) monitor and report, (2) analyze and test, (3) determine policies, and (4) implement policy changes. Figure 12.6 illustrates this credit management and control cycle.

The credit management and control concept is similar to the "process control cycle" of a closed loop computer-controlled manufacturing process.

For example, through special electronic, mechanical, and other measuring devices, the credit management and control process is monitored by the computer. The computer "senses" the data inflow and "records" pertinent data for other uses as well as maintaining a log of the process. Through predetermined logic and mathematical formulations, the computer "analyzes" the data it has monitored, then "calculates" the necessary changes or improvements in the different parts of the process.[3] After calculation, the computer auto-

FIGURE 12.6
Credit Management and Control Cycle

_____

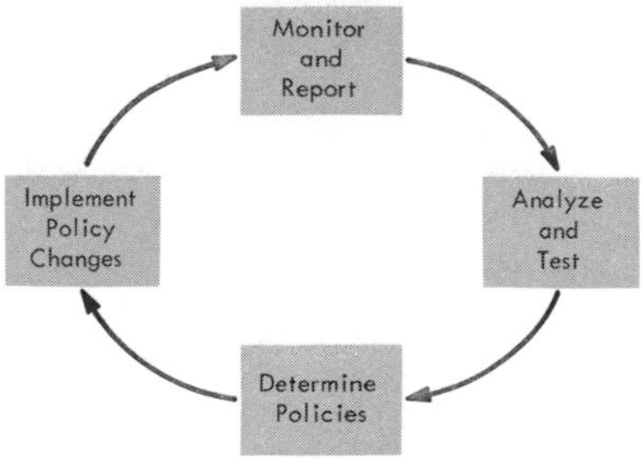

[3] Typical "monitoring" indices are "average credit ratings accepted," "percent refused business," "percent accounts 90 days + overdue," "percent collected of amount due current," and so forth. Collection indices are the key to the effectiveness of credit policies, and very frequently these early indications can be used to forecast profits. Review and analysis of these indices plus good credit management should provide the foundation for control. Furthermore, this system permits the credit manager to experiment with various collection techniques.

matically "sets controls" to effect the improvements, and the cycle repeats.

Obviously, this is a grossly oversimplified description, but it does serve to demonstrate the interrelated control concepts in the credit management and control cycle. The principal difference between the process control cycle and the credit management and control cycle is that the latter process is not automatic but employs management judgment to execute each major phase of the cycle. However, the credit management and control cycle is very similar to the closed loop control system in that it employs measures of the credit process in order to determine the need for action.

Extensions from Basic Model. The credit management and control process is similar to inventory control procedures in that emphasis is given to the heterogeneity of the mass. But instead of specifying control procedures and reorder points for each class of inventory (the ABC Method), the credit management and control system attempts to sort and resort credit applications into several groups for administration purposes. For example, Figure 12.7 shows the relation of dunning procedures to credit reference.

FIGURE 12.7

Relation of Dunning Method to Credit Rating

Credit Rating of Customer	*Dunning Procedure*
High, Group A	Eliminate all Group A accounts from the automatic dunning procedures; handle on an exception basis
Good, Group B	Group B accounts are dunned after missing two payments; handled automatically by the computer
Medium, Group C	Group C accounts are dunned when the account becomes 45 days overdue; handled automatically by the computer
Low, Group D	Group D accounts are dunned when the account becomes 30 days overdue; handled automatically by the computer

Not only will the initial dunning procedures vary by the credit rating of the customer, but the follow-up procedures will also vary by this rating. For example, a Group D account might be dunned on a monthly basis, and if the account becomes six months past due, the account might be transferred to a collection agency. On the other hand, a Group A or Group B account would probably never be transferred to a collection agency; instead, the company would attempt to collect all Group A and Group B delinquent accounts, if and when they occur.

Product Demand and Advertising Management

The source data upon which the credit management and control system in our example operated included a hundred or more prospective customer characteristics for each applicant selected for the sample file. These data were keypunched for inclusion in the computer system, which applied a stepwise discriminant analysis technique for determining the significant characteristics and the weight for each selected characteristic.

Since this mass of data is already keypunched, the alternative cost of using these data is low. These characteristics were subjected to another multiple regression analysis based on the product or products being requested by the applicant. As a result of this procedure, a profile of demand for each product was determined.

With the insights provided by these profiles, marketing management integrated its advertising program with the profile of demand for each product. Not only are these insights used for planning, but they are also useful for control and evaluation purposes. For example, through the accumulation of certain data, management can monitor the sales activity to see if the planned advertising results are being accomplished. If not, the appropriate management actions are taken.

In conclusion, the previous discussion of using customer characteristics in (1) credit management and control and (2) product demand and advertising management are examples of some of the integrated applications that have been successfully used in some business organizations in select markets. The case study at the end of this chapter indicates other applications.

TOPICS FOR CLASS DISCUSSION

1. The management of a major corporation engaged in consumer finance operations desired to establish a credit management and control screen without going through the time-consuming process of accumulating "good" and "bad" risk experience. Instead of using the stepwise discriminant analysis approach, corporate management held

a conference of its 20 "best" credit managers. Each credit manager was asked to draw upon his experience and to select from a list of customer characteristics those which he felt were the most significant. Next, each credit manager was asked to assign weights to the characteristics which he had selected, so that the combined total equaled 100 points. Finally, a composite was made of the 20 credit managers' separate reports, and a tentative credit rating point system was established. A test was made of this tentative credit rating point system, and an 80 percent degree of confidence was assigned to the tentative credit rating point system. Corporate management desires a 95 percent degree of confidence before it will use the credit rating point system.

REQUIRED:

Explain the different approaches that corporate management might use in achieving this desired degree of confidence, and evaluate each approach you suggest in terms of time, effort, and expense.

2. If the source of data for the sample file were exclusively the accounts receivable records and supporting documents, then the resulting credit management and control screen would tend to have an upward bias. Furthermore, the credit management and control screen would periodically have to be restudied.

REQUIRED:

Explain the statistical reasons for these comments.

CASE 12–1.   MIRREX COMPANY*

Management of the Mirrex Company has had several years of use of its specially designed customer experience retrieval system. The system has provided basic customer profile and collection information which has been useful for both marketing and collection purposes. A major question which management is currently facing is: what other relevant information can be developed from the system to aid in directing sales effort or in controlling other aspects of its operations?

Specifically, the retrieval system at present is being used for:

---

* The name and products of this business organization have been disguised; however, in all other respects, the information system and the descriptive setting surrounding this system are the same as those of the "real" company.

1. Basic management statistics on the quality of business
2. Identification of potentially fruitful areas for further investigation for improved credit and collection strategies
3. Testing suggested changes in policies or in credit and collection measures
4. Information on field sales performance in order to assist in keeping the quality of sales high
5. Forecasting, to the extent possible, probable cash flow measuring the cumulative effect of longer contracts and changes in collection performance

Even though the list of current uses of the retrieval system may seem impressive, the management team is convinced that the firm is only beginning to realize the benefits of the retrieval system. Management feels that after more insights have been gained through the retrieval of computer-stored information regarding customer experience it may be possible to state in a precise manner the differentiating characteristics of various types of customers. The relative weight of each of the differentiating characteristics could then be determined. When this is achieved, a computer program can be developed which would classify each customer by interpreting the customer's answers to certain questions. In other words, the computer would classify each customer by interpreting the responses on the application form which each customer must prepare before the sale is completed.

Moreover, because of the speed capacity of the computer, it would be possible to check periodically the customer experience to see if the previously determined classification labels are still valid. Are the special geographical and regional considerations still appropriate?

Or, from a different perspective, is it possible through an analysis of customer experience to identify exceptionally profitable geographical areas for a particular product? The full attainment of this condition would include consideration of customer characteristics (regarding type of item desired and payment behavior) and salesman characteristics (pertaining to type of customer and type of item sold). What other potential applications might be employed?

Members of management continue to examine the current retrieval system for customer experience to see what specific new applications can be adopted on a financially feasible basis. In making this examination, management reexamines the characteristics and operations of the firm.

The Company

Mirrex Company, Inc., a wholly owned subsidiary of a major corporation, designs, manufactures, and sells a wide variety of consumer goods with particular appeal to young, single women and to brides. These consumer goods include all types of kitchen utensils and silver. The Mirrex Company is one of the largest companies in this field of business, with both domestic and international operations.

Except for special arrangements with a few selected firms, all of the Mirrex Company's products are sold door-to-door (which management calls "direct selling"). There are 30,000 representatives in the United States and Canada selling Mirrex Company's products on either a full-time or part-time basis. Current sales volume is $125,-000,000, and management expects this volume to increase.

The average sale is somewhat over $200, and 90 percent of Mirrex Company's sales are time payment accounts. Therefore, the Mirrex Company has a rather substantial amount of effort being used to manage its accounts receivable accounts. In fact, the company has 650,000 open accounts, on the average, which must be balanced twice each month, billed once each month, and if they are delinquent, dunned once each month. On a correspondingly large scale is the task of writing commission checks to any one of the 30,000 representatives whenever they make a sale.

In addition to these considerations of sheer volume, there is the added aspect of growth. Over the past decade, the company and industry have enjoyed a dynamic expansion of sales. As a result of such growth, management has become even more keenly interested in effective ways of managing this rapidly increasing business.

The Integrated Management Information System

In coping with this dynamic growth of the firm over the past decade, a unique integrated management information system has been developed which employs a large computer with several extra magnetic tape units. Order processing, commission accounting, and accounts receivable applications were the initial procedures to be programmed for the computer system. Later, dunning procedures were also mechanized. Recently, the statistical sampling system was established, and this system made extensive use of the computer facilities. This latter application is the unique element of the total system and is the area which appears to have the greatest potential for the future.

The following discussion explains the unique aspects of this statistical sampling system, and the explanation consists of three parts: (1) statistical sampling method (including sample size, data accumulated, and processing procedures), (2) reporting, and (3) graphs.

Statistical Sampling Method

The total installment accounts receivable consists of 650,000 active accounts. For each account (or customer) there is a two-page application form which is prepared by the prospective customer at the time of the sale (see Exhibit A for the format of this application form). In addition to this sales contract (after the application has been approved by the company officials, it becomes a sales contract), there is the transaction experience for each customer (payment activity and so forth). Originally, a customer's history record was

EXHIBIT A

Customer Application Form

INFORMATION ON PURCHASER – PLEASE PRINT – ORDER WILL BE RETURNED UNLESS INFORMATION IS GIVEN IN FULL

Order Signed by
Mr/Mrs/Miss _____

Present
Address _____

Number and Street

City   State   Code

Give Previous Address if Less Than One Year at Present
Address _____

Age ___ ☐ Married   ☐ Single   ☐ Widowed   ☐ Divorced
Number of Years   Telephone
at Present Address ____ Number ____

☐ Owns Home   ☐ Rents   ☐ Other Explain

Ages of Children   Boys
Girls

Owns ☐   Yes
Auto ☐   No

HUSBAND'S
First Name _____
Employed By _____
Business Address _____
No. of Years with Company ____ Job Title ____

WIFE'S
First Name _____
Employed by _____
Business Address _____
No. of Years with Company ____ Job Title ____

BANK REFERENCE
Name of Bank _____
Address _____

☐ Checking Account
☐ Saving Account
☐ Loan

NEAREST RELATIVE
Name _____ Relationship _____
Address _____

BUSINESS REFERENCE
Name of Company _____
Address _____

☐ 30-Day Charge
☐ Time Payment

Name of Insured for Credit Name _____
Life if Other Than Person   Address _____
Signing Contract   Relationship _____
Age _____

Additional
Information
or Remarks _____

Additional
Information
or Remarks _____

I Hereby Certify That This Contract Sets Forth the Entire Agreement between the Purchaser and Me and That the Purchaser's Signature Is Genuine

Sales Representative's Signature

EXHIBIT A (*Continued*)

STATISTICAL DATA				HOME OFFICE USE ONLY
				ACCOUNT NUMBER
				THIS SPACE FOR HOME OFFICE USE ONLY
SHIP TO:	Mr. Mrs. Miss. _____			Special Instructions for Shipping or Terms: _____

This Order Is for the Following Products:		MIRREX COMPANY, INC.			
_____		Date of Order	Rec. with Order	Pay Monthly	First Payment Due Approximately
_____			$	$	☐ 30 Days ☐ 45 Days From Date of Order
Identification Number:	$	(Contract Terms)			
Tax (if any)		Signature _____ Mailing Address _____			
Total	$	Number and Street			
Less Down Payment					
Balance to Pay	$	City State Code County			
(Notice to Buyer)		Representative: _____ Please Print Name	Representative's Number: _____		

manually maintained to reflect the transaction experience. Now, an accounts receivable record is maintained in the magnetic tape unit for each customer. Thus, the transaction data regarding payment action are available for retrieval by the computer.

While management used the customer transaction data (which was retrieved, processed, and summarized by the computer), management recognized the desirability of having other statistical data to compare and correlate with the monetary data. Management assisted by the administrative service staff of a certified public accounting firm developed a statistical sampling system which made available for retrieval not only all the data on the sales contract (see Exhibit A) and transaction experience but also certain correlation analyses determined by comparing all the data available for a given customer.

Sample Size and Sample Selection. Each of the 650,000 active accounts has an account number. A program was developed for the computer to generate random numbers, and this program was designed to achieve nearly automatic sample selection with a small probability of bias. These features were necessary to avoid faulty samples while selecting large numbers of accounts at a low cost. This system of generating random numbers was used to select the sample accounts from the 650,000 file of accounts, and this sample (which was taken at the time the sampling program was initiated) represented all the outstanding accounts.

This same computer program is used daily to select samples from the *new* orders commissioned. The computer daily selects two samples from the new accounts: (1) a control sample and (2) a special sample. The special sample is used for special tests of alternative collection actions.

Data Accumulated for Sample Accounts. A 600-character sample file record was designed for use on magnetic tape which included forty characters available for new information. Following are some of the data included in this 600-character record:

1. Identification number and data regarding location of record on tape unit
2. Initial payment and sales information (date of sale, due date for first payment, monthly payment, total dollar contract, down payment, transportation, taxes, commission, and bonus)
3. Type of purchase (product identification and marketing arrangement—package purchase involving several products, etc.)
4. Sales organization (sales representative's identification number, division, region, district, state, county, and so forth)
5. Descriptive data regarding sales representative (representative's cumulative sales for specified period of time, pay, and so forth)
6. Customer characteristics (an exhaustive accumulation of the data contained on the application form as well as a report of the credit review[4]
7. Transaction history (an exhaustive report of the payment behavior of the customer)[4]
8. Collection action (several "characters" of space are reserved for full coverage of this action if and when it occurs)
9. Attorney action (the 600-character record has several spaces reserved for attorney information and attorney collection activity)

As indicated, this 600-character sample file record contains an exhaustive accumulation of the data on the sales contract and the data regarding the transaction experience for the customer. In addition, a special coding form was designed for the accumulation of

---

[4] A special coding form has been developed for extensive classification of customer characteristics and business transaction data.

interpretative data (statistical classification data) gained through an analysis of all of the customer experience data.

Processing Procedures.   Daily the computer selects from the new order accounts a sample, and a list is prepared of the new order accounts so elected. (This list is subsequently used in reconciliation and verification procedures.) Later, *as time permits,* the sales contract for each new order account (which has been selected) is pulled, and these data are keypunched for inclusion in the 600-character sample file record. As previously stated, a coding form has been prepared for use in the conversion of the data from the sales contract and other documents to the sample file maintained on magnetic tape.

The aggregate daily accounts included in the new order sample during any month are called the "monthly sample" accounts. These selected accounts are supposed to be representative of the new accounts for that month. A sample account file is opened on the magnetic tape for each selected account, and the customer experience with this account is periodically processed on tape for storage purposes. Once an account has been selected for inclusion in the sample, the account becomes part of the "monthly sample," and the data for this account (along with the other new accounts selected during that particular month) are monthly reported over the life of the sales contract.

From another perspective, there are 650,000 active customer accounts. Since each sales contract is for approximately 30 months, there are, on any given day, 30 different groupings of monthly sample accounts which collectively are supposed to be representative of the total (650,000 accounts). In other words, the accounts receivable accounts are identified by month and year of sale, and the accounts are segregated by these criteria. This identification is specified on all reports, and a separate series of reports is prepared for each group. Thus, on any reporting date, there are 30 detailed reports (one for each group) and a summary report to reflect the accounts included in all samples. As will be explained later in the discussion of reports, a statistical inference is made from the characteristics of the sample to the total mass that each sample represents, and each report contains columns for the sample and for the total group represented by the sample. The computer is programmed to make this statistical inference from the sample to the total mass for each item on each report.

At the end of the month, the aggregate accounts receivable information for the month for each customer that has been selected for inclusion in one of the 30 monthly samples is processed in detail to the 600-character sample file records on magnetic tape. The detailed accounts receivable information is already on tape; thus, the computer can process the transaction experience from the accounts receivable records to the sample file records. Some information regarding attorney action and collection activity is processed by clerks and subsequently keypunched for entry on magnetic tape.

In terms of time restraints, the daily selection of new accounts is the only critical item. The pulling of the sales contract for the account, the keypunching of these data, the opening of a 600-character sample file record, and the processing of data to this record can be performed on any day during the period—as time permits. Likewise, the monthly retrieval of detailed data regarding customer experience (transaction experience) from the accounts receivable files can be processed on a flexible basis.

Reports

Seven monthly reports are prepared to provide management with useful information on a regular basis, to assist in decisions on policy matters, and to provide guides in the administration of credit and collection actions. These seven reports make maximum utilization of the regular monthly computer runs (as it becomes apparent that additional information and analyses are required beyond these reports, special computer programs and other processing methods will have to be designed and initiated; however, the current reports are a by-product of the regular monthly computer runs) .

Report 1—New Order Sample File Detail Listing. This report lists each sampled account for the month and a print out of the coded data in the record. This report is intended to aid in checking sample information input and in reviewing account characteristics at a later date.

Report 2—Analysis of Current Status of Receivables. This monthly report breaks down sales contracts and receivables in a variety of summaries by product and in total, for each sample month to date. It is a comprehensive report on the condition of sales contracts outstanding and includes statistics on write-offs, attorney transfers, paid-in-full, paid ahead, paying on time, one to three months late, and so forth. The report contains a projection from the sample to the total for all contracts sold in a month. A report summarizing this information is issued to management monthly, which shows current and past month's condition by product and for all products.

Report 3—Projection of Collections by Month. The expected monthly cash revenue generated by new orders is projected in this monthly report. These projections facilitate comparison of actual collections per month to the collections required by terms for each product and in total. Similarly, net cash flow (collections minus variable costs) for each month can be estimated statistically.

Report 4—Summary of Collection Status by 90-Day Pattern and Section. This analysis is designed to help find the most effective tool to predict an account's collectivity from its early pattern of payment. Eight pay patterns are possible during the first 90 days of transaction history. If *P* means paid and *M* means missed payment, these 90-day patterns are as follows:

0.	*PPP*	4.	*MPP*
1.	*PPM*	5.	*MPM*
2.	*PMP*	6.	*MMP*
3.	*PMM*	7.	*MMM*

Management hopes that through this type of analysis it will be able to determine whether the 90-day report, for example, can be improved upon by earlier reports of a similar type. The report contains analyses on a geographic and ethnic section basis in the hope that some significant differences in collectibility by these characteristics will become apparent from a continuous examination of these data.

Report 5—Analysis of Sales from Statistical Sample. This monthly report summarizes product and total sales by geographic section (not restricted to sales area) and according to terms sold under, for example, "cash sales," "balance payable," and "terms." This information is primarily useful in the statistics department. It is an indicator of sample coverage and has potential as a barometer of future collections based on terms granted and where sold. The report includes information on sample size and percent of total, projected term sales, down payments, and statistical variance of all projections. All of these data are essential for projecting sample data to all accounts.

Report 6—Miscellaneous Totals and Analysis of Attorney Accounts. This monthly report provides statistical information for projecting and making special calculations. It includes information required to calculate variable product costs. A special calculation is made of the month's sample pay code and its statistical variance. The "pay code" is a sensitive indicator of performance and is essentially the ratio of the amount due to the amount actually paid to date. Study of this code should aid in forecasting collection experience.

The attorney analysis is intended to assist in evaluating ways to improve the net return from attorneys, such as improved timing of action. The report relates attorney collections to age when transferred, balance transferred, and company collection experience.

Report 7—Summary of New Account Characteristics. Since the ultimate desire is to relate customer characteristics to account performance, this summary of contract and other data is included. The information is used later in development of improved credit review and collection methods. In other words, this report summarizes current activity in the hope of providing historical data for analysis and correlation purposes which might be used in future time frames for some type of "scientific" credit review and collection method.

Graphs

The integrated management information system currently contains four graphs which highlight significant relationships of different aspects of customer experience.

Graph 1—Collectibility. Of key importance is the actual month-to-month and year-to-year relative collection experience. Current month collection percent data may directly indicate that the business situation has changed and that the firm's profits will eventually be affected, or the percent data may indicate changes in economic conditions that may require tighter credit and collection action. On the other hand, longer term collection trends are necessary as a base for judgment and policy decisions. For short-term history, a more sensitive collectibility statistic has been developed which considers only the current three months' collections against the terms of these same three months. This more sensitive collectibility measure is then augmented by year-to-date percent collected data, and these two groups of data are broken down into product and total collection data.

Graph 2—Cash Collections. Although percent collectibility data are useful for decision-making purposes, management should also be cognizant of the dollar value of the collectibility performance. For this purpose, a special graph of monthly projected cash collections has been prepared. These projections consider the sales volume, mix of products, and terms under which the products are sold. Based upon reasonable sales projections, this cash collection line on the graph can be extended beyond current experience. The incremental dollar significance of current collection performance will be determined by plotting actual dollars collected versus expected collections.

Graph 3—Net Cash Flow. Changes in product mix and sales levels have a significant effect on month-to-month cash position. For this reason, it is important to know net cash income and its fluctuations.

As a by-product of reporting new order samples and collection experience, the basic data are available within the computer system for the preparation of the forecasted net cash flow each month. This forecast considers the directly variable costs as being the most important, and these costs include such items as product costs, average commissions, taxes, transportation, and accessory expenditures.

Graph 4—Sales Volume and Forecast. This graph compares actual sales with forecasted sales on a month-by-month basis. The comparison is in terms of units of sales rather than in terms of dollar volume.

REQUIRED:

Submit a brief report to management which outlines in detail the possible additional uses that might be made of the computer retrieval system for customer experience.

PART V

MOVEMENT TOWARD A TOTAL INFORMATION SYSTEM

CHAPTER 13

Advanced Information Systems

IN AN EARLIER CHAPTER, we recognized that many management consultants use the terms "management information system" to refer to any data supporting network that is more complicated than a typical computer program. This same group of consultants will use the terms "advanced information system" and "total system" as labels, respectively, for an operating system and an information system. Thus, when a TYPE 2.5 information system or a TYPE 3 information system is being designed, these consultants are forced to create a new set of labels to represent these latter systems, such as "a series of large-scale, advanced management information systems operating in a real-time setting."

In our framework (see Chapter 3) an advanced information system was assigned a value of 10 on the scale of digits 1 to 10. Our hierarchy of networks included an operating system, an information system, and an advanced information system. While the label "total system" is not compatible with our framework, this label is frequently used by corporate management, and we should understand what is typically meant by these terms.

Therefore, in this chapter we will first examine the terms "total system." Next, we will analyze the characteristics of an advanced information system, and we will identify the general models of advanced information systems. Then, we will study the special coordinating and administering activities that are required in planning, designing, and implementing advanced information systems. Finally, we will briefly consider some of the common problems that must be resolved in creating such advanced information systems.

Total System

Management consultants frequently use the terms "total system" to indicate that most of the activities in a department or a division will be handled by a major group of computer equipment and communication facilities. Some of the activities may be handled on a manual basis; moreover, there may be only a limited degree of interface among the various subsystems. Thus, the terms "total system" do not necessarily suggest that the company possesses an integrated structure of operating systems, much less any higher order of networks.

About all the management consultants are really saying when they use the terms "total system" is that the overall information flows within the organizational unit have been identified, examined, and evaluated. Based on this scoping study, some of these information flows may be incorporated in newly created operating systems and information systems; however, these latter developments are not prerequisites for the existence of a "total system."

As we begin our examination of advanced information systems, it is helpful to employ some facets of this "total system" approach. Specifically, the inclusion of all information flows within an organizational unit as part of our analysis may encompass some information flows that cannot be efficiently handled by an advanced information system. These flows may be initially processed on a manual basis and then interfaced into the computer network. Through the coordination of manual operations and computer operations, the team of systems analysts may be able to accommodate certain planning activities that would otherwise not be encompassed in this network.

Characteristics of an Advanced Information System

An advanced information system is a large-scale, computer-based network with online communication facilities that supports the major decision-making activities in two or more departments within a corporation. This computer-based network may not initially encompass *each* information flow within these organizational units. Some manual operations may be required to handle special sets of transactions, but eventually there is an interface between the manual operations and the computer-based network.

While the online communication facilities were probably initially established for rapid processing of information, these communication devices are used for inquiring and retrieval purposes. The monitoring and inquiring phase in the TYPE 2.5 information system and in the TYPE 3 information system is indicative of the degree of management's interaction with common data bases and common data files in an advanced information system. Once this level of online interaction begins, then there is a gradual change in the overall nature of the decision-making function.

Many of the management activities represented by the coordination phase and the control phase in the TYPE 2, TYPE 2.5, and TYPE 3 information systems will tend to become routinized. Moreover, the administration and coordination of these activities will begin to be clustered around managers who are not involved in the long-range planning functions. As these extensions occur, there will eventually emerge a realignment of responsibilities, and this organizational change will have some impact on the arrangement of information flows within the large-scale, computer-based network.

At this point, the overall network will begin to reflect two dominant orientations: a planning focus and a housekeeping focus. While these two orientations are interrelated, there are many distinct characteristics of each. When the overall network reaches the point that it encompasses a planning group and a housekeeping group, then we have the creation of a TYPE 4 information system. A general model of a TYPE 4 information system is presented in a subsequent section of this chapter.

The other major attribute in our definition of an advanced information system is that the network must support the major decision-making activities in *two or more departments.* Obviously, there will be many organizational problems inherent in such a network. Special attention is given later in this chapter to some of these organizational problems.

General Models of Advanced Information Systems

From the above statement of characteristics, we can impute a generalized model of an advanced information system. It will approach the point of containing two information systems, with some information flows between these information systems. Specifically, all of those major information flows with a high degree of predictability will be encompassed in a large, integrated production and operation, marketing, and financial management system. In essence, this integrated network will really be a housekeeping system. The other system will be a planning system, both for the unpredictable aspects of marketing and for the unpredictable aspects of the business organization's environment. The planning information system will be supported by an operating system containing a library for information storage and retrieval purposes. The overall advanced information system will be so designed that selected inputs for the housekeeping information system will be preselected for storage in the library of the planning information system.

Beyond these common characteristics, there are unique differences among the various types of advanced information systems, and these differentiating attributes can be effectively depicted by generalized models. In Chapter 11 we have already presented generalized models for two types of advanced information systems; these two advanced systems were the TYPE 2.5 information system and the TYPE 3 information system.

In reexamining these two general models, we should note particularly that the TYPE 3 information system contains many extensions from the TYPE 2.5 information system as well as some other features. For purposes of the present discussion, we might recall the six phases in the TYPE 3 information system:

1. Information gathering, classifying, and storage phase
2. Coordination phase
3. Planning phase
4. Systems processing phase
5. Monitoring and inquiring phase
6. Control phase

The latter phase—the control phase—was especially interesting in that the "human activities" operation in our flow chart provided us with a mechanism for illustrating multidata flows and multitime cycles within one overall system.

The TYPE 4 information system is based on extensions from the TYPE 3 information system plus other features. Figure 13.1 presents a generalized model of a TYPE 4 information system. We note that the TYPE 4 information system contains the same six phases as in the TYPE 3 information system plus the addition of a long-range planning phase. On closer examination, we observe that there are two control phases: control phase for TYPE 2.5 System and control phase

FIGURE 13.1

A Generalized Model of a TYPE 4 Information System

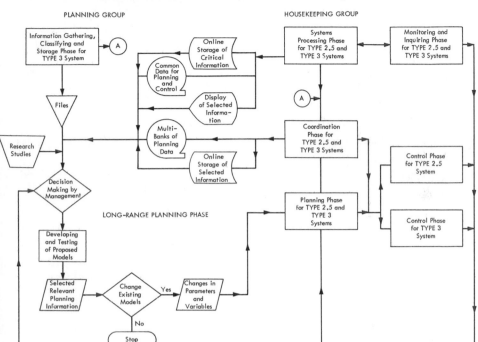

for TYPE 3 System. This means that the unique features of each of these two control phases are separately incorporated and maintained in the TYPE 4 information system.

The TYPE 4 information system clearly shows a planning group that is separate from a housekeeping group. Five of the six phases in the TYPE 3 information system are depicted as being part of the housekeeping group, and only the information gathering, classifying, and storage phase for the TYPE 3 information system is illustrated as being included in the planning group.

This overall arrangement suggests that the planning phases for the TYPE 2.5 information system and for the TYPE 3 information system are representative of short-term planning. The time frame of the overall cycle is for a limited period, such as week, two weeks, or a month. In contrast, the TYPE 4 information system might be for 12 months with the housekeeping group operating on a weekly, two weeks, or a monthly cycle within this 12-month period.

From an organizational standpoint, it is important to note where the information flows go from the long-range planning phase. Specifically, these flows connect the long-range planning phase with the short-term planning phase. These flows do not connect the coordination phase or the control phase with the long-range planning phase. Instead, *all information flows from the planning group to the housekeeping group are processed through the decision makers assigned to the short-term planning phase.* These latter decision makers have the overall planning and coordinating responsibilities for the housekeeping group. If they are to effectively perform these major responsibilities, all recommendations based on long-range planning information must be processed through them.

Long-Range Planning Phase. In reviewing the generalized models for the TYPE 2.5 and TYPE 3 information systems, we note that most of the common data banks for planning purposes are not connected to any decision makers. The expression "common data for other systems" and other similar phrases are used in these models to indicate that the decision makers who will respond to these data are located outside the TYPE 2.5 and the TYPE 3 information systems. In the TYPE 4 information system all of these common data files and common data banks are connected to the decision makers in the long-range planning phase.

In addition to this group of diverse inputs, special surveys and staff studies are performed by individuals assigned to the long-range planning group. Manual inputs into the TYPE 4 system are shown from these research studies.

The other activities included in the long-range planning phase consist of developing and testing models that simulate areas within the housekeeping group. As these models are examined and modified, new management science techniques may be incorporated into existing computer programs. The overall result of these efforts through time will be a gradual upgrading of existing computer programs as new management science techniques are developed and as the reliability and confidence in the data within the system improve.

The decision makers in the long-range planning phase perform another staff function. From the information flows that connect the housekeeping group with the planning group, we note that there is online monitoring of performance by the decision makers in the long-range planning phase. When special problems arise, the decision makers in the short-term planning phase will ask the decision makers in the long-range planning phase for a recommended course of action. This information will be processed from the planning group to the housekeeping group through the regular channel encompassed in this long-range planning phase.

Control Phases. As previously indicated, the TYPE 4 information system contains a TYPE 2.5 control phase and a TYPE 3 control phase. These two control phases must be separately maintained so that the unique features of each phase are not lost. Since the TYPE 4 system is designed to accommodate the major information flows in two or more departments, both the TYPE 2.5 and the TYPE 3 control phases are needed to handle the diverse and complex operations encompassed in this wide area. (It is suggested that the reader review the characteristics of each of these control phases as described in Chapter 11.)

Coordination and Administration of Advanced Information Systems

The Information Systems Coordinating Group was discussed in Chapter 4 as a corporate committee with responsibility for handling all policy issues that arise in planning and coordinating an information system. It is imperative that this type of committee exist when an advanced information system is being designed. Otherwise, the proposed system will not be able to support the major decision-making activities in two or more departments.

During the conceptual systems design phase for an advanced information system, attention is focused on the total set of decision-making activities that are to be supported by the proposed network. But, when the study team moves into the equipment selection and program design phase, different parts of this total network are separately considered. For example, if a TYPE 4 information system is being proposed, this system may contain a TYPE 2.5 information system, a TYPE 3 information system, and a TYPE 1 information system; in addition, there may be a series of supporting operating systems. When this is the case, then separate study teams may be established for each of these systems.

There are several inherent problems associated with any efforts to design an advanced information system. First, the overall project must be segmented into smaller parts if the program design phase is to be completed within a reasonable period of time. (Here, a two-year time interval would appear to be an upper limit.) Second, as soon as the overall project is segmented, then we run the risk of nonuniform and noncompatible subsystems. Third, there may be duplication of efforts when different study teams independently solve the same problem. Fourth, changes in the environment and in the organizational structure may force one study team to redefine this set of information flows while another study team continues to work on extensions from the former set of information flows. This latter situation results in a series of disjointed systems.

Accepting the premise that the overall project must be segmented during the program design phase, then management is concerned with how to overcome these problems. The answer is simple! We must establish some type of continuous dialogue among the study team directors so that through the communication process these pitfalls are avoided. Regularly scheduled weekly meetings of study team directors, frequent interim reports, and monthly meetings of all study team members are three approaches that have been used in coping with this continuous dialogue objective.

There are many other interest aspects in the coordination and administration of advanced information systems. Three of these aspects will be discussed in the remaining portion of this section. The first relates to code structures and data bases. When we are designing an information system, implementing an information system, and operating an information system, we are confronted with requests to establish or modify existing code structures. Frequently, there are many decision makers within the overall organization that are affected by any change in the code structure.

Therefore, when we have progressed to the program design phase for an advanced information system, it is strongly recommended that a Code Structure Identification and Management Committee be established to coordinate these interdepartmental code structures. This interdepartmental committee serves a useful coordinating function in managing the information flows in an advanced information system even after such a system has been implemented for a period of time.

In any type of advanced information system, there are common data bases and common data files being used by more than one department, and this arrangement necessarily poses a significant problem for management of these data bases and files. Decision makers in one department may desire to change or expand some portion of a code structure. While their request has merit, these individuals do not possess an overall perspective of the organization and the system so they can intelligently determine if the proposed change is in the best interest of the total organization. Therefore, some type of interdepartmental committee is needed to resolve this issue.

Code Structure Identification and Management Committee is one name used for this committee; other names are "Common Data Bases Management Committee," "Code Structure Management Committee," and "Data Management Committee." Since we are discussing the need for establishing such a committee during the program design phase for an advanced information system, we will use the name, "Code Structure Identification and Management Committee."

There are two long-run responsibilities for the Code Structure and Management Committee: (1) interdepartmental coordination of existing codes and (2) monitoring and administering changes to the coding systems. During the program design phase, this committee will also have the responsibility for (1) determining the areas to be included within each common data base, (2) specifying the contents and general code structure for each common data base, and (3) monitoring the detail code structure definitions that are developed by the various study teams for conformity with the overall plans. In addition to these coordinating and management activities, this committee must have overall responsibility for and supervision of common data bases. This latter responsibility may be partially performed by the information systems department, and a staff member in the information systems department may serve as the secretary for this committee.

The second aspect relates to staffing for these concurrent systems studies. During the program design phase we may have seven or eight different systems studies in progress. Assuming that we have six or seven members on each study team, then we are talking about a staff of 50 individuals who are working full-time on these studies. From a manpower standpoint, there may be insufficient human resources to staff all of these studies with personnel from the organization. This is one of the reasons that outside consultants are frequently engaged to perform segments of this work.

The third and last aspect relates to management training and development. When an advanced information system is being designed (and especially a TYPE 4 information system) , we tend to see a shifting of responsibilities within the organization eventually resulting in the formation of a planning group and a housekeeping group. Where this has occurred, the management training and development program assumes new dimensions.

Young executives are assigned to the planning group where they work as assistants on various model development projects. In designing and testing models, these individuals acquire a unique overview and perspective of the firm which is typically not possessed by any management personnel below the executive management level. In working with these models, these young executives also obtain a deep insight into the real organizational structure of the company and the goals and objectives of the organization.

These young executives are assigned to the housekeeping group for the purpose of gaining experience in the administrative function of supervising and working with people in carrying out department objectives. In this housekeeping group, all operating types of decisions are monitored by a complex of computer programs using predetermined programmed responses. When a problem occurs for which there is no programmed response (such as a policy question), the young executives in the housekeeping group will not attempt to answer the questions. Instead, the decision makers in the planning group will be asked to resolve the problem. In fact, some individuals within the planning group will be assigned the full-time task of responding to these unprogrammed situations.

If management were to concurrently consider the staffing problem and the management training and development program, then another approach might be created. Specifically, additional personnel in the user departments might be recruited instead of engaging management consultants. Some of these personnel might work full-time on systems studies, and subsequently assume full-time positions in a given user department. Since a consultant is paid at a higher rate than a regular employee, it is economically feasible to be overstaffed in the short run provided there is a normal turnover rate of personnel.

Common Problems

As previously explained, there is a need for continuous dialogue among the study team directors so that an integrated network of subsystems is created. Beyond this administrative problem, there are some common problems that must be resolved in designing advanced information systems. Two of these problems are cited below.

Communication Network. We defined an advanced information system as having online 'communication facilities which include monitoring and inquiring capabilities. This communication network must encompass all segments of the total organizational units that are to be serviced by the advanced information system. In a typical business organization this communication facility must provide a network for incorporating marketing management and planning operations, distribution operations, integrated inventory management and control operations, production and scheduling operations, and financial management operations. The personnel and manpower operations are usually encompassed as subsystems within the other operations (such as production and scheduling management).

If an isolated plant or a remote warehouse is not included in this communication network, then the advanced system immediately encounters a continuous source of pressures to modify the overall system. How will the inputs from these remote locations be integrated into the overall system? This can be accomplished by assigning this processing function to individuals that are part of the network, and the papers from these remote locations can be mailed to them. This type of modification may be initially appropriate; however, when is the volume of activities at these remote locations sufficient to merit their own facilities? The individuals at the remote locations will always be posing this question to management personnel from the home office.

During the past two years, the cost of remote terminals has been significantly reduced, and there are several new manufacturers offering a variety of communication equipment. There are still instances where it is not economically feasible that every remote warehouse can be included within the communication system. Specifically, the data transmission requirements cannot be accommodated by a simple touch-tone facility and the overall volume cannot justify any higher speed facility.

There is another dimension of the communication problem that should be examined, and the following case study is cited for purposes of illustrating this. A major corporation listed on the New York Stock Exchange had recently acquired three wholly-owned diversified subsidiaries. The parent corporation plus the three subsidiaries were all engaged in the manufacture and distribution of consumer goods. However, the marketing methods employed by each firm were different. Each firm had its own separate manufacturing facilities.

A large-scale computer was installed in a major metropolitan city to handle all of the data processing activities on a centralized basis for the parent corporation and the three subsidiaries. Twelve manufacturing plants were involved, some of which were over 1,000 miles from the centralized computer center. Daily, management at each plant would mail all sales invoices and production reports to the centralized computer center. At the computer center, inventory records were updated, invoices were prepared, and all other accounting operations were performed.

Various management groups within this large, corporate complex began to complain that they did not have timely information. In response, executive management of the parent corporation ordered an IBM 360 computer system.

At about this point, a change occurred in the members of the board of directors of the parent corporation. Immediately following this change, the executive vice president of the parent corporation and two senior vice presidents resigned. The new executive vice president, as one of his first tasks, asked a leading management consulting firm to review the total operations of the parent corporation and subsidiaries.

The management consultants, after extensive studies, reported that the primary concerns in the companies were associated with the lack of a communication network, not with data processing speed. It was recommended that the order for the IBM 360 computer system should not be cancelled, but that immediate attention should be given to the design and implementation of a communication network that would not only integrate the 12 production facilities with the centralized computer system, but would also connect the regional sales offices to this computer system.

Although the above description is the experience of one major corporation, if the details were slightly modified the description would apply equally to other major corporations. Information transmission systems have frequently not received the same attention given to information processing systems. This has frequently resulted in unbalanced information processing and information transmission activities.

Personnel Constraints.   In those companies with advanced information systems, the management process is different from the situation where there are only information systems. Specifically, if there is a planning group and a housekeeping group, the assignment of responsibilities to individuals will be different.

It is not unusual to find senior executives with 20 years of "housekeeping type of experience" who are unable to accept the creation of a planning group. Long-range planning is not part of the perspective of these individuals, and they will attempt to perpetuate the existing network. While these personnel constraints are not new considerations, they have prevented the establishment of advanced information systems in several organizations.

Summary

In a few business organizations in select industries, we find teams of systems analysts engaged in the design and implementation of advanced information systems. In a few cases a series of advanced information systems are concurrently being designed. Where this has occurred, we see a significant movement toward a total information system for the company. While overall progress has been made toward a total information system in a few companies, none of these companies has reached this position.

We defined an advanced information system as a large-scale, computer-based network with online communication facilities that supports the major decision-making activities in two or more departments within a corporation. The TYPE 2.5 and TYPE 3 information systems that were presented in Chapter 11 contained all the features of an advanced information system. In the current chapter, we focused our attention on the special attributes of a TYPE 4 information system.

The formal recognition of a planning group and a housekeeping group is one of the critical elements that differentiates a TYPE 4 information system from other advanced information systems. Our generalized model of a TYPE 4 system contained both a TYPE 2.5 control phase and a TYPE 3 control phase; thus, the unique characteristics of each of these systems were separately maintained.

Since an advanced information system supports decision makers in more than one department, there are organizational, administrative, and communication problems inherent in such a system. Some of the common problems encountered in design of such a system were identified. We indicated that a Code Structure Identification and

Management Committee had been established in some companies to cope with one of these problems, and this area of code structure will be further examined in the next chapter.

TOPICS FOR CLASS DISCUSSION

1. One common criticism of any movement toward advanced information systems is that the study team is attempting to automate the management decision process. Is the decision process in an advanced information automated? Explain your answer.

2. A TYPE 3 information system and a TYPE 4 information system continue to contain some manual operations. Identify each of these manual operations and explain the functions performed in each operation.

3. Differentiate between an information system and an advanced information system.

4. Executive management of the American Telephone and Telegraph Company is currently conducting extensive studies of various facets of the company's overall operations for the purpose of developing a series of highly integrated management information systems. The master project under which all of these studies are being coordinated is called "Business Information Systems."

REQUIRED:

Explain the difference between these "Business Information Systems" and a "total system."

5. The Cohen Manufacturing Company has five separate information systems: (1) an integrated profitability accounting and marketing management information system that operates on a daily basis, (2) an integrated inventory control, production control, and sales management information system that operates on a weekly cycle, (3) a responsibility accounting system that operates on a monthly cycle, (4) a financial accounting system that operates on a monthly basis, and (5) a planning information system that operates on a monthly basis.

REQUIRED:

Present a schematic diagram of these different information systems which clearly shows the different time frame of each cyle. Next, sketch a single information network which would incorporate all of these information systems. Explain how your proposed "total system" would operate.

6. Differentiate between the Information Systems Coordinating Group and the Code Structure Identification and Management Committee. Include in your explanation the organizational location of each committee.

7. One systems analyst made the following observation:

The task of applying the information systems approach to the development of a total system for a complex business organization is analogous to the relationship between the plan and the planning process. "The virtue is not in the plan, but in the planning." Likewise, the virtue is not in the attainment of a total system for a business organization, but in the application of the information systems approach to relating the total requirements for information with the data sources.

Do you concur with this observation? Interpret this observation as it relates to advanced information systems.

CASE 13–1. THE MEAD CORPORATION

The Mead Corporation is reported by various management consultants to have the most advanced information system in the paper industry and to have one of the most advanced computerized information systems in any major industrial firm. This present position is the result of many years of planning and effort on the part of system analysts, programmers, operation researchers, management consultants, and representatives from manufacturers of electronic computer equipment coupled with strong administrative support from Mead executive management.

The director—information systems is considering insights gained from a recent study of regional sales offices where an online information retrieval system appeared desirable to obtain customer order status and inventory status. In the past, the systems philosophy of providing information only on an exception basis has been closely followed; thus, a management reporting system, for example, reports only summary customer information and provides for additional supporting detail on demand.

Stimulated by this suggestion, the director—information systems paused and reviewed the progress that Mead has made in the design and implementation of a total information planning and control system for the paper and related group. As part of this review, he reflected upon the company, history of current total information system project, overview of total system, organization changes, current status of paper and related system, and current concerns.

The Company

The Mead Corporation is one of the larger companies in the paper industry with annual sales in 1965 of $548 million. This volume of sales is equally divided among Mead Corporation's three major divisions: (1) paper and related operations, (2) paperboard and related converting facilities, and (3) merchant sales—the wholesaling of paper and paper supplies.

The division for paper and related operations encompasses the manufacturing and distribution of bleached and unbleached chemical wood pulp, white paper mills that produce the world's broadest line of fine printing papers, and the creation, production, and distribution of industrial and technical papers. The division for paperboard and related converting facilities includes multiple packaging, packaging machinery and systems, folding cartons, speciality packages, point-of-purchase marketing aids, multiduty corrugated containers, paperboards and technical fiberboards in a wide range of trims, calipers, treatments, laminations, and combinations, and the international sales of excess board. The merchant sales division consists of seven wholesalers who offer a full line of papers, including both Mead and competitive brands.

The company's annual sales has increased $380 million over the past nine years—from $168 million in 1956 to $548 million in 1965. The rapid expansion of domestic and overseas packaging operations is a significant factor in the growth of sales during the past two years; these operations accounted for over $100 million in sales during 1965.

History of Current Project

In 1960, executive management of the Mead Corporation, assisted by the management consultants from an international certified public accounting firm, embarked on a comprehensive study of Mead's data processing activities. The major objectives of this study were to:

1. Develop a long-range plan for data processing that would take full advantage of commercially available data processing and communication equipment and which would provide for an efficient management information and control system.
2. Review short-term planning in data processing to determine whether it is consistent with the long-range plan.
3. Make recommendations to Mead management as to organization, systems, equipment, and such other points necessary for the implementation of the long-range plan.

This study group's reviews revealed certain basic weaknesses in the flow of management information. For example, data processing was basically a decentralized function guided by loosely defined procedures and methods, particularly with respect to organizations acquired over the last six to eight years. The present management information system for internal happenings had delays, inaccuracies, multiplicity of sources, and a lack of timely decision information. The system for external purposes had an apparent deficiency of data with which to supply the paper and related group customers with timely paper availability information, order status, and answers to other types of inquiries.

Based on these and other findings, the study group concluded that the recommended data processing system would have to include the solution to customer service and related production planning problems. Since the order cycles in the paper and related group and board mills were basically parallel, the study group believed that the solution to the more complicated problem—paper and related group—would, with appropriate modifications, solve the problem of the other. Using this premise the study group concentrated its detailed efforts in the paper and related order cycle with attention being given to board mills insofar as its cycle differed. The order cycles of containers and packaging required additional study to determine the feasibility of a board and related cycle including the converters.

In addition to the study group's detailed plans for the paper and related activities, the study group recommended the establishment of a central information service center, reporting to the director-information systems. The director—information systems would be provided with (1) corporate-wide *functional* (activity) control of all information systems development including systems personnel and (2) corporate-wide administrative and functional control of all data processing equipment and data processing operating personnel. The group proposed that an additional study of data processing requirements in board and related operations should be performed after the system for paper and related activities had been established.

Management of the Mead Corporation accepted the above *Report on Electronic Data Processing* and began to implement many of the recommendations. This action by Mead management in 1961 was not unusual for them, while the same action by management in most other companies in the paper industry would have been revolutionary. For example, one member of executive management could foresee in the mid-1950's that the computer had significant promise for improving operations of a paper company. This executive along with other members of management had given continuous support to Mead's studies and activities in electronic data processing. This environmental setting is an important element to understanding the progress in total information system at Mead.

During the remaining part of 1961 and 1962, most of the recommendations in the *Report on Electronic Data Processing* were implemented, and a group of competent information systems personnel was organized. The director—information systems was recruited from a management consulting firm, and other specialists in systems design and data processing activities were employed. The corporate information systems department also received personnel from within Mead Corporation; individuals with a diversity of background and experience in operations of the paper and related activities were among those transferred to the corporate information systems department.

The information systems department made significant progress in developing the details of the proposed plan for the paper and related activities and in implementing these programs. While the director—information systems was supervising these activities, he was also concerned with the advancements that were occurring in both electronic data processing and communication equipment. He desired to update the master plan for a total system.

In September, 1963, the Mead Corporation entered into an agreement with a major manufacturer of electronic equipment to develop the detailed systems concepts and plan the implementation of the recommendations set forth in the *Report on Electronic Data Process-*

ing, issued in June, 1961, and subsequently approved by Mead management. The overall objective of both the original recommendations and the current study was to design a total information planning and control system which would encompass all of the activities of each other. Thus, information created as a result of an action in one activity would result in a chain of related actions through the other activities on an automated basis. The system envisioned was to utilize complete computer files of dynamically maintained data relating to the current status of the company, and each of its activities. These files would be updated either continuously or on a periodic basis depending on the requirement within the system for up-to-date information.

A study group was formed consisting of 12 members—6 representatives from Mead information systems department, 1 member of Mead internal audit department, 3 representatives from the major manufacturer of electronic equipment, and 2 management consultants from the international certified public accounting firm that participated in the 1960–61 systems study.

The thorough and detailed report of this study group was completed in March, 1964; the general system description from this report is presented in the next section.

Overview of Total Information Planning and Control System for the Paper and Related Group

Introduction. The proposed total information system, according to research performed by the study group, is the most advanced data handling system planned in the paper industry today. It incorporates the latest techniques of data collection by having information on orders and production status flow directly into a computer located in the corporate computer center. It embodies all the features of a completely integrated data handling system for maintaining all necessary records with the single entry of a particular unit of information. It operates on a preplanned control scheme which measures deviations and reports these deviations on an exception basis.

Exhibit A is a pictorial representation of this total system. The left-hand portion of the chart illustrates how management and operating personnel interact with the automated part of the total system. Corporate management determines the direction of the corporation by establishing plans and goals. Operating management converts the

EXHIBIT A
Total Information Planning and Control System

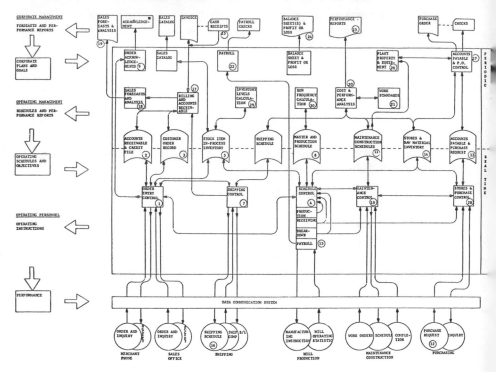

plans and goals into actual schedules and specific objectives. The operating personnel then strive to meet the schedule and attain the specific objectives. This, then, is the oversimplified theory of management and of the system. Under such a system, management must constantly have answers to the question "How are we doing?" because the plan is rarely executed precisely.

To find out "How we are doing," management must first determine what it is trying to do by establishing goals. Examples of such goals might be:

1. Maintain or improve profit for paper and related activities
2. Provide stable employment for all workers
3. Operate paper machines at full capacity
4. Reduce stock inventory to the lowest possible level
5. Provide maximum service to customers from stock inventory

These goals would then form the basis for the planning, reporting, and control techniques to be provided in the total information system. For management to determine if it is attaining the first goal, a sales analysis report would need to be provided that would show Mead paper and related profit and the detailed information used to arrive at this profit, such as gross profit by grade, distribution costs, and warehousing costs. This report would then allow management to review the profit in relation to goals and take action on the items which are causing profit to deviate from the goal. The provision of stable employment and operation of paper machines at capacity are compatible goals since both imply operation at capacity. Stability of employment at less than full capacity may be provided through good scheduling techniques which balance work loads over the periods of less than capacity requirements. However, the goal to reduce inventory clashes somewhat with the concept of providing maximum service. How, then, can these conflicting goals be achieved? Compromise is the answer just as it is the answer to problems in a noncomputer-oriented system. However, in the computer-oriented system, these compromises must be translated into mathematical models which will always produce the optimum solution based on all the goals and resources involved. These goals or objectives then form the underlying foundation for computation of inventory levels and run frequencies and create the basis for developing sound scheduling techniques.

The corporate computer center will be able to assist operating management in arriving at a sound sales forecast and production schedule. The system will then be constantly monitoring operations and aiding operating management in its attempts to meet the schedule or plan as it was assigned. The plan, however, is constantly changing because orders, order changes, quality, and equipment failures must be incorporated into an actual operating schedule. Since the scheduling system will be able to quickly respond to change by examining the interrelationships of various elements in the manufacturing process in order to determine a new optimum schedule.

Operating management will thus be relieved of the many detailed and minor decisions currently required because of the necessity for schedule changes. This will enable operating management to insure that schedules are effected properly and to devote more time to the creative tasks of improving the actual production processes.

Operating personnel are the sensors in the system because they are constantly reporting back on job progress and completed tasks. The feedback of operating status will cause the system to update necessary records, while simultaneously examining the records for any deviations from pre-established schedules and standards. Deviations found will then immediately be reported back to operating management for necessary action.

The chart then depicts how the overall system reacts with its environment of management objectives, outside influences, and internal reporting systems. The various lines on the chart attempt to show which system will provide the necessary data flow between other systems to bring about the desired results.

Information Flow and Interaction. A narrative linked to Exhibit A now follows which presents in summary form the information flow and interactions of the total system, as conceived by the study group. It is suggested that the reader give close consideration to Exhibit A while reading the following description, since the reference numbers in the following description refer to numbers presented in Exhibit A.

Orders, order changes, and inquiries form the triggers to put the system in motion. As these orders flow into the system, they enter the order entry control (1) system. Here the order is checked for completeness. A credit check is also performed using data stored in the accounts receivable (2) files. The order, having passed these initial tests, is checked against the stock item record (5), if it is a stock item, or entered into the schedule control (4), if it is a making item. The stock item record provides complete information about the ordered item. If in stock, the item is scheduled for shipping through shipping control (7). The planned shipping date is returned through the order entry control system back to the original entry terminal. In attempting to fill the stock order, and out-of-stock condition might be discovered in which case the system immediately checks the manufacturing schedule (8), or in-process inventories (5) to see if the item can be supplied from either of these. In this event, the item would be handled in a manner similar to a making item.

Making items are immediately referred to the schedule control (4) where they are fitted into the master and production schedule using information available as to run schedules and in-process inventory. When the appropriate manufacturing date is determined, the date is sent to shipping control (7) where the shipping date is determined and returned to the order entry terminal or customer.

After the order is returned to the entry terminal and accepted by the customer, the order data are transferred to the acknowledgment system (9) which prepares the necessary customer acknowledgments on a daily basis.

All of the above steps occur in a few seconds, and the customer receives immediate response to his order requirements.

Maintenance and construction (10) also effect the schedule. As work orders requesting maintenance enter the system, they are entered into a maintenance schedule (11). Maintenance information on production equipment is automatically relayed to schedule control (4) where the maintenance is fitted into the master schedules.

Maintenance or repairs frequently require replacement parts. By entering a stores stock number and the quantity required with the work order, the stores records are examined (14) and the parts reserved until they are actually required on the job. A materials delivery schedule is prepared daily for use in delivering stores items to the facility. Any deficiency in the balance on hand for a particular item automatically triggers off a purchase request (12) which enters the purchase request file (13) for consolidation with other requests.

Other purchase requests are initiated by appropriate supervisory personnel or automatically created when demands are made against stores or raw materials inventory (14).

Schedule control (4) is constantly updating and monitoring the schedule so that within the system there is always an up-to-date schedule. When the appropriate time arrives, schedule control (4) issues the necessary manufacturing instructions to the mill which include operating instructions as well as raw material requirements. As the mill operations occur, the data describing the completed operations are returned to the computer where they are distributed (15) to the appropriate system. Any of the subsystems detecting an imbalance condition automatically provides management with an exception report describing the imbalance situation.

Daily shipping schedules (16) based on customer requirements are supplied to the warehouses. Completed shipping information is transmitted back to the corporate computer center where it will trigger the preparation of bills of lading. In addition, information will be transmitted to the billing (17) system where the invoice will be prepared and the necessary information for the sales analysis system (18) and accounts receivable system (2) will automatically be created.

Certain files and subsystems are of a more static nature where the information still must be altered or manipulated, but on a periodic, rather than a real-time basis. Earlier attention was given to the establishment of corporate goals. To enable management to establish realistic goals or modify them, provision of information, such as sales analysis, sales forecasts, and economic data must be made. This information (19) is provided for by the sales forecast and analysis (18) system. In addition to providing the data on past and future sales conditions, sound information on production performance must be provided. The cost analysis (20) system in conjunction with the work standard file (21), payroll data (22), storage usage (14), and production status (8) provide the basis for performance reports (23). Management is also provided with the conventional financial reports, such as balance sheets and profit or loss statements (24). Many levels of management are involved in the reporting system, and it will not be until the implementation phase is begun that the study group can determine the exact format, method of submission, level of detail, and frequency required for these management reports.

Other systems of a more static nature are those required to provide the backup information for the balance sheet and profit or loss statement. Cash receipts (25) and billing (17) information will be used to maintain the accounts receivable files (2). The property, plant, and equipment records (26) are maintained by information supplied by the accounts payable (27) and maintenance and construction (11) systems. Accounts payable (27) receives information from the purchasing control system (28) which monitors all requisitioning and purchase order writing operations.

The three most vital subsystems are the inventory levels calculation (29), run frequency calculation (30), and work standards determination (21). These three systems determine the predictive and control power of the schedule control system (4). The inventory levels calculation determines the response the Mead Corporation will be able to give the customer requirements for stock items. These inventory calculations also provide data for the run frequency calculations.

The run frequency calculations provide overall production requirements, and the results form the basis for the master schedule. The production standards will provide the scheduling control system (4) with all the necessary data to determine how long it will take a particular work center or piece of equipment to produce a given amount of paper.

Much historical data will be required to maintain these standards, but while the data will be gathered on a real-time basis, the actual calculations will only be required on a periodic basis to adjust any standards which are out of line. The frequency of calculation will be determined as progress is made into the implementation phase.

The report, *Total Information Planning and Control System for the Paper and Related Group,* was issued in March, 1964, and was endorsed by corporate management. Members of the information systems department had continued to work during the study phase on implementing selected limited-scale information system projects. As a result of this overall study, a revised order of priorities for proposed systems projects was determined, and systems analysts continued to work on the implementation phase of the new master plan.

Organization Changes

To recognize the growing importance of Mead's developing computer technology and, also, to recognize merit and accomplishment, the director—information systems was elected vice president of administration in April, 1964. As a means of providing closer coordination of related corporate headquarters functions, the vice president of administration was given responsibility over three departments in addition to the information systems department: purchasing, traffic, and distribution.

The executive who was in charge of Mead's 1963–64 study group was promoted to the position of director—information systems.

During 1965 several organization changes have occurred. Each of the three major divisions, that were previously discussed, is now organized under a group vice president who is responsible for coordinating production and sales and for producing a predetermined rate of return on the capital employed in his division. The group vice president for paper and related products directs Mead Papers, central planning, customer services, white papers, affiliated pulp companies, Gilbert Paper Co., and industrial and technical papers. The group vice president for paperboard and related products supervises Mead Packaging, Mead Containers, board development, Mead Board Sales (overseas), new board products, and central planning. The other group vice president is in charge of Mead Merchants—the seven wholesalers.

The vice president of finance has retired, and the three individuals who previously reported to him—the treasurer, the administrative

EXHIBIT B. Plan of Organization (December, 1965)

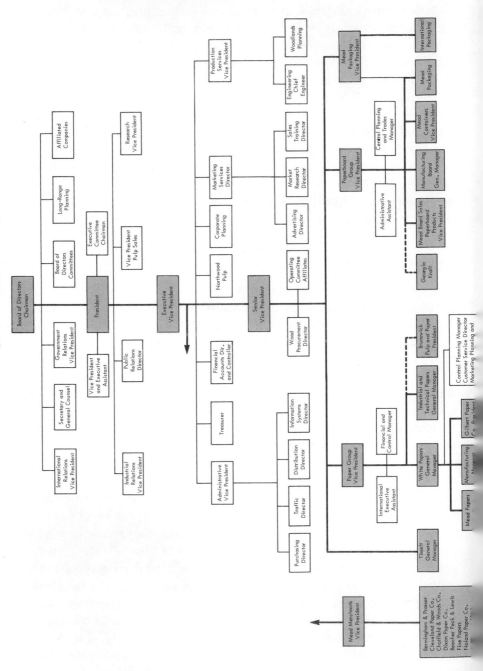

vice president, and the financial accounts director and controller—now report to the executive vice president. The executive vice president previously administered marketing services; recently a director of marketing services was announced.

Exhibit B presents the Mead Corporation plan of organization as of December, 1965.

During 1966 the administrative vice president's area of responsibility was increased. He has staff responsibility over the personnel department and has direct responsibility over the following seven administrators: director of traffic, director of distribution, director of purchasing, director of information systems, manager of operations research, manager of Mead Management Services Division (sells excess computer time and provides other administrative service to small business firms), and manager of the Cincinnati computer center (handles all the data processing for the board group). Exhibit C presents the plan of organization for the administrative vice president as of June, 1966.

Current Status of Paper and Related System

Exhibit D presents the projected status of the paper and related system at the end of 1966. The reader should make frequent use of this chart while reading the following description of the current system.

EXHIBIT C
Administrative Vice President
Plan of Organization
(June, 1966)

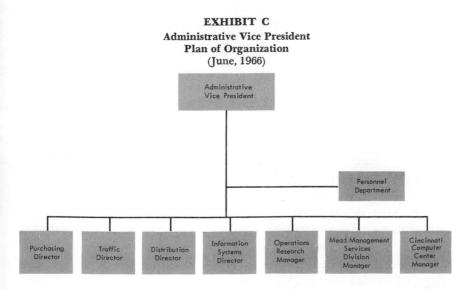

EXHIBIT D

Projected Status—Paper and Related System, End of 1966

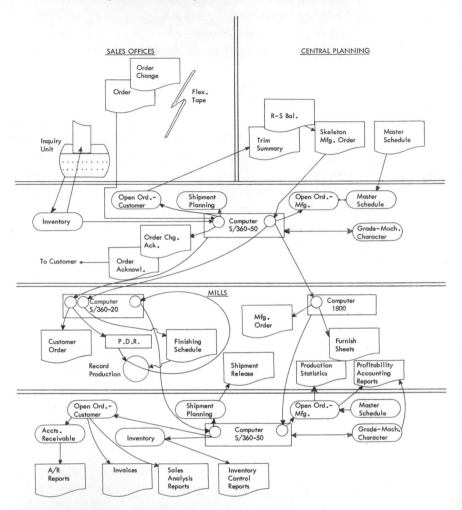

Sales Orders. Each regional sales office has data speed transmitters and data speed receivers for communicating with the corporate computer center. All sales orders are processed by data speed transmitters on paper tape; this means that even sales orders in the Dayton sales office must be processed through these data speed transmitters. The sales order system makes maximum use of constant information, which is contained on various strips of punched paper tape in a storage file adjacent to each data speed transmitter.

At the corporate computer center, the sales orders on paper tape are converted to magnetic tape, and on a batch basis, these sales orders are processed through the computer center. This action encompasses (1) sending order acknowledgment to customer, (2) updating the inventory status of stocked items, and (3) entering the sales order in a customer open order file. Exhibit D also indicates that appropriate information is transmitted to a shipment planning file; this system has not been fully implemented, and the current position of the system is explained at a later point.

Each customer is mailed a sales order acknowledgment containing such information as sales class, terms, freight, office entering sale, status, how to ship, routing, product codes, grade, grade description, finish, item information, and type of packaging. The inventory status system is self-evident. The customer open order file is used by paper and related group's central planning department to schedule manufacturing orders, and this operation is subsequently discussed.

Planning and Scheduling. The central planning department for the paper and related group will schedule each sales order. This scheduling operation is consistent with the monthly assignment of products to machines and with the planned run frequency and sequencing of products by paper machine. In this planning and assignment process, central planning uses four types of planning and scheduling operations: forecasting, long-range planning, master scheduling, and production scheduling.

Forecasting is for a 12-month period. The exponential smoothing technique is applied to the data for the past two years using one of four equations: average, trend, seasonal, and a combination of trend and seasonal. The major paper and related forecasting model is a linear program (LP) consisting of a 700 by a 5,000 matrix. Mead has 190 white paper products. If different product sizes are considered, then there are over 4,000 items. The LP model can only encompass the 190 products, 441 destinations, and 3 group regions (a weighted distribution is computed for each region for each product, including the freight). An LP model is also used for forecasting the assignment of production by machine. At present, Mead has 22 white paper machines (a paper machine and related processing equipment may range in cost from $20 million to $30 million). The LP model uses 24 machines; the two extra machines are used in evaluating proposed plant sites.

Long-range planning is periodically performed on a regular basis in five areas: capital expenditures, plant site, product mix (the estimated maximum and minimum amounts for each product), allocation of production among paper mills for a quarter, and financial planning for next quarter. The production and operation aspects of long-range planning are primarily concerned with which machines will be assigned to which products in which months.

Master scheduling involves determining the exact schedule by machine for the first month and the planned schedule for the second and third months. The master schedule by machine includes both run frequency and sequencing. In operation of paper machines, the learning curve is very important, and the variable cost of manufacturing is higher than transportation cost. Thus, in a short time-period, it is normally more economical to have all units of a product manufactured on one paper machine and shipped to various parts of the country, rather than to have the demand satisfied by production on a decentralized basis.

Production scheduling is performed daily for the next three days. Mead management believes that a three-day exact schedule is typically the minimum time period in which the paper mills can operate efficiently. When a sales order is initially processed by central planning, a scheduler will review the master schedule of frequency and run assignment of products to machines and will determine the planned "available date" for shipment by line item on each order. A copy of the sales order is then sent to the appropriate mill.

A manufacturing order is prepared for a group of sales orders and stock replenishment for like grades of paper, and the information on each sales order is stored in the computer system. Each manufacturing order is transmitted to the appropriate mill by card to card communication equipment.

Central planning uses the corporate computer center to process programs that incorporate the details of each manufacturing order into master production schedules. This exact schedule is also communicated via data speed transmitters to the appropriate mill, and this schedule includes the special operating instructions for the paper machine, cutter, trimmer, rewinder, calendar, coater, and so forth.

Production and Operation. The production process of three paper machines is currently controlled by a process control computer system, and other paper machines will be controlled by such a computerized system in the near future. The Mead Corporation is recognized as being the leader in the paper industry in process control computers (see *Pulp and Paper,* January 31, 1966, or "Total System in the Mill," *Business Automation,* July, 1965). Early in 1962 Mead management began a program to install an IBM 1710 process control computer system on No. 4 paper machine at its Chillicothe Paper Company Division, Chillicothe, Ohio. This process control system has been in full operation since January, 1963, and subsequently, the process control system was expanded to include the adjacent No. 3 paper machine.

Recently, a process control computer system was installed with a new No. 5 paper machine at Kingsport, Tenn. Mead is scheduled to receive an IBM 1800 process control computer at the Central Research Laboratories in Chillicothe, Ohio, during July, 1966. A second IBM 1800 computer system is scheduled to replace the IBM 1710 process control computer system on No. 4 and No. 3 machines in Chillicothe during the fall of 1966.

Management has made many changes and improvements as a result of its experience with process control computer system. The papermaking process has been stabilized; new instruments have been added for measuring and controlling the flow of operations. Manufacturing standards for operation of the various processes have been established, and an alarm program covering important variables has been developed. Mathematical procedure for material balance was established, and computerized process control extended until it encompassed all operations. Currently, management is working on the integration of this computerized process control system with management information systems.

During the production process, on a 36-second cycle the computer records the measurements of the various instruments and gauges, and every 7 minutes an average is computed for each measurement. A detailed production performance report is prepared daily consisting of base yield data, department, cost, chargeable hours by department, average speed, percent of excess trim, percent of down time, grade code, and other information. This production reporting system coupled with good engineering standards for most operations provides the basic data for a wide range of production management activities.

Profitability Accounting. The information systems department assisted by consultants from a certified public accounting firm is installing a profitability accounting system in white paper mills. This system will provide profit contribution by item, by sales area, by customer, by producing mill, and by individual paper machine.

Shipment Planning. The annual volume of traffic is $50 million; thus, close supervision is given to the determination of optimum routes and rates. Shipment planning also involves the relating of customer order status file with the projected date for delivery on shipping dock at the destination. The shipment release operations for each sales area is administered by a separate clerk; thus, each sales office will call this latter individual whenever there is a question regarding the release of a shipment.

Monthly Reports. The accounts receivable reports and inventory control reports are self-explanatory. Marketing management uses the customer open order file as a basis for analysis. An order received analysis is performed by sales office, and a margin is computed by customer. External data are used in marketing potential studies.

Current Concerns

A member of the information systems department visited each regional sales office, and talked with sales personnel about how the information processing and transmitting system could be improved. Regional sales personnel unanimously assigned a first priority to a proposed perpetual inventory information system. Salesmen felt that major customers should have the opportunity of inquiring of this perpetual inventory information system to see if a given item is in the warehouse. The salesmen desired the proposed system to give "no negative answers." If an item was out of stock, appropriate information would be obtained from the customer so that a representative of the regional sales office could contact the customer within an hour. Of course, this information would be obtained before the customer's inquiry is accepted by the information system, and the customer would be notified by the system that a salesman will contact him within an hour about his inquiry.

These interviews indicated that the second priority should be assigned to the development of a different system for acknowledging customer orders. Many orders are less than a carload size; thus, the order must wait for other orders from customers in the same geographical location. Salesmen would like a system that would give a definite commitment for delivery price (regardless of size of order) and delivery date. The present system quotes prices f.o.b. mill and indicates the day the order will be completed at the mill.

EXHIBIT E
Information Systems Department
Organization Chart—February 1, 1966

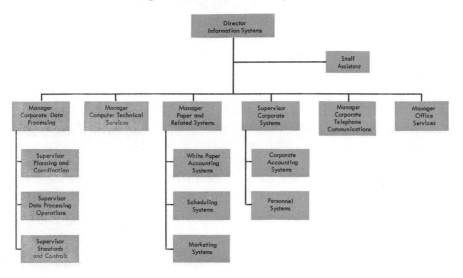

The interviews revealed that the third priority should be assigned to the development of an order status information system. At present, on an exception basis, customers are notified when goods will not be available on promised dates. Salesmen feel that there would be a significant competitive advantage from offering the customer the ability to inquire into the total information system as to the status of his order.

REQUIRED:

1. Study the approach Mead management followed in the design and implementation of a total management planning and control information system for the paper and related group. What are the advantages and disadvantages of this approach? Indicate other approaches that might have been followed, and explain how these suggested approaches would have differed from the approach actually followed.

2. Evaluate the total information system for the paper and related group. Indicate how different information requirements are satisfied by different information sources. As part of your analysis, indicate information requirements that you have imputed for the current environmental setting in the paper industry which are not matched with information sources.

3. As the installed advanced information system becomes one of housekeeping aspects and attention is shifted toward corporate planning considerations, what types of new information systems do you foresee as being required for this environment? Explain the reasons for your selections.

4. The financial accounting director and controller has responsibility for financial analysis, corporate accounting, internal audit, federal and state tax, and external audit. Each information system produces journal vouchers as a final report; thus, accounting is one of the areas the director-information systems services. The current operations of the information systems department as of February 1, 1966, is indicated by Exhibit E. *After* the total management planning and control information system for the paper and related group and an appropriate total information system for the board paper group have been designed and implemented, what types of organization changes do you envision for these two departments? Explain the support for your observations.

5. The director—information systems has followed the procedure of taking major undertakings and dividing these major undertakings into small projects. For example, there are many information systems projects that require two or three men for two or three weeks. At the present time, there are 35 planned projects for the current year. What are the advantages and disadvantages from dividing these major undertakings into small projects? Indicate other methods the director—information systems might follow in administering these activities.

CASE 13–2. GARSIDE CORPORATION

The Garside Corporation is a major manufacturer and distributor of chemicals and fertilizer products. The company has 15 manufacturing plants located in five cities in the eastern part of the United States. The distribution facilities are located throughout the United States and consist of both regional sales offices and warehouses. The home office is located in a major metropolitan city, and the company's common stock is listed on the New York Stock Exchange.

In 1960, the president and chairman of the board of Garside Corporation became interested in computers and business technological developments. He attended several seminars on computers, quantitative methods, and information systems. Later, the mayor of the metropolitan city in which the home office is located appointed the president and chairman of the board of Garside Corporation to a new, special advisory committee on business.

Early in 1961, the metropolitan newspapers contained several statements by the president of Garside Corporation regarding computers and business technological developments. At this point, the executive vice president and other members of the executive management met to discuss what action the Garside Corporation would take in the area of computers and business technological developments.

Organization

The president and chairman of the board of Garside Corporation is not actively involved in the day-to-day management activites of the company. The executive management group handles all the day-to-day activities, and this group consists of 10 individuals. First is the executive vice president and the six individuals reporting directly to him: (1) vice president of marketing, (2) vice president of administration, (3) controller, (4) treasurer, (5) director of research and development, and (6) senior vice president of manufacturing. The latter individual has three assistant vice presidents reporting directly to him: (1) assistant vice president for chemical products, (2) assistant vice president for fertilizer products, and (3) assistant vice president for engineering maintenance and services.

The executive management group decided that a management consulting firm should be engaged to design and implement an advanced information system at Garside Corporation. A few days later the executive management group reconsidered this matter. The executive vice president suggested that Garside Corporation should have its own management services group, and that this latter group should have the responsibility for implementing the advanced information system designed by the management consulting firm.

Furthermore, the executive vice president suggested to the other members of executive management that the director of management services group should temporarily report directly to him. This new management services group would not appear on the organization chart on the same level with the vice presidents, but would temporarily appear in a special position to the right of the executive vice president's box, with a line connecting the two boxes. The executive vice president's suggestions were approved by the executive committee, and the board of directors authorized these temporary arrangements.

Proposed Advanced System

A management consulting firm was engaged to design an advanced information system. The management consultants completed a thorough study of the company's operations, and eventually, they prepared a written report. The management consultants' report recommended that a "total system" should be developed. The report specified that all manufacturing and distribution facilities should be connected to a centralized computer center at the home office. A special communication network should be established to provide this continuous communication channel. Under this proposed system, all information processing would be performed by the centralized computer center, and the communication network would serve to transmit inquiries and information from or to the various decision makers throughout the organization.

Under the proposed system, production planning and scheduling activities would be based on the forecasted sales for each product. A special subsystem would be established that would continuously provide these forecasts. Certain data from day-to-day transactions would be stored in a special information retrieval subsystem, and this library would provide most of the raw data for the projected sales forecasts. The remaining data would come from governmental publications and industry sources.

While the production planning and scheduling activities would operate based on forecasted sales, a production control system would be established to monitor those activities that would be based on reacting to actual sales. This latter system, providing actual sales data, is really an integrated inventory control, production management and control, and sales analysis system. Thus, on a management by exception basis, production management would administer the production activities for those products where the forecasted activity was significantly different from actual.

When the management consultants' report was prepared, existing transmission and communication equipment did not contain the required capacity and speed for coping with the estimated information requirements of this suggested total system. This limitation of existing equipment was equally applicable to both the management of manufacturing facilities and to the management of distribution facilities. The management consultants' report indicated that equipment was being developed which would satisfy these requirements, and that this equipment was scheduled to be on the market in the near future. In the meantime, the production facilities in each of the five cities should have their own data processing capabilities, and summary reports should be mailed to the home office. The report suggested, however, that most of the information processing for the activities of the distribution centers should be performed on a centralized basis at the home office.

Management Services Group

The management services group was established at Garside Corporation, and action was begun on the implementation of the "master plan." Members of the management services group quickly discovered that the management consultants' report was general and did not contain the necessary details for achieving the total information system. Thus, the director of the management services group undertook the task of completing the design phase.

In the completion of the details of the design phase, agreement had to be reached between various management groups on different matters. In one of these areas, a conflict arose between the director of the management services group and the assistant vice-president for chemical products. Finally, the assistant vice president for chemical products decided to retire under a special retirement program that had just been approved by the board of directors. A professor of engineering at the state university was employed as the new assistant vice president for chemical products.

The director of the management services group continued to work toward the completion of the elaborate computer programs and coding systems required by the master plan. This work continued throughout 1962 and the first quarter of 1963.

The executive vice president suggested in March, 1963, that executive management should reconsider the responsibilities of the management services group and should reach a permanent decision on the organization location of this group. After many discussions over the following few weeks, the executive management group recommended to the board of directors (1) that the management services group should be discontinued and (2) that a new "management science and information system group" should be established. This latter group would be directly under the assistant vice president for engineering maintenance and services. After the board of directors approved this recommendation, the director of the former management services group resigned.

Management Science and Information System Group

By June, 1963, the manager for the management science and information system group had been appointed, and he had immediately begun to recruit new members for his group. Many of the former members of the management services group had resigned from the Garside Corporation during May and June. After employing a few individuals, the manager accepted the task of completing the design phase of the master plan.

Subsequently, a point arose in the design phase where agreement was required from the assistant vice president for chemical products, the assistant vice president for fertilizer products, and the controller. The manager sought assistance from his superior, the assistant vice president for maintenance and services, in resolving this conflict. Agreement was not reached, and a stalemate occurred.

A few days later, the executive vice president suggested that a moratorium be placed upon the total information system project. Instead, the management science and information system group was asked to perform a feasibility study regarding the purchase of a large-scale computer for the home office's centralized computer center.

During the third and fourth quarters of 1963, the management science and information system group devoted all their attention to the feasibility study. In December, 1963, the president and chairman of the board of Garside Corporation unexpectedly announced that a given large-scale computer was being purchased by Garside Corporation. This public release also specified that this large-scale computer would be installed and in full operation within a six-month period.

The manager of the management science and information system group was immediately assigned the task of installing this new large-scale computer. The manager developed a critical path schedule of the tasks to be performed if the computer was to be installed in this "record time." Problems arose during the first quarter of 1964, and the installation activities were behind schedule. However, the president restated that the new computer system would be in operation by the scheduled date; he also announced that the existing computer facilities had been sold and would be removed from the premises shortly after the scheduled completion date.

The manager and his associates worked 20 or more hours of overtime per week during the first and second quarter in order to try to achieve the president's announced objective. About 30 days prior to the announced scheduled completion date, the majority of the experienced members of the management science and information system group resigned from the Garside Corporation.

REQUIRED:

1. Evaluate the Garside Corporation's movement toward a total information system.
2. What is the probability of achieving this total information system? Include in your comments the primary constraints you see impeding the attainment of this objective.

CHAPTER **14**

Elements in Large-Scale
Information Systems

"CODE STRUCTURE," "edit routine," "common data bases," and "information retrieval systems" are terms we have used in earlier chapters to refer to different subsystems and procedures within an information system. In Chapter 13 we saw that these subsystems and procedures are monitored, coordinated and managed by the Code Structure Identification and Management Committee. Thus, we already have some appreciation of a few elements in large-scale information systems; however, an increased understanding is needed because of the critical role played by these elements.

In this chapter we will carefully examine two areas: code structure and common data bases. As part of our analysis, two generalized models are presented which focus on selected subsystems and procedures within large-scale information systems. In the last part of the chapter, we will briefly consider information retrieval systems and online and real-time systems.

Code Structure

Members of executive management in many corporations were first introduced to electronic data processing and automatic data processing equipment in the 1950's, and these individuals have observed the gradual progression from data processing systems to computer systems to computer-based information systems. During this period, the records have progressed from paper to tub files to punched cards to magnetic tape to online disk files. Now, data management systems are being proposed to replace the online disk files.

With all of these technological developments, we frequently find that members of executive management are still at the "tub file" state in terms of their level of appreciation of the role played by these systems. It was appropriate in the 1950's for executive management to delegate to computer programmers the decision as to which sets of methods and procedures will be employed for coding inventory and accounts receivable transactions. But when these transactions became incorporated in inventory management control systems and accounts receivable management systems, respectively, then questions as to choice of code structure assumed a higher level of importance.

From an alternative perspective, we can state that many corporations have a "1970 model" computer system, a "1970 model" communication network, and a "1961 model" code structure system. This imbalance cannot be solved through the acquisition of additional computer equipment, online storage facilities, or communication equipment. Instead, a major systems study effort is required to redesign the code structure system based on an examination of decision-making requirements.

From a third perspective, we might describe the code structure system as being responsible for all the *contents* of information flows within our network. If we desire different sets of contents in different information flows, then we must develop sets of programmed rules that will generate these suggested combinations of flows. In the absence of alternative sets of programmed rules, the contents of all information flows will be identical. Moreover, these existing contents may not be the appropriate data for use in selective decision-making processes.

In these three perspectives for viewing the code structure system, we are merely trying to indicate that the code structure system is the "heart" of a large-scale information system. The overall quality of the systems design effort is reflected in how the code structure system is developed.

Coding. The coding process is the assignment of symbols to objects, events and properties according to a set of rules. This set of rules is arbitrarily developed out of the classification process in which relations are expressed among a number of variables. While the overall set of rules is arbitrarily developed, there are many institutional constraints and legal considerations which influence the designing process. These latter factors may be either direct or indirect. For example, legal considerations can be accommodated by designing the set of rules so the desired data are directly provided by the coding system. Alternatively, these specified data may be obtained by further processing and sorting of data initially coded for another purpose. It is becoming increasingly common for institutional constraints and legal considerations to be handled on an indirect basis.

Conceptually, the coding process is based on classification and, as such, can be operationally applied at the lowest level of measurement. It can, of course, be applied at the higher levels of measurement; using Stevens' model, this includes the ordinal scale, the interval scale, and the ratio scale.[1]

Since the coding process is based on classification, it presupposes the existence of a classification system. The arbitrary set of rules used in the coding process is developed from the attributes and elements identified in the classification process. This set of rules will permit the converting and transformation of data from one set of representation to another.

As information systems analysts, we are especially interested in the design of this set of rules. Where there is a choice as to which attributes and elements will be incorporated in the set of rules, we believe that this decision should be monitored by the Code Structure Identification and Management Committee.

The latter recommendation is a reflection of the current "state of the art." The coding process has only recently become a major area of research. Some individuals are applying various management science techniques, including cluster analysis,[2] to the process of identifying relevant attributes and elements for inclusion in the set of rules.

The assigned symbols may be alphabetic, numeric, mnemonic, alphameric or word codes. There are varying efficiencies and error rates with each of these different types of symbols. A computer program can be developed so that the classification and coding process are concurrently performed, and the resulting assigned symbols can be stored online in a code dictionary. There are many other choices

---

[1] S. S. Stevens, "On the Theory of Scales of Measurement," *Science,* Vol. CIII (June, 1946) , pp. 677–80.

[2] Nancy Price and Samuel Schiminovich, "A Clustering Experiment: First Step towards a Computer-Generated Classification Scheme," *Information Storage and Retrieval,* August, 1968, pp. 271–80.

in selecting assigned symbols, but for our purposes, we are especially interested in those *assigned symbols that are in machine readable form.*

Input-Oriented Coding Pattern. In designing a coding pattern, there are two extreme positions: input-oriented and output-oriented. Where there are limited processing and storage facilities, the output-oriented coding pattern is the best strategy. In a manual operation the output-oriented coding pattern is probably the only feasible solution. But, in most organizations we are not confronted with the problem of limited facilities. Instead, we select between these two extreme positions primarily on the basis of how to reduce errors.

In most information systems, an input-oriented coding pattern is employed. Typically, the predetermined data on each source document are transformed into assigned symbols that are in machine-readable form. The raw data contained on the source document will usually be a combination of individual elements and groups. For example, on a sales invoice in a company with three divisions, a single digit might be used to designate which division is making the sale. Twenty digits may be assigned for use in describing the product that was sold, and eight digits may be used for designating the product identification number. Other groups of digits will be assigned for use in recording such data as quantity, per-unit selling price, total, freight, route, shipping instructions, customer name and address, billing instructions, credit terms, salesman identification number, and so forth.

The objective in the input transformation process is to quickly represent the raw data on a source document in machine-readable units. This can be accomplished by coding clerks or by an optical scanner. The source documents can be eliminated and a remote input terminal used in directly recording within the computer system the initial transaction data.

A Second Processing. As indicated in the generalized model of a TYPE 2.5 information system in Chapter 11, after the input transformation process is complete, these selected data are filtered by an edit routine. This is followed by further processing and sorting of these selected data.

The latter operation is really a second transformation process performed by a series of computer programs stored within the information system. This second transformation process can be described as an output-oriented coding pattern. There is another aspect of this second transformation process. The selected data must be sorted and assigned to various common data files, common data banks, and control files.

Obviously, these sorting and assignment processes are performed by a closed set of computer programs that are online in the system. The mere existence of this degree of online capability indicates that some analysis has been made of the information requirements of decision-making activities. Moreover, these information require- ments have been clustered on some basis and related to common data files and common data banks.

From our experience, we have found that this sorting and assign- ment operation usually supports decision-making activities in three distinct time cycles and provides data for internal control purposes in a fourth time cycle. Figure 14.1 presents the systems processing phase which encompasses these four time cycles. The letters, A, B, C, and D are used in this illustration to indicate the information flows in four distinct time cycles that are supported by the same systems processing phase. These four cycles are as follows:

FIGURE 14.1
Systems Processing Phase

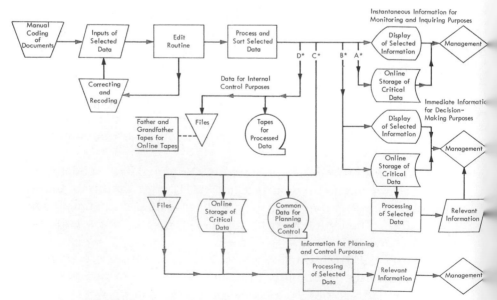

° Note: The letters A, B, C, and D indicate information flows in four distinct time cycles that are serviced by the same systems processing phase.

A. Instantaneous information for monitoring and inquiring purposes
B. Immediate information for decision-making purposes
C. Information for planning and control purposes
D. Data for internal control purposes

Both Cycle A and Cycle B provide online information; the difference is that Cycle B contains the capability of further processing of selected data on command by management, while Cycle A does not possess this capability. The information contents tend to vary between the two cycles. In Cycle A, identification codes or numbers combined with quantitative and statistical data represent the typical contents of these information flows. The prescribed coding pattern for identification purposes may also reflect many critical data that can be immediately used by decision makers. For example, a 10-digit product code might contain the following sensitive information:

1234567890 There are 10 digits in the product identification code.

12xxxxxxxx The first two digits designate the product group.

xx345xxxxx Third, fourth and fifth digits designate the product subgroups. Since there are 1,000 possible assignments within these three digits, we would expect these subgroups to be narrowly defined and not to contain an excessive number of items within any one subgroup.

xxxxx6xxxx Sixth digit designates special physical characteristics of an item, such as, perishable, nonperishable, flammable and nonflammable.

xxxxxx7xxx Seventh digit designates a composite rating of three classification schemes: (1) distribution, (2) packaging, and (3) storage.

xxxxxxx8xx Eighth digit designates a composite rating of two classification schemes: (1) price and degree of importance, and (2) turnover frequency.

xxxxxxxx9x Ninth digit designates the organizational level at which the decision is made for pricing this specific product. (In a different organization another type of marketing data might be reflected in this ninth digit.)

xxxxxxxxx0 Tenth digit is used to specify a particular product among a group of products which have the same assigned numbers in the first nine digits.

In Cycle A, the monitoring and inquiring function is performed by a manager located at a remote terminal. As previously indicated, the contents in Cycle A normally consist of identification codes combined with quantitative and statistical data. Thus, the manager can use the remote terminal to inquire about the status of a specific product, customer, contract, vendor or other object. In evaluating the online response from the system, the manager is provided (through the vehicle of the identification code) with a framework in which to make an informed analysis of a wide range of issues.

In Cycle B, online information is provided for decision-making purposes. The contents of these information flows tend to be decision-oriented and contain marginal cost, marginal price, and profit planning data in the case of a business firm. The contents will contain different types of data in a governmental agency; it will feature sensitive service and performance measures. In our model of Cycle B the manager has the capability of further processing and sorting the online data provided by the network. The latter capability combined with the more complex contents of information flows result in the creation of a slower time period for Cycle B than that present for Cycle A.

In a large corporation with numerous remote terminals, Cycle A might be performed in a maximum period of two minutes. Cycle B might be accomplished in a maximum period of five minutes. Cycle C might be performed on a daily, weekly, or monthly basis. Thus, Cycle A and Cycle B may be accomplished hundreds or thousands of times during a single period of Cycle C.

In Cycle C, the information for planning and control purposes is accumulated in both online and offline locations. In an advanced information system there tends to be a separation between information for long-range planning and that for short-term planning. Information for coordination and control purposes is grouped with the short-term planning information. In the subsequent section of this chapter we will see that the information storage locations supported by Cycle C are grouped into a series of common data files and common data bases which service a wide variety of diverse decision-making activities.

In Cycle D, "father" and "grandfather" tapes are stored so that the online data files can be reestablished in case of machine or system failure. Other data for internal control and internal review purposes are also stored in the files created by Cycle D. However, since we are primarily concerned with decision-making activities, we will not examine these other internal control features. Moreover, in the subsequent paragraphs we will restrict our discussions to Cycle A, Cycle B, and Cycle C.

There are other dimensions of the A, B, and C cycles which are apparent when we concurrently consider all three cycles. We will use a predetermined coding pattern for a sales invoice as a framework for this concurrent analysis. Our coding pattern for this source document contains 59 digits, and the elements within this pattern are as follows:

1234xxxxxxxxxxxx . . .	The first four digits designate the general ledger account.
xxxx567xxxxxxxxx . . .	Fifth, sixth, and seventh digits designate subaccounts based on organizational and responsibility accounting factors.
xxxxxxx8xxxxxxxxx . . .	Eighth digit designates the division of this diversified corporation.
xxxxxxxx90123xxx . . .	These five digits (9th to the 13th digits) specify the customer number.
. . . . . 456789xxxxx . . .	These six digits (14th to the 19th digits) specify the product number.
. . . . . xxxxxx012xx . . .	These three digits (20th to the 22nd digits) designate the date.
. . . . . 3456xxxxxxx . . .	These four digits (23rd to the 26th digits) designate the invoice number.
. . . . . xxxx7890xxx . . .	These four digits (27th to the 30th digits) specify the location code and the cost center.
. . . . . 1234xxxxxxx . . .	These four digits (31st to the 34th digits) specify shipping instructions, such as, ship from and shipped to.
. . . . . xxxx5xxxxxx . . .	This digit (35th digit) indicates the packaging code.

. . . . . xxxxx6789xx . . .	These four digits (36th to the 39th digits) specify sales channel and territory codes.
. . . . . 012345678xx . . .	These nine digits (40th to the 48th digits) specify the quantity.
. . . . . xxxxxxxxx9x . . .	This digit (49th digit) indicates the unit of measure for quantity.
. . . . . xxxx0123456789	These 10 digits (50th to the 59th digits) specify the price.

For purposes of the current discussion, we will assume that these 59 digits are manually coded. In the subsequent section on common data bases we will reconsider this sales invoice from a different perspective.

The monitoring and inquiring activities in Cycle A do not require all 59 digits. The contents of the information flows in Cycle A might include the following elements: customer number, product number, invoice number, date, quantity and price. Managers at various remote locations can request online information on any or all of these elements. It is assumed that these identification codes (like those for the 10-digit product code presented earlier in this chapter) are based on sensitive attributes of the object; thus, the manager obtains additional information from the assigned symbols in these identification codes.

The decision-making activities in Cycle B will include only those marginal and profit planning data which can be utilized by management. This set of data will vary considerably between companies because of the differences in information requirements of decision makers in different environmental settings. In a given environmental setting the contents of the information flows in Cycle B might include customer number, product number, invoice number, date, packaging code, sales channel and territory codes, quantity and price. The decision makers in this latter setting might desire to alter price and packaging in selected territories where planned volume is not being achieved.

In Cycle C, all 59 digits are stored as a group; in addition, separate files are maintained of data on selected elements within the coding pattern. These files serve as a source for a machine-prepared billing of the customer. Weekly, marketing reports are prepared by sales channel, territory, and customer. Monthly, the first eight digits in this coding pattern combined with dollar amounts are used in preparing a series of responsibility accounting reports. The company financial statements are also prepared from files maintained by Cycle C.

While Figure 14.1 has presented the systems processing phase as a distinct unit, we know that it is one of several phases included in TYPE 2.5, TYPE 3, and TYPE 4 information systems. Therefore, the contents of the information flows in the systems processing phase are available within the computer system for online use in other phases. Credit control management, sales analysis management, inventory management and cash management are some of the functions or activities performed in other phases within the network which may use information provided by these 59 digits.

Multiflows within a Network. In the second transformation process we have illustrated how data are concurrently assigned to one or more sets of information flows. We designated these sets of information flows as Cycle A, Cycle B, and Cycle C. The major criteria used in differentiating among the information flows were time cycle, overall purpose, and organizational location of management.

From our previous study of TYPE 2.5, TYPE 3, and TYPE 4 information systems, we know that a large network usually encompasses multiflows of information. We might present Cycle A, for example, as operating in 10 dimensions in which each dimension will contain a group of decision makers with a prescribed set of information requirements. If we are to service the 10 dimensions with a single systems processing phase, then some type of protected file system must be established so that decision makers in a given dimension are not provided with unauthorized information.

The multiflows within a network are not limited to multisets of information requirements. We may have multisets of information sources. When there is a high degree of similarity between two sets of information sources, we may develop a *common data file* or a *common data base* that will satisfy both sets of information requirements.

In conclusion, we might describe Cycle A, Cycle B, and Cycle C as a series of information flows in three time cycles that are supported by common data files and common data bases. Through the use of protected file procedures, this simple model can be extended to include many decision makers in various departments of a company while maintaining the integrity of the original model.

Common Data Bases

The generalized models for TYPE 2.5, TYPE 3, and TYPE 4 information systems contained references to common data files. However, thus far in this book, we have not explained what is meant by a common data file or a common data base. In this section we will define these terms, illustrate some of the properties of a common data base and examine some of the problems encountered in designing and implementing a common data base.

Characteristics. The terms "data base" indicate that a depository of information has been established which is independent of information users. To qualify as a *data base,* the total set of data elements must be stored in machine sensitive media and be accessible by various managers, decision makers, and users. According to this definition, the terms data base include both online and offline situations.

Some of the data bases in a large information retrieval system are usually offline, and they are periodically brought online for processing of inquiries and for updating purposes. We will further examine the characteristics of data bases in information retrieval systems in the next section of this chapter.

In an advanced information system, we typically use the terms data base only in the context of online conditions. If we have an offline depository of information, we refer to it as a "library" or an "information retrieval system." While a data base is a depository of information that is independent of users, we expect this depository or *data bank* (the terms *data bank* and *data base* can be used interchangeably) to be actually used by more than one decision maker. When decision makers in more than one department or division of an organization make online use of the *same data base,* we may label this depository as a "common data base." Moreover, if the terms *common data base* are used, we only expect online use of the common data bank.

In a diversified corporation, each division may have a common data base. When we are referring to several online depositories, we use the terms "common data bases." At the present time it is unusual for a corporation to have common data *bases,* because many corporations are just in the process of having their first common data base implemented. However, other data bases are being planned and designed; thus, in the near future common data bases will be more widespread.

A *file* or *data file* is a collection of records treated as a unit in a data base or a data bank. A data base typically contains several data files. A "common data file" refers to a collection of records in a common data bank; therefore, the terms common data file denote a unit of records within a common data base that are used online by decision makers in more than one department.

In our discussions we will only use the terms common data file and common data bank in the context of advanced information systems. Therefore, our common data bank will also possess online processing capabilities, and these online operations are accomplished through a series of specially developed operating systems.

Example.   Figure 14.2 presents a generalized model of a common data base for financial, manufacturing, and marketing departments

FIGURE 14.2

Common Data Base for Financial, Manufacturing, and Marketing Departments

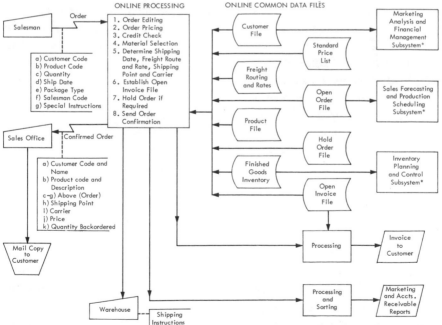

° The order entry subsystem is emphasized in this presentation; marketing analysis and financial management subsystem, sales forecasting and production scheduling subsystem, and inventory planning and control subsystem also have online processing activities and are online with the common data files.

in a particular company. Since this figure is presented for illustration purposes, the online processing activities are only shown for one of the four subsystems: order entry subsystem. The other subsystems—marketing analysis and financial management subsystem, sales forecasting and production scheduling subsystem, and inventory planning and control subsystem—also contain online processing activities.

This generalized model illustrates the information flow for old customers, and it does not show the other procedures required for a new customer. The latter is handled by a subroutine incorporated within the operating system that accomplishes the online processing activities.

In our model we have two manual operations: processing inputs (orders) into system by salesman and mailing machine-prepared order confirmations to customers. All other coding, processing, sorting, and assigning is accomplished by the online operating systems. The latter set of operations clearly indicates that code structure identification and specification activities are prerequisites to the design of a common data base.

Note that the salesman at his remote terminal is coding a minimum amount of data: customer code, product code, quantity, ship date, package type, salesman code, and special instructions. As part of the protected file system, the salesman must have previously identified his organizational unit and sales territory. This combined grouping of data represents the total *variable* information for order entry processing in this given company.

We have illustrated eight online common data files within this common data base. For clarification purposes we will briefly review the contents of two of these files. The customer file includes the customer code, name, address, special billing instructions, unusual product quality requirements, recent transactions, account balance, credit limits, year to date sales, and estimated annual sales by product. The latter data are used in the sales forecasting and production scheduling subsystem.

The open invoice file contains online information on the status of an order. It is automatically updated as changes occur in this status. When the goods are shipped, the online operating system processes these data and sends an invoice to the customer. The record in the open invoice file is closed, and these data are transferred to offline files (in the context of Figure 14.1 this is a Cycle D internal control operation) .

Earlier in the chapter we examined a coding pattern for sales invoice containing 59 digits. This pattern did not include a salesman code (four digits) which is manually recorded on the sales order. We will now examine each of the elements in this coding pattern based on Figure 14.2 and determine which digits are assigned manually and which ones are assigned by the computer system:

Digits	Description	Machine	Salesman
1–4	General ledger account	4	
5–7	Subaccount	3	
8	Division	1	
9–13	Customer code		5
14–19	Product code		6
20–22	Date	3	
23–26	Invoice number	4	
27–30	Location code and cost center		4
31–34	Shipped to and ship from	4	
35	Packaging code		1
36–39	Sales channel and territory codes		4
40–48	Quantity		9
49	Unit of measure	1	
50–59	Price	10	
+4	Salesman code		4
	Total digits	30	33

Thus, we have 30 of the 63 digits being assigned by the computer system. This is possibly a conservative statement because we may be able to create a new set of groupings to encompass location code, cost center, sales channel, and territory code. If this is possible, then the computer system can be used to assign digits to part of this new set. In any case, using the computer system to assign digits in our coding pattern will significantly reduce the error rate.

An Approach for Designing a Common Data Base. When large-scale information systems are being planned, a significant function is determining a common data base. But we must determine the information requirements of decision makers that are to be serviced by a proposed common data base before we can even begin to consider how to design such a data base. In the context of our five phases for planning, designing, and implementing an information system (see Chapter 3), a rough plan for a common data base might be created in phase three: conceptual systems design phase. This rough plan will be revised and modified in the subsequent program design phase.

Hardware-software constraints and economic constraints may force us to drop our plans for a common data base. The proposed common data base may be eliminated entirely by any one of the following factors: (1) location of decision makers; (2) time cycles of various decision-making activities; (3) stability of information requirements for various decision makers; (4) stability of environment in which decision-making activities are performed; (5) extent to which information requirements can be projected, classified, coded, and structured; (6) legal requirements; and (7) security requirements.

Assuming that our rough plan created in the conceptual systems design phase is able to survive the preliminary analysis performed in the program design phase, then we are ready to determine a common data base. At this level the following five steps are necessary for determining a common data base:

1. Identify areas for each common data base
2. Establish logical groupings of areas (such as hierarchy, functional, or activity)
3. Integrate in cross-reference the logical groupings of areas
4. Specify the contents and general code structure of each base
5. Establish study teams for detailed code structure definition

In performing these five steps, we are confronted with a tremendous monitoring and coordinating function. When we faced this same type of problem earlier (see Chapter 13), we recommended that a Code Structure Identification and Management Committee should be established. This type of interdepartmental committee is needed to coordinate, monitor, and administer the common data base.

As the study teams work on specifying common codes and major codes, they must determine the *code element.* If we analyze the major codes in the marketing area, we will focus on the customer, product, sales analysis, and invoice. The invoice codes will include location, shipping instructions, billing instructions, special instructions, product and packaging. Each of the latter might be called an *element,* in the sense of a "code element." If we analyze the related codes in the financial management area, we will examine the accounts receivable record. The accounts receivable codes will include customer code, invoice number, and so forth. Therefore, one of the fundamental problems confronting these study teams is to determine at what level to define the coding units. For example, will we use the accounts receivable level or will we use the invoice location level? Obviously, this degree of specification must occur at as low a level as is feasible.

A matrix is a useful device for determining at what level these coding elements will be specified. We might begin by cross-referencing the major coding documents in each department and placing X's for the intercepts where these same coding elements are being used in other departments. This initial matrix will be followed by a series of matrices where we progressively move to more detailed levels of specification. Through this tedious process we can specify our common data base.

Organizational Considerations. One of the characteristics of a data base is that the depository is independent of information users. In a given company this will probably mean that some members of executive management will be asked to relinquish control over selected data files that they have directly monitored for many years. It is not unusual for this organizational consideration to negate the complete project.

There are two sides to most issues. There are some types of information requirements that executive management *cannot* relinquish control over to the manager of the common data base. For example, there are certain legal requirements and institutional considerations that preclude the treasurer and controller from permitting the manager of the common data base to handle all external reporting requirements. The corporate annual reports, statements for the Securities and Exchange Commission, and manpower reports are some of these reports that must be reviewed by the treasurer and controller prior to their distribution.

If we are to design a common data base, we must face this organizational problem. One approach toward solving this problem is to review with each major decision maker the list of information requirements that have been specified for his decision-making activities. It is assumed that you have previously met with this decision maker and that he concurs with the list of information requirements.

In jointly reviewing this list of requirements, ask the decision maker to please indicate the *extent to which* a common data base might perform certain functions related to each requirement. As an example of what can be accomplished by this approach, in reviewing the sales invoicing and accounts receivable management activities in a given company it was determined that all 13 types of information files could be handled by a common data base. These 13 areas are as follows:

1. Customer files
2. Product files
3. Credit limits and terms
4. Pricing
5. Freight rate and routing
6. Tax reports
7. Systems control (order and shipment information)
8. Accounts receivable aging
9. Credit management
10. Sales returns and adjustments
11. Sales analysis reports
    a) Order analysis
    b) Distribution analysis
    c) Profit contribution by customer/product line/salesmen/district
    d) Budget and actual comparisons
12. Customer tax status
13. Legal constraints
    a) Pricing
    b) Freight payment
    c) Safety and physical

In some organizations an alternative approach is recommended for solving this problem. In reviewing the list of information requirements with each decision maker, ask this individual to try to specify the general nature of his function five years from now when a series of information systems and common data bases will exist. In this alternative approach the decision maker is not confronted with incremental changes in day-to-day activities, but he has the opportunity of conceptualizing about his overall operations. Obviously, we must then assist the decision maker in moving from the proposed state five years from now back to the present.

In a few companies information systems personnel have promised to satisfy all information requirements by some new model, and then subsequently these individuals have achieved only limited results. In this setting, a modified second approach is recommended. Ask the decision maker to leave to you the responsibility of proposing a plan of how we can move from where we are today to where we would like to be in five years. Subsequently, present to the decision maker your specific plan for his approval.

Information Retrieval Systems

In the previous discussion of common data bases, we stated that any offline location of a data bank is usually identified as part of an information retrieval system. In the context of advanced information systems such offline banks cannot be called "common data bases." If we rigorously apply these same criteria, then the offline files in Cycle C (see Figure 14.1) of the systems processing phase may also qualify as part of an information retrieval system.

The latter point is an oversimplification, for according to the professional literature, retrieval of data out of files provided by Cycle C (both online and offline) is a *data retrieval system*. It does not fully qualify as an information retrieval system. According to Lancaster, an information retrieval system is ". . . a complex phenomenon embracing documents, requests, shorthand descriptions of these documents and requests, a mechanism to allow matching of these descriptions, and people."[3] There are two types of activities included under the label of "information retrieval systems": a document retrieval system and a reference retrieval system. A document retrieval system provides for the eventual retrieval of the source document. A reference retrieval system only contains citations; it does not contain the full texts.

In a large corporation we may find information retrieval systems in the following four departments: engineering, legal, long-range planning, and marketing. In evaluating or designing such systems we can benefit from the experience of professional library staffs who have developed some excellent models for indexing and retrieving documents. If the reader is interested in pursuing this area, it is suggested that either Lancaster's book (from which the previous quotation was taken) or the following reference should be studied: A. Kent, *Textbook on Mechanized Information Retrieval* (2d ed.; New York: Interscience Publishers, Inc., 1966).

The *data retrieval systems* associated with TYPE 2.5, TYPE 3, and TYPE 4 information systems are important areas to all decision

---

[3] F. Wilfrid Lancaster, *Information Retrieval Systems: Characteristics, Testing, and Evaluation* (New York: John Wiley & Sons, Inc., 1968), p. 2.

makers in a business firm. The data files provided by Cycle C of the systems processing phase contain a tremendous amount of planning-oriented data. Toward the end of a period, decision makers throughout the business firm will be requesting data from the files provided by Cycle C. Software facilities are available for quickly retrieving these stored data and for preparing a report in good format. MARK IV is the name of one such software package which handles these miscellaneous report requests.

After decision makers in various areas acquire more experience in using these latter data files, then we may find it desirable to establish a series of data files in Cycle C which will be clustered around different types of major requirements. This, of course, will facilitate the quick preparation of desired special reports. Based on this experience, we may establish additional files in Cycle B and assist these decision makers in performing their function in a shorter time period.

In summary, there are some library activities in a business firm that require information retrieval systems. These systems are concerned with either document retrieval or reference retrieval. In most retrieval activities within a business firm, we desire to retrieve coded data that have been assigned on either a manual or machine basis. The latter activities are called data retrieval systems, and they are part of our online and offline files in Cycle C of the systems processing phase.

Online and Real-Time Systems

During the past four years many technological changes and developments in computer equipment and communication facilities have permitted many companies to begin to use online systems. Several industrial firms, banks, and insurance companies have established separate subsidiaries that provide time-sharing services to outsiders. A consumer of these services may store his inventory, accounts receivable or other data in protected files that are online within the time-sharing computer system. In this latter arrangement the consumer uses an online remote terminal for recording his transactions, updating files, processing and sorting data, and printing reports. He has the option of having the report prepared on the facilities of the remote terminal or at the center for the time-sharing computer system.

In many large companies several groups of decision makers may have access to online equipment. By "online equipment," we mean a device that is under the direct control of the central processing unit. If we have an "online system" the network includes part of the central processing unit. Where we have many remote terminals using the same central processing unit, there may be a time delay before a given terminal is brought into an online relation with the central processing unit.

When a company has an advanced information system, it will usually encompass one or more online operating systems. For example, it may include an online order processing system or an online order status system. In other cases, we may have a combination of online order processing, online production scheduling and online distribution. In a given company with this latter combination a customer may be notified within 20 minutes (maximum) that his order has been accepted, will be shipped on a specified date from an identified warehouse by a specified carrier and on what date he should expect arrival at his location.

The latter case is a good example of an online system. In this company it was a 20-minute (maximum) delay for concurrently handling this defined set of activities where we have an annual sales volume of $150 million. There are smaller companies with these online facilities that operate in shorter time periods.

How does an online system differ from a "real-time system"? A real-time system must react to the operation as *it is being processed* or performed; it is not a sufficient condition that the system is capable of reacting to the operation *after* it has been processed or performed. The latter type of network is an online system.

A real-time system will have additional requirements for central processing capabilities that are not present in an online system. The capability of dynamic reaction to an operation as it is being processed will require additional core and online computer programs. Because of these additional computer equipment requirements and special programming efforts, most business firms have elected to use online systems rather than real-time. This situation may be changed in the near future as fourth-generation computer systems are introduced. At present, airline reservations, hotel reservations, banking operations, and a few production and manufacturing activities are currently using real-time systems.

The more common real-time systems are those in operation at

commercial banks and savings and loan institutions. As the customer makes a deposit, the complete accounting transaction is processed, including the updating of the depositor's account balance. In contrast, if this were an online system, there might be a two- or three-minute delay, for example, between the time the customer makes the deposit and the time his account is updated.

There is another special problem in the case of a real-time system. There can be no time delay in processing a transaction, and the network of computer programs do not provide for intermediate storage. What happens in the case of machine failure? We must have duplicate equipment on hand that can be brought online and permit the system to continue to operate in real time. The requirement of duplication of computer equipment makes the real-time system much more expensive than an online system.

Summary

The code structure system is the heart of a large-scale information system. Code pattern identification and specification are prerequisites for the design of a common data file, common data base, data retrieval system, or an information system. Because of the critical role played by this code structure system we strongly recommend that a Code Structure Identification and Management Committee should be established. Other activities of this committee were explained in Chapter 13.

Source documents are typically coded on an input-oriented basis; subsequently, these data are reprocessed and recoded by the computer system. We referred to this second transformation, coding, and assignment operation as the "second processing" of the data.

A generalized model for the systems processing phase was presented which featured four distinct time cycles. We examined the typical information flows in each of these cycles. Later, we recognized that within each cycle there are really multiflows and these provide additional opportunities for designing data files.

A common data base is an online depository of information that is to be used by decision makers in two or more departments. A common data file denotes a unit of records within a common data bank. An illustrative model of a common data base for financial, manufacturing, and marketing departments was presented. From studying this model, the online processing capabilities of a common data base became more apparent.

One of the basic concepts of a common data base is that the data bank is independent of information users. From an organizational standpoint, this means that some members of management may be asked to relinquish control over files that they have directly supervised for many years. In other cases, the manager of the common data base may be requesting more responsibility than he can appropriately handle. We examined two approaches for resolving these organizational problems.

In the last two sections of the chapter, we briefly explained data retrieval systems, information retrieval systems, online systems and real-time systems. These networks have been referred to earlier in our generalized models of information systems; however, the technical characteristics of each had not been examined until the discussion in latter part of this chapter.

TOPICS FOR CLASS DISCUSSION

1. Explain the relationship between the coding process and the classification process.

2. Explain how an identification code can provide a decision maker with additional information.

3. The Internal Revenue Service has an online information retrieval system that reduces the case research time of the attorney to one-tenth the time required by the private lawyer. The case research is, of course, the searching through past decisions for purposes of finding similar incidents that will serve as precedents for the current controversy.

In this situation the Internal Revenue Service can operate with fewer attorneys. However, assume that this online capability were to be inserted in a given company in a highly competitive industry and that an online marketing information system was established. Indicate how the activities and organization of this latter company might change as a result of this new online capability.

4. "In the case of information retrieval systems, the systems analyst is dealing exclusively with *estimated* requirements for information rather than *actual* information requirements." Explain this statement.

5. Differentiate between an online system and a real-time system.

6. "The effectiveness of a coding pattern is a function of (A) how reliably the potential user requirements have been predicted and (B) how effectively the notation of the code is used." Explain this statement.

7. Differentiate between the four distinct time cycles for information flows in the systems processing phase.

8. The edit routine screens and filters input data. After the data have successfully passed the edit routine test, then computer programs may read attributes of these data and may develop additional codes to reflect these composite rankings. Therefore, raw data on a source document in the systems processing phase do not reflect a one-to-one relationship between symbols on source documents and the coded data within the system.

After reviewing Figure 14.2, indicate where the one-to-one relationship between symbols on source documents and the coded data within the system is not being maintained in this illustrated common data base.

9. The manager—transportation department desires to change a transportation code. He consults with the manager—manufacturing department and obtains the latter's consent to make the change. Indicate any other major decision makers that might be affected by a change in the transportation code.

10. Assume that a common data base is proposed for a company. Indicate some of the organizational problems that this may create.

CASE 14–1.   METROPOLITAN INDEPENDENT HOSPITAL GROUP

Executive management at three large, independent hospitals in a major eastern city formed a corporate venture in electronic computers and in information processing and communication systems. The common concern of the "weekend admission" was the original stimulus for getting these three groups of executive management together; however, the joint venture in electronic computers and in information systems encompassed more than admission procedures. The accounts receivable accounting for the three large, independent hospitals was performed on a centralized basis.

Weekend Admission

Periodically, a patient (a nonemergency patient) would be admitted to one of these three hospitals on a late Friday afternoon. At the time the patient was being admitted, he would present an identification card which indicated that he was covered by hospital and medical insurance. The clerk at the hospital would mail a notice to the metropolitan office of the State Medical Service, Inc., and the State Hospital Service, Inc., that a patient with a given identification number had been admitted to the respective hospital.

Because of the time delays associated with mail transmission of information and the nonscheduling of all processing functions over the weekend, the clerks at the combined office for the hospital and medical insurance corporations would not begin to process the above "patient admission notification" until the following Monday or Tuesday. During peak periods, it might be Wednesday before the patient admission notification was processed.

When the above patient admission notification is processed, the office clerks at the insurance corporation discover that the patient is not covered by insurance. Reasons for noncoverage might include (1) policy had expired, (2) new policy was issued which specifically did not cover certain existing medical conditions, and (3) the policy number and card were fraudulent.

Immediately, the hospital would be notified of this situation. But by this time, the "weekend admission" type of patient had incurred a large medical bill for special examinations. Sometimes this type of patient would leave the hospital before the clerks at the hospital were aware that the patient was not covered by insurance.

Regardless of the reason and circumstance, the result is the same. The private, independent hospital probably has a noncollectible accounts receivable. Lawyers, of course, attempt to collect these overdue accounts, but they have only limited success.

Other Considerations

While the impetus for the joint venture in electronic data processing which linked the three hospitals was the common problem of the "weekend admission," other considerations influenced the scope of the new information processing and transmission system. For example, office managers at the respective hospitals were always in the process of training new clerks. The employee turnover rate was high, and the offices were frequently understaffed.

Because of the large volume of "paper" in process within the hospital and the high degree of variation in the contents of this "paper," hospital managements have a difficult task in estimating their current financial positions. Most of management's efforts were in the direction of processing this volume of paper, and little time was given to the management planning and analysis functions.

Another major consideration in this joint venture was the matter of prompt reimbursement from the insurance corporation. At present, there were two significant time delays: (1) the time interval between when a patient receives medical services and the point at which the patient's bill reflects these charges and (2) the time interval associated with the billing and collecting of medical and hospital charges from the combined medical and hospital insurance corporation.

New System

An IBM 1410 computer system was purchased by the corporation formed by the three large, independent hospitals. An extensive network of communication lines was installed to connect various communication points within each hospital to the centralized computer system. With this computer-based system, when a patient enters any of the three hospitals, the relevant information is immediately transmitted through these communication lines to the storage facilities in the computer system. As each hospital and medical service is performed, the appropriate information is transmitted to the patient's record in the computer storage facilities. Finally, when the patient is ready to leave the hospital, he is given a computer-prepared statement which indicates all of his charges.

This computer system is also connected by communication lines with the combined office for the medical and hospital insurance corporation. This insurance corporation has an online information system covering individual policyholder information. Thus, a clerk can place an inquiry in this online system and be immediately informed of the current status of the policyholder. On an exception basis, this information is transmitted back to the appropriate hospital.

The communication lines between the three hospitals, the IBM 1410 computer system, and the medical and hospital insurance corporation are for several purposes. Periodically, the insurance company is billed with the cumulative charges for each insured patient. Since the insurance company has already determined that the so-called insured patient is "covered," the payment of such charges is expedited.

There are other benefits from this system. Since the insurance company has a more up-to-date record of each policyholder's experience, certain types of situations are minimized. For example, some "insured" patients may go to two or more hospitals and spend the maximum period of time in each hospital. The insurance company will only pay for the maximum period of time within a year in the hospital that is provided for by the terms of the insurance policy. Thus this overall system tends to reduce the occurrence of the uncollectible accounts from this type of patient.

This problem is not completely eliminated, because there are still several major private and public hospitals in the metropolitan area which are not connected by some type of information system with the hospital and medical insurance company.

Possible Extensions

Currently, executive managements of these three independent hospitals are considering additional management applications that may be incorporated into this joint computer-based information processing and transmission system. For example, it has been suggested that the history record for each patient might be placed in computer storage.

The management consulting firm with which you are associated was asked to make a high-point review of the existing information processing and communication system.

REQUIRED:

1. Analyze the present system.
2. Indicate how the existing information processing and communication system might be modified in the direction of encompassing more hospital management activities. Be specific.

CASE 14–2.   MIDWEST STOCK EXCHANGE SERVICE CORPORATION

R. John Cunningham, president of the Midwest Stock Exchange Service Corporation, periodically reviews the overall operations of the MSESC for the purpose of evaluating existing operations as a basis for identification of opportunities where additional or improved customer services may be offered. On the basis of such a review in the early part of 1965, Mr. Cunningham was entertaining thoughts regarding the possibility of converting some of the MSESC's operations to an online, real-time system. For example, what would be the nature of the MSESC's operations under a complete real-time system? Would the underlying corporate objectives change under such an advanced information system? On the other hand, without moving toward a more advanced information system, in what areas might the MSESC expand its customer services?

Following is a description of the existing operations of the MSESC.

The Company

The Midwest Stock Exchange Service Corporation, which is a Broker's Centralized Electronic Accounting System, is a wholly-owned subsidiary of the Midwest Stock Exchange. This organization came into being because the members of the governing board for the Midwest Stock Exchange recognized that the typical midwestern broker was in a real profit squeeze. The costs of labor and accounting, as well as the necessity for additional services to customers kept going up and up, while commission rates remained constant. At the same time, it was impossible for the average brokerage firm to economically use computers on either a rental or ownership basis. Consequently, after a detailed study of member firms and their operations, the Midwest Stock Exchange Service Corporation was formed to provide joint accounting services for member firms, using large-scale computers.

The initial study identified every conceivable type of business and way of doing business existing in the brokerage industry throughout the midwestern area. From a number of volunteers, three pilot firms were selected that were very different from each other and encompassed, as much as possible, the variations in business methods that were found among all the firms in the initial study. The objective in this phase of the study was to create a single computer program which was suitable for all the unique requirements of all the brokerage firms. Formerly, there were as many variations in accounting systems and procedures as there were brokerage firms; now, there is one system for all brokerage firms. Currently, all 41 member brokerage firms use the same master set of computer programs.

The 41 member brokerage firms are headquartered in 12 states, even though all the computer processing is performed in Chicago. These firms have 188 branches, and they generate over 8,000 executed orders per day. This daily volume of business is the largest in the country, except for the operations of Merrill, Lynch, Pierce, Fenner, and Smith. Since the Midwest Stock Exchange Service Corporation performs the complete accounting for both the customer and the broker sides of a trade, this volume constitutes over 16,000 trades per day, considering both sides as separate units.

The most remote member brokerage firms range from Minneapolis, Minnesota, to Dallas, Texas; from Denver, Colorado, to the New York City operations of two of the Chicago-based firms; and in the south to Charlotte, North Carolina. From the Pennsylvania border to Denver, and from the Canadian border to Houston, Texas, there are only 11 firms with over 100 trades per day that are not yet members of the Midwest Stock Exchange Service Corporation's system. This 70 percent penetration of the available market is in itself an indication of the acceptance of the Midwest Stock Exchange Service Corporation's product.

The important aspect concerning the success of MSESC's product is that all of the originally identified variations of type and way of doing business are built into *one* set of programs for the computer. This means that MSESC's operators do not have to start and stop the computers to handle each brokerage firm independently; yet, every variation is provided for. Many individual options are available to each participating brokerage firm.

The System

Inputs to the MSESC's system originate after each brokerage firm has initially processed the sales or purchase transaction through the appropriate stock exchange. For example, an investor desires to buy or sell securities. The investor will call his broker and ask the latter to initiate the desired transaction. The broker will call his representative on the floor of the stock exchange who will make the arrangements for buying or selling the securities. After the deal has been completed on the floor of the stock exchange, the brokers are notified by their inside representatives. Then, the brokers notify their clients that the securities have been bought or sold respectively. The investor will pay his broker for the purchase of shares of stock after receiving a written confirmation of the completed transaction. The investor selling the shares of stock will be reimbursed by his broker for the contract amount after deducting the brokerage fee, the federal transfer tax, state tax, and the SEC tax.

As indicated by the above example, each side of the transaction creates a large group of quantitative statistical data that must be accumulated, processed, and reported. The broker's commission, the taxes, the price of the trade, as well as sundry other matters (such as margin trading if applicable) must be accounted for and constantly reviewed, if required. It is precisely at this junction that the electronic computer program of the MSESC enters the framework.

After each broker has been notified by his representative of a completed transaction, the accounting clerk at the brokerage firm will begin to process the entry through the MSESC's accounting system. The broker in his process of handling the transaction will complete a form (an input device) containing the relevant data for the transaction. The accounting clerk will process all of these relevant data over teletype lines to the Chicago Data Center of the MSESC. This information will include names, trades, cash entries, security entries, and inquiries, and these data are transmitted over teletype to the Chicago Data Center for processing.

This type of system is known as "batch processing," as distinguished from "real-time processing." The Chicago Data Center's computer department receives the data from the teletype line as punched paper tape, and these data are converted to magnetic tape for processing. (Data on magnetic tape can be processed by a computer system several times as fast as data on paper tape.)

Only confirmations and batch balancing controls for entries are transmitted back to the brokerage firm from the Chicago Data Center. (After the transaction has been processed by the Chicago Data Center's computer system, data for each brokerage firm are converted from magnetic tape to paper tape; the data on paper tape are transmitted by teletype to the brokerage firm.) The fully addressed confirmations are printed in each broker's office simultaneously. After the accounting clerk in each broker's office has compared and verified the teletype data with the original order, the confirmation is mailed the same day to the customer. Thus, a brokerage firm can bill its customers for the proceeds of a transaction on the same day that the transaction was created on the floor of the stock exchange.

This overall system is illustrated by Exhibit A.

The Chicago Data Center

The Chicago Data Center's problem is gathering data from *many points* and sending to *many points*. The Chicago Data Center receives over four million characters of accounting data daily by teletype and transmits over one and a half million characters per day in confirmation preparation. All other reports are printed at the Chicago Data Center the night of the trade, shipped air freight to the brokerage firms outside Chicago, and delivered via a delivery service to their offices. Practically all locations receive data prior to 10:00 A.M. the morning after the trade.

The teletype lines are duplex (separate send and receive lines) with a 28 ASR and an IBM 870 in the brokerage firm's office. At the Chicago Data Center there are PPT reperfs and tape transmitters, two Digitronics bi-directional converters, and one 80K 8 Tape 710 and two 1401's—36 circuits, over 11,000 miles of private lines, 25 miles of punched paper tape per day, or 6,000 miles per year. Out-of-town brokerage firm's share teletype lines—two brokerage firms to one line.

The basic system is designed so that only a new name and address and the executed order are originated by the accounting clerk in the brokerage firm's office. All other postings and documents of original entry, including all the cashier's entries and reports, are posted automatically. The source of cashier's entries is from punched cards which the Chicago Data Center provides as a result of trades. The punched cards are used to make automatic entries from the brokerage firm's offices for cash and security movement entries. After the executed order is entered into the computer system, the only document originated by the brokerage firm is the proceeds check paid to a customer on the sale of securities.

What are the services actually provided by the MSESC? The

EXHIBIT A
Midwest Stock Exchange Service Corporation

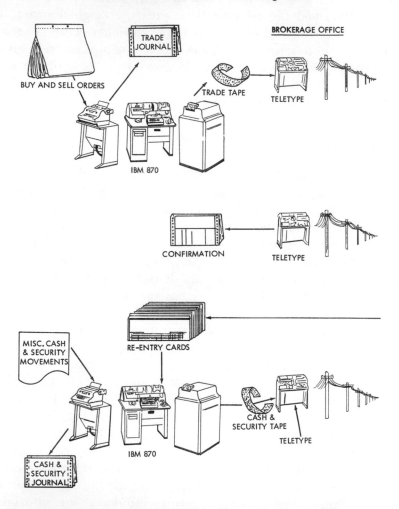

computer system shuffles, reshuffles, sorts, separates, combines, and stores all the information it receives during the course of the day. At night several additional runs of the day's information are made; each brokerage firm receives 28 daily, 6 weekly, and 8 monthly reports. (See Exhibit B for a listing of the more important reports.) All of the accounts of all the brokerage firms are daily updated (for this procedure the computer must search about 750,000 accounts three times daily). Mr. Cunningham summarizes the services provided by the MSESC as follows:

EXHIBIT A (*Continued*)

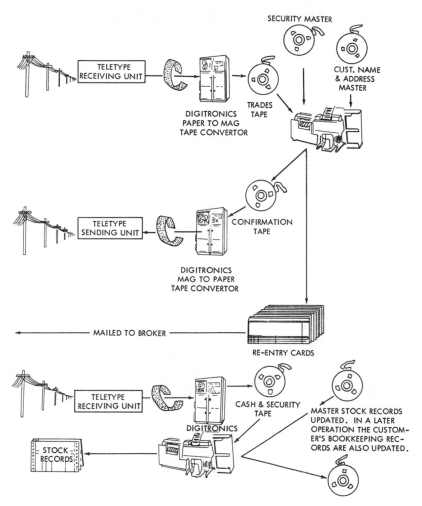

In terms of what we provide in this accounting system, it is easier to relate what we do not provide. We do not confirm open orders, prepare the payroll, or prepare proceeds checks on customer sales, although the system specifies and controls the amount to be paid and when. Every other aspect of brokerage accounting is included and provided for completely in our system, including New York, American, Midwest, other exchanges, over-the-counter, bonds, etc.

The basic charge for all this service is 65 cents per executed order, which includes both sides of the trade. Included for this charge is (1) the equipment in the stock broker's office, (2) all forms printed at the Chicago Data Center except customer statements, (3) communication lines, and (4) the delivery of the daily reports to broker's offices in out-of-town areas.

The 42 different reports that each brokerage firm receives consume, on the average, three fourths of a ton of paper per day. There are 78 computer runs per day involved in the system. These 78 runs are only those involving the big IBM 7010 computer and do not

EXHIBIT B
Midwest Stock Exchange Service Corporation
(A list of the more important reports that the MSESC provides its member brokerage firms)

1. Complete margin accounting on a daily basis.
2. Daily trial balance, which includes for each account
   Trade date balance
   Free credit balance
   Settlement date balance
   Unavailable funds (due to lack of negotiability or receipt of stock)
   Margin due—when issue balance
   Overdue money
   Interest aggregate month-to-date rate
   N.Y.S.E. short form questionnaire totals on a daily basis
3. Daily position reports which show customer and brokerage firms positions by account. Positions are shown according to each security location. Each account contains trade date, settlement date, and memo segregation quantities as they apply.
4. Daily fail lists for both securities and monies for all customers and brokerage firms. Each day's report is complete in itself, so that the previous day's report can be discarded. In addition to reflecting Regulation T requirements, this report enables brokerage firms to manage cash *flow*.
5. Firm trading analysis report, which daily reflects firm trading activity by security and profits for the day, month, and year-to-date by security and by type of trading account.
6. Daily market valuations of stocks borrowed and loaned.
7. In fact, the system is designed in such a way that brokerage firms can determine profits and produce financial statements daily, if they so desire.

include any of the printing runs that are all performed on auxiliary IBM 1401 computers. The MSESC's gross revenue is at the rate of $1,800,000 a year, and the pretax profits are at the rate of $325,000 per year, or 18 percent on gross income.

In addition to providing reports that are vastly more inclusive than any other brokerage accounting system,[4] the MSESC's computers are used to analyze data entered by the brokerage firms and reject the wrong entries. A mirror image of the rejected entry and codes for reason of rejection are transmitted to brokerage firms for their correction and resubmission. There are 750 reasons why the computer will not accept entries for trades and names and addresses. The computer can catch and reject over 50 types of errors in entering cash and security movement entries. This type of editing analysis does not permit erroneous data to enter the accounting records and places the onus on clerks at the brokerage firms to enter data correctly instead of complaining to the Chicago Data Center. Once the data are accepted into the MSESC's system, they are controlled by another feature unique in the system—that of monitoring the brokerage firm's accounting.

Following the billing of the trade, absolute instructions concerning cash and security entries are given to the cashiers in the cage by the computer, after the condition of each account is analyzed by the computer. These instructions are also retained on magnetic tape for follow-up purposes. Thus the computer system instructs the cashiers of the brokerage firms. The instructions are provided in the form of IBM cards that are also used by the broker to make cash and security entries automatically and unattended through the medium of the IBM 870 Document Writer and the teletype lines. This reentry card-principle cuts down the brokers' cost and errors with a ratio of 8 to 1 for these entries compared to the initial trade billing. Each day the computer follows up on these instructions, and if they are not performed on time or correctly, they are reported to the firm on exception reports. Such conditions as transfer prior to payment, sold while in transfer, stock not delivered to customer or safekeeping, securities received from customers and placed in the free box that according to regulations must be segregated, when-issued trades now regular issue were over or under issued in any account, and 47 other similar rules, regulations, and exceptions are monitored by the system. The Chicago Data Center's system also provides similar exception reports on inventory records. Once an item appears on

---

[4] See "Midwest Acts to Let N.A.S.D. Firms Buy Bookkeeping Service," *Chicago Tribune,* June 1, 1965, sec. 3, p. 7: "The N.A.S.D. announcement called the Midwest system one of the 'most sophisticated and completely electronic operations in the securities business.' "

these exception reports, it will remain there daily until corrected. In other words, if a broker ignores these errors, the exception reports will grow and grow. Conversely, if these exceptions are analyzed and corrected daily, the brokerage firm's records will be in better condition than ever before. With this system, it is possible for an accounting manager or partner of a brokerage firm to remain in his office, yet he will know everything that is wrong in the accounting records by just reviewing the exception reports.

Benefits to Participating Brokerage Firms

Following is a list of some of the more important benefits received by participating brokerage firms:

1. Direct cost reduction in terms of "back office" personnel has been 50 percent or more of the staff. In a firm with 250 to 350 executed orders per day, this has meant a *net annual* reduction after the MSESC's charge of $75,000 to $150,000. In a firm with 200 executed orders per day, there were formerly 43 personnel in accounting and cashiering; now there are 20 personnel.

2. Space reduction has been 30 to 40 percent in the back office area.

3. There is practically no overtime under this system. Previously all confirmations had to be prepared, and all the cash and security flow for the day had to be balanced, before the day's work was completed. Sometimes this meant working late in the evening. For example, one brokerage firm that recently joined the MSESC's system reported that when President Eisenhower had his heart attack, employees in the brokerage office had to work until after midnight in order to complete the day's work. But under the MSESC's system when President Kennedy was assassinated, the office closed fairly close to the normal time.

4. Forms and supplies are reduced about 8 to 10 cents per trade. At 200 executed orders per day, this amounts to nearly $5,000 per year.

5. Audit expenses have been reduced anywhere from 26 to 40 percent, depending upon the condition of the brokerage firm prior to conversion and the brokerage firm's use of accounting controls subsequent to conversion.

6. In terms of verification of controls offered and condition of records, about 35 brokerage firms have been audited at least once by

independent CPA firms, since their conversion to the MSESC's system. In all but two instances, the records of the brokerage firms were reported to be in far more perfect order than they were before joining the MSESC's system.

7. In terms of customer service, the brokerage firms have never had more to offer.

Data Transmission Problems

The designers of the MSESC's system expected at the outset and thus planned solutions for predictable problems in the area of operator errors, machine malfunctions, and communication line interference. Following is a list of some of the solutions to expected problems that were included in the original system in order to make the transmission system work:

Solutions	*Problems*
A. Broker Controls	
1. *Batch Control Log* What? Numbering batch Batch totals—records and dollars, etc. Batch can be any size When?	Nonreceipt of data.
2. *Break Key* Control of receiving by broker If bad data, transmission problem, receiver malfunction, can be shut off.	Not ready to receive transmission.
3. *Light Signal* Shared line control Stops spiking, etc.	Simultaneous transmission.
4. *Visual Comparison of Teletype Received Hard Copy* Confirmation matched to order ticket	Transmission to wrong brokerage firm.
5. *Transmission Acknowledgment* Verify receipt of data	Nonreceipt of data.
6. *Edit/Reject List* Complete reference to all input,	Garbled data; missing, added and changed characters; non-

Solutions	*Problems*
indicating batches in, rejections, etc., for comparison to own records	receipt of data; nonentry into system, as well as clerks in firms preparing entries properly.

B. Center Controls

1. *Batch Control Log* Same as (1) above for brokers	Nonreceipt of data.
2. *Computer Edit on All Input* Massive edit to produce Edit/Reject List to each brokerage firm	Garbled data; missing, added and changed characters; nonreceipt of data; nonentry into system.
3. *Punch Paper Tape Count* Match out number of tapes received on teletype to number entered into converter	Nonentry into system.
4. *Signal Bell and Light Alarms* Messages—bell and light Light trouble and open circuit— Warning light Low tape—indicator light Blown fuse—warning alarm	Nonreceipt of data and machine malfunctions.
5. *Transmission Time Record* Proof of transmission, identifying type of data sent from the Chicago Data Center	Not ready to receive transmission and transmission to wrong brokerage firm.
6. *Call Directing Code (CDC)* Automatically turns broker's receiver on/off—first one character and problem until two used	Transmission to wrong brokerage firm.
7. *Pre-prepared Standardized Messages* Drastically reduces time spent preparing messages	Overly heavy message traffic, not ready to receive transmission.
8. *Hard Copy Teletype Monitors* Center and AT&T office control to attempt to locate malfunctioning equipment	Machine malfunction.
9. *Spare Equipment Jack Plug Panel* Permits immediate checkout of suspect equipment. Reduces de-	Machine malfunction.

Solutions	*Problems*
lay when switching is necessary. Why no message exchanger—the MSESC's cost now $5,000 per month including backup. Two message exchangers would run at least $18,000.	
10. *"Printed" Punched Tape* Permits rapid reading of messages and identification of transactions, batch control numbers, etc.	Overly heavy message traffic.
11. *Colored Punched Paper Tape* Input—Pink Output—Green Trouble Check—Gray Messages—Buff	Machine malfunction.

In addition to the above list of planned solutions to anticipated problems, the designers of the MSESC's system considered other matters, but eventually decided that these latter kinds of problems might not occur. However, based on actual experience of operating the MSESC's system, these kind of problems did occur. Following is a list of solutions to these latter types of problems:

A. Broker

(Cannot expect an input function at a remote location to become overly concerned with controls. As much as possible this must be done for them if the MSESC's system is to achieve success. Best we can hope for is that they will retain input tapes.)

Solutions	*Problems*
1. *Retaining Input Tapes* Standard procedure was changed to require a retention period of three days on all tapes transmitted to the Chicago Data Center	Brokerage firms not current in checking out previous day's input.

B. Center

1. *Retaining Input Tapes* Same as (1) above for brokers	Brokerage firms not current in checking out previous day's input.
2. *Receiving Check* At periodic intervals the Chicago	High frequency of failure to receive data.

Solutions	*Problems*
Data Center's communication operator dabs a colored dye on all punched paper tape spewing out of the receivers. The colors correspond to different periods of the day. It is easy to see who has not been transmitting for a period of time. Teletype or telephone contact quickly determines the proper status of the circuit.	
3. *Quality Control* Punched paper tape specifications must be established and rigidly followed. Teletype punch dies must be checked and resharpened on a rigid schedule.	Sensitivity of optical reader on converter.
4. *Equipment Manufacturers Service Personnel Must Work Together as a Team* Ranges for adjustment become quite narrow. As a secondary precaution daily "asterisking" of all magnetic tapes used for collection input from the converter was instituted.	Communications Converter/Computer Tape Drive compatibility.
5. *Confirmation Test* Before daily transmission of confirmations, a proven master is compared to a sample test confirmation to check out the converter.	Converter output requires constant monitoring for accuracy.
6. *Teletype Repair Test* As soon as a Teletype repair man touches any unit, a spare is plugged in and remains on line until the repaired or preventive maintenance unit output is visually compared to the spares output.	High incidence of teletype trouble after preventive maintenance or equipment repairs.

Solutions	*Problems*
7. *Transmission to Wrong Firm Control*	Operator error transmitting to wrong brokerage firm more frequent than expected.

Programs were altered:

   a) Punched paper tape has visual code numbers of the brokerage firm punched in

   b) Reject list has "end print" to recognize when all data is in.

8. *Teletype/Digitronics Test*	Perpetual problem trying to determine if teletype equipment, line, converter, or operator is malfunctioning.

A rigid 5-minute test of 2,000 characters shifting between alpha characters and numeric digits (reputed by AT&T and Digitronics to be the most demanding and comprehensive test ever witnessed). Each morning, every brokerage firm sends in the prepunched (Mylar) tape to the Chicago Data Center. The output is loaded and tape compared to a proven perfect master. If differences are noted, a quick second tape comparison is performed which positively isolates the malfunctioning unit. Immediate corrective action is then taken.

The previous discussion of data transmission problems was included for purposes of giving the reader of this case study some appreciation of the vast array of problem areas that were encountered in the initial operation of this electronic computer and transmission system. While these problems have been resolved, inferences can be made regarding the general types of situations that might occur if the Midwest Stock Exchange Service Corporation's computer system were to be changed from the present online batch processing system to a real-time system.

As an overall indication of the ability of the MSESC's personnel to cope with these problem areas, the following statement by Mr.

Cunningham gives us a clue: "Error factors in teletype transmission among *other users are reported* as 5% plus error factor; with us, the error factor is less than one-tenth of one percent."

REQUIRED:

1. Following the information systems approach, analyze the present system.
2. Comment about the possibility of changing the MSESC's present online batch processing system to a real-time system. What might be the nature of operations under this latter type of system?
3. What additional services might the MSESC provide its customers? (Suggestions: consider such things as online customer account balances for each brokerage firm's customers, online information retrieval system of historical financial data for all firms listed on a recognized stock exchange, etc.) Comment about each of your suggestions.
4. What would be the nature of the MSESC's function under a totally computerized stock exchange condition? For background data on this question, consider the following reference: Richard E. Sprague, *Electronic Business Systems: Management Use of On-Line—Real-Time Computers* (New York: Ronald Press Company, 1962), pp. 96–101.
5. Explain the effect of the following announcement on your responses to the above questions:
   Midwest Acts to Let N.A.S.D.[5] *Firms Buy Bookkeeping Service*
   The National Association of Securities Dealers and the Midwest Stock Exchange have reached an agreement allowing N.A.S.D. members to use Midwest's centralized electronic bookkeeping system, Robert W. Haack, president of the N.A.S.D., announced yesterday.[6]

---

[5] N.A.S.D. has 4,000 members throughout the country, including 3,200 over-the-counter traders.

[6] *Chicago Tribune,* June 1, 1965, sec. 3, p. 7.

CHAPTER 15

Evaluation and Design of Company Total Information Flows

CHAPTER 2 presented a framework for the information systems approach, and Chapter 4 explained how information flows are integrated into successively larger units of analysis until finally an information system is formed. This perspective is excellent for initially designing a series of information systems in a business organization. However, when a business organization is already in existence and has some types of information systems in operation, then the systems analyst will have to modify the sequencing of steps that he follows in his study.

This chapter presents some additional guidelines that the systems analyst may follow in coping with the study of company total information flows. The discussion consists of three parts. First, some practical guidelines are given that the systems analyst can follow in determining what are the present information systems in a large, complex organization. Second, consideration is given to outlining an approach that the systems analyst might employ in evaluating the existing information systems in a business organization. Third, the topic of designing new information systems while working in the constraints of old information systems is explored, with special emphasis given to the justification of changes.

IDENTIFYING AND UNDERSTANDING THE EXISTING INFORMATION SYSTEMS

When the systems analyst undertakes a study of the company total information flows, he must be able to perform two critical functions.

First, he must identify the existing information flows. Second, he must gain a sufficient insight into the operations of the company that he is able to specify the purpose for which each information flow is occurring. The full attainment of this latter function would include the ability (1) to see how various information flows are integrated into information systems and (2) to comprehend the organization objective served by each of these information systems.

Identify the Existing Information Flows

How does the systems analyst identify the existing information flows? He asks questions; he observes the document flow within the organization; he analyzes the internal and external reports; and he pieces together the various clues that he has gained in much the same way that a puzzle is solved.

Frame of Reference. There are no magical methods of performing these tasks; however, many practitioners will argue that flow diagrams, network analyses, and matrices are excellent tools that assist in performing them. Flow diagrams, network analyses, and matrices all have a common advantage. They provide the systems analyst with a frame of reference for studying and evaluating the various clues. This frame of reference is more encompassing than any single organization unit or department. For example, items on the periphery of one framework may be the center of attention in the next framework. Through a series of these frames of reference, the systems analyst can begin to construct an overview of the total operations of the company.

People as Informants. The employees throughout the business organization are, of course, a valuable source of information. However, there are many cautions that the novice systems analyst might benefit from in dealing with employees. First, while members of management are a prime source of information and may be deeply interested in the systems analyst's project, the novice frequently makes too extensive use of management's time. Management expects the systems analyst to be competent and to be able to conduct his own study with the minimum amount of coordination time and effort on its part.

Second, some people in almost any business organization will intentionally mislead the systems analyst. Sometimes a manager may mislead a systems analyst as a way of "testing" his competence; some individuals will make an erroneous reply to a systems analyst's question so as to discourage him from asking any more questions. Other times the reasons for erroneous answers are not always obvious.

Third, people in different parts of the organization may be so closely identified with their day-to-day activities that they may have lost all sense of objectivity. Or they may be working on changing existing operations and will describe for you "what they would like to have" rather than tell you "what currently is." Other individuals may be uninformed about the "total picture" of some operation, or, at least, may have an erroneous conception of it.

Finally, the systems analyst should periodically review basic reference books on human relations, organization, and research design. The reason for studying the latter two areas is self-evident. By reviewing a good reference on human relations, the systems analyst with some practical experience will not only gain a deeper appreciation of the author's ideas, but will also see that much of the "unusual" behavior he has observed in an organization may not be so "unusual" after all. All three basic references assist the systems analyst in maintaining a scientific perspective about his work.

Closed Loop. The novice systems analyst always has the upward flow of information in the business organization. Documents are processed, summarized, sorted, screened, and incorporated in highly condensed reports to executive management. But what backward flow of information closes each "loop"? What administrative actions on a management by exception basis are being followed?

Time Frame. Each information flow occurs in some time frame, and the identification and recognition of this time frame are extremely important for informed analysis. The experienced systems analyst will include the time frame identification in his coding system for a matrix or will have separate flow diagrams, for example, for the various time intervals.

People as Decision Makers. An information flow must involve a decision maker and be specified in terms of a given time frame. This decision maker has to be identified before the information flow can be meaningfully described and interpreted in the next function.

Summary. This brief discussion has attempted to cite some of the common problems the novice systems analyst has in identifying the existing information flows in a large, complex business organization. It is hoped that through this type of discussion the reader will be able to avoid some of these common pitfalls.

Specify the Purpose of Each Information System

At the completion of the previous function, the systems analyst is able to identify the various information flows within the business organization. Each information flow is a closed loop and is described in terms of a decision maker in a given time frame. In the current function, the systems analyst begins by relating the identified information flows with the organization chart. From the many clues he has gained, the systems analyst attempts to impute an organization objective for the various decision makers.

In a "real" company, the systems analyst will test the accuracy of his assumptions and will make the appropriate corrective action. In coping with the lengthy, complex case study at the end of this chapter (Case 15–1, Mercantile Financial Corporation and Subsidiaries) the reader can only evaluate his assumptions in terms of their reasonableness in relation to the factors and information in the case study.

The systems analyst now has specified organization objectives for the various decision makers and has a series of frames of reference that identify by time frame the information flows within the organization. Next, he will change his perspective and ask, "Are these information requirements, or, are they just current uses of information?" This critical question is separately applied to each of the information flows within the business organization. In and through these studies, the systems analyst is endeavoring to try to get at the fundamental, organization purpose of each activity.

The completion of this function might be represented by a report that would be a close approximation to a report prepared at the completion of a small-scale organization study of the company.

EVALUATING THE EXISTING INFORMATION SYSTEMS

The systems analyst must mentally detach himself from the business organization if he is to evaluate objectively the existing information systems. His task is to perform a critical scrutiny of his previous reports that identified the information requirements of various decision makers and specified the existing information systems.

In the process of performing this critical scrutiny, the systems analyst is concurrently making other discoveries. Specifically, the studies thus far have given the systems analyst a good appreciation of the *formal* information systems. As he evaluates the formal information systems, he may discover several *informal* information systems of which he was not previously aware.

The approach taken in performing this critical scrutiny and evaluation will vary, based on the personal preferences of the systems analyst. We are strong advocates of following the processes of administration as a framework of analysis for performing this evaluation.[1] The processes involved in setting objectives, planning, organizing, and controlling should be examined in detail for the total company's activities and for each function within the company. This examination should begin at the highest level with such probing questions as:

1. What is the real nature of the company's business?
2. What niche does management see the company serving?
3. Is this niche included in the long-range plans?
4. What are management's short-term objectives?
5. Are these objectives compatible with the market niche?

As this powerful, top-level organization analysis is performed, the systems analyst will begin to bridge the gap between "what is" in terms of the *formal* information systems and the information flows associated with executive management's long-range decision-making activities. It is not unusual for several voids to be identified by this process where management is not performing certain assumed management activities. In other areas, the systems analyst will discover many opportunities for improvement. These latter opportunities will include both (1) using alternative sources of data in an improved matching of information requirements and (2) identifying unsatisfied information requirements that can now be matched.

DESIGNING NEW INFORMATION SYSTEMS

Whenever the systems analyst is evaluating existing information systems versus proposed information systems, he needs to quantitatively compare these alternative systems. The critical distinctions

---

[1] For an excellent paper on using the processes of administration as a framework for analysis, see Edward T. P. Watson, "Diagnosis of Management Problems," *Harvard Business Review,* Vol. XXXVI (January–February, 1958), pp. 69–76.

between these information systems may primarily consist of (1) differences in speed, (2) differences in quality of information, (3) differences in breadth of information, (4) differences in cost of processing information, (5) differences in cost of transmitting information, (6) differences in extent of information that can be stored for future use, and so forth.

Regardless of the nature of these distinctions, a formal probability model is a useful tool in quantitatively expressing these comparisons. For example, the probability model for a computer feasibility study might include the following factors, in addition to the normal direct, out-of-pocket cost comparisons.

1. What can executive management do with faster information?

    Indicate the types of decisions and activities that could be made (such as increased speed in preparing and mailing invoices). Estimate the marginal advantage that would be realized from each of these types of decisions and actions.

2. What new types of decisions can executive management make using this increased ability to *react* to information that will be provided by the proposed computer system?

    List the new types of decisions that could be made, and estimate the financial benefit that would be realized from each of these decisions.

3. What are some of the indirect benefits that would be derived from the proposed computer system?

    List the indirect benefits that would be obtained, such as (a) reduction in personnel recruitment, (b) reduction in supervisory time spent in training new employees, and (c) reduction in supervisory time spent in performing clerical functions because of personnel shortages. Indicate for each item the estimated financial benefit that would be realized under the proposed computer system.

There are other dimensions to the process the systems analyst uses in evaluating proposed information systems. For example, is executive management seeking new types of personnel for key positions who will be able to make additional new types of decisions? What changes are envisioned in the organization structure in the near future? What changes are forecast in the short run for the volume and complexity of transactions processed by the information systems?

The systems analyst must strive to identify all major aspects of these comparisons. For example, when there is unused capacity in the computer system, some members of management will argue that the marginal cost of adding other applications to the computer system is very low. What these individuals fail to recognize is that other proposed future applications may be unfairly restricted. As an illustration, a company had most of its computer system involved with inventory activities and payroll. Other applications were suggested that would yield a higher financial return from using the computer system. However, each of these latter applications was rejected because of the out-of-pocket cost that now would be required to design and install a manual system for handling the inventory activities.

Summary

This chapter has focused on some special problems that the systems analyst encounters when he is trying to evaluate and design a company's total information systems. This discussion also serves a dual function of providing a frame of reference that the reader might use in coping with the lengthy, complex case study at the end of this chapter.

The Mercantile Financial Corporation and Subsidiaries case study attempts to describe the complete operations of a financial institution. The study presents the organization chart, a detailed description of the document flow within each section of the organization (along with a description of the functions performed within each section), and copies of recent financial statements. The primary objective of the case study is to provide the reader with an opportunity to apply the information systems approach to the overall activities of a company in a controlled setting; it is assumed that the next time the reader applies this approach in such detail will be in a "live" situation.

As a final suggestion, the reader might view the Mercantile Financial case study as though the reader had been engaged to perform a high-point review of the total operations of the company in order to determine if the company's information systems merited a more thorough examination.

TOPICS FOR CLASS DISCUSSION

1. Over the past few years, different activities at a major corporation had been programmed for a large-scale computer system, and

this has resulted in numerous disjointed and unconnected applications in the computer system. In fact, these applications are so unrelated in terms of the actual detailed computer programs that a management consulting firm estimated that the total computing time could be reduced 40 percent through installing a series of integrated information systems. If you were employed to establish a series of integrated information systems in this setting, how would you proceed? What specific factors would you give special consideration to? Be specific.

2. In a proposed computer-based information system, it is estimated that 50 percent of each salesmen's time will be saved by the proposed system. Specifically, the collection activities currently being performed by salesmen will be handled by clerical employees at the home office using up-to-date information from the computer system and the prompt communication channels that will be provided by the proposed transmission system. How can this savings be quantified for inclusion in a probability model? What specific factors might tend to negate this proposed savings?

CASE 15–1.   MERCANTILE FINANCIAL CORPORATION AND SUBSIDIARIES

In the late 1950's the executive vice president of Mercantile Financial Corporation and Subsidiaries was of the opinion that the public accountants who annually audited the firm were more interested in assuring the creditors that their assets were safe, than they were in assisting the management of the firm being audited. Therefore, in 1959, the executive vice president initiated managerial accounting system studies. The studies established proper control patterns and specified the preparation of managerial reports by each location within the overall corporation. In addition, increased emphasis was given to internal auditing. The descriptive procedures of the firm's present operations, as indicated in this case, are highly influenced by these studies.

Currently, the executive vice president is considering the possibility of increased mechanization of the information systems. During the past 18 months, a data processing service center has been used to prepare two statistical reports and to maintain customer ledger cards for one of the firm's operations—small consumer loans. Should other operations be converted to data processing? When should the firm stop using a data processing service center and acquire its own capabilities in this area? These are some of the questions facing the executive vice president.

Frequently, management consultants and representatives of equipment manufacturers ask for interviews with the executive vice president for the purpose of trying to convince him that a particular type of systems review and feasibility study should be undertaken. Each of the different sales presentations emphasizes what some of the larger firms in the financial area are currently doing and that some of the smaller firms, according to reliable confidential sources, are reported to be moving in the same direction. Furthermore, the speaker discusses some of the unusual applications in other industries that might be implemented at Mercantile Financial Corporation, in which case a tremendous competitive advantage and savings might be gained from being the first firm in the industry to adopt these new techniques and procedures. Of course, in the conclusion of each of these interviews, the speaker tries to convince the executive vice president that the speaker is the best-qualified person to make such studies.

Thus far, the executive vice president has refused to have either a general systems review or a feasibility study conducted. However, members of executive management have begun to informally reexamine their operations and consider the cost of the present system.

For example, the executive vice president feels that the major information systems problem facing management is one of assembling data in known areas rather than a problem of not knowing what information it wants. These known areas include the ability to distinguish between desirable and undesirable dealers by source of business. Immediate information is also needed on changes in the volume of new loan applications and the reasons for such changes by type of business—accounts receivable loans, inventory loans, equipment loans, second mortgages, small consumer loans, consolidated loans, combined personal-business loans, furniture and appliance loans, and motor and automobile loans. In the commercial area, immediate information is needed regarding an unfavorable change in the financial status of a customer. The customer's financial status may appear adequate at the time the loan is made, but subsequently the customer changes to an undesirable classification.

The following discussion examines the different aspects of the corporation's overall operations and consists of four parts. First, a brief synopsis is presented on the history of the firm. Second, a highlight review is made of the organization structure, including top management and home office operations and the operations of each of the divisions. Third, a more extensive and thorough analysis is made of the data accumulation, processing and reporting activities of each section within the overall corporation. In this lengthy third part of the case study, consideration is given to (1) customer characteristics, (2) legal aspects of different types of loans, (3) procedures followed in processing data including the format of selected documents, (4) the format, content and uses made of selected reports, and (5) the administrative and internal control functions encompassed within these operations.

The fourth and final part of the case study presents other financial and statistical data including the formats of responsibility reports; historical financial data for the consolidated company from 1954 to 1963; a summary of the increase in net worth, by source, for the same 10-year period; and finally, selected cost and statistical data regarding data accumulation and processing activities.

The Company

This financial institution is engaged in commercial and consumer financing operations and on December 31, 1963, had outstanding accounts receivable and notes receivable from these two divisions totaling $65,000,000. The current level of operation is a substantial improvement over the previous year (which totaled $53,000,000), in spite of the fact that there was a reduction in the total volume of automobile loans because of the aggressive competition by commercial banks, who offered lower interest rates to consumers than the rates offered by consumer financial institutions. (This latter matter is discussed in detail subsequently in this case study.) All indications suggest that a significant rate of growth will be achieved at Mercantile Financial Corporation in each future year.

The original company began in 1917 as an automobile finance company, and in 1924 the commercial finance operations were added. The same management operated the firm from 1917 to 1954, at which time the founder of the firm died. The founder's son, who had a number of years' experience with the firm, began to direct operations, and he was committed to a policy of growth. In 1954 the operations of the then MERCANTILE DISCOUNT CORPORA-

TION AND SUBSIDIARY COMPANIES were restricted to the Midwest, and the firm was privately owned. During the next six years, (1955–60) the total accounts receivable and notes receivable were increased four times ($8,000,000 to $33,000,000), and operations were expanded outside the Midwest area.

In September, 1960, the firm was changed to a public corporation by the issuance and registration of stock under the corporate name of MERCANTILE DISCOUNT CORPORATION AND SUBSIDIARY COMPANIES. In 1962, the corporate name was changed to MERCANTILE FINANCIAL CORPORATION AND SUBSIDIARIES. The stock is sold over the counter, with The First National Bank of Chicago serving as transfer agent and Continental Illinois National Bank and Trust Company of Chicago serving as registrar.

Currently, the firm consists of 22 corporations which are engaged in all types of commercial and consumer financing operations and in insurance brokerage activities.[2] The commercial financing operations are directed from four regional offices: New York City, Atlanta, Chicago, and St. Louis. The consumer division operations consist of 10 consumer loan offices, a motor and automobile discount office, and a furniture and appliance discount office; all of the consumer division's offices are in Chicago. The motor and automobile office also handles insurance transactions, and a given consumer loan office manager may serve as an agent for four different corporations, depending on the type and amount of the consumer loan.[3] Thus, most consumer financing division offices have activity associated with several corporations.

The services offered by the Mercantile Financial Corporation and

---

[2] For internal management purposes, some operations are considered as separate units, when in fact they are only responsibility units and not separate corporations. These different accounting units (there are 32 such accounting units) are discussed in a subsequent section of this case study under the heading of "Responsibility Reports." The large number of corporations is partly indicative of the manner in which the firm has grown (by acquisition of existing financial institutions) and is partly necessary because of legal reasons.

[3] Each consumer loan office may make small loans up to $800 (one corporation), personal loans of $801 to $5,000 (another corporation), semibusiness loans up to $5,000, and nonlicensed (referring to the Illinois State Regulatory Authority) loans over $5,000 (both of these latter types of loans are activities of a third corporation); the office may also finance time-sale paper for the purpose of converting to direct consumer operations (a fourth corporation). A different corporation is used for loans over $800 that were made before the 1962 Illinois law was passed to regulate this type of loan, and consumer loan offices may collect funds due on these accounts.

Subsidiaries cannot be obtained by its customers from regular commercial banks. For example, a given commercial firm might desire to borrow more money on its accounts receivable, inventory, and equipment than can be obtained from a commercial bank; the commercial firm is willing to pay a higher rate of interest for the additional risk inherent in this type of loan. If the commercial firm desires a loan under the terms of a higher interest rate, obviously the commercial firm's management must believe that the investment opportunities are such that the firm will realize a substantial net gain from the employment of these additional funds, or else management would not desire such a loan under these conditions.

The executive vice president recently explained the activities of the Mercantile Financial Corporation and Subsidiaries in the following manner:

The relation of our loan officers to our customers is analogous to the doctor-patient relation of the pediatrician to the infant. The infant becomes too old for the pediatrician and is treated by other types of medical doctors, or else the infant dies. Likewise, a client becomes self-sufficient (including being able to borrow from commercial banks at a lower rate of interest) and no longer needs our services, or else the client becomes bankrupt.

Thus we, like the pediatrician, must constantly obtain new clients to replace our present clients. Unlike most other business firms, we cannot plan on our present customers as being a major group of our future customers. Annually, new customers must be obtained in order to maintain our present level of activity, and if an increase in volume is desired, then a larger volume of new customers is necessary.

Organization Chart

Exhibit A is the organization chart for the top level of management. Note that the vice presidents are at the operating level and actually participate in day-to-day operations.

Commercial Division

Exhibit B is the organization chart for the Commercial Division. The St. Louis branch office is semiautonomous, and the manager of the St. Louis branch office, a senior vice president, is independent as far as internal operating matters. The St. Louis Commercial Branch was opened last year after acquiring an existing corporation, and one of the stipulations of the purchase agreement was that extra shares of stock in the parent corporation would be distributed to former stockholders of the purchased company, depending on the extent to

EXHIBIT A
Organization Chart—Top Management

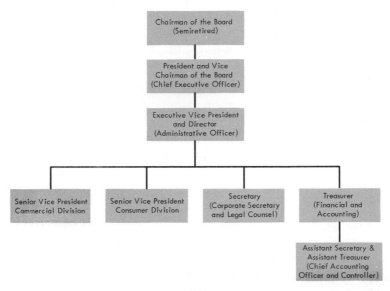

EXHIBIT B
Organization Chart—Commercial Division

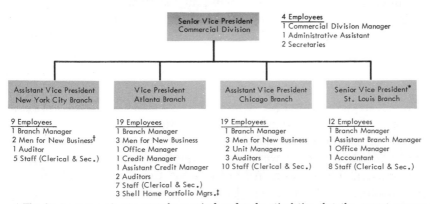

* The St. Louis branch was recently acquired under the stipulation that the current manager would be a senior vice president of Mercantile Financial Corporation and Subsidiaries and a member of the board of directors; of course, there were also other considerations in the pooling of interest agreement.

† New business men are also called "solicitors."

‡ Shell home portfolio managers work out of the Atlanta office, calling on accounts in that area.

which the total earnings for the St. Louis branch were above a certain level for the first three years of operation as a subsidiary of Mercantile Financial Corporation and Subsidiaries.

The managers of the other three commercial branch offices are under the direct supervision of the Commercial Division manager, who is physically located at the home office. However, each branch office is a fully operating office. The accounting functions are decentralized, and each office must develop its own new business. Furthermore, each office is responsible for the audit of its clients; however, the auditors are alternated between the different Commercial Division branch offices for purposes of internal control.

This audit function regarding clients is extremely important for loans from the Commercial Division. Management needs to know if there has been a change in the financial status of the customer since the loan was made (the customer may appear desirable at the inception but subsequently change to an undesirable classification) and if all collections by the client, under certain types of loans, have been forwarded to the branch office. In addition to these areas, the other internal audit functions relate to verification of account balances and the physical location and use of equipment covered by a loan agreement, including both the verification of client's balances with the account balance per branch office's records and the verification of the pertinent account balances of the client's books with the client's customers.

As previously indicated, the St. Louis Commercial Branch Office was opened as a result of acquiring an existing corporation in 1963 under a pooling of interests arrangement. Likewise, expansion into the Atlanta and New York City areas was the result of purchasing existing corporations. In the Chicago area, a separate corporation was created for commercial operations in the state of Wisconsin because of legal considerations.

In total, there are eight separate corporations in the Commercial Division that, from an accounting standpoint, are treated as nine companies—some of the commercial operations in the Atlanta area are handled as if they were the complete operations of the parent corporation. The accounting entities for the Commercial Divisions are as follows: Atlanta area, three companies; New York City area, two companies; Chicago area, three companies; and St. Louis area, one company.

Since the activities of each company do not overlap into other branch office areas, the total operations for a given commercial office is equal to the summation of the company reports under that branch. Furthermore, the types of activities conducted by each company under a Commercial Division branch office do not overlap and are easily identified by type of transaction, which is based on legal considerations. Each transaction document indicates the corporation to which the transaction relates. Thus, the accounting records readily permit the preparation of company reports (which are required to be submitted to the Secretary of the State in which the corporation's charter is granted) and Commercial Division branch office reports.

Consumer Division

When the first branch office was opened, it was organized into three sections: (1) automobile and motor operations, (2) furniture and appliance operations, and (3) small loan operations. There was a branch manager and a collection manager for each section. Each section within an office was considered to be a separate accounting entity. This type of organization for the Consumer Division branch office just did not work. Even though all three sections relate to consumer financing, different techniques and methods are required for activities associated with each section. The techniques used in the small loan operations are not equally applicable to the automobile and motor discount operations, and vice versa. Eventually, a different office was opened for each type of consumer financing operation.

Exhibit C illustrates the current organization chart for the Consumer Division. While the chart shows the senior vice president as the manager of the Consumer Division, the relation between the Consumer Division manager and the heads of the various offices is loose. Each section manager reports jointly to the Consumer Division manager and to the executive vice president of the parent corporation. Furthermore, the Consumer Division manager also serves as head of the furniture and appliance office. A separate office is not maintained for the functions of Consumer Division manager.

Within the Consumer Division, there are many corporations, because of the following reasons: (1) some of the expansion occurred through the acquisition of existing corporations, (2) there are legal considerations which in some instances dictate that separate corporations must be established for the performance of certain types of activities, (3) there are important tax consequences of having several

EXHIBIT C
Organization Chart—Consumer Division

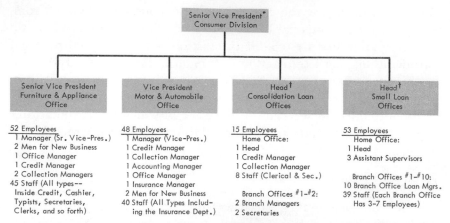

52 Employees	48 Employees	15 Employees	53 Employees
1 Manager (Sr. Vice-Pres.)	1 Manager (Vice-Pres.)	Home Office:	Home Office:
2 Men for New Business	1 Credit Manager	1 Head	1 Head
1 Office Manager	1 Collection Manager	1 Credit Manager	3 Assistant Supervisors
1 Credit Manager	1 Accounting Manager	1 Collection Manager	
2 Collection Managers	1 Office Manager	8 Staff (Clerical & Sec.)	Branch Offices #1-#10:
45 Staff (All types—	1 Insurance Manager		10 Branch Office Loan Mgrs.
Inside Credit, Cashier,	2 Men for New Business	Branch Offices #1-#2:	39 Staff (Each Branch Office
Typists, Secretaries,	40 Staff (All Types Includ–	2 Branch Managers	Has 3-7 Employees)
Clerks, and so forth)	ing the Insurance Dept.)	2 Secretaries	

* The senior vice president of the Consumer Division is also head of the furniture and appliance office. A separate office is not maintained for the overall management of the Consumer Division. The channel between the senior vice president of the Consumer Division and the managers of the three sections is extremely loose. Each section head answers jointly to the division head and to the executive vice president of the corporation.

† The heads of the consolidation loan offices and small loan offices are not officers of the parent corporation; however, they are officers of various subsidiary corporations.

corporations instead of one corporation, (4) the decentralization of operations into separate companies is an advertising point employed by the firm, and (5) this separation into units provides better profit control and determination.

Specifically, there are 13 corporations within the Consumer Division, and they are dispersed by sections in the following manner: furniture and appliance office, one corporation; motor and automobile office, two corporations; consolidation loan offices, two corporations; and small loan offices, eight corporations. Each of the 10 small loan offices is handled as a separate accounting entity; however, 3 of the offices are really divisions of the same corporation. Likewise, one of the corporations in the consolidation loan area has 12 branch offices. All of the operations of the motor and automobile section are centered in one office, and, excluding some collection activities, all of the operations of the furniture and appliance section are centered in one office.

Home Office

Exhibit D presents the administrative staff for the home office operations. Selected members of the home office staff actively partici-

EXHIBIT D
Organization Chart—Top Management Staff

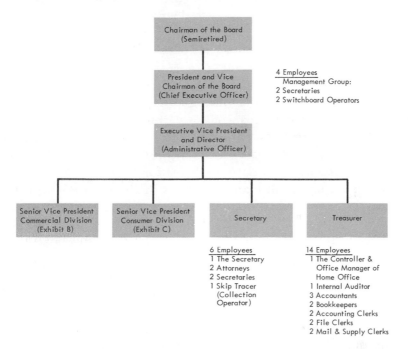

pate in the day-to-day supervision of all types of commercial and consumer financing operations. Even though the parent corporation has exploded in size, most of the key members of management have grown up with the firm and have a "feel" for the data. For example, the treasurer looks at a report submitted by the controller and tells the latter individual, "That figure doesn't look right; recheck it." In many cases the controller discovers that the figure was wrong.

Therefore, when a member of executive management reviews the financial and statistical reports for a branch office, he is reviewing an operation with which he is familiar. Because of this familiarity, he may be able to spot possible trouble areas that may not be apparent even to the manager of the particular branch office responsible for the report being reviewed.

Members of management also review various statistical and financial reports for the purpose of determining if previous management policy decisions should be reconsidered and possibly modified. For example, $400 to $500 is considered to be the ideal small loan in terms of balancing minimum handling cost with maximum return and with a minimum advertising exposure per loan. Do the current reports substantiate this policy? Do the reports of different branch offices vary in respect to the suggested answers to this question? If so, why?

While other loan companies have expanded into new geographical areas, the executive management of Mercantile Financial Corporation and Subsidiaries has decided to concentrate its efforts in small loan operations to the city of Chicago.[4] Expansion has come not only from opening new small loan offices within the city of Chicago, but also by concentrating the efforts by office. For example, offices may offer different types of loans, such as consolidated loans, loans over $800, and joint personal-business loans for over $5,000. In spite of the fact that a few small loan companies in Illinois are several times as large as Mercantile Financial Corporation (measured both in terms of assets and in terms of the number of branch offices), the consumer loan subsidiaries of the corporation collectively are one of the leading consumer loan groups in the state of Illinois, based on the criteria of dollar volume of personal loans over $800.

The expansion has not been restricted to the Consumer Division area. As previously indicated, the operations of the Commercial Division have been extended into three other geographical areas, and the volume of transactions in each area has been increased. The magnitude of these changes is indicated by the comparative financial reports presented in a subsequent section of this case study.

Data Accumulation, Processing, and Reporting Activities

The responsibility for data accumulation, processing, and reporting activities is decentralized to each office manager. While there is uniformity between different offices as to procedures followed in processing transactions of comparable sections, there is substantial difference in the procedures followed by each section within an

---

[4] While small loan operations have been restricted to the city of Chicago, frequently management has the opportunity of acquiring small loan corporations in other cities. Thus far, each of these opportunities has been declined. While each opportunity must be evaluated on its own merits, one management policy has influenced many of these decisions. One or two small loan offices in another city normally are prohibitive because of the administrative cost; ideally, five or six small loan offices should be acquired in a given city if maximum return is to be realized from the administrative cost.

office. Therefore, the data accumulation, processing, and reporting activities are separately examined for each section of the overall corporation.

Commercial Division

Each of the four regional offices of the Commercial Division is similar in respect to data accumulation, processing, and reporting activities. The differences in the administration of activities relate to the type of commercial financing: accounts receivable loans, inventory loans, equipment loans, notes receivable loans, and rediscounting operations. Similar administrative activities are followed in each regional office in respect to each type of loan.

A National Cash Register (NCR model #3300) bookkeeping machine is used at most regional offices in the data accumulation process for all types of commercial loan operations, except equipment loans. While equipment loans aggregate a multimillion dollar volume, there are less than 200 separate equipment loans ranging on the average from $300,000 to $400,000 per loan.

Equipment Loans.   Since the total number of equipment loans is less than 200, the administration of each loan can be maintained effectively and efficiently on a manual basis. The equipment loan contract will specify the amount of the monthly payments, and the home office management of the parent corporation administratively watches (through the reporting system) the payment behavior of these equipment loans.

If there is a serious problem in relation to a given equipment loan, the administrative management of the parent corporation must decide on what action is to be taken.[5] Since there are, typically, only three to four delinquent equipment loans each month, the administrative review of equipment loans is not time-consuming. If a customer is behind in payment of an equipment loan, management may

---

[5] The board of directors of the Mercantile Financial Corporation and Subsidiaries has established an administrative committee that has responsibility for the management and operation of the firm, without removing any direct responsibility from individuals in their designated corporate capacities. The members of the administrative committee are (1) the chairman of the board, (2) the president, (3) the executive vice president, (4) the treasurer, (5) the secretary, (6) the Commercial Division senior vice president, and (7) the senior vice president of the St. Louis Commercial branch office. Except for the latter individual, all of the members of the administrative committee are located at the home office.

telephone the customer and discuss the matter with him—remember the dollar value of each equipment loan.

Throughout the Commercial Division, management must follow a policy of "periodic administrative review" rather than any type of "automatic follow-up policy"; this periodic review is required because of the substantial amount of funds involved in each loan and the degree of uniqueness associated with each customer.

The collateral for an equipment loan—this term is used in the broad sense to include all types of machinery and equipment loans exclusive of real estate—includes a chattel mortage on the equipment.

Accounts Receivable Loans. The accounts receivable loan is the most common type of commercial loan; on the average, there are two accounts receivable loans for every single inventory loan, which is the second most frequent type of commercial loan.

For each new accounts receivable loan, a check is written for the designated amount and recorded by the bookkeeper, through using the National Cash Register bookkeeping machine (model #3300), in the cash disbursements journal. The NCR bookkeeping machine is used to open a ledger card for the customer that summarizes much of the data regarding the loan transaction, as indicated by Exhibit E. Note that the running balance of both the loan and the accounts receivable which are collateral for the loan are separately recorded and balanced.

EXHIBIT E
Format of Customer Ledger Card for NCR System

Solicitor	Bond Premium	Line M ____ Customer's	(Dun and Brad ____
First Payment ____% Date of Contract	Expires ____ 19 ____	Class No. ____ Rating	(Other ____
Final Payment ____% ____	Line of Business ____	Maximum Percentage Off-Rated ____%	

Date	Schedule or Remittance Report No.	Acct. No.	ACCOUNTS RECEIVABLE						AMOUNT DUE M.F.C.			
			100% Accounts Purchased	100% Accounts Paid	Daily Balance	Cumulative Daily Balance	Cash Received		Check No.	Cash Paid	Daily Balance	Cumulative Daily Balance

Name ____					
Address ____					
Town and State ____					

	ADJUSTMENTS			FINAL PAYMENT			Verification Factor
	Debit	Credit	Balance	Debit	Credit	Balance	

The NCR record system is designed in such a manner that selected data from the NCR ledger card are simultaneously printed by the NCR machine on another set of records, and the duplicate copy of the latter set of records serves as the monthly billing document to the customer.

Without going into detail, there are several legal documents that may be prepared to accompany the original transaction for a new loan. The most common documents include a schedule of accounts receivable and a security agreement. The supporting evidence for the transaction may include actual invoices and shipping documents. If shipping documents are not available, the customer prepares an affidavit regarding the terms, conditions, and locations of both properties and receivables. (Subsequently as part of the audit program, the individual accounts receivable will be confirmed.)

Accounts receivable loans are of two types: specific assignment and bulk assignment. Under specific assignment, the collateral for the loan is a specific group of customer accounts receivables which have been selected. The number of customer accounts involved in the specific assignment is usually small. Therefore, a manual ledger card may also be opened for each individual accounts receivable that is pledged by the commercial firm as collateral for the accounts receivable loan. If the commercial firm (which has been granted a specific assignment accounts receivable loan) issues a credit memorandum for returns or allowances, these data are circled on the ledger card for the pledged accounts receivable. While the credit memorandum does not affect the running balance of the accounts receivable loan, it does affect the collateral for the loan—both of these types of data are maintained on the customer's ledger card. A noncash voucher is used to process these data to the ledger card of the pledged account.

On specific accounts receivable loans, the customer must send to the Commercial Division branch office of Mercantile Financial Corporation and Subsidiaries the gross receipts on its collections. A check is prepared for the 20 percent excess (assuming the maximum rate, an accounts receivable loan will not exceed 80 percent of the collateral) and the check is mailed to the customer. This check is for the net amount owed to the customer, which is increased by overpayments (collections on invoices not assigned) and reduced by shortages (discounts and allowances granted by the loan customer to its receivables) . (For accounting purposes, a notation is made on the customer's ledger card to indicate which invoices have been paid.)

The specific accounts receivable loans are generally for 90 days or less. (There are exceptions that might be for five months.) Whenever an accounts receivable becomes 90 days delinquent, the customer must immediately repurchase the account. It is common for the repurchasing activity to occur even when the loan is for less than 90 days, since a given accounts receivable pledged as collateral may be 30 days or more delinquent at the time the loan is made. Monthly, a list is prepared from the cards (specific assignment type of accounts receivable loan) for the delinquent accounts, and the list is mailed to the customer indicating the accounts receivable which the customer must immediately repurchase.

The bulk assignment type of accounts receivable loan is more difficult to administer. The collateral for this type of loan includes all "qualified accounts receivable." Most accounts receivables are "qualified" under the bulk assignment; however, if a given account is a predetermined number of days delinquent on one transaction, this account is considered "nonqualified" on any and all other transactions. In addition, an accounts receivable may be nonqualified because it is a contra account, is specifically rejected by the loan officer for any number of reasons, and so forth.   As part of the collateral for the bulk assigment type of accounts receivable loan, the customer is required to submit a schedule of accounts receivable. A determination is made of the maximum amount of loan that would be made to the customer on this collateral (which is based on *qualified* accounts receivables). A check is issued and mailed to the customer for either the maximum amount or the requested amount of the loan, whichever is smaller.

The bulk assignment type of accounts receivable loan is a continuing type of loan arrangement. The customer is required to submit all of his gross collections to Mercantile Financial Corporation; the 20 percent excess of the collateral over the loan is not automatically returned to the customer. Instead, this amount goes in the customer's reserve until he asks for it.

The availability report (see Exhibit F) is a one-page transmittal document which the customer prepares each time he submits a transaction to Mercantile Financial Corporation. The availability report provides a place for the customer to request a loan for a given amount (a new loan based on the running balance of the collateral) or for the maximum amount. Normally, the customer will wait and borrow the additional funds on the day he has to have it, since interest is computed on a daily basis. Thus, the customer will apply all of his cash collections on the existing loan and will withdraw additional cash from Mercantile Financial Corporation only when it is necessary to meet payroll requirements, on the due date of invoices, or for other needs.

EXHIBIT F

Availability Report

Number_____   Date_____19_____

Accounts Receivable Outstanding Assigned to MFC (Prev. Report) $_____

Additions to Accounts Receivable:

   New Billings (Invoice #   to #   ) $_____

   Less Credit Memos   _____

                                                                    $

Deductions to Accounts Receivable:

   Invoices paid per Collection Report Attached $_____

   Miscellaneous   _____

Accounts Receivable Outstanding Assigned to MFC $

Less:

   Delinquents $_____

   Contras   _____

   Miscellaneous   _____ $_____

Accounts Receivable Balance Available for Loans $_____

Initial Purchase Price _____% $_____

   Loan Balance Previous Report $_____

   Less Cash Remitted Today $_____

      Loan Balance (Before Borrowing) $_____

   Additional Borrowing This Report $_____

      Loan Balance Today $_____

Excess Availability $_____

For the purpose of inducing Mercantile Financial Corporation to grant loans to us, we hereby certify that the foregoing Statement of accounts receivable is true and correct as of this report and is acceptable collateral in accordance with the terms of the agreement dated _____ between

_____

and Mercantile Financial Corporation.

                By:_____

Accounts receivable loans are risky, regardless of type. There can be a quick change in the quality of the collateral, and it is imperative that management is aware of this condition. This administrative function regarding both types of accounts receivable loans is partially achieved through a formal audit program. Periodically, an audit is made of the customer's accounts receivable transactions to verify that all cash receipts due Mercantile Financial Corporation have been properly forwarded and that no unauthorized adjustments (returns and allowances) have been made on customer's accounts. This audit program includes the confirmation of the customer's accounts receivable balances with the individual companies. At a minimum, the audit function is performed every 60 days (that is, all aspects of the audit program exclusive of the actual confirmation of the detailed accounts receivable balances, which is performed more often on a test basis). The customer knows before the loan is made that frequent audits will be made on his books and that the interest rate provides for this type of service.[6]

The auditors are on the staff of each regional commercial loan branch office, and the auditors may be provided with a summary of the loan customer's balances along with other selected documents, which they use to verify the customer's accounting records. These other documents include a list of all pledged accounts for specific accounts receivable loans, which is prepared from the manual cards maintained for each individual account. The auditors also have a list of delinquent accounts for both types of accounts receivable loans. (In the case of bulk assignment, the auditors determine the delinquent accounts from reviewing a list submitted by the customer and from reviewing the accounts receivable records.)

Manual ledger cards are not maintained by Mercantile Financial Corporation for each individual customer's accounts receivable that are pledged under the bulk type of accounts receivable loan. If such manual ledger cards were maintained, it would mean duplicating the customer's complete accounts receivable subsidiary ledger and daily updating this ledger. Instead, attention is given under the bulk type of accounts receivable loan to verification that the customer's records are correct. Periodically, the customer is asked to prepare a schedule of accounts receivable and to age the accounts.[7] Personnel at the commercial loan branch office review the customer's list, exclude

---

[6] Remember the customer did not secure a loan from a regular commercial bank; either he wanted to borrow more funds on the collateral than would be granted by the commercial bank's management or else his application was refused; some commercial banks are hesitant about making loans on accounts receivable. Other commercial banks require a substantial amount of collateral for a very small loan. In some states, commercial banks are restricted by law from making loans on accounts receivable. Thus, the commercial financing operations of Mercantile Financial Corporation and other commercial loan companies provide a service to this type of customer which cannot be obtained anywhere else.

[7] Most payments on accounts receivable loans occur between the 10th and the 20th of each month. Therefore, the monthly report of delinquent accounts receivable is generally prepared around the 20th of the month.

"nonqualified" accounts, compare this report with previous reports (including the daily availability report), and then prepare a formal list of delinquent accounts. The following paragraph appears in the heading of this latter report (which is only for specific assignment accounts):

All the following delinquent accounts require your prompt attention. Please make a special effort to collect those accounts which are "more than 60 days past due." *All accounts over 60 days past due, or where goods have been returned, reconsigned, etc., and against customers who are in any financial trouble whatsoever must be repurchased by you at once. Accounts not repurchased by you will be deducted from schedules or your reserves.*[8]

This auditing function of the customer's activities (transactions) is more than a traditional verification of account balances and proof of cash. It also includes a managerial interpretation regarding the customer's business, such as an implicit forecast of what will probably happen in the next few weeks and how this might change the credit rating of the customer.

At each regional office of the Commercial Division, the collections for all types of accounts receivable are received by the cashier, and a daily report of collections is prepared by this latter individual. The posting to the customer's accounts receivable ledger card is daily recorded by the NCR bookkeeping machine, which provides subtotal detailed data for several control groups. Therefore, the summation of the daily report of collections must equal the appropriate control totals, as determined from the NCR daily proof page.

All disbursements are recorded in the cash disbursements journal, and the aggregate daily disbursements applicable to accounts receivable loans are compared with the appropriate proof totals from the NCR proof page. The NCR separately accumulates daily totals by several categories which provide detailed group control totals. The latter totals are for groupings of ledger cards.

Many transactions are both disbursements and collections. For example, a customer sends in $1,000 as the gross collections on a bulk accounts receivable loan (the $1,000 is compared with the cashier's report and with the change in the customer's account maintained on NCR), the customer requests $100 payment from his reserve (a

---

[8] The formal list of delinquent accounts is submitted to the customer for his immediate attention.

check is issued for this, compared with the check register and the NCR proof page) , and $900 is applied on the account (this latter amount is proved and compared with the change in the accounting balances as indicated by the NCR proof page) .

Inventory Loans. The inventory loan is not based on acquisition cost but is based on the appraised value of the inventory as determined by representatives of Mercantile Financial Corporation. The risk on inventory loans is generally higher than the risk on accounts receivable loans; therefore, the maximum inventory loan is generally 50 to 60 percent of the appraised value of selected items of inventory.

Inventory loans are made under three conditions: (1) where the goods are in a public warehouse, (2) where the goods are in a field warehouse on the customer's premises, and (3) where the goods are on the customer's premises but not in a warehouse. This latter condition is referred to as a "factor's lien." Under the first two conditions, the collateral for the inventory loan would include the warehouse receipt, and the customer will pay Mercantile Financial Corporation at the time the goods are released from the warehouse. Under some circumstances, a schedule of payments is specified for the inventory loan and the customer must make payments according to this schedule irrespective of the release of goods from the warehouse. Under the third condition (a factor's lien), the inventory loan agreement includes a repayment schedule which must be followed. The factor's lien agreement does not contain any release conditions, since the goods are not in a warehouse. (Thus, in this latter case, payments must be made according to the payment schedule regardless of whether the goods are sold.)

The inventory loans under all three conditions are accounted for in approximately the same manner as that followed for accounts receivable loans. Furthermore, if a customer has an inventory loan, he will generally also have an accounts receivable loan. Therefore, the administration of inventory loans is partly achieved through the auditing program; the audit of the inventory transactions occurs at the time the accounts receivable transactions are being examined.[9]

Other Types of Loans. Mercantile Financial Corporation also

---

[9] This generalization can also be applied to equipment loans. If a customer has an equipment loan, then he will generally also have both an accounts receivable loan and an inventory loan. Thus, the auditing for all three types can be performed at the same time; however, there is not a large amount of audit work associated with equipment type of commercial loans.

engages in rediscounting operations and may purchase notes receivable and second mortgages. Periodically, a small loan company or small finance company will have an excessive amount of investments in notes receivable and in second mortgages. Management of the small loan company or small finance company will arrange with management of Mercantile Financial Corporation to rediscount these second mortgages or other documents.

The accounting for the other types of loans is similar to that followed for accounts receivable loans.

Each Commercial Division branch office manually prepares a weekly report of its activities. This report includes a detailed list by name of each portfolio, the loan balance, and the volume generated during the week. This weekly report is three to four pages in length, is purely statistical data, and is sent directly to the executive vice president of the parent corporation and to the senior vice president in charge of the Commercial Division. A liquidation progress report is also prepared, when appropriate, by each Commercial Division branch office to cover the liquidation activities of its customers.

Consumer Division

The data accumulation, processing, and reporting activities are similar in both the consolidation loan offices and the small loan offices. Therefore, for purposes of this case study, attention is given only to the small loan offices. The furniture and appliance office and the motor and automobile office have individually unique administrative procedures. Thus, the data accumulation, processing, and reporting activities for the Consumer Division are described in three sections: small loan offices, furniture and appliance office, and motor and automobile office.

Small Loan Offices.   Each small loan office uses a McBee accounting set for both cash receipts and cash disbursements. This manual accounting system permits the simultaneous recording of entries on several forms by a single writing.

A prospective customer is asked to prepare a loan application form, which is presented in Exhibit G. Within a matter of hours, the references, employment and other data contained on the completed application form have been verified, and the prospective customer's loan request is acted upon. Assuming the decision is positive, the customer returns to the branch loan office where he is given a check

EXHIBIT G. Loan Application Form

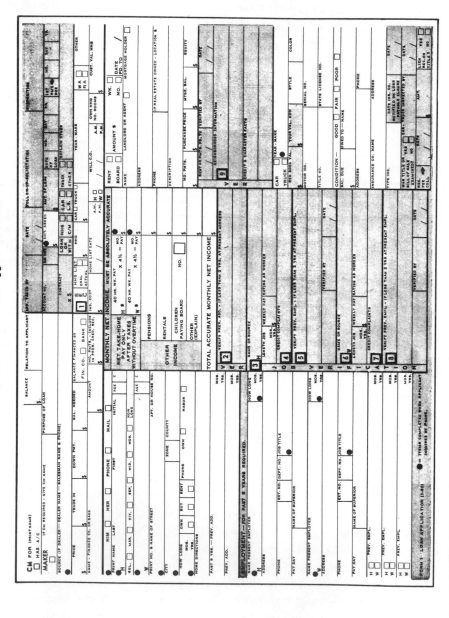

PRESENT & FORMER CREDITORS	PHONE NOS.	DATE OPENED	ORIG. DEBT	BALANCE APPLICANT	VERIFIED BAL. DUE	CONTRACT AND MO. PAYMENTS	SECURITY	SEC.	DATE LAST PMT.	HOW PAID & VERIFIED (SEE RECEIPTS IN OFFICE OR HOME)	VER. BY	CHECKS (EXACT AMT.)
TIME PC☐ FC☐ CM☐												
10 LOAN CO. OR BANK		/ /	$	$	$	X			/ /	11		$
LOAN CO. OR BANK		/ /				X			/ /			
AUTO FINANCE CO. (PRESENT OR BUYING)		/ /				X			/ /			
CREDIT UNION		/ /				X			/ /			
IN CO-MAKER FOR		/ /				X			/ /			
CAR DEALER		/ /				X			/ /			
FURNITURE		/ /				X			/ /			
FURNITURE		/ /				X			/ /			
APPLIANCE		/ /				X			/ /			
JEWELRY		/ /				X			/ /			
DEPT. STORE		/ /				X			/ /			
GROCERY		/ /				X			/ /			
CLOTHING		/ /				X			/ /			
CAR REPAIR		/ /				X			/ /			
HOSPITAL & MEDICAL		/ /				X			/ /			
OTHER		/ /				X			/ /			

	BADGE NO.	PAYROLL NO.	SOC. SEC. NO.	CREDIT CARDS			TOT. MONTHLY NET INC.	$

TOTAL AMT. CRS. ISSUED $

12 TOTAL ALL DEBT $
13 TOTAL SEC. DEBT / UNSEC. DEBT

LESS TOTAL NO. PMTS. TO BE PD. FROM LOAN $

MONTHLY EXPENSES

	$
BAL. MO. PMTS. ON DEBTS	$
RENT OR HOUSE PMTS.	
FOOD $30 PER ADULT — $15 PER CHILD	
CLOTHING	
LIGHT — GAS — PHONE	
HEAT (COAL — OIL — GAS)	
CAR EXP. (GAS - OIL - TIRES $30 MIN. PER CAR - TRUCK)	
BUS TRANSPORTATION	
FAMILY INSURANCE	
CHILD CARE (IF WIFE WORKS)	
CHILD SUPPORT — ALIMONY	
OTHER	$
TOTAL ACCURATE MONTHLY EXPENSES	$
15 ACCURATE EXCESS INC. OVER EXPENSES	$

VERIFICATION IDENTITY

STATE (IDENTIFYING PHYSICAL MARKS) CLASSES

DRIVER'S LIC. NO.

H
W
NO. CHILDREN   AGES CHILDREN   B

BIRTH DATE / /   HT.   WT.   EYES   HAIR

G

NO. DEP YES☐ NO☐ YES☐ NO☐

14 LOAN EXCHANGE VER. BY   DATE / /

LOAN REJECTED FOR FOLLOWING REASONS

CREDIT BUREAU VER. BY   DATE / /

MANAGER DECISION TO   HOW FINDER/DEALER ☐☐☐☐   BY PHONE ☐   IN PERSON ☐

HOME INTERVIEW & LISTING

CORR. SEC.	MonthYear	POOR	YES	NO
		DOES WIFE APPROVE LOAN?		
CORR. NONE		DOES WIFE FEEL LOAN CAN BE REPAID EASILY?		
NONE RENT				

NEIGHBORHOOD INFORMATION

AM'S RECOMMENDATION

COMPLETE BEFORE CHECK BY MANAGER. ALL RECEIPTS ON ALL DEBTS - MUST BE SEEN AND VERIFIED IN PROPER PLACE - UNDER "PRESENT & FORMER CREDITORS" PRECAUTIONS FOR SAFETY OF LOAN

I REJECT ☐ APPROVE ☐ THIS AS "SAFE, GRADE A LOAN" IN AMOUNT OF

$ IN ACCORD WITH 9 RULES AND 3 FUNDAMENTALS.

A.M.'S INITIALS

for the requested amount of the loan (or checks are issued to pay off his obligations, depending on the situation) after he has completed some additional forms. The forms prepared vary by customer, depending on his collateral, and might include (1) the note and chattel mortgage, (2) financial statement listing his present indebtedness and liabilities, (3) application for corrected motor vehicle title, (4) wage assignment, and (5) State of Illinois, Uniform Commercial Code—Financing Statement—Form UCC–1.[10]

A clerk in the loan office types a loan set covering the new loan. Exhibit H presents the original copy of the loan set. The loan set contains an original and seven carbon copies, with each copy containing only selected data which are obtained by using special carbon paper. The different copies are for collateral purposes and include wage assignments, the formal loan note, security agreement, and so forth. The customer must sign various copies of the loan set before he is permitted to leave with the loan check. Subsequently, one of the copies from the loan set will be mailed by the home office of Mercantile Financial Corporation (after the document has been processed) to the customer as a confirmation form.

The original copy of the loan set serves as the customer ledger card, which is maintained in the small loan branch office. The payment behavior of each loan customer is closely observed by the manager of the small loan branch office. If a customer becomes delinquent, five days after the due date, the customer receives a notice in the mail. If there is no payment, three days later the second notice is mailed. If there is no payment, then three days later the customer is contacted by telephone. Thus, 11 days after the actual due date of the payment, the manager of the small loan branch office is trying to contact the customer by telephone.

One of the carbon copies from the loan set is used in the small loan office for an alphabetical present-customer file. This particular copy of the loan set contains both the customer's account number and the due date of the monthly payments. The customer ledger card (original copy of loan set) is maintained in the small loan office by account number according to the due date of the payments. The alphabetical file is used whenever a customer comes to the loan office to make payment and does not know his account number and due date.

---

[10] The latter document is the official form for securing a lien against specified collateral. The document is prepared in an original and four copies, and one of the copies is acknowledged by the appropriate State of Illinois official and returned to the loan subsidiary of Mercantile Financial Corporation.

EXHIBIT H
Master Loan Set

OUTSTANDING DEBTS

PURPOSE OF LOAN:

BORROWERS AGE: RACE: NO. IN FAMILY:

REMARKS: ENTER ALL NOTATIONS - BRIEFLY - LEGIBLY.

Daily, the manager of each small loan office reviews the customer ledger cards; a red flag is attached to any account that is past due; and the manager decides what action will be taken regarding interest and service charges for the delinquent accounts. When a small loan account becomes 10 days' overdue, the Illinois statute prescribes the amount of the penalty that can be charged the customer. If there is a 30-day delay in payment, an extension charge is made. At any time after an account becomes overdue, the manager of the small loan office has the option of converting the customer's original loan from "precomputed interest" to simple interest. The "precomputed interest" is rebated according to the 1278 method, where the interest is computed in advance and each payment is both for interest and principal per the predetermined schedule. By converting to simple interest, simple interest is computed on the daily running balance in the customer's account.[11]

On the 10th day of the month, the manager of the small loan office prepares a brief report from his customer ledger cards. A summary is made of all accounts 60 days or more past due, and these aggregate data are entered on a form containing four column headings: (1) number of accounts delinquent, (2) percentage of delinquent accounts to total accounts, (3) dollar amount of delinquent account, and (4) percentage of dollar amounts of delinquent accounts to the dollar amount of total accounts.

The loan register and disbursements journal (see Exhibit I) is prepared in duplicate, and the duplicate copy is daily submitted to the home office. This document is used for several purposes and will be discussed subsequently in this case study. Note the different types of data included in this daily report, such as volume by type of collateral, volume by type of borrower, and volume by source.

The cash receipts journal (see Exhibit J) is also prepared in duplicate, and the duplicate copy is daily submitted to the home office. The McBee accounting set permits the simultaneous recording

---

[11] Strange as it may seem, the manager welcomes a small delay in payment. Of course, one consideration is the extra service charge that will be received from the same amount of principal. But another consideration is not so obvious. The manager wants to make the maximum amount of loans within restrictions of certain degrees of risk; thus, whenever a loan is paid off, the task now is to put those funds back out as a new loan. If there is a slight delay in payment, then additional funds which draw interest are outstanding for a longer period of time and, for example, there are no additional advertising costs connected with the revenue from this slight overdue period.

of the data on (1) the customer's receipt form, (2) the cash receipts journal, and (3) the customer's ledger card. The duplicate copy of the cash receipts journal is also used for several purposes and represents a daily report of certain types of activities.

In addition to the above reports, the manager of each small loan office prepares a daily report, a monthly delinquent report entitled "2-Month and Over Past Dues," and a monthly statistical report entitled "Mercantile Loan Organization Report." The daily report is a one-page digest of selected data presented in three sections: bank balance, a recapitulation of daily transactions with customers, and different types of summary aggregate data. The "2-Month and Over Past Dues" report shows not only the detailed data by delinquent account but also shows the promises and results of action taken toward the collection of each account.

The mercantile loan organization report is a two-page report which presents a summarization of the monthly transactions with customers; statistical data, the precomputed interest, the late and extension charges for the month for different groups of delinquent accounts; number of employees and the average customer accounts per employee; dollar average of new loans made during month; dollar average of all loans; and a schedule of statistical data by source of loans. This latter schedule contains *rows* for the different types of advertising media, references from different organizational units within Mercantile Financial Corporation, and personal references by type. The schedule contains seven *columns:* (1) number of loans made, (2) aggregate amount of new loans, (3) number of loan applications received, (4) number of loan applications we turned down, (5) number of loan applications prospective customers turned down, (6) year to date, number of applications received, and (7) year to date, number of loans made.

Some of the administration of small loan operations is performed at the home office. Three assistant supervisors of the small loan offices (note organization chart per Exhibit C) are located at the home office, and each supervisor is responsible for a given group of branch loan offices. Daily, the branch office manager sends the home office a duplicate copy of the transactions for the previous day. This includes a copy of the loan register and disbursements journal, a copy of the cash receipts journal, and a copy of the loan set which contains the statistical and other data from the heading of the master loan set as

EXHIBIT I
Loan Register and Disbursements Journal

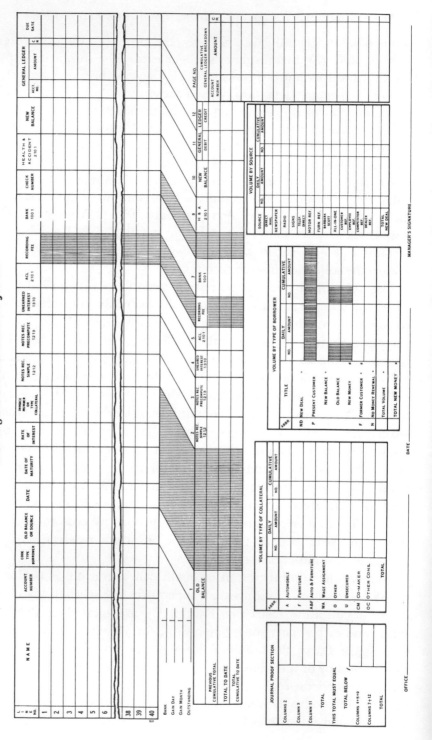

EXHIBIT J
Cash Receipts Journal

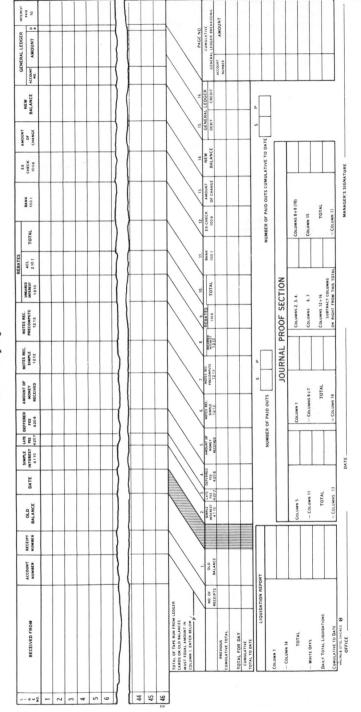

EXHIBIT K
Fourth Copy of the Master Loan Set*

BORROWERS (NAMES AND ADDRESSES)				MERCANTILE LOAN CORP.				
ACCOUNT NUMBER								
OFFICE					CODE			
DUE DATE					RATE			
					3% - 2% - 1%			
DATE MADE	PRINCIPAL AMOUNT OF LOAN	NUMBER PAYMENTS	AMOUNT FIRST PAYMENT	AMOUNT OTHER PAYMENTS	FIRST PAYMENT DUE	FINAL PAYMENT DUE	FEES/SER. CHG.	
PRECOMPUTED INTEREST	FIRST INSTAL. ADJ. CHGE.	TOTAL PRECOMP. INTEREST	TOTAL AMT. LOAN INCLUD'G INTEREST	UNIT CHARGE	H. & A. INSURANCE	COST OF CREDIT LIFE INSURANCE	DATE FILED	DATE PAID

B 40075X

Dear Friend:

* Only the heading of this document is illustrated above. The remainder of the document is a form letter that is mailed to the new customer.

indicated by Exhibit K. This latter document will be mailed to the customer after it has been processed by the home office.

For accounting, the assistant supervisor reviews the daily transaction reports along with the supporting documents. He verifies the footing of both cash disbursements and cash receipts, verifies that check numbers are in sequence, and verifies that cash receipts numbers are in sequence. A spot check is made of the extensions and recapitulations of data.

This review by the assistant supervisor is made for both administrative and clerical purposes. For example, periodically the assistant supervisor will go to the branch loan offices over which he is responsible and verify the cash balance and perform internal checks of customer ledger cards. (The internal control aspects of the assistant supervisor's operations overlap the functions of the internal auditor, who is a member of the treasurer's staff—note Exhibit D.)

After the assistant supervisor has approved the daily transaction reports and supporting documents from his branch offices, the duplicate copies of the loan register and disbursements journal, the cash receipts journal, and the loan set are forwarded to a data processing service center. Punched cards are processed for each customer, by branch loan office, and by type of loan. The outside—external to the corporation—data processing service center also maintains control summary cards for each type of loan by branch office, and these are compared with the balances indicated on the daily transaction reports. Weekly a report of mathematical errors by branch office is prepared by the data processing service center and forwarded to the assistant supervisor who is responsible for the accounting operations of that branch loan office.

The use of a data processing service center was only begun a year ago, and the transition was gradual. Each month one or two small loan branch offices were converted from the complete manual system to the limited data processing system. Data processing cards were punched for each customer of the branch office that is being added to the data processing system. Incidentally, a $6,000 error was discovered in the customer account balances when one branch office was brought under the control of the data processing system. (The bonding company repaid the $6,000.)

At the present time, the last small loan branch office has only recently been added to the data processing system which has been used for only a limited number of operations. The limited data processing activities include control over account balances of each branch office, computation and accumulation of unearned income, accumulation of historical data and preparation of the data for the Robert Morris Associates reports, and the preparation of a statistical report by type of loan for each branch loan office.

This latter report, the loan receivable report, includes the following column headings: (1) account number, (2) borrower, (3) present balance, (4) date purchased, (5) date loan made, (6) original charge, (7) remaining unearned portion of charge, (8) number of installments, (9) last payment, (10) total contractural amounts past due, (11) amount 30 days past due, (12) amount 60 days past due, (13) amount 90 days past due and (14) amount over 90 days past due.

The data processing service center also prepares a list of new borrowers by name, address and telephone number. This list is used in advertising the various services offered by the overall corporation.

Furniture and Appliance Office. All furniture and appliance loans are made through dealers, and these operations can be described as a discounting of customer notes from participating dealers. There is considerable difference in the arrangement made with participating dealers. Some dealers guarantee all customer loans, and if a note is not paid according to contract, the dealer will repurchase the note. Other dealers operate through a reserve agreement, where a certain percent of the note is retained by the furniture and appliance subsidiary of Mercantile Financial Corporation until the customer has paid off the note. In the latter case, if the note is not paid, the dealer can lose only the amount of funds in the reserve. For some dealers, there is an arrangement where a certain portion of the discount rate is placed in a cushion (reserve) and is paid to the dealer only after the customer has paid off the note; in other words, the dealer participates in the revenue from the discount rate after the note has been paid off.

There are other differences in the arrangement with dealers regarding the relation of the customer to the furniture and appliance subsidiary of Mercantile Financial Corporation. Some dealers do not desire that their customers know that they are financing their furniture and appliance accounts through an outside financial institution. In these cases, the dealers will make all collections and forward them intact to the furniture and appliance subsidiary of Mercantile Financial Corporation. If a customer does default in payment and the dealer is not required by the arrangement to repurchase the note, then the furniture and appliance subsidiary of Mercantile Financial Corporation will enter the picture and will notify the delinquent customer that his account has recently been acquired by the furniture and appliance subsidiary of Mercantile Financial Corporation and that all future payments must be made to the latter firm.

Other dealers tell their customers at the time of the sale that their accounts will be financed by the furniture and appliance subsidiary of Mercantile Financial Corporation. In fact, under some financial arrangements the dealer may tell a customer that the proposed sale is dependent upon the acceptance by Mercantile Financial Corporation of the customer's note. In any case, under this second type of arrangement the customer makes his payments directly to the furniture and appliance subsidiary of Mercantile Financial Corporation, and the dealer does not become involved again until the customer pays his account in full or there is a default in payment.

As is suggested by the above discussion, the document evidencing the arrangement with the dealer is the beginning point in the data accumulation, processing, and reporting activities for the furniture and appliance office. There are two solicitors for the Chicago area, and these solicitors work full-time at the task of entering into arrangements with dealers and then monitoring the arrangement. Each solicitor will closely watch the quality and terms of the installment paper submitted by his participating dealers. For example, an arrangement may be made with Dealer A, where his customer's notes will be discounted at a given rate. Subsequently, the company discovers that Dealer A has arrangements with several financial institutions and that Mercantile Financial Corporation is only receiving the low-quality paper. The solicitor will tell Dealer A that he must either send higher quality paper to Mercantile Financial Corporation, or the financial arrangement is terminated.

If a given dealer sends only short-term paper to Mercantile Financial Corporation and sends his long-term paper to another financial institution, then this is bad for Mercantile Financial Corporation. There is not that much difference in the administrative cost for short-term paper versus long-term paper, and under the latter condition, there is a longer period of time over which to receive interest. Furthermore, when any paper is paid off, there is the problem of getting new loans to replace the paid-off accounts. Additional advertising cost may be required for the new account, along with the usual administrative cost.

In this type of business operation, management has the continuous problem of watching the dealers. A dealer can usually take his "choice" customer notes to another financial institution and get the choice notes discounted at a lower rate of interest than the dealer would receive from Mercantile Financial Corporation. The discount rate that has been set by the solicitor for Mercantile Financial Corporation assumes that there will be an averaging out of the choice customer notes with the extremely poor customer notes. The earnings on the choice notes will hopefully more than offset the losses on the extremely poor customer notes.

While the solicitors work full-time in the administration of the financial arrangements with dealers, other members of the furniture and appliance office and selected members of the home office will periodically review the results of given dealer arrangements. In evaluating the dealer arrangements, consideration is given not only to the dealer statistical report (a monthly report of the total transactions by dealer, including the computations of yield by dealer, and this report is based on the statistical data available at the time the loan is made), but also to the repossessions by dealer. If there is a large group of delinquents occurring from a given dealer's customers, this is also considered.

After the document evidencing the financial arrangement with the dealer has been prepared, the "dealer card" is maintained by the credit manager. Each credit manager is responsible for a specified group of dealers, and the credit manager periodically checks Dun &

Bradstreet's *Reference Book* and other credit services' publications for indications of unfavorable changes in the financial position of the dealer. The need for being aware of changes in the financial position of a dealer varies directly with the type and the conditions of the financial arrangement between the dealer and Mercantile Financial Corporation.

When a customer purchases furniture or a major appliance from a dealer, the dealer asks the customer to prepare a one-page credit questionnaire which intentionally does not have a heading on the form so that the questionnaire cannot be identified with Mercantile Financial Corporation in those situations where the dealer prefers to work on an indirect basis with Mercantile Financial Corporation.

A dealer calls the furniture and appliance office and notifies a clerk that he desires to have a given customer's note discounted, and the dealer may request that the credit investigation immediately begin on the customer. (In the latter case the clerk will secure appropriate data from the dealer so that the credit investigation can begin.) Instead of calling, the dealer may mail the customer's credit questionnaire to the furniture and appliance office. The questionnaire contains the complete details of the sales agreement, including description of article, cash price, taxes, trade deductions, cash deductions, insurance charges, finance charges, total contract, amount of monthly payments, and the starting date for payments.

Clerks in the furniture and appliance office immediately perform a credit investigation on the customer, and the results of the investigation are entered on a specially designed office form. The credit investigation report along with the customer's credit questionnaire (maybe the title "sales agreement" might be more appropriate for this document) are submitted to the supervisor who is responsible for transactions with that dealer. The credit manager, assuming he agrees to buy the "deal," attaches a one-page work sheet to the other two documents and assigns an account number to the deal. A major portion of the work sheet is designated for contract analysis and service charge analysis, and these computations are performed by a clerk as soon as the credit manager approves the deal.

The work sheet with the attached documents are given to a typist who prepares a master loan set. This loan set contains an original and six copies. The original serves as the detailed ledger card for the customer. The first copy is a dealer notification report and is mailed to the dealer. The second copy is mailed to the customer, unless there is an indirect arrangement with the dealer, in which case the customer does not receive this copy. The third copy is placed in the numerical file according to assigned account number for the customer. The fourth copy is currently submitted to a data processing service center where data processing cards are punched, and these punched cards are used monthly in the preparation of the dealer statistical report (see Exhibit L for the format of the dealer statistical copy). The fifth copy is placed in the customer's file folder. The sixth and final copy is used for direct advertising purposes.

At the same time the master loan set is prepared, the typist prepares the insurance policy. The customer's account number is also the credit life insurance policy number.

Next, all of the documents are compared; the master loan set is proofed against the work sheet and other supporting documents. The mathematical extensions are recomputed and verified. The insurance policy is compared with the master loan set. The amount of the loan is compared with the check which was issued to the dealer. At the completion of this internal review step, the master set is separated, a customer file folder is opened, a perforated payment-coupon book is prepared for the customer, and all documents are processed to their appropriate locations.

The bookkeeper for the furniture and appliance office only maintains the detail ledger for customers. Control pages are established

EXHIBIT L

Dealer Statistical Copy* of Master Loan Set for Furniture and Appliance Office

				REFERENCE			ACCOUNT NUMBER	
PURCHASER		ACCOUNT NO.	DAY DUE				DATE DUE	
ADDRESS		HOME PHONE	AGE				FURNITURE	☐
CITY AND STATE		OCCUPATION		SELLING PRICE	OTHER ☐		APPLIANCES	☐
EMPLOYED BY	YRS. MOS.	BUSINESS PHONE		DOWN PAYMENT	%		FURN. & APPL.	☐
	DATE PURCH.	AMT.OF NOTE		UNPAID BALANCE	LOSS RESERVE		H.B. $	
	FINAL INSTALL.	DATE OF NOTE		SERVICE CHARGE	OVER–REBATE		D.P.L.R.	
NO. AND AMT. OF INSTALLMENT	WA'S DLR END GUAR. MOS. c			AMOUNT OF NOTE	CHECK OR DRAFT		NET S.C.	

* Normally, this form is 8½ × 4.

for groups of accounts. Daily, the bookkeeper receives an adding machine tape of the total work sheets processed that day; this total is compared with a tape of the new customer ledger cards. If there is a difference, a tape is run on those approved customer loans (as evidenced by the work sheets) which are in process. A comparison is also made between the total checks issued and the new loans.

The accountant for the furniture and appliance office maintains the general ledger and the appropriate journals, which are recorded on a manual basis. The accountant also prepares the normal financial reports for the furniture and appliance office. As previously indicated, there is one report which is not prepared by the accountant but which is prepared by a data processing service center—the statistical report. This latter report shows yield by dealer based on the actual terms and conditions of the customer loans accepted from that dealer.

The volume of business in the furniture and appliance office fluctuates by the day of the week. Monday is the busy day; many sales are made over the weekend and the dealers are on the telephone on Monday asking that credit investigations begin on their customers. If everything is approved, the dealer should receive his check in the mail on Wednesday. Dealers expect this quick service and telephone the furniture and appliance office if their checks are not in the mail on Wednesday. In coping with this uneven work load, the furniture and appliance subsidiary of Mercantile Financial Corporation has three permanent, part-time clerks who work two or three days a week.

The extent of this uneven work load is indicated by the following statistics. On a Monday, 110–120 applications may be approved and 20 applications rejected. The monthly average of applications accepted ranges from 1,100 to 1,500. To complete the statistical data, some of the loans extend for more than a year, and the average volume of active accounts on a given day ranges from 18,000 to 20,000.

The collection procedures on the accounts vary depending on whether the customer will pay the furniture and appliance subsidiary of Mercantile Financial Corporation directly, or whether the customer will pay the dealer. Under either method the collections are posted to the detailed customer ledger cards maintained at the furniture and appliance office. For internal control purposes, there is a daily comparison of the total cash receipts (per the cashier's daily report) with the changes in the bookkeeper's control accounts for customer accounts.

The 18,000–20,000 accounts are separated into books, and seven collectors are responsible for the administration of the collection function. Each collector has a given group of accounts for which he is personally responsible. Monthly, the first Friday of each month, all collectors plus other clerks review the 18,000–20,000 customer ledger cards and prepare a delinquent listing and aging of receivables by book—a specified group of ledger cards. The formal delinquent report is submitted to the supervisor of collections.

The collector will immediately concentrate his attention on the 90-day delinquents. Next, he will try to reduce the 60-day delinquents, and so forth. If the collector does a good job of reducing the short-term delinquents this month, his books will not have many long-term delinquents next month, that is, new long-term delinquents.

When an account becomes 90 days delinquent, if not before, the collector asks the customer to refinance the loan, which will mean additional financing charges and extension charges. When the loan is refinanced, subject to new credit approval, the account is taken off the delinquent listing. In other cases, the dealer may buy back any delinquent account or the customer may be referred to the small loan offices of Mercantile Financial Corporation, where the customer will take out a consolidated loan which he will use to pay off the furniture and appliance note. In either of these cases, the customer ceases to be a problem of the furniture and appliance office collectors.

In furniture and appliance operations, the gross yield and losses are not subject to the variation that exists in the motor and automobile operations. Usually, *new* furniture or appliances are involved, and the rate of interest is constant from one period to the next. Furthermore, the volume of business is fairly constant per participating dealer. There are exceptions to this latter generalization as previously indicated in the discussion of the solicitor's activities.

Motor and Automobile Office. An appreciation of the characteristics and recent changes in motor and automobile loan operations is an essential prerequisite to a thorough understanding of the data accumulation, processing, and reporting activities of the motor and automobile office. Brief consideration is given to these characteristics and changes before an examination is made of the data accumulation procedures.

In contrast with furniture and appliance loans, the mix determines the gross yield. The collateral is not the same—all *new* furniture and equipment. Instead, there are *new* cars, cars *one year old, two years old,* and so forth. The age of the car is a big factor in determining the rate of interest that ideally should be charged. The older the car, the higher the rate of interest should be in order to compensate for the additional risk involved. However, administrative considerations preclude the establishment of completely flexible interest rates on automobile loans that vary directly with customer characteristics and the age of the car. In addition to these factors, consideration is given to the dealer's volume of business and to the quality of automobiles handled by the dealer (used automobiles vary considerably in condition for the same make and age of automobile, and from experience the quality of used automobiles handled by a given dealer can be estimated). Assumptions are made regarding these variable factors, and a given interest rate is established for use in discounting customer notes of a particular automobile dealer.

Mix can only be determined by an analysis of the historical transactions with each dealer. Monthly, a report is prepared by the data processing service center that indicates the mix of automobile loans and the yield per dealer. This first report is a statistical analysis of the available data at the time the automobile loan is made—a copy of the master loan set is furnished to the data processing service center for use in preparation of this statistical report.[12] A second report is prepared by the data processing service center that includes the repossessions by dealer; these latter data are obtained from the motor and automobile's accountant, who manually maintains a repossessions journal. This second report contains the number of repossessions by dealer, losses if any from repossessions, and other statistical data regarding the age of the car and the amount past due at the time of the repossession.

The administration of automobile loans not only requires knowledge of the forecasted yield per dealer, based on a copy of the original loan transaction and knowledge of repossessions by dealer,

---

[12] The monthly reports prepared by the data processing service center are filed in a cumulative ledger called "Dealer's Experience Book," and these reports are frequently used by management of the motor and automobile office in evaluation and administration of dealer transactions.

but also requires knowledge of unusual payment behavior by the customers of a given dealer including losses on uncollectible accounts. The type of recourse that the motor and automobile subsidiary of Mercantile Financial Corporation has with the automobile dealer is also important.

Legally, there are four forms of recourse or contingencies on automobile loans which are followed in the financial arrangements between the motor and automobile subsidiary of Mercantile Financial Corporation and the various automobile dealers: (1) repurchase arrangement, (2) recourse arrangement, (3) guarantee arrangement, and (4) holdback arrangement. Under a repurchase arrangement, it is necessary to actually have physical possession of the automobile *before* the automobile dealer is required to buy back the vehicle. Under a full recourse arrangement, the dealer is required to buy back the vehicle after a certain period of delinquency has occurred, even though the vehicle cannot be located. Under a guarantee arrangement, the dealer guarantees a specified amount of money for a given number of months. Under the holdback arrangement, part of the proceeds on the automobile loan are held by the motor and automobile subsidiary until the customer has made a specified number of payments. At the end of this time period, the dealer is paid the remainder of any balance due him. In the latter case, the dealer is no longer responsible for losses that may result from a delinquent account or from repossession of that particular customer's automobile. The guarantee and holdback arrangements may both be incorporated in a contract with an automobile dealer. (The guarantee type of arrangement is frequently employed, and the dealer may be required to guarantee up to one third of the contract price.)

With some dealers, there is a reserve agreement (which is similar to the reserve agreement with furniture and appliance dealers) where the automobile dealer receives additional revenue when an automobile loan is paid in full. However, the reserve agreements are not as common today as they were two years ago. Commercial banks do not follow the reserve agreement procedure, and the motor and automobile office's management has begun to comply with competition.

The most significant change in automobile loan operations in recent years has been the strong entry by commercial banks into this type of operation. The interest rates charged by commercial banks are substantially lower than those charged by the automobile and motor subsidiary of Mercantile Financial Corporation or than those charged by other financial loan institutions. Surprisingly enough, managers of commercial banks in the Chicago area have followed the policy of making an automobile loan to almost anyone at competitively low interest rates. For example, some loan applicants who were refused an automobile loan by the credit managers of the motor and automobile subsidiary of Mercantile Financial Corporation have gone to commercial banks and immediately received an automobile loan.

The effort by commercial banks in the automobile loan area were not significant until two years ago. Furthermore, the board of directors of commercial banks were thought to have had a rather conservative policy regarding excessive investments in the automobile loan area. Then, the pendulum began to swing to the other extreme. The financial terms and time periods covered by various types of automobile loans were modified, and the commercial banks assumed an increasingly important position in terms of the national volume of automobile loans made.

Management of the motor and automobile office is of the opinion that commercial banks have heavy losses which are currently hidden by the high volume of transactions. There is a lag between the time an automobile loan is made and the time that the typical repossession occurs. This lag averages 9 to 16 months. Commercial banks have been deeply involved in automobile financing for less than two years under conditions of these modified financial terms and extended time periods. Therefore, from a purely statistical standpoint it is almost impossible for a given commercial bank to have had sufficient historical statistical experience upon which to base its rates that pertain to the results of following the bank's current automobile loan policy.

The dynamic increase in the volume of automobile loan operations by commercial banks has produced substantial short-term profits to the commercial banks, and the appropriate losses that should be matched against these short-term profits will not be known until another 9 to 16 months. If the dynamic growth rate continues, the profits 16 months hence from the then higher level of activity will dominate over the losses that might occur by then (these losses would be indicative of the lagged results of lower levels of volume).

Several competent financiers have expressed the opinion that if the volume of automobile loans financed by commercial banks were to achieve even a stable position during the next 18 months, then some boards of directors of commercial banks may revert to their former position regarding automobile loan operations. If this leveling off in volume occurs, some commercial banks who have gone all out in accepting automobile loan customers may have such a large loss from uncollectible accounts and repossessions that the boards of directors will demand that the former credit terms and rates be applied to future automobile loans.

Management of the motor and automobile office tends to agree with this latter position regarding the future and has not adopted a policy of meeting the commercial banks' rates. Instead, management has accepted the short-term forecast of a reduced volume of operations in the automobile loan area.

The following statistical data indicate the degree of impact that commercial banks have had upon the volume of business handled by Mercantile Financial Corporation's motor and automobile office. Two years ago, the monthly average of automobile loans made totaled 700; now, there are approximately 250 automobile loans made each month. Currently, there are 8,500 open accounts, but this level of volume is constantly decreasing at a slow rate. Old accounts which were at the 700 volume level are being paid off at the end of 30 months, and new accounts at the 250 volume level are being added. However, the time period over which new automobiles are financed has been extended beyond 30 months. This latter factor slows the pace at which the total volume of open accounts is decreasing. These 8,500 open accounts have an aggregate balance, on the average, of $11,000,000.

For the corporation as a whole, this substantial reduction in volume in the automobile loan area has been more than offset by substantial gains in the commercial division's operations and in consumer loans, particularly in the area of personal loans for more than $800 (which may be called all-in-one loans or consolidated loans). Furthermore, the entry by commercial banks has permitted management of the motor and automobile office to be even more selective in the screening of customers, and this has resulted in an increase in the profitability of the average automobile loan during the past two years.

For example, a customer's loan application from an automobile dealer is not accepted, and subsequently this customer's loan application is accepted by a commercial bank. The automobile dealer may be upset because of the inconvenience caused by the nonapproval of the loan application but as long as the dealer can get the loan approved elsewhere and sell the automobile, he is happy. A few dealers have expressed their dissatisfaction with the motor and automobile office's operations in disapproving their customer's notes; however, the manager of the motor and automobile office does not believe that the current series of events will damage or affect the long-term relation between the automobile dealers and his office staff. If and when commercial banks become more selective in screening applicants for automobile loans, the volume of transactions by the motor and automobile office will increase.

The positive side of this change of events can be explained as follows. When an automobile dealer has a prospective customer who desires to buy a two-year-old automobile and does not have very many funds for a down payment or desires to repay the loan over an extended period of time, the automobile dealer must get this type of loan accepted by a financial loan institution. Commercial banks will not make such a loan. For example, on a two-year-old automobile, a commercial bank may loan $1,350 to be repaid over 24 months; the motor and automobile subsidiary of the Mercantile Financial Corporation will loan slightly more to be repaid over a longer period. The risk is higher on this latter type of loan, and thus a higher interest rate is demanded. In the aggregate volume of automobile loans, a substantial percent is of the riskier, high interest rate type. This explains the increase in average earnings by the motor and automobile subsidiary on automobile loans during the past two years.

Because of the substantial reduction in volume during the past two years, the number of employees in the motor and automobile office has been reduced significantly. However, the data accumulation, processing, and reporting activities are approximately the same; there are just fewer transactions to process and administer.

An automobile dealer will ask his customer to prepare a purchaser's confidential statement, a one-page document containing both credit reference data and the appropriate decriptive data regarding the proposed automobile sale. This latter data would include all of the financial terms—cash selling price, trade-in, total down payment, and so forth. The automobile dealer will also initiate a bank draft for the net amount payable to him under his arrangement with the motor and automobile subsidiary of Mercantile

Financial Corporation. These bank draft forms are of the envelope type; the automobile dealer will complete the bank draft and enclose in the envelope the automobile sales contract. The automobile dealer takes the bank draft with the enclosed document to his bank.

Eventually, the bank draft arrives at the commercial bank representing the motor and automobile subsidiary of Mercantile Financial Corporation. The motor and automobile subsidiary's management has an agreement with the officers of the commercial bank, and according to this agreement, a bank officer will notify the manager of the motor and automobile office at 2:00 each afternoon of the names and amounts of drafts that have been received by the bank. The manager has 24 hours in which to accept or refuse each draft, and a complete notification procedure is followed. (Even when all drafts are accepted, the manager will notify the bank officer accordingly.)

At the same time the automobile dealer takes the bank draft to his bank, he also sends the purchaser's confidential statement directly to the motor and automobile office. A credit manager in the motor and automobile office will initially review the purchaser's confidential statement. A work sheet is prepared, which is a one-page cover document containing insurance analysis on one segment of the page and draft analysis and collateral details on the other segment of the page. Next, a credit investigation is made of the customer. After the credit references are checked, the work sheet and attached documents are returned to the credit manager, and the credit manager reaches a decision regarding the approval of the automobile loan. (All of this action has occurred before the bank draft is processed through banking channels.)

When the bank officer calls the manager of the motor and automobile office regarding the acceptance of the automobile draft, the manager is ready to make a decision. However, the manager will go to the bank and secure the automobile sales contract for each draft, and during the 24-hour period that the motor and automobile office has to consider the drafts, the clerks in the motor and automobile office will closely scrutinize the terms and details of the actual contract against the application document. If there is any difference, the draft is refused for payment at the commercial bank. (From a statistical standpoint, the number of drafts accepted per day ranges from 10 to 20.)

If the bank draft is approved for payment at the commercial bank, a check is drawn for payment of each draft. A typist prepares a master loan set and a set of Galloway registration cards, which are used for registering the lien against the automobile. The master loan set is similar to the master loan set for furniture and appliance operations, with two exceptions. The fourth copy is also called the "Dealer Statistical Copy"; however, it is not sent to the data processing service center. Instead, the manager of the motor and automobile office uses this copy as the beginning point for accumulating various types of statistical data on automobile loan operations. Subsequently, the manager integrates reports of repossessions, losses, and delinquent account statistics with these data. Thus, confidential managerial statistics which reflect different types of risk are determined from this integrated statistical program, which is administered by the office manager. Exhibit M represents the dealer statistical copy of the master loan set for motor and automobile loan operations.

The sixth copy of the master loan set for motor and automobile loan operations is sent to the data processing service center, where data cards are prepared, processed, and used in the preparation of the monthly reports of mix and yield by automobile dealer.

After the master loan set and Galloway registration cards have been prepared, the insurance policy is typed. An internal review is made of the various documents in much the same manner as was followed in the furniture and appliance office. At the completion of this step, a perforated coupon payment book is prepared for the

EXHIBIT M
Dealer Statistical Copy* of Master Loan Set
for Motor and Automobile Loan Office

NAME OF CAR	SERIAL NUMBER		BODY CYLS.	YEAR	INSURANCE TERM	TYPE OF POLICY	ACCOUNT NUMBER
PURCHASER			ACCOUNT NO.	DAY DUE	NEW USED □ DLR INS. □		DATE DUE
ADDRESS			HOME PHONE	AGE	DEALER		
CITY AND STATE			OCCUPATION		SELLING PRICE	HOLD BACK	INSURANCE CHARGE
EMPLOYED BY		YRS. MOS.	BUSINESS PHONE		DOWN PAYMENT	%	1st YEAR COST
COMPANY NO.	PLAN	DATE PURCH.	DATE OF NOTE	AMT OF NOTE	UNPAID BALANCE	LOSS RESERVE	A C L
NO. AND AMT. OF INSTALL.	FINAL INSTALL			DEALER NO.	SERVICE CHARGE	OVER-REBATE	S C L
SPECIALS			WA'S REPUR. GUAR. MOS		AMOUNT OF NOTE CHECK OR DRAFT		REPURCHASE NET S.C.

* Normally, this form is 8½ × 4.

customer, and all documents are processed to their appropriate destinations.

Seven collectors and two supervisors are responsible for the 8,500 open accounts. As in the furniture and appliance operations, accounts are grouped in books, and a given collector is responsible for one or more books. A few dealers have such a volume of transactions with the motor and automobile subsidiary of Mercantile Financial Corporation that a separate book is established for each of them.

If a customer goes to the motor and automobile office to pay his monthly installment, the cashier will call the appropriate collector. The collector assigned to that customer will meet and talk with the customer while the cashier accepts the installment payment. If the customer is delinquent or there is any problem regarding his account, this collector-customer meeting provides the opportunity for a face-to-face discussion of the matter.

The nondealer books of customer accounts are designated a number according to the due date of the payment. Within the dealer books, the customer accounts are located in the appropriate order based on the due date of the payment. (The 15th, 16th, and 17th days of the month are the largest groupings of accounts, because they are the typical pay days.)

Monthly, a delinquent report is prepared by customer book, and the original copy of the delinquent report is given to the collection manager. The delinquent report is manually prepared by reviewing the payment column of each customer ledger card and observing the "key" designation. The bookkeeping machine records in the payment column the amount and date of the collection. Subsequently, clerks or collectors "key" each collection to indicate the appropriate monthly installment for which a particular payment is related and if there is any amount delinquent on that particular payment. For example, if a review is being made for the May delinquent account report and a given customer is keyed "3–$10," this would mean that the last payment was for the third month—March—and that the customer is $10 delinquent on the March installment; furthermore, the customer is delinquent on the April and May installments. Assuming the monthly installment is $65, the delinquent account list would appear as follows for May:

NAME	Total Delinquent	1–30 Days	31–60 Days	61–90 Days	Over 90
	$140	$65	$65	$10	–0–

The administration of the collection function is similar to that followed in the furniture and appliance office. The pressure is on the collector to reduce the number of delinquent accounts for which he is responsible. The action taken by the collector depends to a large extent upon the arrangement with the automobile dealer—a repurchase arrangement, a full recourse arrangement, a guarantee arrangement, or a holdback arrangement.

Periodically, an internal audit is made of the motor and automobile office's operations, and this includes an examination and confirmation of the balances in the customer accounts. The cash collection and cash payment procedures have internal control and internal check procedures similar to those followed in the furniture and appliance office.

Other Financial and Statistical Data

Consideration is given in this section to other data that are appropriate for a general understanding of the corporation's overall activities. The discussion will consist of three sections: responsibility reports, financial and statistical reports, and selected data regarding data processing activities.

Responsibility Reports

Monthly, a statement of income and expense (see Exhibit N and Exhibit O for the format of the report for all operations) and a statement of financial position (see Exhibit P for the format of the 4-page report) are manually prepared for each of the 32 accounting units. From a legal standpoint, there are 22 corporations contained in the consolidated Mercantile Financial Corporation and Subsidiaries, and each subsidiary corporation is wholly owned by the parent corporation.

The difference between the 22 corporations and the 32 accounting units can be explained as follows. There are three branches of a particular small loan corporation, and each branch is handled as though it were a separate corporation; thus, these three branches would add two accounting units to the compilation (the small loan corporation is already included in the 22 corporations) —22 corporations + 2 extra small loan branch reports = 24 units. Certain types of commercial activities in Chicago and Atlanta are separately ac-

EXHIBIT N

Statement of Income and Expense

Period ————————————

		Current Year		Previous Year	
	Budget	Month	YTD	Month	YTD

Income

Purchased accounts ....
Equipment loans ....
Inventory loans ....
Shell home loans ....
Rediscounts ....
Purchased notes ....
Retail motor loans ....
Wholesale motor & direct loans ....
Retail furniture & appliance loans ....
Small loans ....
Other consumer loans ....
Late charges ....
Bad debt recoveries ....
Insurance commissions ....
Miscellaneous income ....
     Total ....

Operating Expenses

Salaries ....
Administrative travel expense ....
Solicitors expense ....
Telephone & telegraph ....
Office supplies & expense ....
Stationery, printing, & postage ....
Repossession expense ....
Rent ....
Legal expense ....
Legal expense, consumer ....
Taxes, payroll, & misc. ....
Credit reports ....
Insurance ....
Auditing ....
Auditors expense ....
Collectors expense ....
Depreciation & amortization ....
Advertising ....
Entertainment ....
Supervisory expense ....
Commissions ....
Pension plan ....
Profit sharing ....
Service car expense ....
General expense ....

    Total Operating Expense ....
Income before interest, BDP, S&A expense & FIT
Interest expense ....
Income before S&A expense, BDP & FIT ......
Supervisory and administrative expense ....

EXHIBIT N (*Continued*)

		Current Year		Previous Year	
	Budget	Month	YTD	Month	YTD
Bad debt provision					
Income before federal income tax					
Provision for federal income tax					
Net Income					
Branch or Subsidiary ────────────────					

EXHIBIT O

Statement of Income and Expense

Period ──────────────────

		Current Year		Previous Year	
	Budget	Month	YTD	Month	YTD
Small Loan					
Precompute					
Simple					
Extensions					
Total					
Miscellaneous Income					
Dividends					
Regular loans					
Capital loans					
Other					
Total					
Salaries					
Administrative					
Accounting					
Advertising					
Auditors					
Collection/Credit					
Collectors					
Credit					
Service					
Solicitors					
Commercial supervision					
Legal, consumer					
Sales finance supervision					
Small loan supervision					
Total					
Stationery–Postage					
Stationery & printing					
Postage					
Total					

EXHIBIT O (*Continued*)

		Current Year		Previous Year	
	Budget	Month	YTD	Month	YTD

Repossession Expense

Garage ....

Repossessions ....

    Total ....

Taxes

Payroll ....

Personal property ....

State franchise ....

    Total ....

Depreciation–Amortization

Depreciation ....

Leasehold improvements ....

Noncompete ....

    Total ....

General Expense

T/E Accounting ....

T/E Credit ....

Bank exchange ....

Appraisal ....

Donations ....

Miscellaneous ....

    Total ....

Branch or Subsidiary ————————————————————————

EXHIBIT P
Statement of Financial Position
At ————————————

CASH IN BANKS AND ON HAND
  1001 Cash Regular
  1002 Cash Payroll
  1003 Cash Depository
  1004 Cash Dividend
  1005
  1006 Cash Bank Lines
  1007 Petty Cash
  1008 Ex-Check
  1009 U.S. Securities
  1010 Bank Transfers
  1011
  1012

      Total Cash

NOTES AND ACCOUNTS
RECEIVABLE
  1101 Equipment Loans

  1102 Inventory Loans
  1103 Purchased A/R Net
  1104 Purchased A/R Net
  1105 Rediscounts—Net
  1106 Rediscounts—Gross
  1107 Purchased Notes
  1108 Shell Home Loans
  1109 Factored Accounts
  1110
  1112
  1201 Retail Motor Loans
  1202 Wholesale Motor Loans
  1203 Retail Furniture Loans
  1204 Wholesale Furniture Loans
  1205
  1206
  1212 Simple Interest Small Loans
  1213 Precomputed Interest S. Loans
  1214 Simple Int. S. Loans (Acct. #2)

EXHIBIT P (*Continued*)

1215
1216 Other Consumer Loans
1217
1218
1219
1220 Regular Loans
1221 Capital Loans
1224 Employee's Accts. Rec.
1225 Insurance Accts. Rec.
1226 Burglary & Theft Loss
1229 Customer Service Charges
1230 Miscellaneous Accts. Rec.
1320 Dealer Holdbacks
  Sub Total
  Branch or Subsidiary ⎯⎯⎯⎯⎯

LESS
1121 Final Payment—Equipment Loans
1122 Final Payment—Inventory Loans
1123 Final Payment—Purchased Notes
1124 Final Payment—Shell Home Loans
1125 Final Payment—Factored Accounts
1126 Final Payment—Rediscounts
1301 Unearned Service Charge—Equip. Loans
1302 Unearned Ser. Ch.—Purchased Notes
1303 Unearned Ser. Ch.—Shell Homes
1304 Unearned Ser. Ch.—Purchased Accts.
1306 Unearned Ser. Ch.—Retail Motor Loans
1307 Unearned Ser. Ch.—Retail Furn. Loans
1310 Unearned Interest—Precomputed Loans
1312 Unearned Ser. Ch.—Other Cons. Loans
1315 Unearned Ser. Ch.—Regular Loans
1316 Unearned Ser. Ch.—Capital Loans
1320 Dealer Holdbacks
1321 Dealer Participating Loss Reserve
1322 S.C.L. Reserve
1323 Other Reserves
1324 Reserve Accounts—Subsidiaries
1325 Reserve for Doubtful Accounts
  Sub Total (Reserves)
  Net Receivables

FIXED ASSETS (NET)
1401 Furniture and Fixtures
1402 Service Cars
1403 Leasehold Improvements
  Total Fixed Assets

PREPAID OR DEFERRED EXPENSES
1501 Prepaid Expenses
1502 Prepaid Insurance
1503 Prepaid Interest
1601 Deferred Financial Services
1602 Deferred Insurance Expense
1603 Deferred Legal Expense
1604 Deferred Liquidation Expense
1605 Deferred Rebates—Repossessions
1610 Unamortized Debt Discount
1611 Unamortized Documentary Stamps
1612 Unamortized Noncompete Agreement
1701 Cash Surrender Value—Insurance
1702 Borrowed Premiums
1703 Deposit for Redemption—Class "A"
1704 Reserve for Redemption—Class "A"
1705

  Total Prepaid or Deferred
  Expenses
  Branch or Subsidiary ⎯⎯⎯⎯⎯
ADVANCES TO AND (FROM)
AFFILIATES
1801 Investments in Subsidiaries
1901 Current Account M.F.C.—Atlanta
1902 Current Account T.M.F.C.
1903 Current Account M.C.P.C.
1904 Current Account S.M.C.P.C.
1905 Current Account M.S.H.F.C.
1906 Current Account C.B.D.C.
1907 Current Account R.F.C.
1908 Current Account M.F.
1909
1921 Current Account M.M.D.C.
1922 Current Account M.I.B.
1923 Current Account S.M.F.C.
1924 Current Account M.C.F.C. (All)
1925 Current Account M.A.I.O.
1926 Current Account M.L.C. Corp.
1927
1928
1929
1930
1931 Current Account M.L.C. #1
1932 Current Account M.L.C. #2
1933 Current Account M.L.C. #3
1934 Current Account 4th M.L.C.
1935 Current Account 5th M.L.C.
1936 Current Account 6th M.L.C.
1937 Current Account M.C.L.C. (#7)
1938 Current Account 8th M.L.C.
1939 Current Account 9th M.L.C.
1940 Current Account 10th M.L.C.

EXHIBIT P (*Continued*)

1941
1942
1943
1950 Intracompany Insurance
     Total Advances
     TOTAL ASSETS

NOTES PAYABLE
2001 Notes Payable—Unsecured Bank
2002 Notes Payable—Commercial Paper
2003 Current Maturities on Long T.D.
2004
2005
     Total Notes Payable
     Branch or Subsidiary _____

ACCOUNTS PAYABLE AND
ACCRUED EXPENSES
2010 Dividends Payable
2015 Agency Obligations
2020 Collections Due Affiliates
2101 Accts. Payable—Insurance A.C.L.
2102 Accts. Payable—Insurance Auto
2103 Advanced Premiums
2104 Unclaimed Dividends
2105 Accounts Payable—Miscellaneous
2201 Rebates Due Dealers
2202 Suspense (Due Dealers)
2203 Suspense
2301 Accrued Contributions—E.R.P.
2302 Accrued Contributions—P/S
2303 Accrued C.R.I.
2304 Accrued Donations
2305 Accrued General Expense
2306 Accrued Interest Payable
2307 Accrued Legal Expense
2315 Accrued Taxes—Payroll, F.I.C.A.
2316 Accrued Taxes—Unemployment,
     Federal
2317 Accrued Taxes—Unemployment,
     State

2318 Accrued Taxes—Withholding,
     Federal
2319 Accrued Taxes—Withholding,
     State
2320 Accrued Payroll and Bonus
2325 Accrued Taxes—P.P. and R.E.
2326 Accrued Taxes—Franchise and
     Other
2327
2330 Estimated Federal Income Taxes
2331 Estimated State Income Taxes
     Total Accounts Payable & Accr.
     Exp.

LONG-TERM DEBT
2401 Unsecured Notes and Debentures
2402 Unsecured Subordinated Notes—
     Senior
2403 Unsecured Subordinated Notes—
     Junior
2404 Capital Indebtedness
     Total Long-Term Debt

STOCKHOLDERS EQUITY
3001 Preferred Stock—First Series "A"
3002 Preferred Stock—First Series "B"
3003 Preferred Stock—First Series "C"
3004 Preferred Stock—Class "A"
3005 Preferred Stock—Second
3006 $5\frac{1}{2}\%$ Class "A" First Preferred
     Stock
3010 Common Stock
3015 Paid-in Surplus
3016 Contributed Surplus
3020 Income and Loss Summary
3025 Retained Earnings
1802 Parent Current Account
     Total Equity
     TOTAL LIABILITIES
     Branch or Subsidiary_____

counted for as though each were a separate corporation; the compilation is 24 units + 2 commercial division responsibility units = 26 units. The remaining six accounting units are consolidated accounting units (26 units + 6 consolidated accounting units = 32 accounting units).

The administrative cost of the home office's management is prorated among the other accounting units. In the distribution of this administrative cost, the basis is the cash employed in the accounting

EXHIBIT Q
Historical Financial Data
(thousands of dollars)

ASSETS:

Date	Total	Cash	Total Notes	Customers' Equity	Unearned Service Charges	Reserves for Losses	Rec. from Lending Inst.	Invent. of Reposs.	Prepaid Intr., Etc.	Fixed Assets (Net)	Deferred Charges
Dec. 31:											
1954	$ 7,885	$ 1,026	$ 7,905	$ (435)	$ (473)	$ (212)	$	$ 3	$ 35	$ 37	$
1955	9,274	1,117	9,671	(727)	(663)	(219)		7	53	37	
1956	10,845	1,195	11,474	(904)	(785)	(246)		5	63	43	
1957	12,661	1,409	13,164	(986)	(889)	(233)		11	140	44	
1958	16,250	2,233	16,901	(1,983)	(920)	(254)		21	150	81	21
1959	21,349	2,737	21,493	(2,271)	(1,095)	(541)	650	20	186	79	90
1960	29,335	2,679	32,565	(4,988)	(1,599)	(433)	750	23	152	106	78
1961	35,340	4,261	40,831	(7,912)	(1,769)	(471)		13	138	173	76
1962	45,966	4,475	52,572	(7,805)	(3,035)	(722)		10	133	217	120
1963	56,517	5,393	64,377	(8,740)	(4,128)	(1,509)		393	227	262	242

LIABILITIES:

| | | | | | | Long-Term Obligations | | | Stockholders' Equity | | |
| | | Notes Payable Short Term | Accounts Payable & Accrued Expenses | Federal Income Taxes | Dividends Payable | Current Maturities | Nonsubordinated | Subordinated | Capital Stock | Ret. Earnings and Capital in Excess of Par Value of Stock | Total |
Date	Total										
Dec. 31:											
1954	$ 7,885	$ 4,960	$ 116	$ 151	$	$ 203	$ 467	$ 525	$ 555	$ 907	$1,463
1955	9,274	5,280	111	182		255	1,050	770	555	1,070	1,626
1956	10,845	5,225	144	217	19	255	2,050	665	1,058	1,212	2,270
1957	12,661	6,253	174	230	19	355	2,440	704	1,138	1,348	2,486
1958	16,250	9,045	303	203	15	315	2,180	1,583	1,093	1,513	2,606
1959	21,349	10,398	259	221	15	318	4,030	2,801	1,563	1,744	3,307
1960	29,335	15,960	388	306		408	3,825	3,628	1,819	3,003	4,821
1961	35,340	16,820	499	279		853	5,800	5,267	2,577	3,245	5,822
1962	45,966	24,273	479	387		1,292	7,775	5,725	2,577	3,457	6,034
1963	56,517	28,593	812	465		1,243	11,000	6,858	3,209	4,337	7,546

unit plus a direct allocation where applicable. Each accounting unit is charged 5 percent of the estimated average cash employed during the accounting period by that particular accounting unit for interest.

The monthly reports from the 32 accounting units serve dual purposes. They are used first for managerial evaluations and second for legal requirements of a separate report for each corporation. As had been discussed in another section of this case study, the activities of each subsidiary corporation do not overlap from an organization standpoint. For example, the monthly statements for the motor and automobile office are equal to the consolidation report for the two subsidiary corporations doing business in this area.

Financial and Statistical Reports

Exhibit Q presents historical financial data for the consolidated company from 1954 to 1963. These data have been restated to include a subsidiary corporation that was acquired during 1963 and accounted for as a pooling of interests. Exhibit R presents a summary of the increase in net worth, by source, for this same 10-year period.

EXHIBIT R
Sources of Increase in Net Worth

Year Ended	Net Proceeds of Stock Issuances	Consolidated Earnings	Less— Dividends Paid	Increase in Net Worth
December 31:				
1954	$	$159,080	$ 26,775	$ 132,305
1955		189,832	26,775	163,057
1956	502,240	233,480	91,499	644,221
1957	50,000	261,607	95,910	215,697
1958	(45,000)	262,973	97,712	120,261
1959	520,000	290,575	110,082	700,493
1960	1,307,200	363,038	155,380	1,514,858
1961	833,470	426,833	259,514	1,000,789
1962		514,597	303,014	211,583
1963	1,313,297	529,674	330,293	1,512,678

As indicated by the above exhibits, the earnings per share of common stock decreased for 1963 over 1962. Executive management believes that this decrease can be attributed to the increased capital and number of shares outstanding because of the recent acquisitions and expansions. The purpose of this increase in capital is to provide the necessary leverage for borrowing purposes. Furthermore, executive management feels that the firm is now in the relevant range or area where earnings can benefit from this growth pattern.

In the small loan operations, another type of report is prepared quarterly by each supervisor and assistant supervisor. This latter report is a thorough questionnaire type of report on all types of activities for which that supervisor or assistant supervisor is responsible. The questions cover human relation items as well as statistical data. This quarterly report is sent directly to the executive vice president of the parent corporation for his review and consideration.

Selected Data Regarding Data Processing Activities

As previously indicated, three types of activities are currently performed by the data processing service center: (1) customer transactions for each of the small loan offices, (2) a monthly statistical report of yield data by dealer for the furniture and appliance office, and (3) a monthly statistical report of mix and yield data by dealer for the motor and automobile office.

The average monthly service charge for these activities is $1,385. In the small loan area, the charge is $92.50 per 1,000 transactions processed, and the monthly average charge for the small loan area is $1,100. Statistical computations for the furniture and appliance office are billed at the rate of $165 per 1,000 transactions, with the monthly bill for these statistical reports amounting to $185. The computations for the motor and automobile office's statistical reports are more involved, and the rate is $400 per 1,000 transactions, with the average monthly bill of $100 (there are 250 automobile loans per month).

Most of the recording and processing activities in the furniture and appliance office and in the motor and automobile office are performed on a manual basis. Following are the appropriate monthly, clerical cost—the amounts are based on payroll and do not include any fringe benefits—for these two offices at the current volume of operations:

	Furniture and Automobile Office (per month)	Motor and Appliance Office (per month)
Administration	$ 690	$2,423
Accounting	2,848	1,360
Maintenance services	1,982	3,888

The above clerical-cost data include cashiers, bookkeepers, switchboard operators, and so forth. The clerical costs do not include supervisory personnel such as the branch manager. The term "maintenance services" encompasses the cost for the cashier and switchboard operator types of activities (clerical maintenance service). (Note the organization chart for each office as a basis for relating the clerical cost to the number of employees and to "titles.")

REQUIRED:

1. Should a complete systems review be performed? If you were the executive vice president, what action would you take? How much money would you allocate to each part of your action?
2. If you were employed by the executive vice president to perform a systems review, what questions would you ask? Why would you ask each question?
3. If you were employed to perform a general systems review, indicate in outline form the steps you would follow in performing this task.
4. How much of an increase in each type of activity—number of small loan offices and transactions, number of commercial loans, number of commercial regional offices, and so forth—would you desire *before* you would change your present recommendations?

PART **VI**
SPECIAL CONCERNS

CHAPTER 16

Internal Control and Audit of Advanced Information Systems

AN INFORMATION SYSTEM based on electronic data processing will contain four types of internal controls. First, there are controls built into the equipment to detect electronic failures as they occur, and these controls include parity check, duplicate circuitry, double-track reading and recording, and echo check. Second, there are controls over the inputs into the computer system, and these controls include such items as record counts, hash totals, and proof figures. Third, there are the controls that are coded into the computer programs that are designed to perform routine reviews and prevent errors. Program controls include reverse arithmetic, validity check or limit check, sequence check, cross footing, balance check, and label check. Fourth, there are administrative controls over the console operator, tape handling techniques, separation of duties, and assignment of responsibility for program changes.

As the business organization's information systems are shifted from computer-based integrated information systems toward online and real-time information systems, the systems designers, internal auditors, and external auditors encounter a new set of problems in regard to internal control. There is special concern over the control of information in these latter, advanced information systems. The "hard copy" audit trail is not present; in fact, the advanced information system may operate where there is no source document. Transmission equipment, such as American Telephone and Telegraph's Touch Tone card-dialing instruments, may be used as direct input devices to the computer system.

In addition to the problems associated with the lack of an audit trail and the absence of source documents, the online and real-time information systems may not be compatible with many of the traditional internal control procedures. The traditional checks and balances, separation of duties, a network of authorization and approvals, and lines of responsibility have to be reinterpreted and reexamined in light of the new business environment.

This chapter focuses upon some of these problems that the systems analyst copes with in the shift toward real-time information systems. The underlying objective of this discussion is not to suggest specific solutions to problems but rather to increase the systems analyst's understanding of the changed business environment. This latter objective will include increasing the systems analyst's appreciation of the organization aspects of this new business environment. Thus, this discussion is divided into two parts: first, conflicting objectives for advanced information systems, and second, issues facing the audit profession.

CONFLICTING OBJECTIVES FOR ADVANCED INFORMATION SYSTEMS

In the design of advanced information systems, there are really three distinct perspectives. First, there is the point of view of the systems designers who desire relevant and timely information for management's use in decision-making processes. The systems designers are attempting to create an information system that provides relevant and timely information in the most economical manner.

Second, there is the point of view of the internal auditors who desire assurance that the information transmitted to management is valid and that there are appropriate checks and balances, internal controls, and other procedures for protecting the resources of the business organization. While the internal auditors as an organization unit must report to executive management, they have a stated responsibility that is organizationwide. They will argue for a minimum control over the information flows and resources; thus, they may take exception with the systems designers' proposals because of the absence of this minimum control.

The third point of view is that of the external auditors. In the case of all business organizations that are subject to the Security and Exchange Commission's rules, the external auditors' role is that of expressing an opinion about the financial reports for the total business organization. In performing this task, the external auditors will demand more assurance of control over information flows and resources than is normally demanded by the internal auditors. In the final analysis, the external auditors will try to find some objective criteria that they can use as a basis for expressing an opinion about the overall financial statements.

On a continuum, the second point of view—that of the internal auditors—would appear between the other viewpoints. In general, the internal auditors' position will tend to approach that of the external auditors. However, for purposes of this discussion, only the two end positions will be further delineated.

As the business organization's operations are converted from electronic data processing to some combination of online and real-time information systems, the external auditors are confronted with a proposed environment in which they cannot review operations "after the fact." The audit trail is not there. In this setting, the external auditors cannot just be passive observers. They must seek appropriate measures and procedures which are incorporated within the proposed advance information systems so that they can use these measures and procedures as a basis for expressing an overall opinion about the company's financial statements.

In the past, there has been a close relation between executive management and the external auditors, and many practitioners will describe this relation as being that of a "team." This team's collective goal is to do what is best for all interests and parties associated with the business company under examination. This close relation between executive management and the external auditors has permitted many changes to occur in an informal manner, and there is no reason why this situation must change in the future.

But now the business environment has changed. Executive management has a new group of technicians who have an assigned responsibility of appropriately representing executive management's interests. These technicians or systems designers are seeking an information system that meets executive management's numerous requirements at a minimum cost. The systems designers will advocate some types of internal controls over the information transmission and processing activities, for operating personnel can still make human mistakes with a computer system. A magnetic tape may be erroneously erased; the same information may be processed twice; or erroneous information may be entered as inputs into the system. In addition, errors can result from an electrical power failure and machine malfunctions. While the systems designers recognize that different types of errors can occur, they will not concur with the external auditors in terms of the types of internal controls that should be installed. For example, if statistical techniques can be employed for estimating balances, then this procedure might be used by systems designers in lieu of any audit trail or program control criteria.

On the other hand, the external auditors desire some types of objective criteria which are generated within the advanced computer system that they can use as a basis for evaluating the overall information system. Thus, the external auditors must have representatives who are "participating observers" in the design of these advanced information systems if these systems are to contain the appropriate internal control measures. It is not sufficient for the external auditors to assume that the equipment controls, program controls, controls over input and output, and administrative controls which are selected by the systems designers will be satisfactory for the special interests of external auditors.

The case study at the end of this chapter—Case 16–1, State Hospital Service, Inc., and State Medical Service, Inc.—presents in detail a description of this conflict between the systems designers and the external auditors over a minimum level of control for information systems. But before considering this case study, attention is focused on some of the dilemmas confronting external auditors in advanced information systems.

ISSUES FACING THE AUDIT PROFESSION

The professional literature contains numerous papers and several books on how traditional audit procedures can be performed more accurately, timely, and efficiently through using the capabilities of the electronic computer. The literature is, however, almost barren with respect to new audit procedures and concepts for advanced real-time information systems.[1] The reason for this predicament is that

---

[1] Two papers which are exceptions to this statement are: Gregory M. Boni, "Impact of EDP on Auditing," *The Journal of Accountancy*, Vol. CXVI (September, 1963), pp. 39–44, and Franz E. Ross, "Internal Control and Audit of Real-Time Digital Systems," *The Journal of Accountancy*, Vol. CXIX (April, 1965); pp. 46–55.

such advanced information systems have only recently been installed and are not, as yet, widely used. With the increased use of such advanced information systems, special committees of the professional accounting and auditing associations will have to formally address themselves to coping with the new auditing issues associated with real-time information systems.

In the following discussion, some of these auditing issues are cited and briefly explained for purposes of increasing the reader's appreciation of these controversies. No attempt is made in this discussion to specify or even to suggest answers for these dilemmas.

1. Must the external auditors perform a technically oriented review of the major computer programs?

    The external auditors must have an *appreciation* of the overall information systems before they can evaluate the internal controls within the company. This is a prerequisite to the passing of judgment on the general nature of the information within the system and the resulting financial statements. What is the minimum level of inquiry required to gain this general appreciation? Must a selected number of computer programs be examined in detail? If so, what criteria should be employed in selecting the computer programs for such detailed examination?

2. To what extent should test decks be used in reviewing computer-based advanced information systems?

    The use of test decks is widely advocated by practitioners. But when should test decks be used? How should they be used? What are the acceptable ways of having test decks prepared? How often during a fiscal year should test decks be applied to an unannounced examination of the existing real-time information systems operations?

3. In what time period should the majority of the audit work for a company with real-time information systems be scheduled?

    In the past, most of the detailed audit work has been performed after the end of the fiscal year of the time period covered by the audit. Is this schedule still appropriate? Or, might a new concept of auditing procedures be more appropriate that would involve periodic examinations during the audit year, so that maximum use can be made of data while they are in their prime positions for retrieval and examination?

4. What are some guidelines for having a minimum number of built-in program controls?

External auditors desire objective criteria that are created as part of the regular computer programs which can be used by the auditors as a basis for passing judgment on the company's overall financial statements. What are the minimum number of such controls beyond which the external auditor cannot perform a regular evaluation? Within this minimum number, which types of controls are the most crucial?

5. To what extent must representatives of an external auditing firm participate in the design of an advanced information system before they can subsequently "audit" the system?

    Should representatives of the external audit firm serve as participating observers in the design of such systems? Some practitioners argue that if members of the auditing firm are present during the design stage, then members of this auditing firm cannot subsequently evaluate the designed system. These practitioners argue that an individual cannot objectively evaluate something that he has previously, implicitly concurred in in the design of the basic system. Of course, many practitioners will disagree with this latter position.

6. What is the minimum scope of the internal review of an organization with online and real-time systems where nonsource document types of inputs are directly accepted by the system (such as using Touch Tone telephones)?

    In the past, hazy distinctions have been drawn between an internal control examination of the operations of a company and a small-scale organization review. Do the environmental changes necessitate a reexamination of these guidelines?

7. As far as internal control is concerned, how long should magnetic tapes be retained?

    At present, arbitrary guidelines are being followed. Retention of such tapes is expensive, and this total issue merits a rational consideration as to the *why* and *how* in place of the existing arbitrary guidelines.

8. Is unauthorized access to computer-stored information within the scope of the external auditors' examination?

    External and internal auditors are both concerned with the safeguarding of the company's assets, and information is an example of such assets. But, what is the extent of the external auditors' responsibility?

Summary

Systems analysts in the coming years will experience business environments in which increased use is made of real-time information systems. The purpose of this chapter has been (1) to explain some of the general differences that systems designers versus external auditors have with respect to the establishment of controls within such information systems and (2) to raise briefly some of the controversies facing the audit profession.

TOPICS FOR CLASS DISCUSSION

1. In the case of commercial banks, savings and loan companies, and insurance companies that are operating under real-time systems, executive management may desire duplicate records. For example, the original source documents are retained and stored in such a manner that they can be easily retrieved for internal audit and internal control purposes. It is assumed that the general public expects and demands a high degree of confidence in all types of external statements and reports issued by one of the above-cited companies. On the other hand, the typical business company is not a bank, and management is unwilling to spend the extra cost associated with duplicate records for purposes of increasing the degree of confidence in the various internal and external reports.

Suggest some procedures that management might use in achieving a high degree of confidence in the information within the system without maintaining duplicate records. If necessary, please make extensive use of the library in coping with this question.

2. The project manager of a large business organization notified the company's external auditors that management was planning an advanced information system, specifically, a real-time information system. The external auditors were invited to send representatives who would observe the designing and implementation activities. The partner for the certified public accounting firm asked, "How can we subsequently audit a system that we have previously reviewed?" Therefore, the external auditors refused to observe the designing and implementation activities. Later, after the real-time information system had been designed, installed, and in operation for a few months, the external auditors went to this large business organiza-

tion to perform the annual audit. The external auditors were given copies of some of the original flow diagrams for the proposed system and were informed that the system was modified during the implementation phase.

The external auditors had an outside data processing service center prepare a test deck of cards that would check the real-time information system. To the embarrassment of all concerned, none of the test deck of cards was properly coded for the existing, modified information system. Thus, the computer system rejected each card in the test deck. Computer personnel in the company being audited worked overtime during the next month in order to develop test decks of cards which the external auditors can use in reviewing the real-time information system.

REQUIRED:

A. How can the certified public accounting firm verify the activity for the past few months while the company was operating under this real-time information system? Explain fully the problems involved in auditing this type of system under these circumstances.
B. Suggest alternative procedures that might have been followed by both executive management and the external auditors in the company. Justify each of your suggestions.

CASE 16–1.   STATE HOSPITAL SERVICE, INC., AND STATE MEDICAL SERVICE, INC.*

Recently the management of State Hospital Service, Inc., and State Medical Service, Inc., began the transition to an integrated total information system by changing operations from a punched card data processing system to a large-scale computer system. The information flow provided by the punched card system closely resembled the information flow generated by traditional accounting procedures, and management was determined that the new system would not be the blind adoption of the present procedures on another kind of machine. Instead, each operation of the firm was carefully examined

---

* The author and Prof. Hershel M. Anderson of North Texas State University concurrently prepared separate case studies on the business process of the above corporations. Certain parts of this case study are reproduced verbatim from the original draft of Professor Anderson's case study and are used with his permission.

for the purpose of trying to determine (1) "What is it that the people in this operation are trying to do?" and (2) "What information is required for the performance of this operation?" From the consolidation of the findings for each operation, attention was focused on the total information requirements of the firm. Next, management attempted to determine the most timely and accurate methods consistent with low cost that could be employed to meet these total information requirements of the firm.

The most striking departure from traditional accounting procedures contained in the new system was the control over accounts receivable. A rigid system of internal control was imposed over cash receipts, and the system was extended to provide collection data by group of customer accounts. After the total cash receipts had been verified by group of customer accounts, punched cards reflecting the collection data were fed into the computer, and the information system was so programmed that the customer accounts maintained on magnetic tape were updated. If the balance in any customer's account reflects a credit balance, the computer will automatically process a check payable to the customer for this credit balance. On a cycle basis the computer prepares statements used for billing certain customers. Other groups of customers are under a different plan where they pay without being billed. Throughout all of these operations the primary point of control is on cash.

The new accounting procedures are not designed to "prove" that the balance in accounts receivable is equal to the beginning balance plus billings less collections. Instead, a physical inventory procedure is followed. The computer accumulates from the records in the magnetic tape unit the ending balance of accounts receivable, and no attempt is made to reconcile the beginning and ending balance.

As a result of these procedures and the unique information system that was established, the company's independent auditors have been faced with many new problems which will confront other auditors as more companies develop and install integrated total information systems. Currently, the independent auditors and management are arguing over the extent to which controls will be established over the operations of the computer. This matter is an outgrowth of a $1,500,000 difference between the detailed accounts receivable accounts maintained on the computer and the control account which is manually posted.

The Company

State Hospital Service, Inc., and State Medical Service, Inc., began in this midwestern state in the late 1930's for the purpose of providing, on a nonprofit basis, hospital and medical insurance for citizens of this state. The policyholders control the company through the annual election of a board of directors, and this board elects an executive director to serve as the chief executive officer. State insurance regulations provide for control over State Hospital Service, Inc., and State Medical Service, Inc.'s rates. Claim payments are regulated by periodic audits of hospital costs and by a committee composed of doctors, the state insurance agency, and the company. State laws and insurance regulations also set the company's statutory reserves. Thus, by design, the company's primary goal is to provide a vehicle for sharing the risks of sickness and accidents at minimum costs to the citizens of the state.

Both group and individual contracts are written. Currently, there are approximately 3,000,000 members, and 75 percent of these members are covered by group policies. Because of the number of members on family policies, the 3,000,000 members are covered by only 1,300,000 contracts. Of the 3,000,000 members, approximately 20 percent are over 65 years old. The increase in membership this year over last year was 340,000. The number of claims processed has now increased to 1,500,000 a year, representing over $160,000,000. Following are *selected* financial data:

```
Balance sheet, end of current year
  Cash .............................................  $  4,500,000
  Investment in bonds .............................     95,000,000
  Premiums receivable .............................      6,700,000
    Total Assets ..................................  $109,000,000

Income statement for the current year
  Premiums earned .................................  $160,000,000
  Claims incurred .................................   160,500,000
  Underwriting expenses ...........................     4,500,000
    Net Loss .......................................  $  4,000,000
```

Aside from several staff functions, the company is organized around two functional areas: (1) enrollment "sales," which is concerned with maintaining contact with members through district offices, and (2) operations. All departments in the operating division are involved in some manner in either the receipt of premiums or the payment of claims. The new system, therefore, vitally affects every operating department. (Note that divisional status for electronic data processing resulted from the new integrated system.) The organization chart for the operating division is presented in Exhibit A.

The New System

The director of operations, a very able and progressive administrator, has watched the evolution of electronic data processing. In the period following World War II, the company made effective use of punched card equipment; however, the records maintained on this equipment were nothing more than duplicates of the older manual records. Accounting records (such as premiums receivable) and statistical records (such as membership records) were separately maintained. Each operating department used the punched card processing equipment only to eliminate manual work. As the capabilities of electronic data processing equipment increased, the director of

EXHIBIT A

Organization Chart—Operating Division

operations began to consider the feasibility of a completely integrated system which would avoid duplication of effort and provide the information needed by all operating departments. To this end a comprehensive feasibility study for an IBM 7070 was begun by the methods and systems group about three years ago, and its report was favorable. The actual transition began about two years ago.

The director of operations issued a statement of operating policy setting forth the objectives of the new system and the priorities to be assigned to different interests. Exhibit B represents this bold statement.

This policy statement (Exhibit B) was used by the systems analysts and programmers as a basis for selecting data that would be reflected in the new integrated information system. As previously mentioned, the systems analyst in the previous step had identified the pertinent data required in each operation. Exhibit C is an example of the findings of the previous step; the data reflected in the application card are identified and the steps followed in the approval of a hospital admission are indicated. Schematically, the total integrated system is depicted by Exhibit D.

Given the director of operations' bold policy, the manager of the EDP (Electronic Data Processing) divison began by training programmers and developing programs. First efforts were aimed at subscriber records for billing and receivable purposes—to serve the subscriber best by giving him an accurate, timely notice of the premiums due. This part of the system, dealing with earned and unearned premiums, premiums receivable, and subscriber records, was in operation throughout the past year. The programs for claims, hospital, and other payment records are being developed; transition from the old system to the new one in these areas is presently in process.

In the new system there is a significant time lag. For example, individual (nongroup, direct payment) accounts are billed on a quarterly basis 35 days in advance. These subscribers are divided into 13 billing cycles, and one cycle is billed each week. The lead time for changes in the bills of each cycle is about 50 days. If a change is to be made in the cycle which pays for the first calendar quarter, notice must reach the data processing center by November 10.

The built-in lag is not restricted to adjustment to accounts receivable. There are unreported admissions and it is necessary to estimate the amount of such unreported claims at the time of preparing the

EXHIBIT B
Statement of Operating Policy

Our operating policy is to provide the subscriber, physician, and hospital the most timely and accurate service that is consistent with low cost.

The application of computer technology is designed to further this policy.

Designing an "integrated system" is a condition precedent to the efficient application of automation.

Our systems, programming and operating personnel are being guided by the following precepts.

1. We are developing a totally integrated system. This means that we are not attempting to "put present operations on another kind of machine."
2. We want to develop the *best way* to
   a. serve subscribers
   b. serve hospitals
   c. serve doctors
3. After the "best way" is determined, we then shall design as *by-products* of the system the accounting, statistical, and other internal needs for management.

This distinction is important. External orientation is primary, and internal orientation is secondary. It also follows that internal needs and reporting will necessarily undergo substantial alteration.

In case of conflict, the primary (external needs) will take precedence over the secondary (internal needs).

(Signed)
Director of Operations

EXHIBIT C
Examples of Systems Analyst's Findings
Subscriber History File

Each application card contains the following data:

1. Hospital service, effective date.
2. Medical service, effective date.
3. Extended benefits date.
4. Certificate number.
5. Group number or direct payment or pending conversion register number.
6. Name of subscriber.
7. Date of birth of original subscriber.
8. Address (original changed if information received).
9. Employer (not updated and sometimes blank).
10. Sex and marital status (not updated).

On reverse side of jacket:

1. Adjustments with continuity of coverage:

Effective Date	Explanation (if any)	Group No.	Coverage B.C., B.S., Ext.	Clerk's initials & Posting date

2. Adjustments with noncontinuity:
Original effective dates are crossed out and remarks entered that the new dates are the effective dates of membership.

3. Claims:

Dr. or Hosp. No.	Admission Date	In or out Patient or D for Diagnostic	Name of Patient	Relationship 1. sub. 2. spouse 3. child	Clerk's Initials & Posting date

*   *   *

EXHIBIT C (*Continued*)

Hospital Service Admissions

Approval of a hospital admission depends on the following:
1. Correct certificate number.
2. Patient must be included on the membership. If spouse or child:
   a. Coverage must be family type.
   b. Child must not be overage.
   c. Age of spouse must be within reasonable number of years of subscriber.
   d. If subscriber, check name and date of birth.
3. Correct status at time of admission.
   a. Group or direct payment.
   b. Coverage.
   c. Must not be cancelled.
   d. Are there extended benefits?
4. Previous hospitalization.
   a. Check 2 previous admissions within past year.
   b. Check current admission for duplicate.
5. Waiting periods incomplete.
   a. Is there a waiver? Interplan, Medicare?
   b. Is it a 3XB deletion? (19 yr. old child deleted from parent's membership)
   c. Is it a state membership?
   d. Is there a cross-reference to another number?
6. Restrictions.
   a. Health waiver.
   b. Tabbed as delinquent.
   c. Flagged for department head.
7. Maternity information.

*   *   *

annual report. Furthermore, individuals will have submitted a claim and possibly received payment on the claim even though they have not paid their premium for the quarter (this will be discovered later when the data in the magnetic tape unit are updated and the appropriate collection action will be initiated).

The director of operations accepts the time lag as being an inherent aspect of an integrated information system. His objective is not to establish new procedures to try to eliminate the time lag, but rather to try to reduce the time element of the lag. The current goal is to try to reduce the time lag to 30 days. The director feels that 30 days will be about as far as he can profitably go in reducing the time lag. Any further reduction would cost more than the benefits derived from such efforts.

Under the current system, a general ledger (including control accounts for the group and individual accounts) is maintained in the accounting department. Charges to the accounts receivable control are based on the weekly totals of premiums billed as shown by the computer runs. Credits are based on the cashier's daily reports.

EXHIBIT D
Data Flow

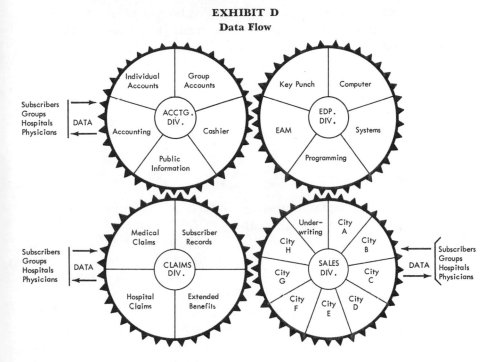

Input data originate in four external areas:
  1. Subscribers
  2. Groups
  3. Hospitals
  4. Physicians

They are introduced into the system and prepared for processing through three divisions:
  1. Sales
  2. Claims
  3. Accounting

All data are processed in one division:
  1. Electronic Data Processing

Output data are distributed to external areas (subscribers, hospitals, physicians, groups) through three divisions:
  1. Sales
  2. Claims
  3. Accounting

Information on rejects, changes in coverage, additions, cancellations, and errors go directly into the computer runs. The accounting department does not maintain control over these items. Because these items do not go through the accounting department, the general ledger balance of accounts receivable does not agree daily with the balance in the magnetic tape unit. (Remember that even for the accounts on magnetic tape, no attempt is made to reconcile the beginning and ending balance by considering all of the adjustments, additions, cancellations, collections, and billings. Instead, a physical inventory is taken at the end of the year as to the ending detailed accounts receivable balance per the magnetic tape unit, and the general ledger account is adjusted to reflect this amount.)

The Auditor's Appraisal

The state insurance commission conducts an audit of the company every three years. However, members of the board of directors and the executive director believe that an annual audit by a certified public accounting firm more than pays its cost by increasing public confidence in the company's fiscal soundness. New auditors were selected at the time the computer was installed.

During the interim work, which the audit firm started in the 11th month of the fiscal year, the in-charge manager of the audit was disturbed to note that the total of the detailed accounts receivable was $1,500,000 over the balance shown by the control accounts. A closer look at the new system uncovered several unorthodox procedures which led him to prepare a memorandum for the company's consideration (Exhibit E). Investigation revealed an error in the program for group accounts which resulted in an understatement of the billed premium amount used to charge (debit) the control account. After the correction of this error, data for the first eight months of the year were reprocessed and the company's accountant arrived at a $1,000,000 increase in the control account. The auditor felt that the additional difference could be traced to the same source, but the company would only agree to an adjustment of $1,000,000. Furthermore, the load on the computer did not permit further inquiries.

The audit manager's concern goes beyond this single error. His questions center around three permanent features of the new system:

1. The accounting department has no control over the billed premiums. Amounts supplied by the computer cannot be checked to an independent source.

2. Rejected cash receipts are ignored by the accounting department. At no time does the cash credited to the control agree with the sum of the credits to the detail.

3. Time lags result in the reflection of some changes in the detail before reflection in the control and vice versa. The records kept are insufficient to permit reconciliations.

The audit manager's recommendations are included in his memorandum. These recommendations are based on the position that internal check and control are essential in every system; an integrated system, like any other system, must be controlled to avoid errors. Furthermore, control does not mean that the company must "put present operations on another kind of machine."

The Company's Rebuttal

Generally, the director of operations and his division managers reject the auditor's recommendations. They contend that no important administrative decisions are based on accounts receivable balances, that the degree of accuracy indicated by the auditor's memorandum would not improve administrative action, and that tighter controls would not be worth their costs. The company depends on the audit of groups and individual subscribers to uncover major errors. Minor errors will eventually come to light as claims are filed and other changes made. The director of operations stated that implementation of the auditor's recommendations would result in as much manual processing (and costs) as experienced under the punched card system.

EXHIBIT E
Memorandum on Accounting Procedures and Internal Control of the Data Processing Department

As a result of our observations during the course of our recent review of the accounting procedures and internal control of the data processing department in preparation of our audit work for the current year, a number of ideas and suggestions were developed which we are presenting in this memorandum for your consideration.

We hope the suggestions contained in this memorandum will be helpful to the companies in improving operations and strengthening internal control in the data processing department.

Positive Controls of Information Processed

During the course of our examination of the financial statements of the companies, we noted that very substantial differences existed between the general ledger control balance and the total of the premiums receivable detail maintained on the computer. In our opinion, this situation has developed, in part, because adequate positive controls have not been established to provide assurance that the processing of information on the computer system is correct. Currently, the only means of checking the system are the reviews for reasonableness of the volume of data prepared and the time required to process it. While the monitoring of volumes by the test of reasonableness is important and should be continued, positive control should also be established.

We recommend that these controls include the following:

EXHIBIT E (*Continued*)

A. Source Data Control

(1) New Business—Item counts of new subscribers should be made manually and these counts should be reconciled to the number of new accounts set up by the computer.

(2) Miscellaneous Transactions (Dollar Adjustments)—Precomputer processing totals should be established of dollar amounts which should be reconciled to the amounts processed by the computer.

(3) Nondollar Miscellaneous Transactions—Item counts should be reconciled to the count of nondollar transactions accepted by the computer.

Transmitting this data in batches of workable sizes with preestablished controls will help substantially in isolating errors and in locating missing data.

B. File Control

(1) Receivable Amounts—Normal balancing procedures should be followed after each weekly processing as follows: Previous week's balance, plus billings, less cash received and adjustments equal present ending balance.

(2) Policy Count—Normal balancing procedures should also be followed for these counts.

(3) Billing Amounts—Independent control over the billing should be established. For example:

   (a) Accumulate on the computer file run the number of policies to be billed the following week.

   (b) Provide totals by groups of certificate numbers, for example, every 100,000 numbers, and compare these to the previous quarter's billing figures.

   The count prepared on direct payments should be monitored and double checked until the bills are actually put in the mail. Having the computer serially number these bills would be desirable.

(4) Transfers between Billing Methods—Control the receivables, in dollars, and the item counts which are transferred between the group billing and the individual billing accounts.

(5) Rejects—Totals of amounts rejected by the computer which are still pending should be controlled as a separate account. Weekly trial balances of the unprocessed detail should be made and reported as to the number of items and the dollar amount to disclose that an unusual buildup in rejected items has not occurred.

   We noted that there are some reports containing the type of data indicated above which would facilitate the establishment of controls over rejects. The tie-in of the reprocessed items to that processed by the computer could be simplified to provide the basis of establishing the controls suggested.

General Ledger Control Accounts

The records of the accounting department should control the amounts as processed by the computer in each stage of operation in order to isolate computer errors. It is not adequate to accept computer amounts without the ability to independently verify the amounts on an overall basis as suggested above through batch controls. Control totals should be directly traceable to the detail supporting them.

A suggested setup of the accounts and a description of the journal entries relating thereto follows:

General Ledger Accounts

  Cash
  Cash Clearing
  Premiums Receivable—Computer
      Groups
      Direct Payment
  Premiums Receivable—Manual
  Rejects Receivable—Items Pending Investigation

Journal Entries

(1) As deposits are made—
   Dr. Cash
      Cr. Cash Clearing
(2) As the computer accepts cash—
   Dr. Cash Clearing
      Cr. Premiums Receivable—Computer

The balance in the Cash Clearing account would represent deposits which the computer has not processed. A trial balance of this account should be prepared at least monthly and reconciled with the actual unprocessed cash items on hand.

   (3) As the computer processes refunds, rejects, and sundry write-offs, an entry would be required to reflect the disposition of these items by the computer:
   a. Dr. Premiums Receivable—Computer
         Cr. Cash (Refunds)
         Cr. Rejects
   b. Dr. or Cr. Premiums Receivable—Computer
         Dr. or Cr. Write-off of Sundry Debit or Credit Balances
   (4) As items are processed out of the reject file:
   Dr. Rejects
      Cr. Premiums Receivable—Computer

The balance in the rejects account represents unprocessed items which should be in the trial balance weekly.

   (5) As writings are calculated by the computer:
   Dr. Premiums Receivable—Computer
      Cr. Premiums Billed (Income)

The detail listing of accounts receivable balances on the computer should be reconciled monthly with the general ledger control account for premiums receivable—computer.

Master Tape Routine

We believe the Company would realize substantial benefits by adopting a technique known as master tape routine. This technique facilitates more rapid correction to program instructions, and of greater importance, changes can be made only under strict conditions as established by the controls provided in the master tape routine. Another advantage of this technique is that the master instruction tape minimizes setup time and reduces the potential for operator error.

While we recognize that it would be a substantial undertaking to revise the existing programs to effectively insert control and linkage instructions, we believe the Company should seriously consider that as a project and schedule it for evaluation by its programming group. This technique, of course, could be used with little additional effort in developing programs for new applications.

Test Program

The Company should provide for a comprehensive and coordinated test program using test data monitoring a computer program in a test session. It is a major effort to prepare this material for testing purposes but it is imperative to identify as many error conditions as possible before processing actual transactions. In addition, this test program data would reduce computer time for debugging and it would facilitate revision and control changes to the program once the system has been put into operation.

Other

We suggest that the individual activity list be condensed to two items a line and that the list provide more "coverage" and "paid-to" information on all accounts. This would reduce printing time and would provide a complete listing of the file which could eliminate the manual maintenance of the card file.

CHAPTER 17

Simulation and Management Information Systems

In the XYZ Corporation, a production and operation information system has been installed that reacts daily to changes in stock level. This system contains a computerized, integrated inventory control and production scheduling subsystem that maintains perpetual inventory control and triggers the reorder quantities which should be produced. Another segment of the information system relates on a daily basis the total group of items that should be produced with the existing plant capacity and restrictions of machines and personnel.

The XYZ Corporation is operating in a marketing environment where the sales for each item cannot be forecast with a high degree of confidence, and, at the same time, the plant is operating at, or near, full capacity. In this situation, how does the systems analyst forecast the monthly (or weekly) financial requirements that are necessary for the operation of the production department?

The traditional statistical technique of *expected value* could be used wherein ranges would be specified for each product and the daily demand for each product determined. After the daily demand for each product has been determined, the expected time at which the reorder point will be reached for each product can be computed. Next, the machinery, raw materials, and equipment can be daily forecasted for the previously computed reorder quantities.

Although this statistical technique does generate a complete budget, the technique does not give any suggestion of the range of variation that is expected in the actual day-to-day behavior of the system. Furthermore, a statistical technique is desired which is not based on a single expected value for each variable but, instead, permits each variable to vary in respect to its assumed frequency distribution. These and other reasons are responsible for the development of the *simulation* technique.

Simulation

The term "simulation" is used to designate a special characteristic of some models. A certain segment of reality must be represented by the model before it can be labeled a "simulation model."[1] The simulation model must also possess a close approximation to the real situation.[2] For example, some management scientists argue that the simulation model should be such a close approximation of the real situation that a given "simulation" occurrence is a predictable, possible occurrence of the real situation. If this degree of "close approximation to the real situation" does not exist, then the model should be labeled a "statistical model" instead of a "simulation model." In other words, the mathematical factors in the simulation model should be related in such a manner that the mathematical results of the simulation model can be meaningfully, directly interpreted in terms of the real situation.

This simulation technique may be applied to different business situations for various purposes, and the general character of the simulation model will vary by the purpose. This discussion considers three purposes: (1) short-term planning, (2) long-term planning, and (3) integrating information systems into a computerized total system.

Although the simulation technique is normally used when a computer program is available for processing the information, the reader needs to gain an appreciation of what the computer does in terms of processing the information through the simulation routine before the reader can intellectually interpret and evaluate the output from the simulation model. Therefore, the following discussion presents the simulation models as though they were going to be manually

---

[1] The following paper contains an excellent discussion of the different general types of simulation models: Joel M. Kibbee, "Management Control Simulation," in Donald G. Malcolm, Alan J. Rowe, and Lorimer F. McConnell (eds.), *Management Control Systems* (New York: John Wiley & Sons, Inc., 1960), pp. 300–320.

[2] C. West Churchman succinctly describes the conditions that a simulation must possess in "An Analysis of the Concept of Simulation," in Austin C. Hoggatt and Frederick E. Balderston (eds.), *Symposium on Simulation Models: Methodology and Applications to the Behavioral Sciences* (Cincinnati, Ohio: South-Western Publishing Co., Inc., 1963), p. 12.

processed. After the reader has a general understanding of the simulation process, then, computerized applications of the technique can be explored.

Short-Term Planning

The general simulation models are modified as dictated by the business situation. Thus, it is difficult to group simulation models because of the numerous modifications and adjustments that have been made. However, if these various simulation models were to be sorted in reference to their environment, the following two groupings might be the end points on a continuum. The first group can be labeled "simulation under certainty." In these simulation models, all of the alternatives are known and management desires to determine the outcome under different combinations of alternatives.

The second group can be labeled "simulation under risk." In these simulation models, each alternative cannot be precisely specified but, instead, only the frequency distribution of the range for each variable is known or can be estimated.

Simulation under Certainty. In a given project there may be 20 or more variables that corporate management can change at their discretion. A computer program can be used in coping with the project, and this program would express the mathematical relation among these 20 variables. Each of the variables is modified in turn and an outcome is determined for each possible combination of variables. By this process, management can select that group of choices which most nearly coincides with its objectives.

The use of simulation is similar to the technique of preparing a budget. The major difference is that the budget technique is applied over and over again, with different values being specified for the variables. This relation between budgeting and simulation is emphasized in the following illustration.

The Alpha Company has four regular products. A consultant has just completed the computation of the reorder quantity and the reorder point for each of the four regular products. These four products are similar and are equivalent units for production scheduling purposes. At present, there are 620 units of inventory in stock. The plant capacity for any eight-hour shift is 370 units if no setup is required; 355 units if one setup is required; and 340 units if two setups are required. It is against company policy to have more than two setups per eight-hour shift. The average daily sales for the four products equals 315 units.

Management desires to employ the reorder quantities and the reorder points in the daily scheduling of production. Therefore, since the production capacity is greater than average daily sales, there will be a gradual increase in the balance of inventory in stock. Management's objective is to have an average balance of 1,100 units in inventory. Whenever the average daily balance reaches 1,200 units or more, the next day a 100-lot size quantity of the marginal product (a fifth product) is scheduled for production, and this lot size quantity is sold the following day to a local manufacturer.

Using the following rules, management desires to simulate the production cycle for purposes of determining (1) how soon the 1,100 unit balance will be reached and (2) how frequently the fifth product will be manufactured once this average balance (1,100 units) is reached:

1. Less than lot size quantities may only be scheduled during the first three cycles. It is recognized that this predicament may occur in the initial conversion to the reorder quantity and reorder point procedure.
2. If at the completion of the production of a regular reorder quantity for a given product, no other product's inventory level is at the reorder point, then the remaining capacity for that cycle may be scheduled as a "special" quantity for the product currently being produced. However, a test will be made during the next four cycles and if a negative value is forecasted for any product, then the special quantity for the former product will not be scheduled. Instead, after the regular economic lot size quantity is manufactured, the program will determine which product is forecasted to reach the reorder point first, and this product will be scheduled for production.

Simulations for the first seventeen cycles are shown in the accompanying chart:

		Products				
	A	B	C	D	E*	Total
Reorder point	140	145	150	170		605
Reorder quantity	210	220	230	250		910
Beginning inventory	80	210	200	130	—	620
1st Cycle: Production	210†			145		355
Sales	70	75	80	90		315
Balance	220	135	120	185		660
2nd Cycle: Production		15	220‡	105		340
Sales	70	75	80	90		315
Balance	150	75	260	200		685
3rd Cycle: Production		370§				370
Sales	70	75	80	90		315
Balance	80	370	180	110		740

| | | \multicolumn{5}{c}{Products} | | | | |
		A	B	C	D	E*	Total
4th Cycle:	Production	210			130		340
	Sales	70	75	80	90		315
	Balance	220	295	100	150		765
5th Cycle:	Production			235§	120		355
	Sales	70	75	80	90		315
	Balance	150	220	255	180		805
6th Cycle:	Production				355§		355
	Sales	70	75	80	90		315
	Balance	80	145	175	445		845
7th Cycle:	Production	210	130				340
	Sales	70	75	80	90		315
	Balance	220	200	95	355		870
8th Cycle:	Production		90	265§			355
	Sales	70	75	80	90		315
	Balance	150	215	280	265		910
9th Cycle:	Production			370§			370
	Sales	70	75	80	90		315
	Balance	80	140	570	175		965
10th Cycle:	Production	210	130				340
	Sales	70	75	80	90		315
	Balance	220	195	490	85		990
11th Cycle:	Production		90		265§		355
	Sales	70	75	80	90		315
	Balance	150	210	410	260		1,030
12th Cycle:	Production				370§		370
	Sales	70	75	80	90		315
	Balance	80	135	330	540		1,085
13th Cycle:	Production	210	130				340
	Sales	70	75	80	90		315
	Balance	220	190	250	450		1,110
14th Cycle:	Production		370§				370
	Sales	70	75	80	90		315
	Balance	150	485	170	360		1,165
15th Cycle:	Production	355§					355
	Sales	70	75	80	90		315
	Balance	435	410	90	270		1,205
16th Cycle:	Production			240§		100	340
	Sales	70	75	80	90		315
	Balance	365	355	250	180	100	1,230
17th Cycle:	Production			370§			370
	Sales	70	75	80	90	100	415
	Balance	295	260	540	90	—	1,185

° A 100-lot size quantity of the marginal product (Product E) is manufactured in the following cycles: 19th, 21st, 24th, 27th, 29th, 32nd, and so forth.
  † Machine setup for A.
  ‡ Less than lot size.
  § Special lot size.

The rules cited in the previous example could easily be incorporated in a computer program. After this computer program has been written, then management can quickly recompute the simulation under alternative conditions. For example, the daily sales for each product in the example were estimated, and these values can be changed, and a new simulation computed under revised estimates.

In other words, the computer program for simulation is viewed by the systems analyst as being analogous to the computer program for a critical path planning and scheduling model. In both cases, the major cost is the establishment of the computer program. The second, third, and subsequent uses of this computer program have a relatively low marginal cost. Thus, management can use the simulation model of a project for coordinating, monitoring, and controlling the activities associated with the project while these activities are being accomplished. In achieving this latter objective, the computer program is rerun frequently using revised information.

In addition to scheduling of production, the technique of simulation under certainty is frequently used in evaluating and managing a special project. For example, a land development company might be formed for the purpose of constructing and selling commercial and residential properties on a given tract of land. The simulation technique can assist in determining (1) the best parceling of the land between different types of houses and buildings, (2) the extent to which a given plot should be filled and improved, (3) the best terms and conditions under which the properties are sold, (4) the weekly cash flow for the duration of the project, and so forth.

Simulation under Risk. A project may have 20 or more variables, but the value that each variable will take may not be determined by management. The technique of simulation under risk permits management to specify a range and the nature of the frequency distribution for each variable. Values for each variable will be selected at random from that variable's estimated frequency distribution and used in computing a total value for the project. This procedure is repeated over and over again. The reason for repeating the process is that the systems analyst desires to know the range of the probable outcomes based on the interaction of all the variables. The following example illustrates this type of simulation:

The Beta Company is considering the introduction of a new product for purposes of having a better product mix and using idle capacity.

	Product A	Product B
Selling price	$48	$32
Variable production cost	$16	$10
Variable marketing cost	12	8
Overhead expense	8	6
Total expenditures	$36	$24
Net profit per unit	$12	$ 8
Number of units (annually)	10,000	15,000
Total net profit for product	$120,000	$120,000

After a thorough study, management has found that two new products—Product A and Product B—both meet these objectives and have the same estimated profit.

Management decided to use the technique of simulation under risk in evaluating these two products. The range and frequency distribution for each variable were estimated by management. Next, random numbers are assigned to each class interval in proportion to the class's frequency distribution. Finally, random numbers are drawn or selected by some process, and the random number so drawn is compared with the previous grouping of random numbers for purposes of determining what number for the variable should be used in the first simulation cycle. This procedure is repeated as often as the system analyst feels appropriate.

Figure 17.1 illustrates the assignment of random numbers to each of the variables for Product A and Product B. Figure 17.2 presents 25 simulations that, for purposes of illustration, show the same random number being used for all variables in a given simulation cycle. Statistically, it would be preferred to have a random number separately selected for each variable, even though the assignment of random numbers for each class range has been systematically performed.

Based on the 25 simulations illustrated in Figure 17.2, the average profit for Product A is $125,200 and for Product B is $116,080. Product A has a range of $90,000 to $168,000, a median of $120,000, and a mode of $99,000. Product B has a range of $64,000 to $180,000, a median of $120,000, and a mode of $135,000. Thus management has much more information on the interaction of the variables which it can use in choosing between Product A and Product B.

As indicated by the previous example, the technique of simulation under conditions of risk is easy to apply. The difficult and critical part of this technique is the management task of specifying the range for each variable and the appropriate frequency distribution for each variable.

This latter type of simulation procedure is especially suitable for testing alternative marketing strategies. For example, in the Mirrex Company case study, after the multiple regression technique has been applied to customer characteristics and payment behavior, to customer characteristics and products, and to customer characteristics and salesmen, then the simulation technique can be used in estimating the reaction of prospective customers in a given geographical area to a given type of promotion program. The risk would be with estimating the customer characteristics of readers of the promotion literature.

FIGURE 17.1

Assignment of Random Numbers to Each of the Variables

	Product A				Product B		
	Value	*Fre-quency*	*Random Numbers*		*Value*	*Fre-quency*	*Random Numbers*
Selling	$45	8%	790–869		$29	7%	112–181
Price	46	16	630–789		30	12	992–111
	47	22	050–269		31	18	562–741
	48	30	330–629		32	28	182–461
	49	18	870–049		33	19	802–991
	50	6	270–329		34	10	462–561
					35	6	742–801
Variable	$14	15%	516–665		$ 9	15%	285–434
Production	15	15	166–315		10	65	635–284
Cost	16	50	666–165		11	20	435–634
	17	20	316–515				
Variable	$10	5%	373–422		$ 7	15%	048–197
Marketing	11	16	023–182		8	70	198–897
Expense	12	60	423–022		9	15	898–047
	13	19	183–372				
Overhead	$ 6	5%	897–946		$ 5	15%	759–908
Expense	7	13	947–076		6	70	059–758
	8	65	247–896		7	15	909–058
	9	17	077–246				
Number of	8,000	5%	484–533		12,000	10%	751–850
Units	9,000	16	324–483		13,000	10	551–650
	10,000	50	824–323		14,000	15	101–250
	11,000	20	624–823		15,000	30	251–550
	12,000	9	534–623		16,000	15	951–100
					17,000	10	651–750
					18,000	10	851–950

FIGURE 17.2
Twenty-five Simulations

Random Number:	601	167	814	519	976	444	735	228	353	820	791	542	941
Product A													
Selling price	$ 48	$ 47	$ 45	$ 48	$ 49	$ 48	$ 46	$ 47	$ 48	$ 45	$ 45	$ 48	$ 49
Variable production cost	$ 14	$ 15	$ 16	$ 14	$ 16	$ 17	$ 16	$ 15	$ 17	$ 16	$ 16	$ 14	$ 16
Variable marketing cost	12	11	12	12	12	12	12	13	13	12	12	12	12
Overhead expense	8	9	8	8	7	8	8	9	8	8	8	8	6
Net profit	$ 14	$ 12	$ 9	$ 14	$ 14	$ 11	$ 10	$ 10	$ 10	$ 9	$ 9	$ 14	$ 15
No. of units (000)	12	10	11	8	10	9	11	10	9	11	11	12	10
Net profit (000)	$168	$120	$ 99	$112	$140	$ 99	$110	$100	$ 90	$ 99	$ 99	$168	$150
Product B													
Selling price	$ 31	$ 29	$ 33	$ 34	$ 33	$ 32	$ 31	$ 32	$ 32	$ 33	$ 35	$ 34	$ 33
Variable production cost	$ 11	$ 10	$ 10	$ 11	$ 10	$ 11	$ 10	$ 10	$ 9	$ 10	$ 10	$ 11	$ 10
Variable marketing cost	8	7	8	8	8	8	8	8	8	8	8	8	9
Overhead expense	6	6	5	6	7	6	6	6	6	5	5	6	7
Net profit	$ 6	$ 6	$ 10	$ 9	$ 8	$ 7	$ 7	$ 8	$ 9	$ 10	$ 12	$ 9	$ 7
No. of units (000)	13	14	12	15	16	15	17	14	15	12	12	15	18
Net profit (000)	$ 78	$ 84	$120	$135	$128	$105	$119	$112	$135	$120	$144	$135	$126

FIGURE 17.2 *(Continued)*

Random Number:	382	058	437	116	925	310	662	706	278	875	023	589
Product A												
Selling price	$ 48	$ 47	$ 48	$ 47	$ 49	$ 50	$ 46	$ 46	$ 50	$ 49	$ 49	$ 48
Variable production cost	$ 17	$ 16	$ 17	$ 16	$ 16	$ 15	$ 14	$ 16	$ 15	$ 16	$ 16	$ 14
Variable marketing cost	10	11	12	11	12	13	12	12	13	12	11	12
Overhead expense	8	7	8	9	6	8	8	8	8	8	7	8
Net profit	$ 13	$ 13	$ 11	$ 11	$ 15	$ 14	$ 12	$ 10	$ 14	$ 13	$ 15	$ 14
No. of units (000)	9	10	9	10	10	10	11	11	10	10	10	12
Net profit (000)	$117	$130	$ 99	$110	$150	$140	$132	$110	$140	$130	$150	$168
Product B												
Selling price	$ 32	$ 30	$ 32	$ 29	$ 33	$ 32	$ 31	$ 31	$ 32	$ 33	$ 30	$ 31
Variable production cost	$ 9	$ 10	$ 11	$ 10	$ 10	$ 9	$ 10	$ 10	$ 10	$ 10	$ 10	$ 11
Variable marketing cost	8	7	8	7	9	8	8	8	8	8	9	8
Overhead expense	6	7	6	6	7	6	6	6	6	5	7	6
Net profit	$ 9	$ 6	$ 7	$ 6	$ 7	$ 9	$ 7	$ 7	$ 8	$ 10	$ 4	$ 6
No. of units (000)	15	16	15	14	18	15	17	17	15	18	16	13
Net profit (000)	$135	$ 96	$105	$ 84	$126	$135	$119	$119	$120	$180	$ 64	$ 78

Long-Term Planning

The simulation technique in long-term planning is significantly different from that used in short-term planning. In the short-term case, the output of a daily production and operation system may be inputs to a management simulation model. For example, at the El Segundo Division of Hughes Aircraft Company in El Segundo, California, a simulation model is used as a study tool to evaluate the effects of various management decisions on the operation of the fabrication shop, and the inputs to the IBM 7090 computer simulation model are actual shop operating data contained in an existing data processing system.[3] In the long-term case, no attempt is normally made to connect the simulation model to the day-to-day management information systems within the business organization.

For purposes of long-range planning, the systems analyst begins with an overall perspective of the business organization and then attempts to express in a mathematical model those factors which he feels are the most important. Each factor becomes an element in the model, and the analyst assigns relative weights to each element.

This approach to long-range planning has been followed by several research groups, and each research group has made certain modifications in the general approach because of the group's own special interest. The first interpretation is associated with Jay Forrester's *Industrial Dynamics.*[4] In the original work in the late 1950's, Forrester developed a basic model of six interconnected networks: materials, orders, money, personnel, capital equipment, and the interconnecting information. As Forrester continued to work with these interconnected networks, he increased the number of variables in each network. For example, in 1963 he addressed a symposium at the 13th CIOS International Management Conference at the New York Hilton Hotel, where he spoke of working with a model containing 250 variables.[5]

---

[3] Earl LeGrande, "The Development of a Factory Simulation System Using Actual Operating Data," *Management Technology,* Vol. III (May, 1963), pp. 1–19.

[4] Jay W. Forrester, *Industrial Dynamics* (Cambridge, Mass.: The M.I.T. Press, 1961).

[5] Jay W. Forrester, "Simulative Approaches for Improving Knowledge of Business Processes and Environments," 13th CIOS International Management Conference, September, 1963, New York.

The objective of the *Industrial Dynamics* type of simulation model is limited to the total perspective of the business organization. Through conferences with corporate management, an attempt is made to identify the significant factors in the simulation model and to identify the relative weight of each factor. The *Industrial Dynamics* type of simulation model has been successfully used to simulate the growth behavior of a business organization, the implications of a change in marketing strategy, the implications of a change in products and product mix, the fluctuations of price and supply in commodity markets, and other applications.

Another interpretation of the long-range planning type of simulation model is the basic research performed by the System Development Corporation. Early in 1959 the Management Control Systems Project was initiated at the System Development Corporation for the purpose of studying management controls in the context of a total complex system. The objective of this latter study was to ". . . learn something of what such controls are and how they work."[6]

A third interpretation of the long-term planning type of simulation model is identified with the work of Charles Bonini. In his doctoral dissertation, *Simulation of Information and Decision Systems in the Firm,*[7] Bonini integrated a behavioral model with the regular simulation model. His behavioral model contains a pressure index which represents the interrelation of one level of organization upon another level and the influence of a given activity's previous performance upon that activity's current performance. After developing a pressure index for each level of organization, Bonini then computed a company index of pressure which was ". . . intended to represent the pressure felt by the executive committee, as a group, about prospects for the company in the next quarter."[8]

A popular interpretation of the long-range planning type of simulation model is represented by the general purpose business game. "The first business game was introduced by the American Management Association, being initially demonstrated in December, 1956, in Los Angeles."[9] Other organizations using business games at an early date include the following: University of California, Los

---

[6] John Kagdis and Michael R. Lackner, "A Management Control Systems Simulation Model," *Management Technology*, Vol. III (December, 1963), p. 145.

[7] Charles P. Bonini, *Simulation of Information and Decision Systems in the Firm* (Englewood Cliffs, N.J.: Prentice-Hall, Inc., 1963).

[8] *Ibid.*, p. 57.

[9] Joel M. Kibbee, *op. cit.*, p. 304.

Angeles (UCLA), International Business Machines, and the Pillsbury Company. By 1962, there were over 160 business organizations and universities which had their own business games.[10] The number of such general purpose simulation models has been increasing in a similar manner since the 1962 report.

There is another approach toward the development of simulation models that has been followed in a few instances. This latter approach is a mathematical application of Russell Ackoff's *Scientific Method: Optimizing Applied Research Decisions.*[11]

Currently the managements of two business organizations are attempting to employ Ackoff's method. First, they follow a conceptual approach toward identifying the major, operational goals of the business organization. The major goals are identified, and the relationships between goals are expressed by mathematical equations. Next, the subgoals are identified under major goals. An attempt is made to express mathematically the relationship between subgoals and the major goals and between one group of subgoals with another group of subgoals and so forth. The next step is to weight these mathematical elements in the equations and to program these elements for the computer. Thus, the simulation model of the business organization has been created.

What is unique in the above situation is that the Ackoff's type of simulation model can simultaneously provide both total hypothetical results and the detailed data for subsystems. It should be pointed out that neither of these two business organizations' special type of simulation model has been reported to be successful, in the sense of reasonable reliability. However, it is encouraging that such basic research is being performed by business management.

Recently, a practical version of an overall simulation model was submitted by Mattessich for use in financial budgeting.[12] The Mattessich model does not contain the behavioral elements which play such a dominant part in both Bonini and Ackoff's models and to

---

[10] Paul S. Greenlaw, Lowell W. Herron, and Richard H. Rawdon, *Business Simulation in Industrial and University Education* (Englewood Cliffs, N.J.: Prentice-Hall, Inc., 1962).

[11] Russell L. Ackoff (with the collaboration of Shiv K. Gupta and J. Sayer Minas) *Scientific Method: Optimizing Applied Research Decisions* (New York: John Wiley & Sons, Inc., 1962).

[12] Richard Mattessich, *Accounting and Analytical Methods: Measurement and Projection of Income and Wealth in the Micro- and Macro-Economy* (Homewood, Ill.: Richard D. Irwin, Inc., 1964).

a lesser extent in Forrester's model. In addition, the Mattessich model does not attempt to represent all of the business organization's operations, but only those activities that directly relate to financial budgeting.

Although the simulation technique has been applied to several diverse types of questions in the framework of long-term planning, we believe that the primary benefit from this technique is achieved in the process of identifying the significant elements in the model and assigning the weights to each element. In other words, the systems analyst increases his understanding of the total business organization and the interrelationships within the organization. With these insights, he can do a better job of coping with whatever task confronts him.

Integrating Information Systems

The simulation technique is frequently used in practice for testing a proposed information system to see if the information system copes with the unique business situation. Subsequently, after the proposed information system has been modified and refined, the designed information system is again tested by numerous simulations for the purpose of discovering as many of the defects as possible before actually placing the information system into operation.

The above use of the simulation technique is equally applicable to the integration of inventory control information systems and production control information systems as it is to the integration of production and operations information systems with marketing information systems. Of course, the highest application of this technique would be the task of constructing a single, total information system for the entire business organization.

In addition to this type of simulation technique being used in the design and testing of integrated information systems, the long-term planning type of simulation model can also be used. Specifically, Edward Roberts, a colleague of Jay Forrester, argues for using industrial dynamics as a means of testing the proposed system to see if it copes with the real situation.[13] While this purpose is similar to that previously expressed as the objective of the other type of simulation

---

[13] Edward B. Roberts, "Industrial Dynamics and the Design of Management Control Systems," *Management Technology*, Vol. III (December, 1963), pp. 100–118.

technique, the manner of achieving this objective is different. The industrial dynamics approach tries to determine the *parameters* of the information system as well as the significant *internal variables.* Harmony must be achieved between the parameters and the internal variables before this type of simulation technique will pass the test of being reasonably accurate. In contrast, the other approach to simulation focuses only on the internal variables.

This distinction is subtle, but important. The industrial dynamics approach, by focusing on both the parameters and the internal variables, tends to determine if the "real problem situation" has been described by the simulation model. If the parameters are not included as an important part of the simulation model, then the information system may pass the test when, in fact, the information system may not be suitable for the "real problem."

Conclusions

As the systems analyst begins to cope with complex business environments, the need for using the different types of simulation techniques becomes increasingly important. For example, in the case of production and operation information systems, the systems analyst does not desire to design an information system which cannot be successfully maintained in operation because (1) capacity restrictions do not permit the establishment of the initial stock levels required prior to the conversion of the new system (in other words, "we cannot get to the new position from where we are today") and (2) short-term monetary constraints are incompatible with the probable range of financial requirements that the unrestricted production and operation information system might need. Both types of short-term simulation models can be used in trying to eliminate this type of occurrence.

At present, the systems analyst sees the long-term simulation models as a means of testing the effect of different management policies as well as a means of evaluating the effect of alternative strategies with respect to products, advertising, personnel, and so forth. In addition, the long-term simulation models are viewed as being primarily an educational vehicle for the systems analyst to increase his understanding of the "real beast"—the business organization under question.

The different types of simulation models can be used in all facets of the process of designing, testing, and implementing a new information system. However, the industrial dynamics type of model is advantageous in this latter use because the technique tends to test the model of the situation with the real situation. (The industrial dynamics type of model, of course, is more expensive to construct, both in terms of man-hours and machine time.)

In the future, it is possible that the systems analyst will change his approach toward designing integrated information systems. Instead of designing a series of integrated information subsystems and then gradually integrating all of the subsystems into a single total information system, the systems analyst may attempt to construct a simulation model that possesses the essential elements of both Forrester's and Ackoff's models. After this complex model has been constructed and tested, then the systems analyst may attempt to design and install a total computerized management information system without the necessity of going through the traditional steps of integrated activities to integrated subsystems to an integrated total information system.

TOPICS FOR CLASS DISCUSSION

1. There are many similarities between the construction of a critical path schedule and the development of a simulation model for short-term planning. Explain how a critical path network is different from each type of simulation model for short-term planning.

2. Explain how a simulation model for short-term planning under conditions of risk is different from a financial budget model.

3. Management scientists will frequently attempt to represent separate areas of concern by means of a series of simulation models. These efforts will normally not meet the strict criteria of the "pure" management scientists, because each simulation run in one of these simulation models does not represent a plausible occurrence of reality. Instead, the pure management scientists will classify many of these so-called simulation models as "statistical models." Regardless of whether they are labeled "simulation models" or "statistical models," management scientists continue to apply this technique to different areas of concern, even though they are not attempting to fully represent reality. Why?

4. Executive management of a major corporation recently applied the simulation technique to each step of a new plant construction

project. Simulation models were used for (1) site selection, (2) architectural planning of buildings and facilities on the new site, (3) coordinating construction of buildings and facilities, (4) installation of machinery, (5) training of personnel, and (6) overall financial management of the project. Explain some of the benefits that management might have obtained from using the simulation technique in each of these six cases.

5. How does a simulation model permit management's experience and insights to be brought to bear upon a problem? Be specific.

CASE 17–1. SIMULATION PROBLEM

Management of the Beta Company still has some questions regarding which new product should be introduced—Product A or Product B. The example presented in this chapter contained only 25 simulations, and some members of management desire more simulations before they will accept the insights gained from this technique.

Therefore, a computer program in Fortran IV was prepared for this case. (Please review the facts of the Beta Company case as given in the example in this chapter.) This computer program contains a subprogram for a random number generator. Ten random numbers are generated for each combined simulation run for Product A and Product B. The computer program calls for 1,000 simulations or an array of 1,000 values for Product A and Product B.

This computer program was run 10 times, each time beginning the random number generator library program at a different point. The results of these 10 runs are as follows:

		Product A	Product B
Run	1	$ 121,112	$ 119,223
	2	119,917	117,930
	3	120,421	116,164
	4	121,047	119,128
	5	120,286	118,214
	6	121,279	116,895
	7	120,795	119,104
	8	121,040	117,569
	9	119,318	119,359
	10	120,410	118,476
Total	....	$1,205,625	$1,182,062
Average	....	$120,562	$118,206

While the average for Product A was larger than the average for Product B, some members of management were concerned with the distribution of values for each product. The computer program was expanded to include a subroutine for computing the frequency distribution by class interval.

Exhibit A presents this modified computer program. Exhibit B presents the frequency distribution for 35,000 simulations of Product A and Product B; this latter exhibit shows the results obtained by running the computer program 35 times.

EXHIBIT A

Computer Program

```
      PROGRAM BETA                        213   PRODC = 17.
      DIMENSION PA (1000) , PB (1000) ,   300   X = RANF(−1)
         C(1000), D(25, 4), E(25)         301   IF(X−.05000)310,310,302
      DO 95 J=1,1000                      302   IF(X−.21000)311,311,303
 95   PA(J) = 000000.0                    303   IF(X−.81000)312,312,313
      DO 96 J=1,1000                      310   XMARC = 10.
 96   PB(J) = 000000.0                          GO TO 400
      READ(60,898)R                       311   XMARC = 11.
898   FORMAT(F5.4)                              GO TO 400
      CALL RANFSET(R)                     312   XMARC = 12.
      PAT = 0.0                                 GO TO 400
      PBT = 0.0                           313   XMARC = 13.
      DO 800 J = 1,1000                   400   X = RANF(−1)
100   X = RANF(−1)                        401   IF(X−.05000)410,410,402
101   IF(X−.08000)110,110,102            402   IF(X−.18000)411,411,403
102   IF(X−.24000)111,111,103            403   IF(X−.83000)412,412,413
103   IF(X−.46000)112,112,104            410   XOVEC = 6.
104   IF(X−.76000)113,113,105                  GO TO 500
105   IF(X−.94000)114,114,115            411   XOVEC = 7.
110   SLPRC = 45.                              GO TO 500
      GO TO 200                           412   XOVEC = 8.
111   SLPRC = 46.                              GO TO 500
      GO TO 200                           413   XOVEC = 9.
112   SLPRC = 47.                         500   X = RANF(−1)
      GO TO 200                           501   IF(X−.05000)510,510,502
113   SLPRC = 48.                         502   IF(X−.21000)511,511,503
      GO TO 200                           503   IF(X−.71000)512,512,504
114   SLPRC = 49.                         504   IF(X−.91000)513,513,514
      GO TO 200                           510   UNITS = 8000.
115   SLPRC = 50.                              GO TO 600
200   X = RANF(−1)                        511   UNITS = 9000.
201   IF(X−.15000)210,210,202                  GO TO 600
202   IF(X−.30000)211,211,203            512   UNITS = 10000.
203   IF(X−.80000)212,212,213                  GO TO 600
210   PRODC = 14.                         513   UNITS = 11000.
      GO TO 300                                GO TO 600
211   PRODC = 15.                         514   UNITS = 12000.
      GO TO 300                           600   PA(J) = (SLPRC −PRODC
212   PRODC = 16.                                   −XMARC −XOVEC)* UNITS
      GO TO 300                           700   X = RANF(−1)
```

EXHIBIT A (*Continued*)

```
701   IF(X—.07000)710,710,702
702   IF(X—.19000)711,711,703
703   IF(X—.37000)712,712,704
704   IF(X—.65000)713,713,705
705   IF(X—.84000)714,714,706
706   IF(X—.94000)715,715,716
710   SLPRC = 29.
      GO TO 720
711   SLPRC = 30.
      GO TO 720
712   SLPRC = 31.
      GO TO 720
713   SLPRC = 32.
      GO TO 720
714   SLPRC = 33.
      GO TO 720
715   SLPRC = 34.
      GO TO 720
716   SLPRC = 35.
720   X = RANF(—1)
721   IF(X—.15000)730,730,722
722   IF(X—.80000)731,731,732
730   PRODC = 9.
      GO TO 740
731   PRODC = 10.
      GO TO 740
732   PRODC = 11.
740   X = RANF(—1)
741   IF(X—.15000)750,750,742
742   IF(X—.85000)751,751,752
750   XMARC = 7.
      GO TO 760
751   XMARC = 8.
      GO TO 760
752   XMARC = 9.
760   X = RANF(—1)
761   IF(X—.15000)770,770,762
762   IF(X—.85000)771,771,772
770   XOVEC = 5.
      GO TO 780
771   XOVEC = 6.
      GO TO 780
772   XOVEC = 7.
780   X = RANF(—1)
781   IF(X—.10000)790,790,782
782   IF(X—.20000)791,791,783
783   IF(X—.35000)792,792,784
784   IF(X—.65000)793,793,785
785   IF(X—.80000)794,794,786
786   IF(X—.90000)795,795,796
790   UNITS = 12000.
      GO TO 800
791   UNITS = 13000.
      GO TO 800
792   UNITS = 14000.
      GO TO 800
793   UNITS = 15000.
      GO TO 800
794   UNITS = 16000.
      GO TO 800
795   UNITS = 17000.
      GO TO 800
796   UNITS = 18000.
800   PB(J) = (SLPRC —PRODC
             —XMARC —XOVEC)* UNITS
      DO 801 J=1,1000
      PAT = PAT + PA(J)
801   PBT = PBT + PB(J)
      WRITE(61,899)
899   FORMAT(1H1,35X, 10HPRODUCT
            A ,31X, 10HPRODUCT B )
      WRITE(61,900) (PA(J),PB(J), J =
      1,1000)
900   FORMAT(36X,F8.0,32X,F8.0)
      AVA = PAT/1000.
      AVB = PBT/1000.
      WRITE(61,902)AVA,AVB
902   FORMAT(1H2,30X, 16HAVERAGE
            FOR A = ,F8.0///31X,16
            HAVERAGE FOR B = , 1F8.0)
      DO 59 I=1,25
59    E(I) = 0000.
      DO 60 I=1,25
      DO 60 J=1,4
60    D(I,J) = 000.0
      DO 61 J=1,1000
61    C(J) = PA(J)
      CALL CLASS (C,E)
      DO 62 I=1,25
62    D(I,3) = E(I)
      DO 63 I=1,25
63    E(I) = 0000.
      DO 64 J=1,1000
64    C(J) = PB(J)
      CALL CLASS (C,E)
      DO 65 I=1,25
65    D(I,4) = E(I)
      DO 70 I=1,1
      D(I,1) = 0000.
70    D(I,2) = 9999.
      RATE = 10000.0
      DO 71 I=2,25
      DO 71 J=1,2
71    D(I,J) = D( (I—1),J) + RATE
79    WRITE(61,80)
80    FORMAT(1H1,32X,12HCLASS
            LIMITS,9X,9HPRODUCT
            A,7X,9HPRODUCT B)
81    WRITE(61,82) ( (D(I,J), J=1,4),
      I=1,25)
82    FORMAT(31X,F6.0,4X,F6.0,10X,
            F4.0,12X,F4.0)
```

EXHIBIT A (*Continued*)

```
      STOP
      END
      SUBROUTINE CLASS (C,E)
      DIMENSION C(1000), E(25)
      DO 30 I=1,25
30    E(I) = 0000.
      DO 26 J=1,1000
31    G = 1.0 + C(J)/10000.
      GO TO(1,2,3,4,5,6,7,8,9,10,11,12,13,14,
          15,16,17,18,19,20,21,22,23,
      1 24,25)G
1     E(1) = E(1) + 1.0
      GO TO 26
2     E(2) = E(2) + 1.0
      GO TO 26
3     E(3) = E(3) + 1.0
      GO TO 26
4     E(4) = E(4) + 1.0
      GO TO 26
5     E(5) = E(5) + 1.0
      GO TO 26
6     E(6) = E(6) + 1.0
      GO TO 26
7     E(7) = E(7) + 1.0
      GO TO 26
8     E(8) = E(8) + 1.0
      GO TO 26
9     E(9) = E(9) + 1.0
      GO TO 26
10    E(10) = E(10) + 1.0
      GO TO 26

11    E(11) = E(11) + 1.0
      GO TO 26
12    E(12) = E(12) + 1.0
      GO TO 26
13    E(13) = E(13) + 1.0
      GO TO 26
14    E(14) = E(14) + 1.0
      GO TO 26
15    E(15) = E(15) + 1.0
      GO TO 26
16    E(16) = E(16) + 1.0
      GO TO 26
17    E(17) = E(17) + 1.0
      GO TO 26
18    E(18) = E(18) + 1.0
      GO TO 26
19    E(19) = E(19) + 1.0
      GO TO 26
20    E(20) = E(20) + 1.0
      GO TO 26
21    E(21) = E(21) + 1.0
      GO TO 26
22    E(22) = E(22) + 1.0
      GO TO 26
23    E(23) = E(23) + 1.0
      GO TO 26
24    E(24) = E(24) + 1.0
      GO TO 26
25    E(25) = E(25) + 1.0
26    CONTINUE
      RETURN
      END
```

EXHIBIT B
Frequency Distribution of Simulated Profits

Range	Product A				Product B			
	Number	Cumulative	Percent	Cumulative	Number	Cumulative	Percent	Cumulative
20,000– 29,999	0	0	0	0	3	3	.01	.01
30,000– 39,999	0	0	0	0	38	41	.11	.12
40,000– 49,999	2	2	.01	.01	178	219	.51	.63
50,000– 59,999	21	23	.06	.07	234	453	.67	1.30
60,000– 69,999	93	116	.27	.34	1,023	1,476	2.92	4.22
70,000– 79,999	453	569	1.29	1.63	2,147	3,623	6.13	10.35
80,000– 89,999	1,586	2,155	4.53	6.16	1,994	5,617	5.70	16.05
90,000– 99,999	3,906	6,061	11.16	17.32	4,596	10,213	13.13	29.18
100,000–109,999	3,900	9,961	11.14	28.46	4,179	14,392	11.94	41.12
110,000–119,999	5,381	15,342	15.38	43.84	3,383	17,775	9.67	50.79
120,000–129,999	6,003	21,345	17.15	60.99	5,324	23,099	15.21	66.00
130,000–139,999	5,479	26,824	15.65	76.64	3,240	26,339	9.26	75.26
140,000–149,999	4,001	30,825	11.43	88.07	2,601	28,940	7.43	82.69
150,000–159,999	2,416	33,241	6.91	94.98	2,202	31,142	6.29	88.98
160,000–169,999	1,141	34,382	3.26	98.24	1,860	33,002	5.31	94.29
170,000–179,999	274	34,656	.78	99.02	706	33,708	2.02	96.31
180,000–189,999	236	34,892	.67	99.69	782	34,490	2.23	98.54
190,000–199,999	76	34,968	.22	99.91	347	34,837	.99	99.53
200,000–209,999	26	34,994	.07	99.98	75	34,912	.21	99.74
210,000–219,999	6	35,000	.02	100.00	65	34,977	.19	99.93
220,000–229,999	0	35,000	0	100.00	12	34,989	.03	99.96
230,000–239,999	0	35,000	0	100.00	9	34,998	.03	99.99
240,000–249,999	0	35,000	0	100.00	2	35,000	.01	100.00
Total	35,000		100.00		35,000		100.00	
Average	$120,535				$118,197			

REQUIRED:

1. Which product would you select? Quantitatively support your answer.
2. Why do the frequency distributions in Exhibit B not approximate a normal curve? Explain in detail.
3. *Possible extensions:* (*A*) Reproduce the computer program. Change the degree of expected occurrence for certain costs (without changing the overall range of values) and run the computer program to see how sensitive the results are to this change. (*B*) Repeat this procedure, but eliminate some current extreme point or extend the range of other extreme points. In other words, through the simulation process you are attempting to see how sensitive the overall results are to changes in one or more factors in the model.

CASE 17–2. FERGUSON MILLS CORPORATION

The management consulting firm with which you are associated has been engaged in a series of information systems projects at the Ferguson Mills Corporation over the past decade. Thus, it was not surprising when the executive vice president telephoned your management consulting firm and asked one of the senior consultants to join him for lunch. The executive vice president had read an article in *Business Week* explaining how simulation models had been used in another industry, and he saw many similarities with the problems in the textile industry. He is wondering how simulation models might be used at Ferguson Mills.

The Company

Ferguson Mills Corporation is one of the 15 largest corporations in the textile industry, and it is a company that has continued to make a reasonable profit while many of its competitors have been dissolved. For example, over 800 textile companies have been liquidated during the past decade and 125 other textile companies have been merged with other textile companies. The result of this general movement has been that the remaining larger corporations have increased their share of the market. For instance, the 10 largest corporations currently have about 25 percent of industry sales, whereas a few years ago they had less than 20 percent.

Technological Factors and Market Changes

Ferguson Mills has invested a substantial amount of funds in new laborsaving equipment utilizing technological advancements. This equipment contains high-speed frames for spinning fiber into yarn that have increased productivity by over 50 percent. Improved looms for weaving fiber into cloth are also incorporated in this equipment, and these looms permit the operator to produce larger strips of fabric in less time. This new equipment is augmented by changes in production procedures. For example, the computer system, utilizing operations research techniques, supervises the mixing of different colored dyes.

In recent years, Ferguson Mills has experienced significant changes in market mix and in market demand. Some of these changes were the result of management's marketing and production activities; others were based on external factors. Management has intentionally shifted from natural fibers to man-made fibers, such as acrylic, polyester, and triacetate, which have supplemented the traditional synthetic standbys—nylon and rayon. Through the use of man-made fibers, marketing management can be more sensitive to changes in consumer preferences.

The textile industry has experienced a general change based on three factors. First, garment manufacturers have perfected a new manufacturing process which permits delicate fabrics to be bonded with another substance and then manufactured on a mass scale production basis (the price of some finished items, for example, can be reduced by more than 50 percent). This change in garment manufacturing process has resulted in shifts in the demand for certain products from the textile industry. Second, all domestic textile companies have benefited from the "Cotton Bill," under which these domestic companies are reimbursed at $6\frac{1}{2}$ cents per pound for the cotton they use. This reimbursement rate is supposed to approximate the difference between the world market price of cotton and the U.S. government price-supported level. Third, new types of management personnel have been recruited for the textile industry, and these individuals have brought new management techniques and procedures to bear upon different problem areas. This new type of management group has resulted not only in greater stability of earnings by companies, but in greater stability of earnings by the textile industry.

Information Systems

The management consulting firm with which you are associated has assisted Ferguson Mills personnel in the application of operations research and linear programming techniques to various problem areas, such as warehousing, transportation, production scheduling, and sales forecasting. The latter application consists of a system which relates sales forecasts by style, including the salesmen's confidence estimates, with production capacity and profitability factors.

These management consultants were also instrumental in the design and implementation of an inventory anticipation system for style goods. The basic sales pattern for each product line was determined, and experience data were accumulated regarding the probability of deviation by each item within a product line from the average. Prediction factors have been derived for estimating the duration of the season for each product. All of these insights and relations have been incorporated in a set of tables which management can use in making day-to-day decisions.

These tables, for example, indicate the odds of selling enough goods to fill the looms' profitability objective, and these odds would vary based on the week of the season involved. Other tables show the odds of allocating various styles to different looms so as to have a good assignment for profit purposes. Management must continuously use these tables and others in making day-to-day decisions if a satisfactory profit level is to be achieved, which, incidentally, requires a zero level of style-goods inventory at the end of the season. (This latter comment is based upon statistical studies presented in the industry's professional literature.)

In the nonstyle-goods area, another type of system had to be developed. Orders are daily received for production with a three-month delivery date, and each of these orders is at a negotiated price. In the early part of each production season, the sales price per order is lower than it is later in the season. After many of the companies in the textile industry have committed their production capacity for three months ahead, then the remaining production capacity brings a premium. However, if management waits too long before accepting orders, there may be insufficient orders to satisfy full production; thus, the company will have unused capacity.

In coping with this general problem in the nonstyle-goods area, a system for setting refusal profit levels was established. The system shows the value per loom week for specific styles, taking into account the costs, loom speeds, and sales commissions. Thus, each style has a different refusal price in terms of cents per yard. Furthermore, this system provides an acceptance price based on the forecasted average profit level of the loom class. Separate refusal profit levels and prices are established for delivery in each future quarter.

Recently, the management consultants assisted management in the design and implementation of an information system which connects the various regional sales offices with the home office. This communication network is not only used in marketing management, but also permits an immediate response to sales orders. This immediate response is extremely important in the peak of each season.

REQUIRED:

1. Indicate how simulation models might be used at Ferguson Mills. Be specific and, if appropriate, attempt to relate one application of the simulation technique with the next application.
2. What are the advantages and disadvantages of employing simulation techniques at Ferguson Mills as compared to the statistical techniques that they are currently using?

CHAPTER 18

The Systems Analyst and Organization

THE INFLUENCES of organization on different aspects of the systems analyst's work have been examined in detail at various points throughout this book. In addition, attention has been given to possible future organization structures that might be developed as a result of advanced information systems, such as housekeeping types of advanced information systems and planning information systems. The changing training ground for executive development has also been noted. Thus, the reader may wonder what additional aspects of organization will be discussed in the present chapter.

The majority of the case studies and the discussion thus far have been viewed from the standpoint of an outside management consultant. This chapter is from the opposite viewpoint and examines the role of the systems analyst within an organization. Consideration is first given to the formal organization location of the information systems function, and this is followed by a discussion of project selection and management by the systems analyst.

ORGANIZATION AND THE INFORMATION SYSTEMS FUNCTION

Within a business organization with advanced information systems, where is the information systems function organizationally located? To what extent does this organization arrangement vary between companies? This discussion presents a brief statement on the intermediate reactions that select business companies have made to the information systems function. In the previous sentence, the adjective "intermediate" should be emphasized. Business companies have only recently begun to design and install advanced information systems on a large-scale basis; prior to 1962, there were only a limited number of such systems in existence. Thus, it is too early to speak of final reactions by organizations to the information systems function.

The organization location of the information systems function in business companies with advanced information systems has changed significantly during the past two years. Power struggles, personnel conflicts, and other organization considerations are continuously changing the location of this function. For example, in one major corporation, two years ago there was an administrative services group at the assistant vice president level that was organizationally independent and had the total corporate responsibility for the information systems function. Today, the corporate controller in this major company has assumed this total corporate responsibility, and the former members of the administrative services group are part of his staff.

In another major corporation, two years ago the information systems function was performed by an information systems group on the staff of the corporate controller. Today, this group has been elevated to the vice president level, which is the same level as the corporate controller and the treasurer. As far as status is concerned, the vice president for information systems is higher than either the corporate controller or the treasurer. Since the president and the chairman of the board are inactive positions in this company, the only active positions with higher status are those of the executive vice president for manufacturing and the senior executive vice president.

With these types of changes occurring in major companies, it is impossible to present any single, dominant organization reaction to the information systems function. Instead, the four major current arrangements are briefly described.

Under the Corporate Controller.   One of the most common organization reactions is for the information systems function to be performed by the corporate controller's staff. When this arrangement exists, it appears that there is more emphasis on accounting types of information in the advanced information system than is the case with other arrangements. For example, when the information systems function is under the responsibility of the vice president of manufacturing or the vice president of marketing, the types of information in the advanced information systems tend to be significantly different than under the above arrangement. But perhaps these are only temporary conditions, and as advanced information systems are more widely used within the corporate enterprise, the types of information included in these systems will tend to be more encompassing under all organization arrangements.

Administrative Services Group. A few companies have established an independent administrative services group at either the vice president or assistant vice president level to act as management consultants to the other organization units. The particular arrangement has been extremely successful in some companies. The project manager for an advanced information system in this type of organization arrangement will tend to be comparable with a product brand manager for marketing operations. The project manager's personality, temperament, and abilities are significant factors in influencing the scope and breadth of the advanced information system being designed. When there is an administrative services group, it is typical for the other organization units to be billed at some predetermined cost rate for both "consulting" types of assistance and for "information services" provided by the advanced information system.

Vice President of Information with Decentralized Operations. At the corporate level, there is a small central staff that provides the basic expertise for the information systems function. This central staff typically includes operations researchers, statisticians, system designers, programmers, managerial accountants, and management scientists. However, each division or department has its own "information systems controller." This latter individual serves as the organization unit's communication link with the central staff. He is responsible for appropriately representing the special interests of his own organization unit when any advanced information system is being designed and implemented. After the advanced information system has been installed, he has the responsibility for understanding the system and being able to explain the system, when appropriate, to the other members of management within that organization unit. For example, the system may prohibit certain types of comparisons and operations from being performed; if so, he is supposed to know about that.

Vice President of Information with Centralized Operation. This type of organization arrangement is similar to that for the vice president of information with decentralized operation, except that the division or department information systems controllers do not formally exist. Various members of the central staff perform these services; in fact, there may be a regular assignment of responsibility for the various divisions to specific members of the central staff.

Incidentally, this "vice president of information" is not a new title for either the corporate controller or the treasurer. Both of these latter positions continue to exist concurrently with the vice president of information.

At this point in time, there are too many organization pressures for change in respect to the information systems function for an individual to predict with a high degree of confidence what the typical organization response will be a decade from now. However, we believe that there will be a substantial increase in the number of corporate officials with the position "vice president of information systems."

PROJECT SELECTION AND MANAGEMENT
BY THE SYSTEMS ANALYST

Organization considerations are involved in each and every aspect of the project selection and management process, and these considerations are frequently the dominant factors responsible for the project's success or failure. This discussion will suggest some guidelines that the systems analyst can follow in steering away from the most common pitfalls. These guidelines are presented under three groupings: (1) project selection, (2) project management, and (3) project audit and evaluation.

Project Selection.   If the information systems function is just being established within the business organization or if the systems analyst is a new member of the corporate staff, then the matter of initial project selection is extremely important. From an organization standpoint, the systems analyst cannot afford the risk of failure on the initial group of projects. Thus, the major project with the estimated greatest benefit to the company is not the type of project to select initially. Instead, smaller types of projects that can be handled more quickly and that provide a reasonable amount of benefit to the company should be selected initially. After a few of these types of projects have been successfully designed and implemented, then the systems analyst can and should undertake the major projects that are more risky but with a much higher potential benefit to the company.

During the past decade, there has been a significant employee turnover of corporate systems analysts. While each situation may be slightly different, one reoccurring type of story is told. In this company, three years ago (the time element would vary by company) the director of the information systems group undertook a major project. This project involved advanced operations research techniques and normally involved most of the activities in a major organization unit. When this initial major project did not work according to the director's expectation, because of one reason or other, the director became disgruntled and left the company. Recently, management consultants or members of a new systems group have rediscovered the former director's major project. Even today, this old project is just beginning to be installed in some companies with advanced information systems. Various corporate officials will comment, "I wonder what ever happened to George (the former director of the information systems group) ; he had some good ideas; it is a shame that we didn't benefit from his suggestions, but you have to be a member of a team."

From the above story and related experiences, four suggestions are offered as guidelines in the initial selection of projects. First, as previously discussed, the information systems group should initially select a few small-scale projects which can be quickly accomplished with a low degree of risk. Second, the information systems group should develop a working relation with corporate officials and managers of the various organization units. Talk with them, find out their current concerns, ask questions about procedures. In other words, plant seeds that may result in new, advanced information systems. When a manager of an organization unit is *working for* a new type of information system, such a system has a high degree of success. Without this manager's full appreciation and participation in the design and implementation of a new, advanced information system, the chances of failure are high. In fact, if the systems analyst cannot secure the active participation of a manager in a project affecting his area, he is well advised to drop the project temporarily and to look elsewhere within the company for another project.

Third, the systems analyst's group should intentionally select some of the initial projects in each of the various departments in the company. While a given department may have several choice projects, the systems analyst's group may become too closely identified with a given department. For example, in one major corporation, a new information systems group had initially performed several

projects in the production management area, without doing any-
thing in the marketing area. The vice president of marketing received the permission of the senior executive vice president to hire a
management consulting firm to perform some studies in the marketing area. Because of this occurrence and other organization considerations, the future of this corporate information systems group is
at present rather cloudy.

There is another viewpoint for this third suggestion. Through
actually performing small projects in the various departments, the
systems analyst's group may discover that its previous conceptions of
the department's activities were erroneous. For instance, it may
discover that, in the above example, the marketing department really
had more "choice" projects than those it was working on in the
production department.

Fourth, while the systems analyst's group is intentionally performing small projects in various departments, it should be compiling a
list of possible future projects. Each entry on the list should not only
describe the nature of the possible project but should include estimates of cost, benefit, and risk.

After the initial group of projects has been selected and accomplished, then the ground rules change. Now the various proposed
projects are evaluated in the same manner as research and development proposals. However, a different point of view is suggested for
calculating the estimated benefit of each project. Instead of determining the benefit of a proposal, the systems analyst should calculate
the *benefit required to justify the project.* By calculating the benefit
required to justify a project, it may not be necessary to actually
quantify the many intangible benefits associated with a proposed
project. In many situations, the determination of the benefit required to justify a project will immediately suggest the appropriate
decision regarding project selection, without attempting to measure
the intangible benefits.

Project Management. Before work is begun on any selected
project, the director of the information systems group should perform the following three functions. First, he should talk again with
the operating management involved with a selected project. The
director should reiterate the primary advantage or objective of the
selected project, and he should obtain operating management's approval that accomplishment of this advantage or objective is worth-
while.

Second, he should ask operating management how they foresee their operations and activities a few years hence. The systems analyst's group, even though it performed a detailed examination, may be unaware of some major change scheduled to occur that might result in the proposed project not being able to cope with the increased volume, for example. This latter procedure is an internal check on the quality of the systems analyst's staff's research. In addition, this procedure would update the staff's research report if the scheduled change has only recently been announced.

There is another aspect of this second function. When operating management mentions some estimated change, the director of the information systems group should "think through" this change with operating management. A step-by-step analysis of the effect that some change may have on the business activity should be jointly performed, and then they should jointly determine whether or not this proposed change will affect this selected project. The negative aspect of this latter discussion is as follows. If for any reason some change that operating management casually mentioned were to accelerate in importance and impact, then at some future date the director of the information system group may be left "holding the bag." Under these circumstances, operating management has been known to have forgotten that it deemphasized the importance of a proposed change. Or, worse, operating management will emphasize that it told the director about the change; it just cannot understand why the director did not change the information systems project. Again, when operating management mentions a change, the director should go through the effects that the change may have on the business in a step-by-step manner.

Third, in consultation with operating management, the director of the information systems group should develop a procedure for measuring the benefit of the selected project. He should gain agreement from operating management that these procedures will be followed in the final measurement of benefit (at the evaluation stage). This prior agreement is extremely important for the long-run success of the information systems group. Otherwise, especially on lengthy projects, operating management has a tendency to "forget" what was the primary purpose of the project. Instead, new criteria are offered by operating management, and the information systems group is criticized because the project does not meet the new measurements.

Project Audit and Evaluation. When the project has been accomplished, the total cost of the project should be charged to the department involved or prorated between one or more departments, depending on the nature of the project. We advocate using the original estimated cost as the basis for the charge; any difference would be charged to the information systems group. For costing purposes, this total project should be expensed over the original estimated benefit period.

If the above cost accounting procedures are followed, then the system has a built-in project evaluation procedure. However, a more thorough audit should be made of each completed project. For example, has operating management performed its tasks? If the project was justified on the basis of a reduction in staff, has the number of employees been reduced? Using the previously agreed-upon criteria, the benefit of the completed project should be determined. An after-the-fact analysis should be performed of the estimates associated with the original project cost, risk, and benefit. From these audits and evaluations, the information systems staff will have a higher degree of confidence in its future estimates.

TOPICS FOR CLASS DISCUSSION

1. The vice president of information with decentralized operation and the vice president of information with centralized operation were briefly discussed in this chapter. However, there is another dimension which was not discussed. The environmental settings in which these two types of organization arrangements exist are different. Typically, there are predictable differences in terms of the extent, degree, and scope of decisions made by corporate officials under each of these arrangements. Indicate examples of types of decisions that you would expect to be different, depending on the organization arrangement, for each of the following six corporate officials. Be specific.

   a) Vice president of manufacturing
   b) Vice president of marketing
   c) Director of research and development
   d) Corporate controller
   e) Treasurer
   f) Vice president of information systems

2. Assume that a major corporation's management had recently decided to establish an information systems group and that you were employed as the first director of this group. Sketch a model that would contain the *eight* most important factors that you would consider in the initial selection of a group of projects. Indicate the relative weight for each factor. Justify your model. Repeat this same process for the project selection model you would use two years later.

3. List alternative ways that the cost accounting for an information systems project might be handled. Cite the advantages and disadvantages of each alternative you listed.

INDEX

Index

This book has been set in 11 and 10 point Baskerville, leaded 2 points. Part numbers are in 14 point Bodoni and 24 point Bodoni Bold; part titles are in 18 point Bodoni. Chapter numbers are in 11 point Baskerville and 24 point Bodoni Bold; chapter titles are in 18 point Bodoni Bold. The size of the type page is 27 by 45 picas.